Power Sharing in a Divided Nation

ISEAS – Yusof Ishak Institute (formerly the Institute of Southeast Asian Studies) was established as an autonomous organization in 1968. It is a regional centre dedicated to the study of socio-political, security and economic trends and developments in Southeast Asia and its wider geostrategic and economic environment.

The Institute's research programmes are the Regional Economic Studies (RES, including ASEAN and APEC), Regional Strategic and Political Studies (RSPS), and Regional Social and Cultural Studies (RSCS).

ISEAS Publishing, an established academic press, has issued more than 2,000 books and journals. It is the largest scholarly publisher of research about Southeast Asia from within the region. ISEAS Publications works with many other academic and trade publishers and distributors to disseminate important research and analyses from and about Southeast Asia to the rest of the world.

The **Strategic Information and Research Development Centre (SIRD)** is an independent publishing house founded in January 2000 in Petaling Jaya, Malaysia. The SIRD list focuses on Malaysian and Southeast Asian studies, economics, gender studies, social sciences, politics and international relations. Our books address the scholarly community, students, the NGO and development communities, policymakers, activists and the wider public. SIRD also distributes titles (via its sister organisation, **GB Gerakbudaya Enterprise Sdn Bhd**) published by scholarly and institutional presses, NGOs and other independent publishers. We also organise seminars, forums and group discussions. All this, we believe, is conducive to the development and consolidation of the notions of civil liberty and democracy.

JOHAN SARAVANAMUTTU

Power Sharing in a Divided Nation

Mediated Communalism and New Politics in Six Decades of Malaysia's Elections

ISEAS YUSOF ISHAK INSTITUTE

Strategic Information and Research Development Centre

First published in Singapore in 2016 by ISEAS Publishing
ISEAS – Yusof Ishak Institute
30 Heng Mui Keng Terrace
Singapore 119614
E-mail: publish@iseas.edu.sg
Website: bookshop.iseas.edu.sg

Co-published for distribution in Malaysia only by
Strategic Information and Research Development Centre
No. 2, Jalan Bukit 11/2, 46200 Petaling Jaya, Selangor, Malaysia
E-mail: gerak@gerakbudaya.com
Website: www.gerakbudaya.com

ISEAS Library Cataloguing-in-Publication Data

Saravanamuttu, Johan.
    Power Sharing in a Divided Nation : Mediated Communalism and New Politics in Six Decades of Malaysia's Elections.
    1.   Elections—Malaysia.
    2.   Malaysia—Politics and government.
    I.   Title.
    II. Title: Energy Security Assessment in Indonesia's Power Sector
JQ1062 A95S24   2016

ISBN 978-981-4695-43-5 (soft cover)
ISBN 978-981-4695-42-8 (e-book, PDF)

Perpustakaan Negara Malaysia Cataloguing-in-Publication Data

Johan Saravanamuttu
    Power Sharing in a Divided Nation : Mediated Communalism and New Politics in Six Decades of Malaysia's Elections / JOHAN SARAVANAMUTTU.
    Includes index
    Bibliography: page 287
    ISBN 978-967-0960-47-0
    1.   Ethnicity--Malaysia.
    2.   Malaysia--Politics and government.
    3.   Malaysia--Ethnic relations.
    4.   Malaysia--Social conditions.
    5.   Malaysia--Race relations. I. Title.
305.8009595

Typeset by International Typesetters Pte Ltd
Printed in Singapore by Mainland Press Pte Ltd

In memory of
colleagues recently departed, that their work may inspire future
generations of socially engaged scholars

CONTENTS

PREFACE

This is a book I had always wanted to write but had to keep on hold for one reason or another. Arguably, as a "work in progress", it has been coterminous with my career as, first, a journalist, then as a lecturer and professor, as a senior research fellow and finally as an independent scholar.

Majoring in political science at the University of Singapore in the mid-1960s predisposed me to the intricacies of Malaysian politics and its discontents. Then working as a young journalist in the *New Straits Times* around the time of the May 1969 riots confirmed my belief that studying politics was a vocation I could not elude, which in turn no doubt spurred my desire to pursue graduate studies in political science at the University of British Columbia (UBC), Vancouver from 1970 to 1976. However, at UBC I was drawn to develop my main field of interest in international relations and to write my doctoral thesis on Malaysia's foreign policy. Thus my interest in electoral politics remained on the back burner, but, in truth, it never waned. Malaysian political developments seemingly climaxed during my years as a lecturer at Universiti Sains Malaysia (Penang) and, with my colleague Francis Loh, I put together a book on the emergence of *new politics* during the 1999 general election. The term, *new politics*, a corollary of the Reformasi Movement, has now earned considerable currency in the Malaysian studies literature. It has been associated with the wave of democratization in Malaysia that saw the salutary engagement of ordinary citizens in the electoral process alongside an unprecedented level of political activism.

New politics in no small way brought about the outcome of the landmark 2008 general election which saw the ruling coalition lose for the first time its two-thirds majority of seats in Parliament. During my second year at the Institute of Southeast Asian Studies (now known as the ISEAS – Yusof Ishak Institute), I analysed the outcome of this election together with Ooi Kee Beng and Lee Hock Guan in a book published that same year, and wrote many op eds and several articles about its impact. It was evident that the 8 March 2008 election was a critical juncture in Malaysian electoral politics and charted a path-dependent trajectory of future success for the newly emergent coalition of oppositional forces aligned against the ruling Barisan Nasional. Most importantly, the outcome of 2008 signaled the prospect for what political scientists termed the development of a "turnover" political system in Malaysia, wherein voters are able to periodically exercise a reasonable choice of selecting at least two sets of potential ruling parties. Then came the 2013 general election which some may argue was an anticlimax as the "turnover test" of democratic politics failed to obtain. In a volume edited by myself, Lee Hock Guan and Mohamed Nawab Osman, our contributors offer explanations for the 2013 outcome.

By now it seemed perfectly logical for me to finally undertake my own book on Malaysia's electoral politics. In fact, ISEAS had already kindly agreed in 2012 to my proposal to write such a book, which I had planned to finish writing only after the 13th general election, and which has taken me another two years to complete. In its contents covering six decades of electoral politics in Malaysia, I offer both the specialist and the general reader a thoroughgoing historical and theoretical narrative behind electoral success and failure in Malaysia since the 1950s, and try to answer the perennial question of why the ruling coalition has had a hegemonic grip on the electoral process.

After many years of observation and study I have now come to accept the realist view that ethnic politics or communalism remains at the core of electoral politics in Malaysia because of this country's unique history and social fabric. Because of this, power sharing through a strategy of *mediated communalism* has always been an imperative of political coalitions seeking electoral success. The book delves into this question by narrating and theorizing communal politics over six decades of elections, up until the emergence of *new politics*, which has arguably put Malaysia on the track of further democratization. While not superseding mediated communalism, *new politics* offers a pathway to transcend the most deleterious effects of communalism. It is the discursive instrumentality for subverting the overdetermination of ethnicity in Malaysian politics. In these pages the reader will be presented narratives that deliberately tilt towards a critical theory providing pointers for progressive change to Malaysian electoral politics and ultimately to elevate Malaysian social and political discourse. I make no apologies for this bias and I hope the reader will find that the book's long gestation has not been in vain.

First, let me take the opportunity to thank the former ISEAS director, K. Kesavapany, who was responsible for my appointment as Senior Visiting Research Fellow in 2007 and also the present director Tan Chin Tiong for extending my stay till 2013. Many thanks go to Head of ISEAS Publishing Ng Kok Kiong, his senior editor Rahilah Yusuf and copyeditor Stephen Logan, who have been very helpful every step of the way to see through this publication. My thanks also go particularly to Malaysia Studies coordinators Ooi Kee Beng (now deputy director) and Lee Hock Guan, and also to Terence Chong who prodded me on and provided constant encouragement. Many other ISEAS fellows and researchers, past and present, have also been supportive of my work and I have enjoyed their camaraderie and goodwill. In particular I would like to mention Tan Keng Jin, Daljit Singh, Rodolfo Severino, Omkar Lal Shrestha, P. Ramasamy, Mark Hong, Tin Maung Maung Than, Leon Comber, Francis Hutchinson, Loh Kah Seng, Rusazlina Idris, Ian Storey, Mustafa Izzuddin, Bernhard Platzdasch, Michael Montesano, David Koh, Geoffrey Wade, Hui Yew-Foong, Lee Poh Onn and Theresa Devasahayam.

Much appreciation goes to the many Malaysian colleagues, friends, interviewees, informants and politicians, and my comrades in the Aliran community, who have spared their time and shared their knowledge and insights on electoral politics with me. In particular I would like to thank all of those who were kind enough to talk with me during my fieldwork for the March 2008 general election, for the many by-elections I observed after 2008, for the April 2011 Sarawak state election and for the May 2013 general election. There are just too many individuals to mention in the numerous encounters I have had over the period of my fieldwork. I do hope they will forgive me for this mass attribution, but wherever I have found it pertinent and necessary to make attributions, I have done so in my footnotes. I do want to mention that during important stages of the fieldwork, Adil Johan and Robert Oon provided me with much needed assistance and companionship.

A vote of thanks goes to the "Lunch Group" (Choo Liang Haw, Manicam Saravanamuthu, Ten Chin Liew, Tan Keng Feng, Chu Tee Seng and Choo Han Teck), comprised of practising and former distinguished academicians and professionals of impeccable standing. Thanks to the group's regular discussions about Malaysia, this contributed in no small way to keep my work intellectually primed and on track, with sharp queries and questions about Malaysian developments and with friendly but persistent reminders about progress. I should also mention that my good friend and regular companion, Professor Lim Chin, who has left us, kept my mind engaged about economic issues.

I dedicate this work to former academic colleagues and Malaysian specialists who have passed on in years not long past; namely, Ishak Shari (1948–2001), Hashim Yaacob (1949–2009), Khoo Khay Jin (1948–2011), Barry Wain (1944–2013), Ismail Hashim (1940–2013), Lim Chin (1947–2014), Badriyah Salleh (1942–2015) and Cheah Boon Kheng (1939–2015). Many of these individuals were not just close friends but fellow intellectual travellers and I believe their work will continue to have a profound influence on future generations of critical academics as well as the general reader. Like me, I am sure they would have subscribed to a positioning that writing and research serves not to just explain social phenomena and practices but to critique them in our pursuit of human progress.

Thanks are also due to three anonymous reviewers who gave very helpful suggestions on improving the original manuscript, including ideas to enhance its arguments and its potential contribution to the existing theoretical literature.

Finally, I would like mention the support given by my immediate family. Adil and Rosa often provided solicited feedback for my ideas and I thank them for their love and encouragement. But as always my deepest thanks go to Maznah, whose unsparing intellectual support and selfless assistance were irreplaceable in the writing of this book.

Johan Saravanamuttu
April 2016

ABBREVIATIONS AND GLOSSARY

ABIM	Angkatan Belia Islam Malaysia, or Malaysian Youth Islamic Movement
ACCIN	Allied Coordinating Committee of Islamic NGOs
Aliran	Aliran Kesedaran Nasional, or National Consciousness Stream
Alliance	Also known as *Perikatan* in Malay. The original coalition of UMNO, the MCA and the MIC.
API	Angkatan Pemuda Insaf
APU	Angkatan Perpaduan Ummah, or Ummah Unity Front
ASWJ	*Ahlus Sunnah Wal Jamaah*. The official Sunni-Sha'fie school of Islam practised in Malaysia, prescribed by the Malaysian Department of Islamic Advancement Malaysia.
AWAM	All Women's Action Society
BA	Barisan Alternatif
Barisan Sosialis	Socialist Front of Singapore, formed as a splinter from the PAP
BARJASA	Barisan Ra'ayat Jati Sarawak (Muslim Bumiputera party)
BCIC	Bumiputera Commercial and Industrial Community
Berjasa	Barisan Jemaah Islamiah, PAS splinter party formed in Kelantan in 1978
Berjaya	Parti Bersatu Rakyat Jelata Sabah
BERSIH	The Coalition for Clean and Fair Elections

BMF	Bumiputera Malaysia Finance, associated with the BMF scandal of a RM2.5 billion loss to Bank Bumiputera
BN	Barisan Nasional (National Front), which was the successor to the Alliance
bumiputera	A Malaysian term meaning "sons of the soil" referring to the Malays, indigenous peoples of Peninsular Malaysia and the natives of Sarawak and Sabah
CAP	Consumer Association of Penang
CCM	Council of Churches Malaysia, the national body that represents mainstream Protestant churches in Malaysia
ceramah	Political meeting or forum used in electoral campaigns
CFC	Christian Federation of Malaysia
Danaharta	Asset Management Corporation
Danamordal	Special Purpose Vehicle for recapitalizing banking
Darul Arqam	House of Arqam, a group considered deviant by Malaysian Islamic authorities and banned by the Malaysian government
DNU	Department of National Unity
Dong Jiao Zong	Malayan Chinese Education Movement comprising the United Chinese School Committees Association and the United Chinese School Teachers Association
DPU	Department of National Unity
EC	Election Commission, or SPR (Surahanjaya Pilihanraya)
EPSM	Environmental Protection Society of Malaysia
EPU	Economic Planning Unit
FELDA	Federal Land Development Authority
FPTP	First-past-the-post, referring to Malaysia's electoral system
Gagasan Rakyat	Coalition for People's Democracy. Also known as "People's Concept".

Gerak	Malaysian People's Movement for Justice
Gerakan	Parti Gerakan Rakyat Malaysia (Malaysian Peoples' Movement Party)
HAKAM	National Human Rights Association of Malaysia
Hindraf	Hindu Rights Action Force
HAMIM	Parti Hizbul Muslimin Malaysia, or Muslim People's Party of Malaysia
Kaedah-kadeah hukum sebat	Caning methods sanctioned by *hudud* law
hudud	The class of punishments under shariah fixed for theft, robbery, illicit sex, consumption of alcohol and apostasy
ICA	Industrial Coordination Act
IFC	Inter-Faith Commission
IIUM	International Islamic University of Malaysia
IMP	Independence Malaya Party
ISA	Internal Security Act. The ISA was repealed and replaced by the Security Offences (Special Measures) Act 2012 on 18 June 2012.
Islam Hadhari	Civilizational Islam
JAKIM	Jabatan Kemajuan Islam Malaysia (Malaysian Department of Islamic Advancement)
JAIS	Jabatan Agama Islam Selangor (Islamic Department of Selangor)
JAWI	Jabatan Agama Wilayah Perseketuan (Islamic Department of Federal Territory)
JIM	Jamaah Islah Malaysia
Ketuanan Melayu	Malay supremacy, or Malay overlordship
khalwat	Term used in Malaysia to mean the compromising proximity of single men and women, chargeable as an offence for Muslims.
KMM	Kesatuan Melayu Muda
Konfrontasi	Indonesia's "Confrontation" against the formation of Malaysia
LDP	Liberal Democratic Party
LP	Labour Party, also known as Parti Buruh Malaya, which disbanded after the 1969 election

Malay	Constitutionally defined as those who practice Malay customs (*adat*), habitually speak the Malay language (*Melayu*) and are adherents of Islam
MBA	Malaysian Buddhist Association
MCA	Malaysian Chinese Association
MCCBCHST	Malaysian Consultative Council for Buddhism, Christianity, Hinduism, Sikhism and Taoism
MCP	Malayan Communist Party
Menteri Besar	Malay term for chief executive of the state government, equivalent to Chief Minister.
MIC	Malaysian Indian Congress
MISC	Malaysian International Shipping Corp
MP	Member of Parliament
NEAC	National Economic Action Council
NECC	National Economic Consultative Council
NEP	New Economic Policy
NOC	National Operations Council
NUJ	National Union of Journalists
OIC	Organisation of Islamic Cooperation. Formerly the Organisation of the Islamic Conference.
Operasi Lalang	Operation Weeding, in which 106 politicians and activists were detained under the ISA in 1987.
OSA	Official Secrets Act
PAJAR	Parti Anak Jati Sarawak
Pakatan Rakyat	People's Alliance, the political coalition made up of opposition parties that were formed in 2008. The parties in this coalition are Parti Keadilan Rakyat/People's Justice Party (PKR), Democratic Action Party (DAP) and the Islamic Party of Malaysia (PAS).
PANAS	Parti Negara Sarawak (National Party of Sarawak)
PAP	People's Action Party of Singapore
PAS	Parti Islam Se-Malaysia (Islamic Party of Malaysia)

PBB	Parti Pesaka Bumiputera Bersatu, or United Traditional Bumiputera Party
PBDS	Parti Bansa Dayak Sarawak
PBS	Parti Bersatu Sabah
Pekemas	Parti Keadilan Masyarakat Malaysia, or Social Justice Party
PEMBELA	Muslim Organisations in Defence of Islam
PERKIM	Pertubuhan Kebajikan Islam se-Malaysia (Malaysian Islamic Welfare Organization)
Permas	Persatuan Raykat Malaysia Sarawak
Pesaka	Parti Pesaka Anak Sarawak (Dayak party)
PKMS	Persatuan Kebangsaan Melayu Sarawak
PKR	Parti Keadilan Rakyat (People's Justice Party)
PKN	Parti KeADILan Nasional (National Justice Party)
PMIP	Pan-Malayan Islamic Party, predecessor of PAS
PN	Party Negara, also Parti Negara
PPP	People's Progressive Party
PR	Pakatan Rakyat, or People's Alliance, and also known simply as "Pakatan"
PRM	Parti Rakyat Malaysia
PRS	Sarawak People's Party
PSM	Parti Sosialis Malaysia, or Socialist Party of Malaysia
PSRM	Parti Sosialis Rakyat Malaysia (originally, Parti Rakyat of Malaya)
PUM	Persatuan Ulama Malaysia (Association of Islamic Scholars Malaysia)
qisas	Offenses that involve bodily injury or loss of life punishable by death and imprisonment but which can be compensated by money or property
Radical Party	Party formed for 1951 George Town election
reformasi	Protest and reform movement initiated after Anwar Ibrahim's dismissal from UMNO and from the government in 1968
ROS	Registrar of Societies
Rukunegara	National Ideology or principles

saluran	Voting "streams" organized for each polling centre or district
SAPO	Sarawak People's Party
SAPP	Sabah Progressive Party
S46	Semangat 46 (Spirit of 46)
SF	Socialist Front formed among opposition parties for 1964 election
SIS	Sisters in Islam
SNAP	Sarawak National Party
SPR	Suruhanjaya Pilihanraya, or Election Commission (EC)
STAR	State Reform Party
SUARAM	Suaram Rakyat Malaysia, Malaysian human rights organization
Sunnah	Teachings, sayings and practices of the Prophet Muhammad.
SUPP	Sarawak United Peoples Party
Suqiu	"17-Point" Election Appeal
Syariah (*shariah*)	Islamic law
Sy'ia (*Shia*)	Followers of Ali, who regarded him as the legitimate successor to the Prophet Muhammad
Tabligh groups	Islamic missionary groups springing from the Deobandi movement, Tabligh Jumaat, of the Indian subcontinent
Tabung Haji	Muslim Pilgrims' Fund
UDP	United Democratic Party
UMNO	United Malays National Organisation
UNKO	United National Kadazan Organisation (later UPKO)
UPKO	United Pasokmomogun Kadazandusun Murut Organisation
USNO	United Sabah National Organisation
UUCA	University and University Colleges Act
WAC	Women's Agenda for Change
WCI	Women's Candidacy Initiative
WDC	Women's Development Collective
Yang di-Pertuan Agong	The Paramount Ruler or King in Malaysia

1

THE IMPERATIVE OF MEDIATED COMMUNALISM

At 3 p.m. on 10 February 2015, Anwar Ibrahim, the leader of the Malaysian Opposition Front, Pakatan Rakyat (PR), was driven in an unmarked vehicle from the Malaysian Federal Court at the Palace of Justice in Putrajaya to the Sungai Buloh prison to be jailed for the second time in his political career. Five federal justices led by Chief Justice Arifin Zakaria unanimously rejected his appeal against a prison sentence of five years for sodomy. The case was a virtual facsimile of his earlier conviction of 1998 when he was sentenced to six years jail but released in 2004 after a federal court overturned the earlier decision. Anwar's incarceration the second time around — indeed, he was detained in 1975 as a social activist too — shows not just the occupational hazard of being a politician in Malaysia but also the extremely high stakes of political contests and outcomes. Malaysia's electoral politics over six decades has seen the tumultuous struggles of political figures, none more prominent than Anwar, to change and drive the country in a more democratic and accountable direction. It has been a politics of repressive tolerance dominated by the ruling coalition of the Alliance and then the Barisan Nasional (BN) after. At the point of writing, the opposition alliance of the Pakatan Rakyat (PR) had twice denied the BN its customary two-thirds command of parliamentary seats and, most spectacularly, won more than 50 per cent of the popular vote in the 2013 election.

This study examines the manner in which Malaysia's multicultural, largely democratic politics have manifested through elections and the factors that drive electoral success and failure. So far there have been thirteen general elections, along with an accompanying number of state elections. The most recent and much anticipated general election was held on 5 May 2013. These elections, the preceding political campaigns and the post-electoral ramifications provide a rich source of materials for the study of procedural and electoral democracy in Malaysia. These two concepts have found their way into the political science literature; the former referring to a process of incorporating technical, transparent electoral procedures while the latter connotes a notion of popular or voter sovereignty. Yet another term is "participatory democracy", usually taken to mean a substantive form of democracy beyond mere electoral processes. Malaysia has failed to make the cut in the U.S.-based Freedom House definition of electoral democracies, but it cannot be denied that it possesses some elements of an electoral democracy despite some obvious flaws, which will be explained in the next chapter.[1]

A particular genre of literature has categorized Malaysia as a form of "competitive authoritarism"; namely, a sort of hybrid regime which marries democratic electoral processes with a measured dose of repressive politics (Levitsky and Way 2010).[2] This sort of politics, as Slater puts it, is effected through an "authoritarian leviathan" (Slater 2010) often resistant to democratic "breakdowns" (Pepinsky 2009). The generalizability of the Malaysian case for broad theorizing related to democratization is highly suggestive and the works cited above demonstrate this. I will touch upon this further in the final chapter but, suffice it to say for now, that in analysing electoral politics over some six decades in Malaysia, I have certainly found many aspects of the authoritarian politics alluded to by writers such as Slater and Pepinsky to be highly evident. My own work in the late 1980s focused on Malaysia as an example of bureaucratic authoritarianism (Saravanamuttu 1987). The burden of my analysis in this book, however, is to show how elections are won or lost in a severely divided plural polity, and thus much of the theoretical underpinnings of the book hark to the scholarship concerned with ethnic politics and elections, which I review further below.

Certainly, electoral exercises cannot also be divorced from deeper political and societal processes which provide the context for electoral contests. While its electoral system inherited from the British may still be found wanting, Malaysia possesses many of the elements of electoral democracy, and is also somewhat exemplary of how a multi-ethnic Asian society has succeeded by and large to mediate ethnic contestations through the ballot box. Moreover, since its emergence as an independent state in 1957, Malaysia has become one of the prime examples of ethnic power sharing and coalition politics in the world. Save for 1969 when a general election sparked racial riots and bloodshed, all other elections have been peaceful and have seen no undue violence. Nonetheless, a major criticism has been that the electoral system, a first-past-the-post (FPTP) single-member constituency plurality choice model, unfairly favours incumbent political parties and has kept the ruling coalition of parties in power for an unbroken six decades (Rachagan 1993; Lim 2002; Brown 2005).

That said, on 8 March 2008 the opposition parties deprived the ruling coalition of its two-thirds majority of seats and defeated it in five out of thirteen state elections. This result has led analysts (including this one) to suggest that electoral politics may have breached a threshold that augurs for the development of a fully fledged two-party system. Turnover political systems are seen by political theorists to be the *sine qua non* of democratic politics. In Malaysia's case, after decades of one-party dominance, 8 March seemingly carried the promise of a new trajectory towards a two-party electoral system. However the 5 May 2013 general election did not see a turnover of the ruling coalition, although the opposition coalition won the popular vote. The prospect of attaining a real turnover political system and "consolidated democracy"[3] clearly remains elusive as long as certain structural obstacles of the electoral system or the substantive and formal development of an effective alternative alliance of forces to the incumbent ruling coalition is not achieved. Huntington (1991) views a stable democracy as one which has passed the "two turnover test"; that is a state which has undergone two peaceful democratic changes. Linz and Stepan (1996) hold that consolidated democracies are those where the citizenry has acquired democratic norms and major actors believe that democracy is the "only game in town". However, these standard political theories do not take account of the problems encountered in ethnically divided societies where democratic processes, as in Malaysia's case, are constitutive of complex ethnic, religious as well as regional bargaining processes.

POPULATION AND COMMUNITIES

In order for the reader to understand adequately the general thrust and arguments of the book with respect to ethnic politics and power sharing, I provide below a number of charts showing Malaysia's population, its ethnic and religious communities and current levels of urbanization in its thirteen states. The information is taken from the latest Population and Census report of 2010. I also provide in Appendix 1A a list of political parties within the different political coalitions in the present and the past.

Figure 1.1 denotes the population of Malaysian citizens distributed by ethnic group (8.2 per cent of the population are non-citizens). The largest single grouping of citizens is the Malay bumiputera, which accounts for 54.6 per cent of the population, followed by Malaysians of Chinese origin, who make up almost 25 per cent of the total population. These are followed by non-Malay bumiputera and Indians who constitute 12.8 per cent and 7.4 per cent of the population, respectively. Figures 1.2 and 1.3 give a further breakdown of this division in accordance to residential location. Among those classified as urban population, Malay bumiputera make up 50.8 per cent, while Chinese Malaysians make up 31.3 per cent. On the other hand, among rural residents non-Malay bumiputera make up the second largest group (24.6 per cent) next to the Malay bumiputera rural population of 63.9 per cent.

Another significant demographic factor is religious identity (Figure 1.4). Muslims predominate at 61.3 per cent, followed by Buddhists comprising 19.8 per cent, Christians 9.2 per cent and Hindus 6.3 per cent of the population. Finally, Figure 1.5 shows the level of urbanization in accordance to states. The most urbanized being the federal territories of Putrajaya and Kuala Lumpur, followed by Selangor and Penang. Based on the 2010 census, Malaysia's population

Figure 1.1
Malaysia: Population Division by Ethnic Groups, 2010

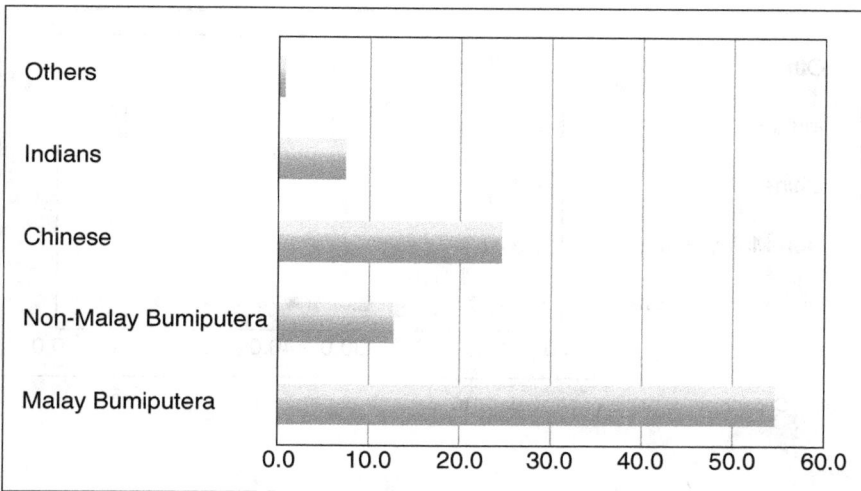

Source: Department of Statistics Malaysia 2010.

Figure 1.2
Malaysia: Population Division by Ethnic Groups in Urban Areas, 2010

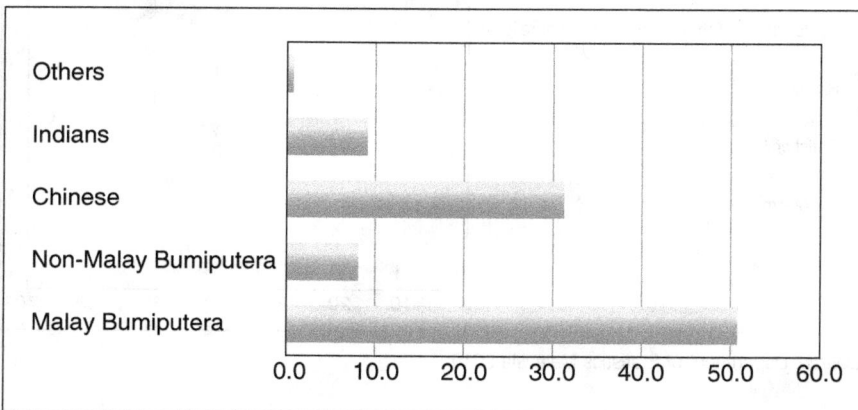

Source: Department of Statistics Malaysia 2010.

Figure 1.3
Malaysia: Population Division by Ethnic Group in Rural Areas, 2010

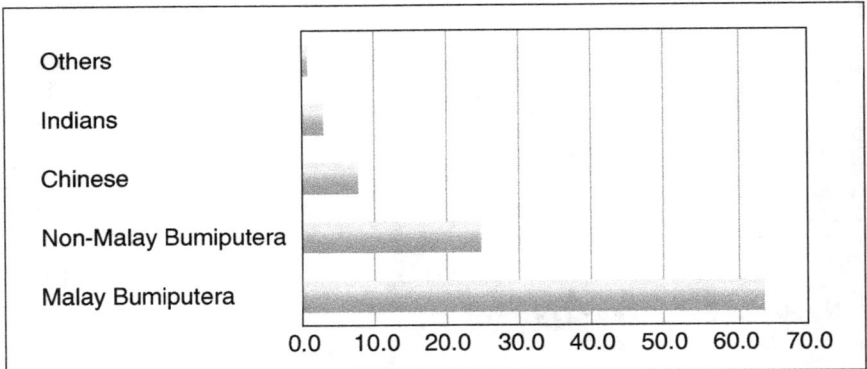

Source: Department of Statistics Malaysia 2010.

Figure 1.4
Malaysia: Percentage of Population by Religion, 2010

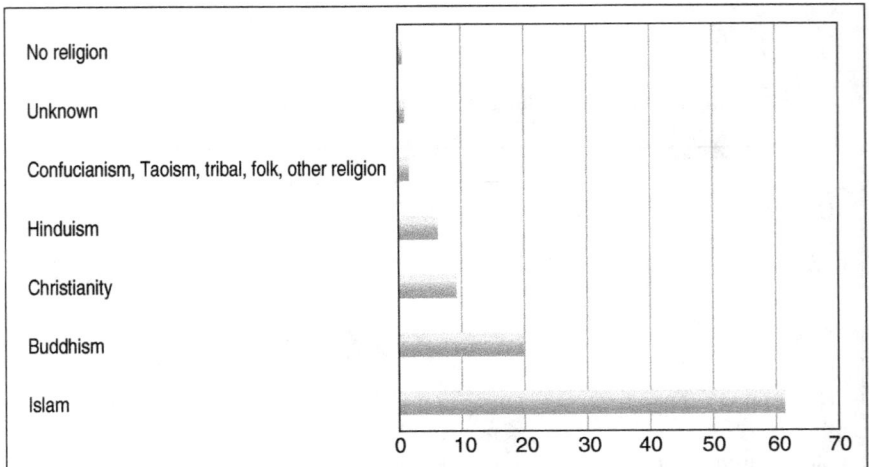

Source: Department of Statistics Malaysia 2010.

Figure 1.5
Malaysia: Level of Urbanization by State, 2010

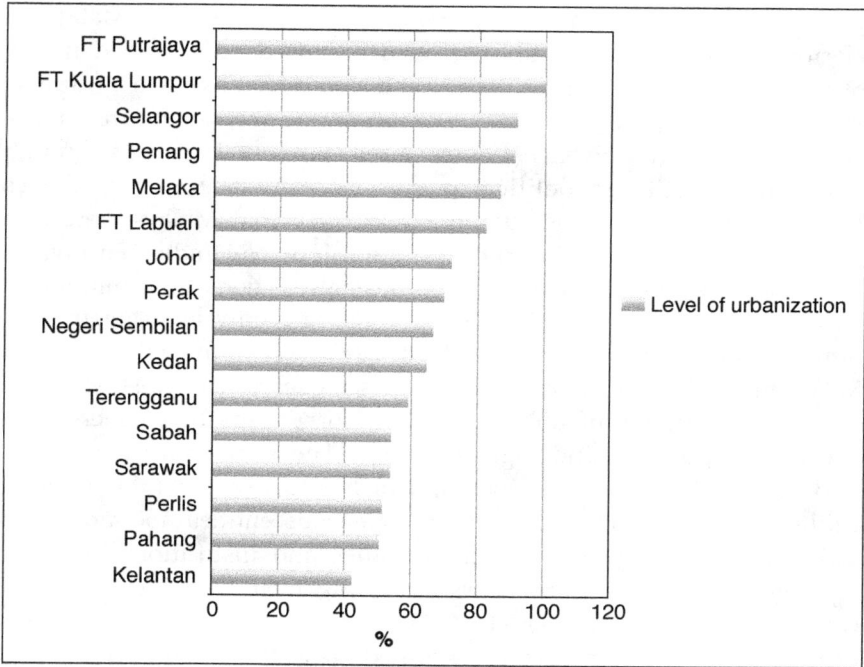

Source: Department of Statistics Malaysia 2010.

topped thirty million in February 2015 and the population has more than tripled since its formation in 1963.[4]

It is against this backdrop of cultural and regional diversity that the contestation for political control has taken place. The convergence of ethnic identity with spatial location (rural versus urban) and the preponderance of the Malay bumiputera is a major reason for the need to secure the support of this community, as well as to mediate all other forms of diversity in the power-sharing model of electoral competition.

COMMUNALISM AND THE PLURAL SOCIETY

This book draws on the deep well of work on communal and electoral politics, as well as theoretical work on "plural societies".[5] Malaysian electoral politics have historically been premised on a hybrid model of "communalism" (Ratnam 1965) and "consociationalism" (Liphart 1977). According to Ratnam, communal politics, a feature of the "plural society" (Furnivall 1948), valorized communal interests through ethnically constituted political parties. Moreover, ethnic cleavages were reinforced with religious affiliation, such that Malays were also Muslims, Chinese were also Buddhists, and Indians Hindus. Furnivall's notion of the plural society comprised small sections or communities living side by side but without integrating, and only held together by dint of colonial power. Alternatively, it was based on the anthropologist M.G. Smith's (1965) notion of divided societies having distinct cores of basic institutions of different sections or groups that cohere only because of political and legal coercion. The same may have been said of the early Malayan society, which was divided into different cultural sections conceived of as homogeneous entities not capable of acting cooperatively within shared values and institutions but only separately through cultural markers among their own members that were "primordial" in character.[6] An inevitable consequence of this primordialism, it was further assumed, was the manifestation and rise of intractable conflicts among groups. Communalism was thus a social feature of plural societies detrimental to social and national integration (Geertz 1963). In Malaya's case, communalism came to be mediated by political processes of ethnic power sharing since the mid-1950s, which analysts have associated with Lijphart's notion of consociationalism. Lijphart argued that ethnically divided societies could live with their ethnic cleavages, that conflict could be contained by leaders of the ethnic communities and that democracy within such divided societies could be managed through formal institutional arrangements — such as federalism and proportional representation — to contain ethnic conflict. He suggested four conditions for the successful implementation of consociational democracy; namely, a grand coalition of all ethnic groups, a mutual veto in decision-making, an ethnic proportionality in allocation of opportunities and offices, and ethnic autonomy, often through federalism.

The corollary to Lijphart's argument was that the adversarial democracy of the Anglo–American variety was unsuitable for plural societies. Writers like Milne and Mauzy (1980) have tried to show that Lijphart's model could be applied to Malaysia with some modification. While consociationalism may explain why and how power sharing arrangements are made, it fails to explain why electoral success is achieved in ethnically and regionally divided societies with a complex distribution of votes and constituencies comprising ethnic majorities, which can be large or small, as well as those with a mix of ethnic voters. The basic consociational model also glosses over the diversity existing within each ethnic group, based on class, place, education and even ideology. The simplification of the older consociational model makes it inadequate as a singular approach for understanding the complexity of intra-communal variations and differences.

A newer theory of political engineering deploys "centripetalism" as a countervailing concept to communalism and consociationalism (Reilly 2006). Essentially, this approach suggests that a centripetal spin of moderate policies to a centre can blunt divisions in ethnically divided societies and thus lead to more sustained systems of electoral democracy. Centripetalism entails the formation of "bridging" rather than "bonding" political parties based on practices of compromise, accommodation and integration across ethnic divides. Bonding parties tend to consolidate ethnic identities in the political system. When bonding becomes predominant in party formation, as is well known in a country like Malaysia, political rewards are given to ethnic constituents at the expense of public goods (Reilly 2006, chap. 4). Reilly considers Papua New Guinea and Fiji to be examples where centripetal systems were adopted. Indonesia after 2004 is also thought to have introduced such a system based on devolutionist politics. Even Singapore with its group representation constituencies, which ensure ethnic inclusiveness, can be said to be an example of such a model of politics. Reilly suggests that governments in Asia are increasingly attempting political reform based on centripetal strategies rather than the older consociational or communal approaches to ethnic peace (Reilly 2006, pp. 85–86).

When we turn to Malaysia it is obvious that the BN, with its consociational model, has dominated central political structures, while the emergent PR, which collectively advocates more moderate, arguably more centripetal politics, remains weak institutionally. The implied notion of centripetalism, that moderate policies tend to garner a larger pool of support, can be applied effectively to the ethnically divided situation of electoral politics in Malaysia along with its need for basic consociational arrangements. Both the BN and now the PR have become effective in pooling the votes of Malaysia's ethnic communities in elections by moving or "spinning" to the centre of the political terrain and advocating moderate ethnic policies. That said, the tendency for Malay-Muslim political parties such as UMNO (United Malays National Organisation) and PAS (Islamic Party of Malaysia) to pull towards extremist and purist ethnic and religious lines have escalated over the last few years.[7]

MEDIATED COMMUNALISM

Taking into account the notions of centripetalism as well as the older notions of communalism and consociationalism, I would like to introduce an approach that could account more fully for electoral success in the Malaysian case. This is the notion of *mediated communalism*, defined as a process which softens the most extreme ethnic, religious and cultural demands and gravitates its actors towards win-win or variable sum outcomes rather than zero-sum ones.[8] Mediated communalism valorizes *bridging* rather than *bonding* dimensions of ethnic relations and is related to the considerable body of social capital literature, particularly the work of Robert Putnam, which stresses that such bridging social capital also brings about a high level of civil engagement to democratic politics.[9]

For Malaysia and other ethnically divided societies, the notion of mediated communalism incorporates consociational and other bridging arrangements of ethnic groups working towards social policies as a stratagem for electoral success. This process also concomitantly moves actions and outcomes to a moderate centre. Unlike Reilly, I do not see centripetalism, consociationalism and communalism as mutually exclusive "ideal types" but as generic stratagems on a continuum of ethnic mobilization. As such, the approach of mediated communalism uses the necessary stratagems implied in these concepts for electoral success. Riker's classic work on political coalitions with its central notion of "minimal winning coalition" is of relevance here. However, beyond minimal imperatives, inter-ethnic political negotiation usually involves both necessary as well as sufficient conditions for desired outcomes.[10] In the Malaysian case, I would argue that consociational arrangements are a necessary first step for communal political parties to establish centripetal practices of moderation. Thus, I posit that there are two *necessary general* conditions for the practice of mediated communalism:

1.   A grand coalition of major communal parties
2.   A centripetal spin to moderate ethnic/religious policies

However, observations show that for a political coalition in Malaysia to achieve electoral success, given the country's history and the persistence of communal politics, there needs to be three *specific sufficient* conditions for mediating communalism:

1.   Strong and effective Malay leadership
2.   Strong non-Malay bumiputera support for coalition parties
3.   Strong non-bumiputera support for coalition parties

In relation to the BN, the current ruling coalition, a strong and effective Malay leadership refers to the hegemonic bloc that has been controlled by UMNO from the outset. While ruptures in the hegemonic Malay bloc occurred in 1969, after the 13 May riots; in 1987 in the party's Team A–Team B conflict; and in 1998 after Anwar Ibrahim's ouster, the UMNO leadership was always able to regroup and re-establish itself in time for the next general election. Leadership splits in UMNO seemingly had minimal effects on the ruling coalition's stable practice of mediating communalism as long as a new leadership prevailed. It is now axiomatic that the ruling coalition has its sustained support in the East Malaysian bumiputera communities, notably the Iban, Bidayuh, Melanau and Orang Ulu in Sarawak and the Kadazan-Dusun and Bajau in Sabah. Indeed, UMNO has become the dominant party in Sabah, although its membership is of non-Malay bumiputera rather than Malays as such. In these East Malaysian states the indigenous coalition parties have remained strong. On the Peninsula, Chinese and Indian support has fluctuated more than that of the other groups. Whenever the BN has tended to veer from its moderate policies, which is one of two *necessary general* conditions (a centripetal spin of policies towards moderation), Chinese and Indian votes on the Peninsula have receded. Up till the 1990s, on the opposition side, the main parties, such as the DAP (Democratic Action Party) and PAS (Islamic Party of Malaysia), have been unable to fulfil almost all of the *necessary general* conditions for a successful mediated communalism. However, from 1999 onwards there was a breakthrough in the formation of the grand coalition; firstly the BA (Barisan Alternatif, or the Alternative Front) in 1999 and then later in 2008 and 2013, the PR. Having had this success, the opposition parties were then able to enhance their support among the non-bumiputera voters and to further fragment the Malay vote, denying UMNO its customary hegemonic control.

In the ensuing chapters of this book I will show that in all elections in which the BN has been successful, the above *necessary general* and *specific sufficient* conditions were mostly present. The two *necessary general* conditions, i.e., the grand coalition and centripetalism in practising mediated communalism, apply *mutatis mutandis* to the opposition coalition, and were achieved in the 2008 and 2013 elections. Likewise, the lack of some of the *specific sufficient* conditions usually presaged poor electoral performances for contesting political parties, whether on the BN or opposition side. The PR succeeded in fulfilling the three specific conditions for winning state contests to form five state governments in 2008 and three in 2013. In short, the *necessary general* conditions can determine marginal electoral success, but, arguably, the *specific sufficient* conditions make for superlative electoral performances. Finally, it should be noted that intervening though not insignificant factors such as external national threats, control of the media, party organization (party machine), finance and money politics (to be discussed in ensuing chapters) are also major factors contributing towards electoral outcomes.

I would like to further deploy the heuristic concept of "path dependence" to reinforce and embellish this theory of mediated communalism. Path dependence theorizing has become associated with a sub-field of politics or school of thought known as "historical institutionalism".[11] This literature puts the accent not on just institutional stability but on institutional change. I would argue that its genealogy harks back to the early work of S.P. Huntington on political institutionalization and his notions of "political development" and "political decay" as well as his subsequent work on democratization.[12] In adopting path dependence as its approach to explaining electoral success and failures, this book could arguably fall within the rubric of this genre of work. Beyond this, however, I am particularly interested in explaining the character of coalition politics in ethnically divided polities, of which Malaysia is a prime example.

A path dependence meta-analytical framework can serve to illustrate trajectories of electoral politics and also explain how electoral successes are continued and enhanced in a multicultural social formation such as Malaysia. Such an overarching framing also warns and guards against analyses that are fully predicated on rational choice and that "satisficing" solutions could often obtain based on more realist assumptions of politics.[13] Moreover, path dependence could show the limits to institutional design to address politics given that contingent events sometimes lead to major changes in political regimes. That said, paths taken as opposed to paths not taken tend to develop positive feedback loops as long as actors are able to capitalize on initial advantages. Thus, an important notion of path dependence theory is "first-mover advantage" (FMA), normally used in economics and business studies to refer to the technological advantage of a pioneering firm or a new entrant in a field of enterprise. Paul Pierson has adapted this notion for the analysis of politics in a seminal article followed by a book.[14] Coupled with FMA is the notion of "increasing returns" which, in brief, refers to the probability that further steps along a particular path tend to lead to increases down that path. Both concepts are central to path dependence theorizing.

The BN's electoral successes, as I will try to show in ensuing chapters, were achieved by its mediated communalism being on a trajectory of increasing returns, or, to put it differently, it was able to capitalize on actions and policies which were electorally successful which further enhanced its model of multi-ethnic politics. Such path-dependent success continued in spite of ruptures of the hegemonic Malay bloc in 1969, 1987 and 1999, as argued above, because of well-managed and well-executed mediated communalism involving the consociational partners of the ruling front. Thus, I would argue that path-dependent electoral success was premised on the maintenance and management of mediated communalism even when coalition partners — be they UMNO, MCA, MIC or East Malaysian partners — were experiencing internal conflicts.

An element lacking or understudied is the political economy of electoral politics. The book also deals with the phenomenon of money politics and invokes the notion of "party capitalism" as a major factor impinging on electoral politics. This factor is dealt with in Chapter 5 and alludes to a form of rentier economics that had become a concomitant of the New Economic Policy (NEP) involving the engagement of UMNO and its coalition partners in business. Akin to "pork barrel politics", money politics qua party capitalism deeply embeds and melds ruling political parties into political businesses and the corporate economy (Fields 1995). In Malaysia, party capitalism saw its apogee in the Mahathir years and remains prevalent in the Najib Razak years. It may be conceived of as both a positive and negative phenomenon in terms of causing increasing or diminishing returns to electoral success, as will be explained in Chapters 5 and 6.

Broadly, electoral politics in Malaysia could be viewed as transitioning through three chronological periods:

1. Emergent Mediated Communalism: 1950s to 1960s
2. Corporatized Mediated Communalism: 1970s to late 1990s
3. Contested Mediated Communalism: Late 1990s to 2013

In the first period Malaysian politics may be said to be cast within the frame of an initially somewhat pristine strategy of mediated communal politics, which was anchored on a form of basic consociational politics. The discursive trope of mediated communalism during this first phase was the politics of "The Bargain" — the compact among ethnic political elites at the point of Independence, where supposedly non-Malay citizenship was "exchanged" for Malay political primacy[15] — which saw the politics of ethnic competition and compromise, well captured in much early work on Malaysian politics. In this early phase, electoral politics were sharply divided by ethnic schisms within the ruling coalition of the Alliance Party and its rival the Independence Malaya Party (IMP) and between them and the non-Malay opposition parties. However, the ruling coalition somehow was held together by the informal rules of a basic form of consociation, not least of all by the strong and dominant personality of its first leader Tunku Abdul Rahman. Although not using consociational theory, Von Vorys (1975, chaps. 6 and 7) describes this model well as one with the oversight of a "Directorate" of the major leaders of ethnic communities headed by the Tunku. The Directorate's task was one of ensuring "vertical mobilization" (i.e., getting support of respective ethnic communities) and "horizontal solidarity" through building trust among ethnic leaders. Compared to the Alliance, opposition parties had no such nationally driven stratagems. The Islamic party (PMIP, then) failed to significantly penetrate national politics and later ensconced itself in the East Coast of Malaya. Other parties that opted out of this consociation were the professed ideological parties, namely the Labour Party and the Malay-based socialist party, PSRM (Partai Sosialis Rakyat Malaysia). In a period when the ruling Alliance Party invested heavily into consociational power sharing arrangements, positive returns were reaped to keep the ruling coalition comfortably in power until the late 1960s. However, these arrangements tended to be highly elite-biased and failed to provide increasing returns, especially to its larger rural-based Malay constituency.

In hindsight the racial riots of 13 May 1969 were a predictable outcome of the stark nature of Malayan communal politics and the failure of consociational arrangements to contain extreme ethnic politics outside of the Alliance. In the words of Von Vorys (1976), it was a "democracy without consensus" that would structure the next phase of politics. Thus, investment in political arrangements began to swing to the other extreme. In this second phase of Malaysian politics one saw how Malay supremacy became both the discursive trope and the primary political tool of the main Malay political party. UMNO refurbished its role as *primus inter pares* and patently dominated all aspects of political life through the implementation of the NEP. However, despite or even because of the NEP, a new form of mediated communalism was effected through party capitalism. The BN was highly successful in this phase in melding politics with business and rewarding its own political parties and cronies. An expanding pie ensured that the distribution of spoils was more than satisfactory. This phase of electoral politics could aptly be termed "corporatized mediated communalism". However, while the ruling coalition successfully expanded into the more encompassing National Front, electoral democracy was clearly hamstrung by a highly micromanaged form of politics, which placed a premium on the creation of bumiputera institutions, businesses, legislation and regulations to promote the NEP goals. While UMNO was able to capitalize on the increasing returns to its NEP-driven policies, its non-Malay partners began to lose political ground. The expanding economic pie coupled with a comprehensive network of politically linked corporate entities ensured that all BN parties received a suitable share of the economic largesse to the extent that several UMNO-linked non-Malay figures rose to or remained at the commanding heights of the economy.

The second major rupture of the hegemonic Malay bloc occurred when Tengku Razaleigh challenged Mahathir for the UMNO leadership, leading to the deregistering of UMNO itself. In spite of this rupture the BN's mediated communalism was managed well and given much sustenance through UMNO and its partner parties' corporate and business linkages, and this was enough to secure an electoral victory in 1990 because of the inability of the opposition parties to form a united front. Instead, two opposition fronts were created to mobilize Malay and non-Malay parties and pressure groups and, as shown by outcomes, this was less than satisfactory.

Perhaps the most significant rupture of the Malay bloc occurred after the sacking of Anwar Ibrahim as deputy prime minister and his incarceration. This episode, another manifestation of intra-party rivalry within UMNO's leadership, is not unconnected to fallouts and crises of UMNO's party capitalism. This opened the floodgates of a participatory *new politics*. This new participatory politics of the third period was symbolized by the Reformasi Movement, which sparked unprecedented multi-ethnic and cross-ethnic engagement in politics on the part of civil society and oppositional forces.[16] In this book I use the term *new politics* as a modality rather than an outcome to denote an ongoing participatory politics of civil engagement in the public sphere with the objective of valorizing democratic values and human rights over and above ethnic interests.[17] *New politics*, however, does not necessarily supersede the need for political actors, particularly political parties, to deploy stratagems of mediated communalism for electoral success.

The developments associated with *new politics* spilled over on to the electoral process. The political shift that occurred with the surfacing of such politics in the late 1990s culminated in the political watershed of the 8 March general election of 2008. At this juncture it became obvious that with the rise of a coherent united opposition and the alternative alliance of the PR, BN's mediated communalism was seriously challenged.

An analysis of the landmark 2008 general election shows why the BN lost its first-mover advantage, an edge it had held for decades with its copious investments, both political and economic, in institutions which reproduced its form of mediated communalism for electoral outcomes. The fact that this path dependence was broken on 8 March suggests an alternative path dependence based on a new mode of political mobilization executed through the mediated communalism of the PR. A major plank of the PR's mediated communalism was its engagement of people-oriented and civil-society-driven agendas. It has become increasingly clear in the early years of the PR's success that newer more effective forms of political investments were being introduced by the opposition coalition in spite of a previous steep learning curve. While still relying on the older consociational arrangements of ethnic power sharing, the PR has invested time and effort in political institutions which have aimed to provide good governance, economic welfarism and civil rights in the tradition of delivering more universal "political goods" to the citizenry.[18] This new trajectory was one that put the premium on participatory politics while debunking the deleterious effect of a rentier political economy based on the ruling coalition's party capitalism. The trajectory of new politics did not at all mean a total departure from ethnicized politics, but rather a political shift in the direction of an investment in more universalist and democratic politics coupled with economic sensibility and even-handedness in the distribution of political goods within the context of a neo-liberal economy. These were the new elements of political engagement which layered the practice of a contested mediated communalism. After 2008 the BN no longer monopolized the terrain of the latter, with the PR as its new, credible competitor. Political developments in mid-2015 have seen the disbandment of the PR, but there were immediate attempts to revive a similar opposition alliance, as narrated in a later chapter.

STRUCTURE OF THE BOOK

Following this introduction, Chapter 2 examines the literature on electoral politics and the origins of an electoral system introduced and reconstituted within the parameters of Malaysia's "plural" or divided society. The constant tweaking of the electoral system has led some to suggest its departure from democratic norms. However, it should be remembered that Malaysia's first-past-the-post, single-member constituency system was from the outset a legacy of British rule and tutelage and its historically unique features have remained intact. Electoral politics has been broadly anchored to elements of procedural democracy such as transparent and autonomous electoral institutions and procedures, freedom of political association and campaigning and the like, guaranteed by law and the Constitution. This said, the erosion of some of these constitutional guarantees and best practices through electoral manipulation and amendments to electoral laws are now thought to have reached unacceptable proportions. Such amendments to the electoral system, and particularly the practice of the malapportionment of greater rural weight to constituencies, have seemingly ensured the longevity of the ruling coalition, which has held power since Independence. The maintenance of such a system is clearly premised on political investment in arrangements that have largely kept *ethnic peace*, without necessarily valorizing electoral democracy.

Having examined the origins and various critiques of Malaysia's first-past-the-post system, in Chapter 3 the book next analyses and critiques ethnicity manifested as "communalism" (Ratnam 1965) and how this defined the parameters and discursive terrain of Malaysian electoral politics. This chapter traces the origins and entrenchment of Malaysia's first consociational arrangement through the grand coalition of the Alliance. Basic elements of mediated communalism were successfully incorporated into this model of politics and helped to keep the electoral process on an even keel until the fateful May 1969 general election. This chapter presents the results and interprets the elections of 1959, 1964 and 1969. The Alliance was able throughout this period to capitalize on its power sharing arrangements, although the parliamentary leftist forces, the Socialist Front, mounted a veritable challenge.

The next two chapters, Chapters 4 and 5, study the post-1969 situation, namely the rise of a reconstituted Alliance in the form of the BN as a response to communal riots in 1969 and the breakdown of the first power-sharing model. Undoubtedly, the framing of Malaysian politics under the NEP and the discursive device of *Ketuanan Melayu* (Malay supremacy) impacted heavily on how a new mediated communalism was to be institutionalized. Admittedly, it did have the salutary effect of constituting a highly stable if authoritarian political order anchored around the dominance of UMNO within the BN governments of those years. Along with Malay supremacy came along the notion that the BN could never afford to lose its two-thirds majority of seats in Parliament or, for that matter, control of any state government. The general elections of 1974 and 1978 are analysed in Chapter 5. The Islamic party (PMIP, then later, PAS) was incorporated into the ruling coalition from 1974 until 1978, as well as the previously oppositionist party, the Gerakan. The period ended with PAS's departure from the BN but with the strengthening of Gerakan as a Chinese-centric party in control of the Chinese-majority state of Penang.

Following from this, Chapter 6 analyses the impact of a new element in the mediation of communalism — its corporatization in the form of money politics under the premiership of Mahathir Mohamad. The character and persistence of money politics is examined by invoking the concept of "party capitalism" to dissect how this had become a contributory factor in keeping mediated communalism intact, yet not immediately destructive of the ruling coalition in this initial phase. Malaysia has become a prime example of how political parties are directly involved in business wherein capitalist practices themselves are a function of political agendas. In this period, investment in bumiputera institutions also helped to a great extent to keep the East Malaysian states of Sabah and Sarawak firmly within the BN. UMNO, under the leadership of Mahathir, took party capitalism to its zenith in the 1990s, and the BN's landslide victory in the 1995 election perhaps marked the high point of this type of politics. As with the economic notion of "boom and bust", the 1995 election also symbolized the beginning of diminishing returns for the ruling coalition. The financial meltdown of 1997–98 occurred in tandem with this decline. The limits to and deleterious impact of money politics is shown against the backdrop of the 1982, 1985, 1990 and 1995 elections.

Chapter 7 examines the rupture of the hegemonic Malay bloc, the mainstay of UMNO, which occurred after the sacking of Anwar Ibrahim as deputy prime minister. This event and his incarceration led to the emergence of a new participatory politics, manifested in the 1999 general election, also the last election held under the premiership of Mahathir. The political shift that occurred in the late 1990s culminated in the political watershed of 8 March. The chapter delves into the genesis of the Reformasi Movement, the burgeoning of civil society organizations and their involvement and engagement in the electoral process. The new factor of cyberspace and social media and their implications for and impact on electoral politics via the expansion and engagement of civil groups in the public sphere provide a significant trope for analysing this period. The chapter discusses the formation of the People's Justice Party (PKR), the emergence of the multi-ethnic Barisan Alternative just prior to the 1999 election, the election's outcome and the political fallout of the ensuing years.

Chapter 8 begins with a narrative on the political retirement of Mahathir and the emergence of the Abdullah Badawi government. It examines the results of the 2004 elections to explain how in the context of new politics this election may merely have represented an aberration, a sort of "swan song" before an egregious decline of the ruling coalition. On 8 March 2008 the opposition parties in Malaysia deprived the ruling National Front coalition of its two-thirds majority of seats and defeated it in five out of thirteen states it contested. The chapter argues that March 2008 augured the beginning of a new path-dependent development of a turnover electoral system in Malaysia. Path dependence analysis is used here to explain why the BN progressively lost its first-mover advantage. March 2008 represented a decline of this earlier path dependence for the BN. Put differently, the BN was not able to reap "increasing returns" from its established practice of mediated communalism. This was largely because of the emergence of the PR, which succeeded in establishing its own practice of mediated communalism. The PR's path-dependent success in 2008 was reinforced by the fact that that it won eight of the sixteen by-elections held after March 2008. It became increasingly clear that newer forms of political processes and sensibilities were being introduced by the opposition coalition. This new trajectory was one which put a premium on urban-based participatory politics.

The post-2008 period saw the continued expansion of the public sphere, the engagement of civil society and youth in the political process and the significance of social media. In the four years preceding the 2013 general election, the changed political landscape became more than evident. The tracking of two-coalition politics continued at the federal and state levels. The outcome of the Sarawak state election of 16 April 2011 saw the development of two-coalition politics in this state, with the swing of urban votes to the PR. The Achilles heel of the PR was its lack of capacity to penetrate the vast and geographically removed rural constituencies where traditionally powerful parties like the PBB (Parti Bersatu Bumiputera, United Traditional Bumiputera Party) maintained its strong path dependence. Money politics and party capitalism at the state level no doubt contribute greatly to the victories of the state BN parties. On the Peninsula, the leadership of Najib Razak saw attempts to introduce reforms, including the abolition of draconian laws like the ISA (Internal Security Act). The impact of such reform seemed minimal in the changed political landscape. Citizens continued to take to the streets to demand electoral reforms in two massive BERSIH[19] rallies held in 2011 and 2012.

In the context of these political developments, Chapter 9 analyses the general election of 5 May 2013. While the 2013 election proved to be a significant development in the progress of electoral democracy, there was no electoral turnover of the BN and, in hindsight, the 2008 outcome may be said to be a more critical conjuncture of political change than 2013, as it had created the onset of the two-coalition system. However, 2013 did mark further progressive movement in terms of more than 50 per cent of the popular vote attained by the PR. One could argue that this was a technical breach towards a turnover electoral system, although one still without substantial political significance. The rural–urban divide that appears to be deeply embedded in Malaysia's configuration of electoral politics is the main cause for the current electoral impasse, as the rural weighting of seats as well as the large number of East Malaysian seats continue to favour the ruling coalition.

Political developments post-2013 turned out to be highly chaotic for both the government and the opposition, and events are still unfolding at the point of writing (mid 2016). Two political developments which will have a major impact on society and elections are, first, the beleaguered position of Prime Minister Najib Razak and, second, the break-up of the Pakatan Rakyat. The first development has seen yet another schism within the ruling UMNO party with the sacking of deputy premier Muhyiddin Yassin and his replacement by Ahmad Zahid Hamidi. This came after revelations surfaced on the 1MDB scandal involving an RM42 billion debt and alleged malfeasance on the part of executives and advisers of the federal fund. Most damaging were media revelations pointing to the flow of RM2.6 billion into Najib Razak's private bank account and the likely use of some of the money for campaigning in the 2013 general election. This development may not necessarily lead to a breakup of UMNO and the BN but will no doubt have grave implications for its cohesion and institutional capacity for the next election. The other major development was the breakup of the PR after the 61st PAS Mukthmar (party congress), of June 2015, when a resolution was passed to sever relations with the DAP. This action by PAS and the responses to it by the DAP and PKR effectively brought an unceremonious end to the opposition alliance. I deal with these developments in Chapter 10 with the view to bringing the reader up to speed on the manner the opposition alliance tried to reconstitute itself for the next general election. The book ends with a substantive conclusion which reinforces the importance of consociation and mediated communalism in electoral politics, demonstrating the particular constraints encountered in the special case of Malaysia in constituting centripetal electoral arrangements, as well as the problem of using generic theories of politics to explain the Malaysian case.

In summary, the book through Chapters 3 and 4 explores the idea of emergent mediated communalism of the early period, from the 1950s to the late 1960s. Chapters 5 and 6 make a case for the onset and entrenchment of a mediated communalism in a corporatized mould via Malay primacy and party capitalism from the 1970s till the late 1990s. Chapters 7, 8 and 9 subsequently trace the origins of a contested mediated communalism and new politics, spanning the period between the late 1990s till 2013. Developments beyond 2013 are dealt with in Chapter 10, while Chapter 11 reiterates the major arguments and draws out the conclusions of the book. Through its discursive and empirical explorations the book attempts to test the saliency of a distinct approach to ethnic power sharing and electoral dominance, notably through a process of mediated communalism, a practice that is particularly suited to a social formation such as Malaysia, which is ethnically, religiously and regionally divided, yet which has been remarkably if tenuously integrated throughout its electoral history.

APPENDIX 1A

Barisan Nasional (BN) Component Parties

	Name	Acronym	Year founded
1	United Malays National Organisation*	UMNO	1946/1988
2	Malaysian Chinese Association	MCA	1949
3	Malaysian Indian Congress	MIC	1946
4	Malaysian People's Movement Party	Gerakan	1968
5	People's Progressive Party	PPP	1953
6	United Traditional Bumiputera Party	PBB	1973
7	Sarawak United People's Party	SUPP	1959
8	United Sabah Party**	PBS	1985
9	Liberal Democratic Party	LDP	1988
10	United Sabah People's Party	PBRS	1994
11	United Pasokmomogun Kadazandusun Murut Organisation	UPKO	1994
12	Sarawak Progressive Democratic Party	SPDP	2002
13	Sarawak People's Party	PRS	2004

Pakatan Rakyat (PR) Component Parties

	Name	Acronym	Year founded
1	People's Justice Party	PKR	1999
2	Democratic Action Party	DAP	1966
3	Pan-Malaysian Islamic Party***	PAS	1955

* UMNO was founded in 1946. In 1988 it was deregistered over breach of party rules. A new UMNO (UMNO Baru), under Prime Minister Mahathir Mohamad, was registered in the same year.
** PBS left the BN coalition in 1990 and rejoined it in 2002.
*** PAS joined the BN coalition in 1974 and left it in 1977.

APPENDIX 1B

Electoral Coalitions in Malaysia, Past and Present

	Name	Acronym	Founded	Dissolved
1	Alliance (Perikatan)		1951	1973
2	National Front (Barisan Nasional)	BN	1973	
3	People's Concept (Gagasan Rakyat)	GR	1989	1996
4	Ummah Unity Front (Angkatan Perpaduan Ummah)	APU	1989	1996
5	Alternative Front (Barisan Alternatif)	BA	1999	2008
6	People's Pact (Pakatan Rakyat)	PR	2008	2015
7	Sabah People's Front (Barisan Rakyat Sabah)	SPF	2010	
8	Coalition of Hope (Pakatan Harapan)	PH	2015	

Sources: Barisan Nasional website <http://www.barisannasional.org.my/en>; Wikipedia "List of Political Parties in Malaysia" <http://en.wikipedia.org/wiki/List_of_political_parties_in_Malaysia> (accessed 25 May 2015); *Straits Times*, 23 September 2015.

Notes

1. See Campbell (2008, pp. 18–30) for a discussion of the minimal and maximal definitions of "democracy".
2. Competitive authoritarianism is defined as follows: Competitive authoritarian regimes are civilian regimes in which formal democratic institutions exist and are widely viewed as the primary means of gaining power, but in which incumbents' abuse of the state places them at a significant advantage vis-à-vis their opponents. Such regimes are

competitive in that opposition parties use democratic institutions to contest seriously for power, but they are not democratic because the playing field is heavily skewed in favour of incumbents. Competition is thus real but unfair (Levitsky and Way 2010, p. 5).

3. On the notion of consolidated democracy, see Linz and Stepan (1996) and the useful survey of work on the subject by Rose and Shin (2001). On democratization processes from an Asian perspective, see Saravanamuttu (2006). The classic work on democracy qua "polyarchy" is by Robert Dahl (1971). Samuel P. Huntington's (1991) work on the "third wave" of democratization sparked the broad discourse and theorizing about new democracies and Larry Diamond (1999) and others have carried the discussions forward in the *Journal of Democracy*. Our interest here is how electoral democracy, as a subset of consolidated democracy, could be attained in Malaysia. In later chapters I also deal with how the expansion of the public sphere impacts on and deepens electoral politics.

4. See report of Statistics Department, cited in <http://www.themalay mailonline.com/malaysia/article/population-to-hit-30-million-today-statistics-department-says> (accessed 13 August 2015).

5. The literature on ethnic politics and elections in Malaysia is voluminous; the more prominent studies being Ratnam (1965), Ratnam and Milne (1967), Vasil (1972), Von Vorys (1976), Pillay (1974), Means (1976, 1991), Milne (1978), Milne and Mauzy (1980), Crouch and Lee (1980), Crouch (1982, 1996), Zakaria Ahmad (1987), Gomez (1996), Case (1996), Milne (1999), Loh and Khoo (2002), Loh and Saravanamuttu (2003), Verma (2004), Puthucheary and Noraini (2005), Ooi, Lee and Saravanamuttu (2008), Maznah (2008), O'Shaunassy (2009), Pepinsky (2009), Loh (2009), Faisal Hazis (2011), Weiss (2013, 2006), Chin (2013), Ahamd Fauzi and Muhamad Takiyuddin (2014), and Saravanamuttu, Lee and Mohd. Nawab (2015).

6. In Clifford Geertz's well-cited essay (1963), primordial sentiments and attachments are ascriptive ties of blood, race and religion, which can obstruct societies from developing civil loyalties to larger entities such as the "nation".

7. Ever since the BN's loss of its two-thirds parliamentary majority in 2008, UMNO has adopted a strategy of winning greater Malay support through its exhortation of more extreme racial and religious causes. It has also tried to form a unity government with PAS to consolidate the Malay-Muslim bloc. On the tendency to re-communalize, see Case (2013).

8. I am invoking here a familiar concept of game theory, which is premised on rational choice.

9. See Putnam's two classic studies (1993, 2000). In a research project I undertook with USM colleagues (Chan Lean Heng, Yen Siew Hwa and Tan Lee Ooi) in 2005–6, we found that the associational life created by ethnically based NGOs in Penang were crucial steps towards the generation of subsequent bridging social capital to bring about some level of "ethnic peace" in society. We presented our findings at the 5th International Malaysian Studies Conference held in Kuala Lumpur on 8–10 August 2006 in a panel on "Building Social Capital through Associational Life". See Campbell and Yen (2007) for an exposition and summary of the research results.

10. Riker's famous work based on game theory and rational choice advances the idea that politicians will choose the minimal size of coalitions necessary for governance with minimal expense of resources (Riker 1993). While this may be true of politics in more homogenous societies, I believe that the classic work of anthropologist F.G. Bailey (1969) on "stratagems and spoils" of politics relates better to the nuances and complexities of ethnic politics in a country such as Malaysia.

11. See, for example, Mahoney and Thelen (2010) which has a collection of essays dealing with institutional change in terms of critical junctures and breakdowns of established processes.

12. See Huntington's classic work, *Political Order in Changing Societies* (1968) and his *The Third Wave of Democratization* (1991).

13. Herbert H. Simon was first to deploy the notion of "satisficing" to explain decision-making behaviour of public institutions. It refers essentially to arriving at approximate best results given administrative and political constraints; i.e., results that are satisfactory rather than optimal (Simon 1947).

14. Pierson (2000, pp. 251–67). See also Pierson's larger work, *Politics in Time* (2004) for a comprehensive exposition of path-dependence theorizing. Work cast in terms of historical sociology is found in Mahoney (2002, pp. 507–48).

15. However, there has been considerable debate over whether such a quid pro quo was in fact struck among the political elites or that it was the basis for the formalization of the provisions for Malay privileges in the Malayan Constitution. See Cheah (2002), especially Chapter 2.

16. In fact there have been two broad connotations of the term. The more broadly used meaning is that of the rise of participatory politics with the increased engagement of civil society in the public sphere (Loh and Saravanamuttu 2003). However, in his earlier work, Loh had used *new politics* to refer to the politics of developmentalism (Loh 2001, 2002) but later he adopted a more encompassing definition: "[New] politics

refers to the increasing fragmentation of the ethnic communities, on the one hand, the contestations between the discourses and practices of the politics of ethnicism, participatory democracy, and developmentalism, on the other" (Loh 2003, p. 297).

17. See also Loh's collection of essays (2009) in a book entitled *Old vs New Politics in Malaysia*. On the back cover he states that old politics was essentially ethnic based and characterized by money politics, coercive laws and other restrictions, while new politics "demands more democratic participation and social justice, accountability and transparency, and is more multi-ethnic in orientation".

18. For the notion of political goods, see the work of Pennock (1966).

19. BERSIH is the electoral reform movement which emerged just prior to the 2008 general election (see Chapter 9). For a pictorial account of one of the biggest of these rallies, BERSIH 3, see Yeoh (2012). Some have suggested that the 2015 BERSIH 4 rally topped BERSIH 3 in numbers (see Chapter 10).

2

THE ELECTORAL SYSTEM
Origin, Rationale and Critique

This chapter will examine the origin of Malaysia's first-past-the-post (FPTP) system and the manner in which elections have been conducted. Malaysia, with its unique distribution of ethnic political parties, has a generic FPTP single-member constituency system, which was originally implemented by the British in 1955 at the national level under self-government. After Independence in 1957, following the recommendations of the Reid Constitutional Commission,[1] a federal form of government and elections, based on Westminster-styled institutions, was implemented.

The electoral system is broadly anchored to elements of procedural democracy such as transparent and autonomous electoral institutions and procedures, freedom of political association and campaigning and the like, guaranteed by law and constitutional provisions which devolve duties of conducting elections to an independent Election Commission (EC). By and large the system introduced at Independence in terms of broad procedure and institutions has remained intact. The erosion of some of these constitutional guarantees owing to political developments along with changes and amendments to some of these procedures and the introduction of new elements will be discussed in this chapter.

Malaysia's electoral system as its stands today harks back to the report by the Constituency Delineation Commission for the Federation of Malaya of 1954, headed by Lord Merthyr (hereinafter, Merthyr Commission), which recommended the delimitation of the fifty-two constituencies in Malaya's first federal election of 1955.[2] The report goes into considerable detail in making its recommendations, including the reasons for the adoption of the FPTP single-member constituency model and the reasons for the appropriate system of electoral representation that should be adopted in the then Malayan Federation. The issues of apportionment or distribution of voters and *rural weightage* and its rationale along with the role and powers given to the EC were arguably the most crucial matters taken up by the Reid Commission. The Reid Commission, which crafted the Malayan Constitution, recommended an electoral system based on that proposed by the 1954 Merthyr Commission, but it was no doubt also influenced by the conduct of the First Election of the Members of the Legislative Council of the Federation of Malaya and the detailed report submitted on it (hereinafter, the Smith Report). The issues of the eligibility and citizenship of electors and other rationales for adopting this system will be given due focus in this chapter. The FPTP single-member plurality system was deployed for all the federal elections from 1959 onwards, with important amendments made in the 1960s and, with the formation of the Federation of Malaysia in 1963, a new apportionment of seats for Singapore, Sabah and Sarawak had to be made. Other amendments made in 1973 and in 1984 will also be studied along with the delineation exercises of the EC. The broad argument could be made that the FPTP electoral system, despite its merit of simplicity, has tended to distort voter choice and to favour incumbent political parties. This sort of system has given rise, in the parlance of electoral studies, to "manufactured majorities", i.e., electoral outcomes that confer a majority of seats (simple or large) to a single party or a coalition of parties which do not command a majority of the popular vote. As stated by Douglas Rae in his classic work on the political consequences of electoral laws, parliamentary majorities can be achieved in two basic ways, namely by winning a majority of the popular vote and receiving a proportionate number of seats or by winning less than a majority of the popular vote but receiving a bonus of seats as an artefact of the electoral system. The first type of majority is "earned" while the second type is "manufactured".[3]

Further below I will delve into changes to the system and critiques of the system by academics. There will also be a section that deals with the abolition of locally elected councils by the Malaysian government. The removal of this tier of electoral politics constitutes a major erosion of procedural democracy in Malaysia. The final part of the chapter will be devoted to various calls and suggestions for electoral reform.

EARLY ELECTIONS

The first election ever to be held in Malaysia was in George Town, Penang, at the municipal level on 1 December 1951 after the Local Authorities Elections Ordinance 1950 was passed. This election was not based on single-member constituencies but a system based on a number of constituencies, called "wards", which elected more than one candidate per ward. The election gave the first taste of electoral democracy to Malayans and was the first attempt at introducing self-government by the British.[4] The 1951 election proved to be eminently successful from the colonial perspective. Adult suffrage given to 10,500 voters was implemented in three wards, which returned 9 councillors, while the High Commissioner appointed 6. There were altogether 24 candidates from the Radical Party, UMNO, and the Labour Party and 3 independents. The Radical Party took the honours with 6 wins, while the Labour Party took 1 and another went to an independent.[5]

The George Town election was followed by the Kuala Lumpur municipal election of 16 February 1952. This election witnessed the birth of the ethnically based Alliance coalition, which initially comprised the United Malays National Organisation (UMNO) and the Malayan Chinese Association (MCA), without the Malayan Indian Congress (MIC), which was then in an alliance with the Malayan Independence Party (IMP). Twelve out of the 18 councillors were elected from four constituencies, with the remaining 6 being appointed by the Sultan of Selangor. Thirty-two candidates contested in four constituencies; of the 12 elected, 3 were from UMNO, 6 from MCA, 2 from IMP and 1 was an independent.

The 1952 Kuala Lumpur election paved the way for the first federal election of 27 July 1955. The Alliance Party helmed by Tunku Abdul Rahman virtually swept the board, winning 51 seats, losing only 1 seat to the Pan-Malaya Islamic Party (PMIP, later PAS). The Alliance fielded 66 candidates, Parti Negara helmed by Dato' Onn Jaafar fielded 33 candidates, while PMIP fielded 11. Other participating parties were the Labour Party, Perak Progressive Party (later known as the People's Progressive Party), Pertubuhan Kebangsaan Perak and Pertubuhan Melayu. In this election the Alliance Party consisted of UMNO, the MCA and the MIC (which joined the Alliance in 1954). More than 80 per cent of voters gave their support to the Alliance Party. In its general election manifesto the Alliance called for Independence within four years, compulsory education for all races, a local civil service, adherence to human rights and a constitutional monarchy based on Malay rulers. The Tunku, as the leader of the Alliance Party, was appointed as the first chief minister of the Federation of Malaya and within two years he was able to successfully gain Malaya's Independence from the British.[6]

As already noted above, the 1954 Merthyr Commission's constituency study and the detailed report on the 1955 election by T.E. Smith, the supervisor of that election, would have provided the basis for the Reid Commission's recommendations for the FPTP system of elections for an independent Malaya. I will now draw on the narrative of the 1955 Smith Report, which gives a full account of the 1955 election.

THE CONDUCT OF THE 1955 ELECTION

Malaya's first general election was held on 27 July 1955 after the government had accepted the 1954 Merthyr Commission's recommendations. The chief secretary of the government took charge of conducting the election. A princely sum of $1,125,000 was expended to conduct the election of 52 federal representatives. The numbers of polling districts and stations are given in Table 2.1.

The registration of voters under the Registration of Electors Ordinance, 1954 started on 18 October and formally ended on 16 November 1954. However, due to the low registration rate by

Table 2.1
Distribution of Seats and Polling Districts/Stations, 1955

State/Settlement	No. of federal constituencies	No. of polling districts	No. of polling stations
Penang	4	68	141
Malacca	2	85	85
Perak	10	201	239
Selangor	7	125	134
Negri Sembilan	3	85	97
Pahang	3	120	125
Johore	8	263	275
Kedah	6	183	184
Kelantan	5	245	245
Terengganu	3	107	127
Perlis	1	22	27
Total	52	1,504	1,679

Source: Smith Report 1955, p. 5

the end of this period, a special supplementary period lasting nine days from 1 January 1955 was added. Eventually, a total of just over 1,280,000 people were registered as electors. The distribution of voters by ethnicity was as follows: Malays, 84.2 per cent; Chinese, 11.2 per cent; Indians, 4.5 per cent. Only in two constituencies (George Town and Ipoh) did Malays form less then 50 per cent of the electorate. In no constituency did Indians form more than 15 per cent of the electorate. In thirty-seven constituencies, Malays formed 75 per cent of the electorate.

Nomination Day fell on 15 June 1955, giving candidates a six-week campaign period. The campaign period saw the Alliance candidates holding numerous public meetings and conducting door-to-door canvassing, which was the method used by the other parties. Radio Malaya arranged for a number of party broadcasts and forums. Other than that the campaign was unremarkable. The deposit for each candidate was $500 and postal voting was arranged with some difficulty for military and police personnel. There was no incident of major significance on Polling Day. Town halls and school halls were used as counting centres. From 11.30 p.m. onwards there was a steady stream of results and the Alliance was assured victory when in the early hours of the morning of 28 July it had won 27 constituencies. It eventually went on to win all but one seat and obtained 80 per cent of the popular vote. Some 43 candidates failed to secure one-eighth of the valid vote and lost their deposits. Party Negara fared badly, losing 13 deposits, while 14 independents also forfeited their deposits. No election petitions were presented within the twenty-one-day window of the publication of results in the *Gazette*.

BIRTH OF AN ELECTORAL SYSTEM

The smooth conduct of the 1955 election coupled with the detailed study by the Merthyr Commission no doubt provided the basis and gave the Reid Commission the grounds for their recommendations for the kind of electoral system to be established for an independent Federation of Malaya. The commission first recommended that the 1955 legislature be dissolved by 1959 (under provisions of Article 154 of the new Constitution) so that elections for the newly constituted Malayan Parliament could be held between 1 January and 30 August 1959.[7] The delimitation of constituencies was to be undertaken by an independent Election Commission of three members appointed by the Yang di-Pertuan Agong, with the authority and status equivalent to Supreme Court judges (Article 108).[8] The first important issue that the commission delved into was the number and size of constituencies and the problem of ensuring that the distribution of electors was not unduly skewed. The commission alluded to the problem of constituencies like Kuala Lumpur Barat, which had a large number of residents who were not citizens or voters, while constituencies like Kelantan Utara had a large number of voters but proportionally fewer residents.[9] The commission suggested that in time to come this anomaly would be corrected as more residents qualified for citizenship. It was emphatic that regard should be paid to the sparsity or density of population, ethnicity in delimiting constituencies and the like, but *"in order to prevent too great weight being given to any of them, we recommend that the number of voters in any constituency should not be more than 15 per cent above or below the average"* (Reid Commission 1957, p. 31,

emphasis added). The main rationale for the electoral system adopted
and for the manner of delineations, as argued by the commissioners,
was as follows:

> We think that the delimitation of constituencies should take place in
> two stages (Art. 109): the Election Commission should first allocate
> the total of 100 seats among the States giving each State a quota so
> that the sum of the 11 quotas is 100. It should then delimit in each
> State the number of constituencies equal to the quota of that State.
> We do not think that it would in present circumstances be fair to
> the various communities to determine the State quotas either solely
> by reference to the population in each State or solely by reference
> to the number of voters in each State. In normal circumstances the
> main object of delimitation is to ensure, that so far as practicable,
> every vote is of equal value and we think that the principal factor
> to which the Commission should have regard is the number of
> voters in the State; but we think that it is necessary also to have
> regard to the total population of the State (Reid Commission, 1957,
> p. 31).

Based on these considerations and the 1955 election, the commission
retained the original 52 constituencies but split them into two, giving
the Federation 104 seats (Article 109). Thus the number of constituencies
created were as follows: Johore 16, Kedah 12, Kelantan 10, Malacca 4,
Negri Sembilan 6, Pahang 6, Penang 8, Perak 20, Perlis 2, Selangor 14,
Terengganu 6. Under Article 110 the commission also fixed the number
of state-level constituencies by subdividing the federal constituencies as
follows: Johor 32, Kedah 24, Kelantan 30, Malacca 20, Negri Sembilan
24, Pahang 24, Penang 24, Perak 40, Perlis 12, Selangor 28, Terengganu
24. It is apparent that the Reid Commission had relied on the reasoning
and arguments of the Merthyr Commission, which, in deciding on
the 52 legislature seats for the 1955 general election, had followed
the principle of apportionment based on the populations of the states
and the allowance of a 50 per cent cap on disparities between urban
and rural seats. The Reid Commission later established a 100-seat
apportionment for the federal parliament and a 15 per cent cap on
rural weightage, both of which were overturned by executive decisions
of the first Malayan government, overriding the originally intended
functions of the EC, as we shall see later.[10]

I will now delve into some of the major recommendations and rationales of the Merthyr Commission for adopting the FPTP single-member electoral system.

RATIONALE FOR THE FPTP SYSTEM

The commission argued against having a multiple member constituency system because of its complexity and also avoided cross-state delineations. Using the 1947 census, there could be 52 constituencies with an average size of 94,386 for each constituency (Merthyr Commission 1954, p. 4). By rounding the population averages using 1953 population estimates, the final allocation of constituencies that the commission arrived at is as shown in Table 2.2.

The Merthyr Commission admitted that there were substantial differences between the average populations of constituencies in several states owing to their rejection of cross-state boundaries. Some of the smallest constituencies on the East Coast were well below the average,

Table 2.2
Seat Allocations, 1955

State or settlement	No. of constituencies	Average population of constituencies (1947)
Penang	4	111,580
Malacca	2	119,678
Perak	10	95,394
Selangor	7	101,541
Negri Sembilan	3	89,223
Pahang	3	83,393
Johor	8	92,281
Kedah	6	92,407
Kelantan	3	89,714
Terengganu	3	75,332
Perlis	1	70,490
Total	52	Avg. 94,386

Source: Merthyr Commission 1954, p. 12

while West Coast constituencies had above average sizes. For example, Terengganu Selatan, the smallest, had a population of 53,700, while George Town, the largest, was at 137,000.[11] Nonetheless, the commission was satisfied that under the circumstances the overall distribution of electors for the whole country was acceptable.

It cannot be more emphatically stated that the Reid Commission, in adopting the FPTP single-member constituency electoral system, considered the role of an impartial Election Commission to be of paramount importance. It was charged with ensuring the smooth conduct of all elections at the federal, state and municipal levels, including the registration of voters, appeals against exclusion in the electoral roll and the like. The commission also stressed that if the result of any constituency should be disputed, such a dispute would be subject to adjudication by no less than the Supreme Court (Article 113 [3]).

There was also the question of whether the Upper House, the Senate, should have fully elected representatives or members indirectly elected by state assemblies. The commissioners were evidently conflicted over this matter, but by a majority decision decided on a Senate of indirectly elected members, 2 from each state, and 11 members nominated by the Yang di-Pertuan Agong. Parliament would have the power to reduce or abolish the nominated members as it deemed fit.[12]

CHANGES TO THE ELECTORAL SYSTEM[13]

There have been several broad phases in the way the Malaysian electoral system has been changed and its procedural features and constraints on executive control eroded. Although significant changes were introduced, the simple plurality single-constituency FPTP model has remained intact. The pre-Independence period, as mentioned earlier, saw the holding of municipal elections in George Town in 1951 and Kuala Lumpur in 1952 and a federal election under self-government under British supervision in 1955. According to Lim (2002), the initial formulation established a practice of malapportionment and "rural weightage", probably at the insistence of UMNO. This was likely based on a political compromise and a quid pro quo by UMNO to non-Malays for more relaxed citizenship strictures (Lim 2002, p. 105). Many of the contentious issues were threshed out by the 46-member federal legislative committee established in 1954 prior to the setting up of the Merthyr Commission. According to Lim, the committee suggested that rural constituencies could have as little as one-half of the population of urban counterparts. This was included in the terms of reference for the Merthyr Commission and "rural weightage together with Malay predominance in the electorate resulted in Malay constituencies in all but two of the constituencies" (Lim 2002, p. 105). In its terms of reference, the Merthyr Commission stipulated the following, basically following what was suggested by the legislative committee:

> The inhabitants within each constituency should be approximately equal except that, having regard to the greater difficulty of contacting voters in the country districts and the other disadvantages facing rural constituencies, a measure of "weightage" for the area should be given to the rural constituencies. In view of the very great distances involved in some of the sparsely settled portion[s] of the country, it could not be regarded as unreasonable if in some instances a rural constituency contained as little as one half of the inhabitants in the more populous urban constituencies returning single members. (Merthyr Commissiom 1954, p. 1)[14]

Be that as it may, the Reid Commission, as I have noted, set the upper limit of 15 per cent for the difference between constituencies and thereby would have more than halved the amount of rural weightage previously allowed.[15] The reader will learn that these limits were altered and ultimately removed in latter-day delimitation exercises owing to new political imperatives.

The first major change that was made to the electoral system occurred in the early 1960s. The first review of the electoral constituencies was initiated by the EC soon after the 1959 general election, but was not well-received by UMNO which had lost Malay ground to the PMIP, particularly in the East Coat states of Kelantan and Terengganu.[16] The government then introduced the Constitutional (Amendment) Act 1962, "that not only annulled the revised constituencies but also removed the EC's final power of decision on electoral constituencies and transferred it to a simple majority in parliament" (Lim 2005, p.253). This meant that henceforth the EC could only submit reviews to the prime minister, who can make revisions before it is presented to Parliament. The 1962 Act also effectively annulled the EC's new delineations, reverted them to the 1959 situation and virtually emasculated the EC's impartial and independent role in constituency delimitations. The Act drew the ire of the constitutional expert H.E. Groves, who wrote:

> The vital power of determining the size of constituencies as well as their boundaries is now taken from a Commission, which the constitution-maker had apparently wished, by tenure and status, to make independent and disinterested, and had been made completely political by giving this power to a transient majority of parliament, whose temptations to gerrymander districts and manipulate the varying numerical possibilities between "rural" and "urban" constituencies for political advantage is manifest. (Groves 1962, as cited in Lim 2002, pp. 109–10)

A major change made to the electoral system came with Malaysia Act 1963. Extensive amendments were made to the Federal Constitution to allow for the inclusion of the new states of Singapore, Sabah and Sarawak. Lim (2002, p. 110) writes that "[t]he key to understanding the adaptations to the electoral system was UMNO's desire to overcome the threat to a favourable ethnic–political balance posed by Singapore's 1.7 million largely Chinese inhabitants." R.S. Milne (1968), among others, has also made the point that the inclusion of Singapore had meant a skewing of the Malaysian population in favour of the Chinese, and the inclusion of Sabah and Sarawak into the federation (and initially also Brunei) was partially aimed at balancing the Chinese presence, on the assumption that the "natives" of these Borneo states would be allies of the Malays. With respect to the apportionment of seats in the 159-member parliament, the distribution was as follows: Singapore 15, Sabah 16, Sarawak 24, and 104 to the Malayan states. On the basis of population, Singapore (with almost 17 per cent of the Federation's population) would have got the largest number of seats, of about 27, and Sabah and Sarawak would have received 7 and 12 seats, respectively (Lim 2002; Rachagan 1980, p. 274). However, it should be noted that in the 20-point agreement (Sabah) and 18-point agreement (Sarawak) with respect to the Borneo states joining

Malaysia, Point 17 states that in determining federal representation, not only population but also "size" (geographical) and "potentialities" should be considered and that representation for these two states should not be less than that of Singapore.[17] This said, the actual final numbers were negotiated and not predetermined. All stipulations concerning Singapore were annulled when it left the Federation in 1965.

What is of further note is that the new member states of Malaysia were considered to be distinct or separate units for the purpose of constituency delineations, and reviews were to be conducted every eight to ten years, which meant that the reviews for these territories could be carried out at different times from those of Malayan states. A fourth member of the EC was allotted for the new states.

THE AMENDMENTS OF 1973 AND 1984

The next round of amendments to the electoral system came in 1973. The context was the 1969 general election, which had sparked ethnic rioting on 13 May. Following the Alliance's worst ever outcome, amendments to the constitution included the proscribing of discussion of "sensitive" issues such as the position of the Malays and the rulers, and the stopping of all public rallies during election campaigns. The Alliance was reconstituted into the current Barisan Nasional (BN) which brought many more parties into its fold on the Peninsula and in East Malaysia. The New Economic Policy (NEP), the affirmative action policy for bumiputera, was also subsequently proclaimed and implemented in 1971. Obviously it was not just the electoral system that was restructured but the very character of the political regime had also changed. The material change that occurred with regard to electoral politics came in the form of the Constitutional (Amendment) Act (No. 2) of 1973. This Act removed the EC's power to apportion parliamentary constituencies among states and the number was now specified in Article 46 of the federal Constitution, amendable by the government with a two-thirds majority vote. The 1973 Act also removed numeral or percentage limits to rural weightage, with the wordings "a measure of weightage ought to be given" to such (i.e., rural) constituencies (Lim 2002, p. 111). Another change was the creation in 1974 of the federal territory of Kuala Lumpur, whose non-Malay voters had probably caused the 1969 Selangor state election impasse, which, some argue, sparked the Kuala Lumpur riots.

Next came the Constitutional (Amendment) (No. 2) Act of 1984. The Act changed the upper ten-year limit for constituency reviews to an interval of not less than eight years. According to Rachagan (1993), the new Act enabled the party in power to effect changes to constituencies, whether at the federal or state level, by varying the number of seats at the government's choosing during district delimiting or re-delineation exercises. This was possible as long as the government had control of a two-thirds majority of seats in Parliament. By 1984, as Lim (2005) avers, the ruling party had reduced the constraints and arrogated to itself effective control over the apportionment and delineation of electoral constituencies.

SALURAN SYSTEM FROM 1990

An important change to the electoral system came in 1990. An amendment to the Elections Act of 1958 enabled votes to be counted at polling stations and voters would vote according to their respective "streams" (*saluran*), each of which initially was capped at a maximum of seven hundred voters.[18] According to the EC, this change improved efficiency and avoided the problem of ballot boxes being brought to a counting centre, thus reducing the possibility of interference with them and in some instance the loss of ballot boxes being delivered from far-flung areas of large rural constituencies. The opposition and critics were quick to point out that the *saluran* system would allow the government to identify who had voted against them, and the fear of reprisals would favour the government parties. Over time the *saluran* system has turned out to be a positive rather than negative development which has allowed for more efficient administration of voting. The fear of victimization is more likely to be of importance in rural, rather than urban, constituencies, where streams are small in number and voting preferences can easily be identified. The sword cuts both ways, as the opposition could also use the fine data obtained from *saluran* votes to identify and target areas of support and weakness.

CONSTITUENCY DELIMITATIONS UNTIL 2003

From time to time — and, after the latest amendment, in intervals of no less than eight years — the EC must undertake to review and delimit electoral boundaries. The most extensive enhancement of constituencies occurred after the 1999 general election, from July 2002 till May 2003. Prior to this there had been delimitation exercises in 1974, 1984 and 1994. Up until 2003 the EC's own strictures allowed for disparities of 3.5 times between the smallest and the largest constituencies. Controversy always revolved around the EC's implementation of a highly liberal measure of rural weightage, with the DAP voicing objections every time a delimitation exercise was carried out. After the 1984 exercise, DAP leader Lim Kit Siang argued that rural weightage had in fact nullified the one-man-one-vote principle, and even the MCA was unhappy with the extent of the de-amplification of the urban vote (Lim 2005, pp. 266–67). Alarm bells were also sounded by civil society groups prior to the 1999 general election, with the *suqiu* group of Chinese organizations calling for a return to the 15 per cent upper limit of discrepancy between constituencies (Loh and Saravanamuttu 2003, pp. 13 and 284).

Delimitation exercises have evidently hugely benefited UMNO through rural weightage and a disproportionate number of Malay-majority constituencies, which today is arguably also a potential advantage for PAS. Interestingly, what has become salient and crucial to peninsular politics is also the disproportionate electoral power given to the bumiputera communities of Sabah and Sarawak. This could of course be justified as affirmative action owing to the economic underdevelopment of the two states. However, as noted by analysts, federal electoral manipulation of these states also produces its own reflexive local impacts, intended or otherwise (Loh 2005). As noted by Lim (2005, p. 270), the 1994 exercise in Sabah raised to 26 out of 48 the previous 18 bumiputera-majority constituencies, thus effectively placing control of the state government in the hands of the Muslim bumiputera who comprised 40 per cent of the population. The Sabah re-delineations provided the structural basis for UMNO's entry into Sabah state politics, and by 1999 it effectively captured state power via the BN.[19] In the more complex situation of Sarawak, it was allotted 62 state constituencies in the state-level exercise of 1995, but no group controls a majority of them, with Muslim-Melanau bumiputera in effective power with about 28 per cent of the population, even though Dayaks (mainly divided between Iban and Bidayuh) comprise about 40 per cent of the population. According to Lim (2002, p. 271), re-delineations in Sarawak have also benefitted the Pesaka Bumiputera Bersatu (PBB), UMNO's consistent electoral partner, giving it clout to resist Dayak electoral inroads into its strongholds.

I will now examine the 2003 delimitation exercise in some detail, drawing on studies that have been conducted about it. The outcome of the 1999 general election, which saw PAS making considerable inroads into UMNO territory, no doubt gave great impetus for the delimitation exercise, conducted from July 2002 to May 2003, which created 25 new parliamentary seats and 53 new state seats. As the Dewan Rakyat (House of Representatives) was about to approve the delineations on 8 April 2003, 44 opposition members walked out in protest against both the proposal and the BN's abuse of parliamentary procedure.[20] The DAP's challenge against the delineations under the EC's grievance process had earlier been rejected by the EC's chairman on the ground that "although [the DAP] did submit a personal letter asking me to reconsider the State's proposal on the delineation, [it] could not come up with a counter proposal which can grant a representation to be made and enable the EC to conduct [a] local inquiry to hear and consider appeals or objections".[21]

Many of the new delimitations seem to ignore population trends. For example, the state of Selangor, with a population of 4.19 million and an annual growth rate of 6.1 per cent since the 1991 census, received 5 new seats, while Johor, with a population of 2.74 million and an annual growth rate of 2.6 per cent, was granted 6 new seats. The 2003 delimitation produced the highest population variations of any previous delimitation exercise. The constituency of Johor Bahru had an electorate of approximately 90,000 voters, while Lenggong had about 21,000 voters, a disparity of over 325 per cent. Table 2.3 shows the difference between the 1994 and 2003 delimitations by states, showing Selangor and Kuala Lumpur (Wilayah) as the major losers in both exercises.

The study of the Kedah delineations by Ong and Welsh (2005, p. 317) came to the broad conclusion that the exercise "involved moving 'safe areas' in traditional UMNO strongholds and non-Malay

Table 2.3
Delimitations, 2003

State	No. voters in 1994	No. voters in 2002	% change	Difference	Over/Under allocation in 1994	Over/Under allocation in 2003
Perlis	97,978	109,750	12.0	11,772	1	1
Kedah	675,790	793,517	17.4	117,727	1	-1
Kelantan	528,679	655,602	24.0	126,923	3	1
Terengganu	337,918	411,453	21.8	73,535	1	0
Penang	563,039	659,155	17.1	96,116	-1	0
Perak	1,047,175	1,138,010	8.7	90,835	1	2
Pahang	456,834	554,534	21.4	97,700	1	3
Selangor	**949,317**	**1,368,693**	**44.2**	**419,376**	**-3**	**-5**
Wilayah	**591,806**	**664,233**	**12.2**	**72,427**	**-3**	**-2**
N. Sembilan	298,178	417,712	40.1	119,534	1	0
Melaka	269,198	331,327	23.1	62,129	-1	-1
Johor	982,484	1223,532	24.5	241,048	-1	2
Total	6,798,396	8,327,518	22.5	1,529,122		

Source: Grace 2008.

seats into constituencies that would strengthen the BN's electoral position". The study goes into great detail about changes to constituencies. The 2004 electoral outcome seemed to confirm their analysis, as UMNO picked up the largest number of seats, winning 12 parliamentary and 23 state seats, up from 5 and 16 previously. However, Ong and Welsh also conceded that the 2004 gains were not solely the result of the delimitation exercise, and the results were also the product of stronger support nationally for the BN. This is an important caveat, as we now know that in the 2008 outcome Kedah was captured by the opposition front but it reverted to the BN in 2013. The outcomes suggest to this author that some of the electoral manipulations through gerrymandering and malapportionment need not always favour incumbents, particularly when there are major waves of Malay support moving from one coalition to the other. As noted in Chapter 1, securing a majority or a large proportion of the Malay vote is crucial to electoral success. Moreover, in highly contested situations like Kedah, and in large ethnic-majority constituencies, even minor single-digit swings can deliver significant changes.

The study by Brown (2005) zooms in on the 2003 delineations but draws extensively from data of the 1986, 1990, 1991 and 1999 elections. Brown makes the argument that the 2003 delineations could have actually reduced ethnic bias (i.e., Malay electoral strength) and given more advantage to particular geographical areas and distributions of ethnicity thought to be favourable to the BN. This may have been the BN's manner of checking the advances made by PAS in the 1999 general election, but it also had the unintended consequence of Malay votes shifting back to PAS by 2008. Brown's interesting thesis provides the basis for an explanation as to why the 2003 delineations may not have been structurally detrimental to the opposition coalition, which had begun to adopt electoral strategies much like those of the BN to gain cross-ethnic votes in mixed seats. We will return to this point later.

Brown's study shows that up until 2004 the FPTP system had favoured the BN in that it had consistently won a two-thirds majority in Parliament despite capturing much less than that proportion of the popular vote, as shown in Table 2.4. It is thus of no surprise that in 2013, although the opposition won about 51 per cent of the popular vote, it won no more than 40 per cent of the seats — much as occurred in 1969.

The point made by Brown about ethnicity being less of a significant factor in re-delineations by 2004 is worth pursuing, as it runs counter to previous arguments made by Rachagan (1984), Crouch (1996), Lim (2003) and others, who tended to consider ethnicity (namely, Malay dominance) to be the main driver of such re-delineations. First, it should be noted that after Singapore's departure from Malaysia, Malay

Table 2.4
East Malaysian Weightage (%)

	1974	1984	1994	2004
Electorate	14.7	15.0	16.8	16.5
Seats	26.0	25.5	25.5	24.9
Over-weightage	1.77	1.70	1.49	1.50

Source: Brown 2005, p. 6

electoral dominance was re-established on the Peninsula, and perhaps did not need to be further amplified for the ruling coalition. As for Sabah and Sarawak, bumiputera weightage has remained paramount, as shown in the table, with the caveat that UMNO presence, hence "Malay" pre-eminence, had also been established in Sabah. The argument made in Chapter 1 about the importance of certain conditions for mediated communalism as practised by the BN applies here. Malay and bumiputera predominance must be guaranteed for the success of the strategy, given the apportionment of constituencies to these two groups.

Brown (2005) shows that over-weightage of the Malays in the Peninsula had stabilized and then been reduced in the latest delimitation of 2003, as shown in Table 2.5. Brown avers that because the BN had over time performed well in mixed constituencies, re-delineations — which historically favoured rural, largely Malay constituencies — were shifted towards ethnically mixed seats, the majority of which are in urban areas. From 1986 to 2004 the largest category of seats was of the mixed variety, accounting for 43–46 per cent of peninsular seats, although their over-weightage was reduced considerably by the 2003 re-delineations. Brown's calculations show that the correlation between constituency size and the Malay proportion of the electorate fell, even when factoring in the exceptional case of Putrajaya. As shown in Table 2.5, positive Malay weightage had come down from 7 per cent in 1999 to 5.3 in 2004.

Extrapolating from Brown's analysis, I would argue that the new delineations of 2003 were of definite benefit to the BN up until the 2004 election, when it was able to capitalize on the mixed seats in the massive swing of votes to the Abdullah Ahmad Badawi (Pak Lah)

Table 2.5
Peninsular Ethnic Weightage (%)

	1986	1990	1995	1999	2004
Malay	7.1	7.4	7.0	7.0	5.3
Chinese	−10.0	−10.2	−10.0	−10.1	−8.2
Indian	−5.9	−7.2	−7.5	−7.9	−5.9

Source: Brown 2005, p. 8

regime. However, when the electoral swing went against Pak Lah in 2008, the vast majority of mixed seats went to the opposition, thus explaining the "political tsunami" of that election. In 2013, as my analysis will show in a subsequent chapter, the opposition coalition continued to hold sway in the mixed seats, while losing some ground in the Malay constituencies. To put it in terms of the central hypothesis of this book, the BN under Pak Lah swung from a period of a perceived excellent centripetal policy of moderation in its strategy of mediated communalism to the diametrical opposite when this strategy was seen to fail badly during his tenure, coupled with the rise of Pakatan Rakyat's newly mounted centripetal new politics. What this meant in electoral terms was that the middle ground, the mixed seats, became fair game for the opposition.

THE DEMISE OF LOCAL ELECTIONS[22]

An important tier of electoral politics was removed in Malaysia by the early 1970s. Up until the 1960s, Malaysia had some 373 local authorities that had well over 3,000 elected representatives out of a total of some 4,223 local councillors. This number excluded those of the Kuala Lumpur municipality, which came under a separate jurisdiction because it was the federal capital. The three most prominent municipalities were George Town, Ipoh and Malacca. Elsewhere, there were 37 town councils, 37 town boards, 289 local councils and 7 district councils. Penang and Malacca were the two states which had state-wide local councils, and only Penang had fully elective councils throughout its territory on both the island and the mainland.

George Town had a particularly eminent history in terms of democracy at the local level, to which we have already alluded briefly. The first elections in Malaya were held there in 1951 to elect 9 councillors. George Town was a "city council" (the only one) by virtue of the fact that it was granted city status by the British in January 1957. With the passage of the Local Government Act, 1960, a new Constitution was granted to the City Council of George Town from 1 April 1961. George Town was fully autonomous financially and was the richest local authority, with annual revenue almost double that of the State of Penang. Its reserve fund at the end of 1965 stood at some 6,037,535 Malaysian dollars. However, in 1966, under a Transfer of Functions Order, the functions of the City Council were transferred to the Chief Minister to enable a Commission of Inquiry "to inquire on [sic] the acts of maladministration and malpractices and breaches of law committed by the City Council of George Town" (Saravanamuttu 2000).

Kuala Lumpur, the next municipality to assume city status, also had a thriving elected local government. The KL Municipal Council was created in 1951, with 18 councillors — 12 elected and 6 nominated. In the 1952 elections the Alliance Party won 9 seats, the IMP won 2, and 1 was won by an independent. Other active city councils with elected representatives, not to mention a host of councils in the New Villages, were found in Seremban, Malacca, Kuantan and Ipoh, which by the 1960s had fully elected councils (Goh 2005, p. 54). When the Kuala Lumpur council elections were suspended in 1958 it was a sign of things to come. Kuala Lumpur was handed over to the Federal Capital Commissioner and was declared a Federal Territory in 1974. Other councils lost their elected status by the late 1960s.

The local council elections that were scheduled for 1965 and 1966 were suspended on the grounds of an emergency situation due to Indonesia's Confrontation against Malaysia. The two material regulations were the Emergency (Suspension of Local Government Elections) Regulations 1965 and the Emergency (Suspension of Local Government Elections) (Amendments) Regulations 1965. These Acts allowed state governments to assume control of local councils, usually on the ground of maladministration. In June 1965 the government set up a "Royal Commission of Inquiry on Local Authorities" headed by Senator Athi Nahappan. The commission's members included D.S. Ramanathan (the former George Town mayor), Awang Hassan (a future governor of Penang), Chan Keong Hon, Tan Peng Khoon and Haji Ismail Panjang Aris. The commission held numerous sittings and hearings, received memoranda from far and wide and completed a comprehensive study of the workings of West Malaysian local authorities. It completed its work in December 1968, coming out strongly in support of elected councils. However, the central government chose to completely ignore the findings and recommendations of the commission. Although the commissioners found that local councils were inefficient and prone to some corruption, they felt this was insufficient cause to abolish elected officers.

After the Nahappan Commission's work was completed, the Cabinet appointed a committee to study the implications of its report. This Cabinet Committee was headed by Hassan bin Mohd Noh, the secretary general of the Ministry of Technology, Research and Local Government. Among its members were Hashim Yeop Sani, the then representative of the Attorney General, who was later to become Chief Justice of Malaya. To the credit of this committee, it went along with the spirit and most of the recommendations of the Nahappan Commission. However, another report submitted by the Development Administration Unit (DAU) of the Prime Minister's Department effectively set aside the Nahappan recommendations in 1971. The DAU's main arguments were that elected local councils were no longer consonant with the current national objectives such as the New Economic Policy, and that they provided for "an over-democratized over-government at the local level" (sic). Furthermore, the DAU claimed that the system led to "oligarchic elites" facilitating the domination of the "haves" over the "have-nots".

More objective observers, however, have cited two ostensible reasons for the collapse of locally elected councils. First, the Indonesian Confrontation led to the de facto suspension of local level elections since 1965 and, second, the 13 May 1969 racial riots provided the perfect excuse to kill off opposition elective local councils. In reality, although ethnic factors had something to do with the demise of elected councils, the push for more centralized control of politics by the Razak government was the more significant factor. Opposition politics, the large number of local governments and the issues of inefficiency or maladministration ultimately led to the decline of local government. Consider the fact that both George Town and Ipoh consistently elected opposition parties — the Socialist Front and the People's Progressive Party — to head and run the city councils. The same happened in Malacca. Also consider the fact that in the 1962 local council elections held in Perak, the PPP won 57 per cent of the vote and 112 of the 150 seats contested in the Kinta District. The Alliance won only 27 seats, while 11 seats went to the Socialist Front. Tennant (1973), in his study, takes the view that "[t]he existence of corruption and inefficiency ... within the elected councils paved the way for state officials to eliminate the nuisance of independent local decision makers, and to expand the sphere of state influence by abolishing the major elective local governments". But Goh adds that the abolitions would not have occurred in Penang and Kelantan had the same party been in power at both the state and local levels (Goh 2005, p. 58). The then prime minister Abdul Razak took a rather cavalier (perhaps disingenuous) view of the whole matter:

> It has become clear to us, after having examined the position of the last twenty years, that with the existence of elected local authorities this small country of ours has in fact been over governed.... It is quite clear to us in the government that it would be a waste of time, money and resources for elections to be conducted at this level when ... there is full opportunity for the people to participate in the government during elections at the state and national levels. (as cited in Goh 2005, p. 60)

Another prominent personality connected to this saga of the demise of local democracy was the erstwhile Socialist Front Mayor of George Town, D.S. Ramanathan, who later become an independent and then an Alliance councillor. Ramanathan, who has a road named after him in Penang, caused a major sensation in 1963 when he alleged serious malpractices on the part of George Town councillors. One charge was that the construction of the city's largest market involved fraud. The flap led to a vote in the council, which, although rejecting Ramanathan's complaints, agreed to a commission of inquiry.

However, it was only three years later in 1965 that the Royal Commission headed by Nahappan was formed, and considerations for the move went well beyond Penang politics. The Nahappan team finally submitted its report in 1968. Its recommendations were crystal clear. It called for the restoration of elected local government but with a variety of administrative changes and a new set of rules. On hindsight, one could surmise that the commissioners were acting in good faith but were perhaps naive to expect that their suggestions would be followed. Some of the more important Nahappan recommendations were:

- Every state capital should be administered by a local authority and have elective representation. The same principle should also be extended to all local councils outside state capitals.

- There should be a single law applicable throughout the country relating to and governing local authorities, and every state should adopt and enforce the law within six months after it has been passed by Parliament.
- A local authority should be decentralized and should be an autonomous corporate body consisting of fully elected members with financial and administrative autonomy but subject to the control of the state government on matters of national importance and interest.
- Party politics should be allowed to continue despite its good and bad aspects and those who wish to remain non-conformist should have the right to stand as "independents", as in the past.
- A Local Government Tribunal should be constituted by the State Authority of every local authority.

Despite the submission of the Nahappan report and its considered and reasoned recommendations for the revival of local democracy, the government stepped in to snuff out elective local government in complete contradiction to the spirit of the recommendations.

The then local government minister Ong Kee Hui played a significant role here. Long after Confrontation ended in 1971, he recommended the setting up of a Cabinet Committee to study the Nahappan commission's recommendations. And again, against the grain of the Cabinet report on the Nahappan commission's findings, proclaimed that there was consensus among the states to oppose restoration of elected local government. He then did nothing in particular for a number of years except to allow existing councillors to be replaced by members of the same party upon death or inability to continue. Then, the Local Authorities (Temporary Provisions) Act was enacted in 1973, which in theory implemented some of the administrative and restructuring recommendations of the Nahappan Report.

The writing was on the wall and the *coup de grâce* came three years later when the government enacted the Local Government Act of 1976. The new Act only allowed for the establishment of 12 municipalities and 90 district councils within three years, but most detrimentally members of these councils would be appointed and not elected and in most cases the chairman would be the district officer or some other civil servant. This is the system of local government Malaysia now has.

REFORMING THE FPTP SYSTEM?

In this section I will examine critiques of the Malaysian electoral system, some of which has been already implied in the foregoing text of this chapter.[23] The FPTP system, inherited from Britain, has been the object of a considerable amount of debate and criticism, particularly in recent times with the rise of election watch groups such as BERSIH. Critiques revolve around the question of whether Malaysian elections are "free and fair", but more specifically on the following pertinent issues: the FPTP system itself; delimitation exercises; the conduct of elections; electoral rolls (clean and valid procedures); electoral law and petitions; the independence of the EC (and public confidence in the electoral process). Some of these issues clearly overlap and I will only be able to touch on the main issues of the FPTP system in this chapter. Nonetheless, it is important to see each of the above as distinct areas of concern, which will be taken up in subsequent chapters. One area of particular concern is the tendency of the FPTP system to create manufactured majorities beyond acceptable limits and how this could be ameliorated.

Because of its inbuilt inequity, as early as 1974 the redoubtable opposition figure Tan Chee Khoon argued for a mixed voting system such as that of Germany, "where fifty percent of the seats are elected under the first-past-the-post system and fifty percent by proportional representation". Tan's Party Pekemas (People's Justice Party) won only one parliamentary seat despite winning 5.3 per cent of the vote in the 1974 Election.[24] The FPTP system has been largely blamed for the ease with which malapportionment in the distribution of voter in the Malaysian electoral system has been executed.[25] Were Malaysia to follow a proportional representation electoral system, the issue of excessive rural weightage would not arise. In a balanced essay on Malaysia's FPTP system, Horowitz (2005) suggests implicitly that no electoral system could be a perfect mirror of voter preference or choice, nor would that necessarily be desirable from particular political perspectives. He posits that six goals are essential to a good electoral system for a country such as Malaysia; namely, proportionality of seats to vote, accountability to constituents, durable governments, victory of the *Condorcet* winners,[26] inter-ethnic and inter-religious conciliation, and minority office-holding. Without going into the details of his arguments, it would be fair to say that Horowitz thinks that the FPTP system of Malaysia does have its merits based on the goals he specified. For example, the issue of the fragmented party system is of some concern. In a proportional representation system, where single-digit percentages (as opposed to higher thresholds) count, there would be "great inducements for parties to split into component factions, and it may enable very small parties that can make or break governments to have disproportionate impact in determining policy and receiving patronage" (Horowitz 2005, p. 397).

However, Horowitz does point out some problems and surprises in the Malaysian electoral system. First, is the well-documented issue of disproportionality, that "the largest party habitually receives bonus seats"; second, party fragmentation has occurred despite the FPTP system because of Malaysia's ethnic, religious and regional pluralism; third, it has had a mixed record in inter-ethnic conciliation. If I read him correctly, no amount of tweaking of inter-ethnic conciliation has ameliorated a highly centralized leadership and its dominance. Contrariwise, I have argued that with the emergence of an alternative opposition coalition since 2008, we have seen the establishment of more centripetalized politics, suggesting that some alteration of the FPTP system could augur for more balanced and fairer ethnic outcomes.

In a contrarian essay, Kessler (2005) advocates the debunking of the FPTP system altogether for one based on "preferential voting". In what he himself dubs a "fantasy/scenario", Kessler (2005, pp. 416–17) speculates on the benefits of a system based on an "Australian-type preferential voting procedure, combined with ... redrawing of electoral boundaries to maximize the number of mixed-ethnicity electorates, and a corresponding reduction in the number of heavily Malay-majority constituencies, and an accompanying reduction in the constitutionally mandated pro-Malay rural areas".

In fact, what Kessler has suggested has been a sort of wish list of critics of the Malaysian FPTP system who would rather choose the more realistic path of "making the system work" (Lim 2005). The main issue for critics like Lim is a subservient Election Commission which fails to inspire public confidence:

Public confidence in the electoral system depends importantly, even if not solely, on public confidence in the EC. It should not escape attention that what has become the subject of controversy in Malaysia with respect to elections is not the first-past-the-post electoral system per se but the manner in which it has operated. (Lim 2005, p. 284)

Among the most problematic issues of Malaysia's FPTP system is that of constituency delineations, which we have already discussed at great length. The other major issue is that of clean and valid electoral rolls, which undergirds electoral democracy and the principle of "one person one vote" (Puthucheary and Noraini 2005, p. 430). The most serious concern has been that of "phantom voters", i.e., illegitimate names — including deceased voters whose identities have been transferred to others — making it into the electoral rolls through disingenuous acts of interested parties. Rachagan recounts the curious situation of a massive drop of some 330,864 voters in 1973–74, which the chairman of the EC attributed to "the removal from the rolls of the names of persons who have died or migrated and cases of double registration". But on polling day on 24 August 1974, thousands of voters failed to find their names on the register and were thus disenfranchised (Rachagan 1980, p. 265). The issue of clean and valid electoral rolls sparked Malaysia's BERSIH Movement[27] and has been the subject of many probes and studies. After the 2013 general election, BERSIH constituted a "People's Tribunal", from 18 to 22 September 2013, to hold hearings on testimonies and grievances ranging from vote manipulation, procedural matters such as the use of indelible ink, custody of ballot boxes, to bribery and the actual buying of votes.[28] An important study by Sadiq (2005) shows how in Sabah "documentary citizenship" had been a highly prevalent phenomenon whereby illegal immigrants were incorporated into the state as voters. After many years of stalling, a Royal Commission of Inquiry was set up in Sabah on illegal immigration, completing its work in 2013. The commission heard many testimonies about the phenomenon revealed by Sadiq in his study.[29] If indeed true, the political expediency of converting illegal immigrants to voters makes a travesty of the notion of clean and valid electoral rolls and strikes at the heart and essence of the nation and national processes such as elections. Moreover, the issues of registration of voters, "phantom voters", the postal vote, deletion

of voters, overseas votes and, most recently, the use of indelible ink
have remained problematic and have continued to exercise critics of
the Malaysian electoral system. Suffice it to say, the EC has failed to
inspire public confidence in the manner in which it has dealt with these
issues to date.[30] Thus, without doubt, even within the current FPTP
system of Malaysia, much needs to be done to introduce correctives
towards an implementation of best practices.

CONCLUSION

This chapter began by examining the roots of the Malaysian electoral
system. Its main features, inherited from a Westminster model, also
exhibit some unique features crafted by the Reid Constitutional
Commission, which was accepted and implemented by Malaysia's
independent government but with significant changes as the years
went by. From 1959 until 2013, quite a few new features have been
added to it, just as some older features have seen attrition due to
amendments by the ruling coalition. However, the basic FPTP single-
member plurality model remains intact. What is patently clear is the
erosion of the powers of the Election Commission, the confidence
of the public on its independence, and a practice of constituency
re-delineations of dubious merit or fairness. These issues have created
a serious flaw in the current Malaysian electoral system. It has been
famously said that Malaysia's electoral system may be "free but not
fair". More severe critics suggest that it is neither free nor fair. It is
debatable which problem is more serious; the implementation of broad
principles that would ensure freedom of choice, or the procedures
and institutions that ensure fairness. Without doubt the most serious
problems that require immediate reform are the correction of the undue
level of malapportionment of electors through the practice of rural
weightage and the general practice of the disproportionate distribution
of electors without adequate rationale. The proper, timely and valid
registration of voters and the maintenance of clean electoral rolls
constitutes the next most serious problem. While is it true that no electoral
system could be a perfect mirror of voter choice, an approximation
of that cardinal principle is to be expected. Particularly in a country

like Malaysia where ethnic power sharing is a given, the delimiting of constituencies should try to ensure fairness and minimize any distortion of results to minority communities, maintain fair representation of rural and urban dwellers and keep a healthy balance of weightage among regions. Of course, there is no magic bullet to resolve these issues, and it is to the credit of Malaysian political actors and voters that despite the flaws of the electoral system, two roughly equal coalitions of ethnic power sharing have emerged to represent these differences through strategies of mediated communalism in the country's evolving consociational politics.

Notes

1. Lord William Reid chaired the Commission. Its other members were Sir Ivor Jennings (Britain), Sir William McKnell (Australia), Justice B. Malik (India) and Justice Abdul Hamid (Pakistan). It met 118 times between June and October 1956 and received 131 memoranda from individuals and organizations. It completed its work on 21 February 1957, submitted as the Report of the Federation of Malaya Constitutional Commission (hereinafter, Reid Commission).
2. The commission was appointed by Sir Donald MacGillivray, the British High Commissioner for Malaya. The commission was chaired by Lord Merthyr and the other members were Mr W.C.S. Corry, Mr E.G. Farrington and Mr T.E. Smith, who acted as secretary. Prior to the setting up of the commission, a forty-six-member committee of the Federal Legislative Council deliberated on the type of electoral system Malaya should adopt. On the basis of their deliberations, the terms of reference was set for the Methyr Commission. See Lim (2002, pp. 103–4) for an account of the issues, debates and recommendations of this committee.
3. See Rae (1967, pp. 74–77). See also the prodigious work of Lijphart on democracy in plural societies and on electoral and party systems, where he alludes to manufactured majorities and their relevance to plural societies and consociational politics (1977, 1994, 1999). Further, see the comprehensive study of electoral systems by Nohlen (1996).
4. The Report on the "Introduction of Elections in George Town, Penang", submitted by the Supervisor of Elections, A.S.M. Hawkins (hereinafter, Hawkins Report), gives a full narrative and details of the election. See also Goh (2005).

5. By 1956 George Town had become the first municipality in the Federation of Malaya to have a fully elected council, with G.H. Goh of the Alliance as its first president. By 1957, after being proclaimed a city by Queen Elizabeth II, it had its first mayor, D.S. Ramanathan of the Socialist Front (Goh 2005, p. 56).

6. Arkib Negara <http://www.arkib.gov.my/en/pilihanraya-umum-pertama-1955> (accessed 17 October 2013).

7. The narrative here is drawn from pages 29–35 of the Reid Commission (1957).

8. See the Reid Commission (1957, p. 30), which notes that an EC member can only be removed in the manner one removes a Supreme Court judge.

9. Kuala Lumpur Barat had only 8,862 voters but 132, 300 residents, while Kelantan Utara had 42,510 voters and 93,300 residents.

10. See Rachagan (1980, p. 271–79) for a discussion of these points, including the malapportionment to Sabah and Sarawak after 1963.

11. It is interesting to note that this disparity (60.8 per cent) is still much less than the 2013 situation, with the largest constituency of Kapar (144,159) far exceeding the smallest, such as Putrajaya (15,791; disparity of 89 per cent) or Igan in Sarawak (17,771; disparity of 88 per cent). The second case of Igan is justified on the ground of rural weightage, even if excessive, but Putrajaya, as the administrative centre of Malaysia, can have no such justification.

12. The two dissenting commissioners who opposed the indirectly elected Senate were Sir William McKnell and Justice Abdul Hamid, who argued that such a procedure was "out of step with a system of parliamentary democracy" (Reid Commission 1957, p. 34).

13. Sothi Rachagan (1980, 1984, 1993) and Lim Hong Hai (2002, 2003, 2005), from whom I draw on for some of the narrative of this section, are the two main scholars to have undertaken extensive work on this subject.

14. It is interesting to note that the commission's terms of reference included the possibility of multiple member constituencies for urban districts, but the commission decided against this in their final submission (See Merthyr Commission 1954, pp. 1 and 9). The argument made for choosing the single-member plurality system was the necessity for "simplicity and uniformity of procedure".

15. See Lim's (2002, p. 106) detailed discussion of this.

16. Lim (2002) notes that UMNO was particularly peeved by the EC's adherence to the Reid Commission's stipulations on limits to weightage, which would have drastically reduced urban–rural disparities and given major disadvantages to the ruling party.

17. As official texts of the agreements are hard to come by, see legal activist Charles Hector's explication of the points at <http://charleshector.blogspot.com/2012/09/malaysia-agreement-20-pointsabah-and-18.html> (accessed 22 October 2013). For a discussion of the twenty points with regard to Sabah, see Loh (2005, pp. 92–96).

18. See Crouch (1996, p. 61) for an explanation of the rationale for this change. The secretary of the EC offered this reasoning: "we do not want the voters to wait in long queues, especially under the burning sun" (ibid.). In more recent times the cap of 700 voters has been removed, with some *saluran* having more than 1,000 voters.

19. See Loh (2005, pp. 107–14) for a chronology of delimitation exercise in Sabah and their effects.

20. I draw on a report written by Jeremy Grace, part of a USAID-sponsored Delimitation Equity Project, at <http://aceproject.org/ace-en/topics/bd/bdy/bdy_my> (accessed 21 October 2013).

21. See ibid.

22. This section draws on material from Saravanamuttu (2000) and the report of the Royal Commission of Inquiry headed by Senator Athi Nahappan (hereinafter, Nahappan Commission 1968). I have also referenced the highly informative article by Goh (2005), who uses material from the Nahappan Commission and various other studies, including an important article by Tennant (1973).

23. For critiques of the electoral system, I draw from the comprehensive volume on electoral issues by Puthucheary and Othman (2005).

24. As cited in Rachagan (1980, p. 257).

25. For two detailed studies of how malapportionment had contributed in particular to the BN's electoral success in the 13th general election, see Lee (2013, 2015) and Otswald (2013).

26. That is, the candidates who would automatically win a majority in a two-person contest. It often happens in multi-cornered contests that a presumed Condorcet winner loses because of the splitting of votes.

27. BERSIH started out in 2006 as a movement of civil society forces and political parties calling for clean and fair elections. Its demands for cleaning up the electoral rolls, reviewing postal votes, allowing voting from abroad, fair access to the media and the elimination of corrupt practices has inspired major street demonstrations — in 2007, 2011, 2012 and 2015 — of proportions hitherto unseen in Malaysia.

28. The tribunal comprised international and local specialists and was chaired by Yash Pal Ghai, a constitutional law expert and former professor of Law at Hong Kong University. Other members were Ramlan Surbakti (Indonesia), Kraisak Choonhavan (Thailand), Azzat Kamaluddin, Mavis Puthucheary

and Herman Shastri (Malaysia). See <http://www.bersih.org/?p=6216> (accessed 26 October 2013).

29. A report was finally submitted to the government that blamed errant officials for the problem, but at the point of writing no apparent action has been taken based on the recommendation to set up a permanent secretariat to oversee the problem of illegal immigrants.

30. See Ong (2005, pp. 292–315) for a measured depiction and analysis of these problems up until the 2004 election. For more up-to-date reports, news and statements, see the BERSIH webpage at <www.bersih.org>.

3

CONSOCIATION AND THE ELECTORAL PROCESS, 1952–55

This chapter traces the birth of the Alliance and the establishment of its unique sharing model in the two early pre-Independence elections of 1952 and 1955. In so doing, it will be shown how the Alliance was able to overcome its opponents, particularly the professedly non-communal forces represented by the Independent Malaya Party (IMP), later Party Negara (PN), and the Islamic and the left-leaning parties. These two early elections paved the way for the Alliance to develop a path-dependent success based on its model of ethnic consociation in subsequent elections after "Merdeka" (Independence) was attained in 1957. In this period of emergent consociational politics, the Alliance was able to establish a first "grand coalition" of the major ethnic groups premised on its basic form of mediated communalism.

In the previous chapter, I sought to establish that Malaysia's electoral system is unique, with its distribution of ethnic political parties and first-past-the-post (FPTP), single-member constituency system. Despite obvious flaws, electoral politics has been broadly anchored to elements of procedural democracy such as transparent and autonomous electoral institutions and procedures, freedom of political association and campaigning, guaranteed by law based on the Constitution. By and large, electoral politics and competition with the oversight of an Election Commission had remained relatively free and fair until the late 1960s. It was only after the 1969 general election, which saw the eruption of racial riots in Kuala Lumpur, that a host of restrictions and constraints were placed on electoral processes and a more authoritarian state structure was instituted. The evaluation of the electoral system by a notable group of Malaysia specialists seems to confirm this broad view:

> The general conclusion reached in this assessment of the current state of Malaysia's electoral system is that Malaysian elections cannot be considered reasonably free and fair because they do not fulfill the functions required of them in formal democratic theory — or at least that our elections have become, over the years since the 1960s, rather less free and fair than they once were, and that they now are much less free and fair than they might or should be. (Puthucheary and Othman 2005, p. 14)

Be that as it may, according to Khoo, writing in the same volume, the broad features of parliamentary democracy adapted from British practice still "matched most requirements of a modern democratic system" (Khoo 2005, p. 20).

Beyond questions of procedural democracy, there has also been considerable discourse about the character of electoral politics in the early years. The manner by which political parties were constituted reflected a practice of what Ratnam termed as "communalism" (Ratnam 1965). However, as I have argued, there were attempts to ameliorate the most deleterious conflicts of a plural society in the electoral process through a form of *mediated communalism*. Electoral politics drove ethnic groups to arrive at compromises rather than zero-sum outcomes. Barraclough (1984) complains that Ratnam and other academics who have used the term *communalism* have failed to define it well or at all. In his view, Esman's definition appears to have the most conceptual clarity; namely, that communalism "can be defined as competitive group solidarities within the same political system based on ethnic, linguistic, racial or religious identities" (as cited in Barraclough 1984, p. 418). In practice, communalism was married with a form of power sharing or "consociation" (Lijphart 1977) that was peculiar to Malaysia's cultural make-up of its British heritage and history.

It bears repeating here that Lijphart argued that ethnically divided societies could live with their ethnic cleavages, that conflict could be contained by leaders of the ethnic communities and that democracy within such divided societies could be managed through formal institutional arrangements, by establishing a grand coalition of all ethnic groups, mutual veto in decision making, ethnic proportionality in allocation of opportunities and offices and ethnic autonomy, often through federalism. We have already noted earlier that writers like Milne and Mauzy (1978) have tried to show that Lijphart's model could be applied with modification to Malaysia and, I would add, with an injection of a high dosage of processes of communal mediation. The broad elements of a consociation were successfully incorporated into a model of politics initiated by the Alliance, and this helped to keep the electoral process on an even keel until the fateful general election of May 1969. The event, as observed by Von Vorys, marked the collapse of the "inter-communal directorate" held in rein by the Tunku, whom he termed a "supra-communal arbiter" (Von Vorys 1976, p. 14, passim).

BIRTH OF THE ALLIANCE

In some ways the Alliance party was given life almost fortuitously, but also through the political guile of United Malays National Organisation (UMNO) president Tunku Abdul Rahman. It was his foil against his nemesis Dato Onn Ja'afar, the leader of the Independence Malaya Party (IMP), and he was well aided by Onn's poor public relations with Chinese leaders. This was ironic, as Onn was the founder of Malaya's first multi-ethnic party. What Onn lacked, the Tunku had in abundance, in terms of personal acuity and political acumen. The event which proved to be the pivotal moment for Malayan, hence Malaysian, history was the Municipal Council election of Kuala Lumpur on 16 February 1952, because, through it, the country's ruling political coalition (although somewhat reconstituted since then) began its path towards six decades of electoral success.

Most analysts thought that the non-communal IMP would defeat the hastily constructed political "alliance" of UMNO and the MCA (Malayan Chinese Association), but on polling day voters delivered to it 9 of the 12 contested seats and handed only 2 to the IMP and 1 to an independent. The 6 Selangor Labour Party candidates were all defeated. The Alliance won 10,240 votes compared to the IMP's 6,641, by any measure a resounding victory for UMNO and the MCA. The Malayan Indian Congress (MIC) at this point of time chose to throw its weight behind Dato Onn's IMP.[1] It was only in 1954, as we shall see later, that the Indian party decided to join the Alliance.

What then were the factors and events that led to the success of the first alliance of UMNO–MCA? The political alliance was formed to overcome the growing attraction and influence of the IMP. It was a tactic of the Tunku's so as to preserve UMNO's political presence in the face of Dato Onn's challenge. Without going into the reasons for Onn leaving UMNO and his setting up of the IMP,[2] his new party's pitch of "non-communal" politics and its liberal attitude towards non-Malays and citizenship rights was thought to be a winner with the electorate, especially the Chinese. Indeed, the leader of the MCA, Tan Cheng Lock, was chairman of the founding meeting of the IMP and had toured the country with Dato Onn to organize IMP branches. This positive IMP–MCA relationship seemed to have soured at some point. Diane Mauzy alludes to the "minor" event which could well have provided the gambit for the Tunku to draw the MCA away from the IMP. Colonel H.S. Lee, the influential president of the Selangor State MCA organization, was not consulted about the formation of the IMP, and at the inaugural meeting he was not even invited to sit on the platform. By these acts of omission the IMP created a powerful enemy it could ill afford (Mauzy 1983, p. 16).

Karl Von Vorys suggests that political calculation may well have been the motive for the MCA's abandonment of the IMP. Tan Cheng Lock intoned the intellectual rationale for the turn to a communal approach in the following manner:

> I don't advocate that the MCA should encourage a spirit of communalism
> as racialism but I see people using words like communalism without
> being precise or understanding the real implications and significance of

the term... For instance, a form of communalism exists in Switzerland with a great deal of success and yet Switzerland remains a single, successful and harmonious national state. (Von Vorys 1976, p. 112)

The frustrated Onn was livid in his remarks after the MCA departure, accusing the party of trying to make Malaya a province of China, while claiming that 98 per cent of the Chinese were loyal to Taiwan and the rest were communists (ibid.). It became apparent that Onn was even unable to mobilize significant support among the Malays or draw supporters away from his erstwhile party, UMNO.

Thus, on 8 January 1952, the Selangor branches of UMNO and the MCA made a not too surprising joint declaration that the two parties would contest as a common front in the Kuala Lumpur Municipal election.

Table 3.1
Results of Municipal Elections, 1952–53

	Date	Seats	Alliance	IMP	Prog. P	Ind.	Labour	Muslim
Kuala Lumpur	Jan. 52	12	9	2	—	1	—	—
Johor Baru	Dec. 52	9	9	—	—	—	—	—
Batu Pahat	Dec. 52	9	5	—	—	3	—	1
Maur	Dec. 52	9	7	—	—	2	—	—
Malacca	Dec. 52	3	2	—	—	—	1	—
Kuala Lumpur	Dec. 52	4	3	1	—	—	—	—
Seremban	Aug. 53	12	10	—	—	1	1	—
Alor Setar	Aug. 53	9	7	—	—	2	—	—
Sungai Petani	Aug. 53	9	7	—	—	2	—	—
Kuala Baru	Aug. 53	9	6	—	—	3	—	—
Segamat	Nov. 53	9	9	—	—	—	—	—
Kluang	Nov. 53	9	9	—	—	—	—	—
Muar	Dec. 53	3	3	—	—	—	—	—
Malacca	Dec. 53	9	4	—	3	—	2	—
Kuala Lumpur	Dec. 53	4	4	—	—	—	—	—
Total		119	94	3	3	14	4	1

Source: Von Vorys 1976, p. 109.

Means interprets the IMP–MCA breakup as a clash of the personalities of Onn Jaafar and Tan Cheng Lock and the unwillingness of Tan to allow the domineering Onn to hold sway (Means 1976, p. 134). Or, it could also be the influence of H.S. Lee, as suggested by Mauzy, that dealt the lethal blow. Be that as it may, the alliance of UMNO and the MCA made it difficult for the IMP to overcome the communal thrust of Malayan politics. Although all the parties contesting argued for communal harmony, the collaboration between two ethnic parties, I would argue, clearly showed voters that power sharing would be assured *institutionally* in a political game of dominant and domineering political personalities.

The sweet victory of the UMNO–MCA alliance propelled path-dependent electoral success in other municipal elections and led to the progressive downslide and eventual demise of the IMP. Clearly, the Alliance had established that a process of mediating communalism through ethnically constituted parties was an effective path to electoral success. In the 37 municipal council seats in six cities of the Federation elections conducted in December 1952, UMNO–MCA captured 26 while the IMP was only able to win 1. In Penang, UMNO went into partnership with the Muslim League and, without the MCA, was able to win 1 of 3 contested seats, ousting the Radical Party and ranking second in that contest to the Penang Labour Party. In Johor, of 9 seats contested, the strongest IMP candidate polled less than half the votes of the UMNO–MCA candidates, dealing a humiliating defeat to Onn's party on its home turf. More defeats were to follow for the IMP in 1953 (see Table 3.1).

From the outset it was clear that the temporary UMNO–MCA alliance could easily flounder due to differences in their communal interests. Early friction came because of the visit in August and September of 1952, on the invitation of the MCA, of Dr Victor Purcell, the well-known British scholar and champion of Chinese interests. UMNO took strong exception to Purcell's visit while the MCA stuck to it guns and, in the ensuing quarrel, withdrew an earlier offer of M$500,000 to set up a Malay Welfare Fund to be administered in cooperation with UMNO (Means 1976, p. 135). It appeared that the level of trust between Alliance partners was still razor thin.

More was to follow in the three years leading up to the first federal election of 1955 in the way of intra-Alliance friction, but the more serious and escalating rivalry with Onn's IMP kept the Alliance intact. Ironically, the non-communal IMP began to act more and more as an anti-Chinese party, attacking the MCA for its running of welfare-oriented lotteries and seeking its ban. At some point in 1953, Onn also attacked UMNO for "selling the country to the Chinese", citing Chinese demands for the creation of a Chinese university, Chinese opposition to nationality laws, their threats of hartal and the like (Means 1976, p. 139). Onn also moved to undercut UMNO by establishing links with Perak's Dato Panglima Bukit Gantang, who had led a revolt against the Perak branch of UMNO. Both the Alliance and the IMP vied to lead Malaya into Independence from the British, and the IMP took the step to call two separate "national" conferences. The first, under the leadership of Dato Panglima Bukit Gantang (together with a number of other Menteri Besar), met on 27 April 1953 with four organizations in attendance — the IMP, the MIC, the Selangor Pakistan Association and the Straits Chinese British Association. The MIC later exited this group over a number of disagreements, including educational policy for Tamil schools and the timing of the first federal election. In its failed attempt to create a "national front" for the attainment of Independence, the Menteri Besar Conference instead gave birth to Party Negara.[3]

The rival "national convention" of UMNO–MCA was held in August 1953. Joining the Alliance were the Peninsular Malays Union (PMU), the Pan-Malayan Islamic Association and Persatuan Persetiaan Melayu (Union of Malay Patriots). Matters became even more chaotic when PMU decided on its own course and called for the "All-Malaya National Congress" comprising minor Malay political groups. This Congress proposed that Malay be the official language, Islam the official religion and a Malay be elected monarch — policies which did not differ significantly from those of the IMP or Alliance (Means 1976, p. 147). The British decided to act in the midst of these complex developments (not all of which have been fully adumbrated here) by appointing a forty-six-member multi-ethnic Elections Committee, which produced a report released at the end of January 1954. On the basis of this report and, by its own deliberations, the Merthyr Commission (discussed in the previous chapter), proposed the terms, format and date for the first federal election of 1955.

In the political fisticuffs that followed, the Alliance objected strenuously to the recommendations of the committee, which it considered to be still too restrictive. In its own national convention the Alliance made the following demands:

1. Elected members must not be less than 75 per cent of the total members.
2. Government servants should be allowed to take part in politics.
3. Those born in the Federation who had lived there for five years without a break should be allowed to vote and those working in Singapore, if they had lived no less than seven years in the Federation.
4. The election should be held no later than November 1954.
5. The election must be based on majority vote.
6. Those members returned would be eligible for ministerial posts in the federal cabinet. (Tunku 1986, p. 43)

Meanwhile, the Alliance had begun to take the institutional shape that would eventually characterize it. Soon after the Kuala Lumpur success, UMNO and the MCA held roundtable conferences to institutionalize the Alliance. The roundtable talks were held on 3 and 21 February and on 15 March 1952 in Kuala Lumpur, Singapore and Johor Baru, respectively. The participants, apart from the Tunku, were Dr Ismail Abdul Rahman, UMNO vice president Sardon Jubir, UMNO youth leader Bahaman Shamsuddin, Syed Nasir Ismail, MCA president Tan Cheng Lock, MCA vice president H.S. Lee, MCA secretary Leong Yew Koh, S.M. Yong, Ong Yoke Lin and T.H. Tan. According to the Tunku, the talks proceeded smoothly (Tunku 1986, pp. 35–36). This was followed by a conference in March 1953 that set up a "National Alliance Organization", which was then formalized on 23 August 1953. Liaison committees were established at local levels. In September 1954 a thirty-member National Council was set up and the Tunku was named "leader of the Alliance". In the meantime, the MIC had begun to approach the Alliance. On 17 October, after a closely contested vote, the MIC Executive Committee elected to join the Alliance. By 10 April 1955 the Alliance National Council met to make arrangements for the first federal election. The National Council consisted of 16 UMNO, 16 MCA, and 6 MIC representatives, while its smaller Executive Committee was made up of 5 UMNO, 5 MCA and 2 MIC representatives. All decisions required unanimity and were generally arrived at informally (Mauzy 1983, p. 18).

THE 1955 ELECTION

The intense politicking of the two sets of forces already touched upon above led the British government on 15 July 1953 to set up the 46-member committee, mentioned earlier, from the existing Federal Council members to seek solutions and compromises towards setting the stage for the first federal elections. The committee delegated its work to a 20-person group made up of 10 Malays, 3 Chinese, 3 Europeans, 2 Indians, 1 Ceylonese and 1 Eurasian, and produced in 1954 much of the basis and the rationale for the system of elections instituted for the first general election of 1955. As noted by Ratnam (1965) and others, the committee rejected the idea of communal rolls and advocated a common roll of electors. However, the committee did make a communal gesture by recommending that three seats be reserved for the lesser communities, albeit as a temporary measure. The communities that met the requirement were the Ceylonese, the Eurasians and the aboriginal Orang Asli (Ratnam 1965, p. 179). At the end of the day, the Alliance, with its stronger claims, won the right to lead a delegation headed by the Tunku to make demands on the British. Although not granted permission to meet with the Colonial Secretary Oliver Lyttelton, the delegation forced itself on him in London (Ratnam 1965, p. 182). As noted earlier, among the major Alliance demands was the call for a 75 per cent fully elected Council and an early federal election, but it came away only with some vague assurances that all these matters would be addressed.[4] Alliance–British frictions continued unabated, with Alliance members threatening to resign en bloc from the legislature, until the High Commissioner Donald MacGillvray stepped in with a letter to the Tunku to save face for both sides. MacGillvray stated that the course he intended to pursue was to consult the leader (or leaders) of the majority of the legislature on the appointment of reserved members.[5] The British, of course, would have the final say in these matters, but 5 were promised to the winner of the election. Ultimately, there were 32 appointed members to the first Federal Council but, because the Alliance won in the election, 5 of these were appointed on the advice of the chief minister of the new government, the Tunku.

As noted in the previous chapter, the actual format of the first federal election, and the delineation of constituencies by size and number, was all left to the Merthyr Commission, which either ignored or avoided factoring in considerations for the communal character of the Malayan political terrain through a simple first-past-the-post electoral format. A critic opined that the commission's report was the result of a "growing ostrich-like belief in Malaya that communalism can best be scotched by refusing to recognize its existence".[6] Analysts such as Ratnam, for example, seem to suggest that no amount of universalizing of voting through a common roll could avoid the communal characteristics of Malayan electoral politics.

In the event, Nomination Day was set as 15 June 1955, which allowed for about six weeks of campaigning. By this time, as we have shown, much water had flowed under the bridge and the political groups in contestation were now aligned largely in two major groups, one in support of the Alliance, which had grown in stature and prominence under the Tunku, and the second behind the now much weaker forces of Party Negara (PN), the successor to the IMP, led by Onn Jaafar. One may even say that these two major, if still inchoate, political blocs were drawn to seek political legitimacy from somewhat similar political forces in that contemporary Malaysian political landscape; a large rural sector, a growing but still small urban middle class, and the three ethnic communities. Today, of course, the middle class has grown by degrees. In the 1950s the Alliance and the PN were both seemingly vying for the middle ground in Malaya's communalized politics, much as the BN and Pakatan Rakyat were attempting five decades later. In 1952 the Alliance proved it was more effective than its rival to win an election with its strategy of ethnic compromise of mediated communalism and consociational politics.

As noted in the previous chapter, the Alliance candidates held many public meetings and door-to-door campaigns, as did the other parties, and Radio Malaya arranged for a number of party broadcasts and forums. On the morning of 28 July the Alliance had won 27 constituencies and it eventually went on to win all but a single seat. Some 43 candidates who failed to secure an eighth of the valid vote lost their deposits. Party Negara, with 30 candidates, fared badly, losing 13 deposits, while 14 independents also forfeited their deposits.

The most distinct aspect of the Malayan electorate in 1955 was its skewed ethnic composition, given that most non-Malays remained unregistered as voters. Of the 1,280,000 electorate, 84.2 per cent were Malay, with Chinese comprising 11.2 per cent and Indians 4.6 per cent (see Table 3.2). The Alliance Manifesto called for Independence within four years, Malay as the National language, Malayanization of the civil service, and better social services, but it eschewed the thorny question of citizenship. The main aim of the Alliance was to win a large enough majority to be the party with the mandate to lead Malaya to Independence from the British and, concomitantly, to assign its nemesis Party Negara and its leader Onn Jaffar to history. This it succeeded in doing with élan when, on 27 July 1955, the results of the election showed that it lost only one seat to the PMIP and swept some 80 per cent of the popular vote. The Alliance polled four times the votes of all opposition candidates and ten times that of the PN, dealing a humiliating defeat to Onn Jaafar, who was only able to capture 22.4 per cent of the vote, even in his home turf of Johor Baru (Means 1976, p. 167).

I shall now analyse the major factors behind the remarkable success of the Alliance in 1955 and the implications of the outcome in terms of its model of consociation and mediated communalism, taking into account also the peculiarities of that time and the structural features of the electoral system.

Table 3.2
Ethnic breakdown of 1955 Electorate

	Number of voters	Percentage
Malays	1,078,000	84.2
Chinese	143,000	11.2
Indians	50,000	3.9
Others	9,000	0.7
Total	1,280,000	100

Source: Ratnam 1965, p. 187.

Table 3.3
Parties, Candidates and Results, 1955

Party	No. of candidates	Malays	Chinese	Indians	Seats won	Votes polled	Percentage
Alliance (UMNO, MCA, MIC)	52	35	15	2	51	818,013	76.6
Party Negara	30	29	1	–	–	78,909	7.6
Pan-Malayan Islamic Party (PMIP)	11	11	–	–	1	40,667	3.9
National Association of Perak	9	8	1	–	–	20,996	2.0
Labour Party	4	–	2	2	–	4,786	0.4
Perak Malay League	3	3	–	–	–	5,433	0.5
Perak Progressive Party	2	1	–	1	–	1,081	0.1
Independents	18	16	1	1	–	31,642	3.0
Total	129	103	20	6	–		

Source: Smith Report 1955, p. 18 and Ratnam 1965, p. 196.
Note: Figures exclude spoilt votes.

Alliance Institutional Clout

The first point to be made about the 1955 outcome was the growing political strength of the Alliance just prior to the election. In path-dependence parlance, the coalition capitalized on its "first mover advantage"[7] in setting the tone and format for ethnic relations in the plural society of Malaya through its politics of compromise and moderation. As described by one of the astute early observers of Malayan politics, the model was none other than a consociational one of mediated communalism, although the author himself does not employ these concepts:

> The power of the Alliance was dependent upon cooperation and agreement among its three partners ... internal discipline and cohesion became the major task of the leadership of the trio of parties comprising the Alliance. Each communal organization contained within its ranks elements which resisted the concessions made to their communal partners. Thus each constituent party had to retain the support of its communally conscious members without antagonizing the other two to the point where their common political front would be jeopardized. The intra Alliance tension was greatest when its "National Council" set about the task of allocating seats on the ticket to each respective party. The internal politics of Alliance can best be described by reference to the problem of compromise and discipline encountered by each of its constituent members. (Means 1976, pp. 161–62)

And how true it was that even in the midst of campaigning against its opponents, internal friction would hound the Alliance. Thus, in March 1955 a serious incident threatening MIC participation in the early Alliance came about as a result of a political faux pas by the secretary and the publicity chief of the MCA, who had attacked the *Singapore Standard* newspaper for posting an article which was "pro-Tamil" and "anti-Chinese". This led the Tamil paper *Tamil Murasu* to upbraid the MIC for its subservience to the Alliance and to call on all Indians to boycott the Alliance. Earlier, and even more critical, was the fact that the Tunku had to fend off what he called the tendency towards a "Malays only" approach by his party, when its members asked for 42 out of the 52 seats to be contested by Malays. Only the Tunku's threat to resign could silence his detractors.[8] There was also the major issue of Chinese not being an official language —

brought up by the United Chinese Schools Teachers Federation (Jiao Zong) at the height of the campaign period — which needed the intervention of Tan Cheng Lock to resolve, since the MCA had already accepted Malay as the sole official language and English as the other language used for official purposes (Tunku 1986, p. 53).

While maintaining its internal cohesion, the Alliance seemingly made the most radical demands on the British, with an almost no-holds-barred, albeit civil, approach towards gaining independence from the colonial rulers. Its strong stance and non-compromising position vis-à-vis the British and its ploy of calling for amnesty talks with the Communists were clear winning strategies with the electorate. Means (1976) argues that the issue of amnesty stole the limelight, particularly in the final weeks of the political campaign after the British revealed that peace feelers had been received from the Malayan Communist Party on 24 June 1955. Because of the British government's rejection of the Communists' offer of peace, the Alliance was able to capitalize on its own call and campaign to pursue amnesty.

Party Negara's Organizational Weakness

The Alliance's strength stood in sharp contrast to Party Negara's weaknesses on various fronts. First, the PN showed softness towards the British and had become identified with the government in not pressing for an early date for Merdeka. In the public eye the PN appeared to be the party of the entrenched, Western-educated elite, with little connection with the grass roots, and virtually a party of government servants (Means 1976, p. 158). By the time it turned to gain support from the smaller Malay parties, it was too little too late and, worse, this move was guaranteed to irk its non-Malay supporters. One such disillusioned supporter was E.E.C. Thuraisingham, the leader of the Ceylonese, who was quoted as saying that the communalism of the party "left him cold" (ibid., p. 159). The manifesto of the party played up popular issues of the Malays, such as restricting immigration, with Onn using and condoning such phrases as "Chinese threat" and, with regard to the language policy, the PN proposing Malay as the sole official language. Onn was able to thus gain the support of groups like the All-Malaya Youth Congress and the Malay National Front, and some former Malay radicals of the Kesatuan Melayu Muda and Angkatan Pemuda Insaf. However, he was unable to secure the support of PMIP's Burhanuddin Al-Hemy. Instead, there was an informal understanding to back each other's candidates, as the PMIP was strong in the North and on the East Coast while the PN was able to channel it some funds, so it was alleged by the Alliance. A debate ensued in the legislature over the use of cars and whether polling day should be a holiday. The PN opposed both these measures because of the Alliance's superior organization and political machine. In the event, the PN carried the car issue by one vote and three leading Alliance members — the Tunku, H.S. Lee and Dr Ismail Abdul Rahman — resigned from the council. The paradoxical use of communal tactics and unpopular measures such as the above vote on polling day policy, its aligning with radical Malay political parties, and its strong association with the British government were no doubt factors which compounded the PN's problems beyond its organizational weakness. The astute stance of the PMIP in demurring Onn's overtures and in maintaining its neutrality vis-à-vis the two coalitions may be an important factor to explain its subsequent rise as a third political force in Malaysian politics.[9]

The Disparate Left

Finally, something needs to be said about the political Left. The Malayan "Parliamentary Left" (i.e., excluding the Malayan Communist Party, MCP) started mobilizing itself as a plethora of local parties, largely in urban areas, and began to establish some presence at the national level by the 1950s. Means unkindly terms many left-wing parties as "paper organizations" (1976, p. 156), but by the time of the 1955 election there was an attempt to amalgamate the Left into the Pan-Malayan Labour Party — later superseded by the Labour Party of Malaya — on the initiative of the Penang and Perak Labour parties. From the looks of it, the Left was riddled with internal and geographical divisions, not to say ethnic problems. The Penang Labour Party had in 1951 joined forces with the All-Malay Peasants Organization (led by Mohamed Sopiee), representing the *padi* farmers of Kedah, to become the Pan-Malaya Labour Party. In Perak, one faction of the Labour

Party became the Perak Progressive Party, which in 1954 joined the UMNO–MCA Alliance to contest town council elections. In the 1955 federal election, the People's Progressive Party contested two seats on its own. Means summarizes well the plight of the Malayan Left circa 1955:

> The weakness of the labour parties was not so much in their programs as in the nucleus of their support. They tended to rely too heavily upon the trade union movement which was not yet strong enough to command large blocs of voters. Because these parties were generally unwilling to compromise their programs or share leadership with other important elements of society, they had almost no hope of winning a single seat in the federal elections. (Means 1976, p. 158)

IMPACT AND IMPLICATIONS OF 1955

As the 1955 federal election was atypical of Malaysian elections, given the overwhelming Malay electorate, one needs to be circumspect in drawing broader implications for the future, although undeniably its political impact was crystal clear. The Alliance had gained the overwhelming support of the Malayan electorate and established itself as the dominant force in Malayan politics. However, the comprehensive defeat of its opponents, particularly Party Negara, may have been unhealthy for the democratic trajectory of the new state, and the result dealt a mortal blow to the already incipient two-party system. There were an insufficient number of non-Malay candidates to truly test the Alliance's overall appeal as a multi-ethnic coalition, while Party Negara became virtually mono-ethnic, offering only one non-Malay candidate. The Alliance's victory was symbolized by Khir Johari, the UMNO secretary, taking the honours by winning the largest majority of the day by eliminating his opponent with a margin of 29,646 votes (Ratnam 1965, p. 195).

What was particularly interesting though was the performance of 15 Chinese and 2 Indian Alliance candidates, who won despite standing in mostly Malay-majority constituencies, only 2 of which had Chinese majorities, namely George Town and Ipoh-Menglembu. The Islamic party PMIP made its mark, if pyrrhic, by winning only 1 seat out of the 11 candidates it offered. Apart from stressing Islam, its manifesto was perhaps deliberately vague, even though it had earlier called for equal citizenship rights for all. Its candidate Haji Ahmad Haji Hussain defeated his Alliance opponent in Krian (Perak) by merely 450 votes. The Labour Party fared poorly, and even the Malayan Trades Union Congress did not rally behind the anti-Alliance electoral front.

Cross-ethnic voting[10] clearly favoured the Alliance. This pattern of voting was to become one of its most enduring and effective electoral strategies in a Malaysian electoral system that had eschewed communal rolls. Ratnam provides us the prime example of cross-ethnic voting in the victory of the MIC's S. Cheelvashingam MacIntyre in Batu Pahat:

> Of the 27,323 registered electors in this constituency, there were only 530 Indians and 5,679 Chinese. And yet, of a total of 21,685 valid votes that were cast in this constituency, Mr. MacIntyre collected 18,968, while his sole opponent, a Malay representing Party Negara, was able to get only 2,717. (Ratnam 1965, p. 197)

Ratnam goes on to analyse Chinese voting and to posit that despite an overall tendency for the Chinese to support Chinese candidates, "like the Malays, the Chinese had also voted along party and not communal lines" and helped to return Alliance candidates (p. 199). However, in the 1956 by-election in Ipoh, a predominantly Chinese constituency, the Alliance candidate lost to D.R. Seenivasagam of the People's Progressive Party, who had aligned himself closely with Chinese sentiments (the same man who had lost his deposit in 1955). Be that as it may, there is little doubt that a middle ground of moderation and rational choice which factored in "communalism" had clearly become the overall formula for success of the Alliance Party. Such a notion would be consistent with the concept of "consociation", which, as explained at the outset of this book, is the form of *mediated communalism* which deliberately softens the most extreme demands and moves them towards win-win or variable sum outcomes rather than zero-sum ones.[11] I have also referred in Chapter 1 to the overarching idea of the ethnic "bargain" between the communities and its quid pro quo politics of ethnic compromise which has been the concept most commonly used by many analysts of Malaysian politics to explain the Alliance success of 1955 (cf. Mauzy 1983, pp. 20–22).

Without doubt the Alliance landslide victory in 1955 prefigured its role as the main negotiator with the British for the constitutional provisions of 1957 incorporating the "bargain" it had worked out with its constituent ethnic parties. The gist of this was that the non-Malays would be given liberal citizenship rights while the Malays would be recognized as the "indigenous" community of the country and accorded a special position, including a constitutional monarchy based on Malay kingship. In this first period of electoral politics, although it was obvious that UMNO was the chief orchestrator of consociational politics, there was seemingly less of a suggestion at this stage, or none at all in the formal sense, of Malay "hegemony" or dominance. Communalism was mediated often in the face of highly fractious ethnic politics. The trajectory and path of politics that had begun to develop was one which established institutional stability and strength under ethnic leaders like the Tunku, Chinese leaders like Tan Cheng Lock, and Malaysian-oriented Indians like Sambanthan.

Leadership has no doubt been a major factor in the manner in which this model of mediated communalism had been given cohesion in the first period of electoral politics. The Tunku's personality was needless to say a crucial factor in sealing and maintaining the "constitutional contract". As stressed and celebrated by Von Vorys, the Tunku was indeed Malaya's *supra communal arbiter*: "His style was leisurely, his manner benevolent, and his attitude flexible. He used his political power gently, always sensitive to the interests of others. Yet, all along he was determined to concentrate final authority in his own hands" (1976, p. 125).

CONCLUSION

The birth of the Alliance, Malaysia's first multi-ethnic ruling coalition, was somewhat unexpected and almost fortuitous, made possible by a strong and enlightened leadership who saw the wisdom in establishing a consociational form of politics given the realities of Malayan ethnic divisions. After two important pre-Merdeka elections, the Alliance was able to maintain its institutional strength and stability. Indeed, its landslide victory in the first federal election of 1955 gave the Alliance an unassailable first-mover advantage in electoral politics. It allowed for its subsequent path-dependent success in the elections during the Independence period. By the same token, the Alliance's comprehensive victory in 1955 augured poorly for the development of a more democratic polity and smashed the early prospects for a two-party or two-coalition electoral system.

Notes

1. For the facts relating to the 1952 and 1955 elections, I draw from the following sources of information and perspectives: The Tunku's own narrative about the events are found in his *Political Awakening* (1986); Means' detailed account in his first book on Malaysian politics (1976, Chapters 10 and 11); Von Vorys' insightful accounts, spliced with anecdotes (1976, Chapter 5); Ratnam (1965, Chapter 6) and Mauzy (1983) who provide crucial information about early and later-day alliance formation politics.

2. There has been the suggestion that the British influenced the establishment of the IMP. Von Vorys suggests it was George Maxwell the former chief secretary of the Federated States who had planted the idea, urging the MCA's Tan Cheng Lock to cooperate with Onn (Von Vorys 176, p. 106). However, Onn's involvement in the Communities Liaison Committee of 1949, initiated by Commissioner General Malcolm MacDonald, was probably the seed of the IMP. See Mauzy (1983, pp. 12–16).

3. As noted by Ratnam (1965, p. 178), having lost non-Malay support, the Malayan National Conference initiated by the IMP then became a Malay-oriented organization in its new persona as Party Negara.

4. The Alliance members threatened a boycott of all legislative councils, but a meeting with the British High Commissioner Donald MacGillivray on 2 July 1954 averted the action. See Tunku (1986, pp. 41–48) and Means (1976, pp. 147–50) for narratives of the protracted Alliance–British negotiations and friction over the 1955 election.

5. The opinion and assessment about the situation and about the Tunku by the previous High Commissioner Gerald Templer (who replaced Henry Gurney, assassinated by the Communists) may have made the difference in the British relationship with the Alliance party. The Tunku revealed the following words Templer penned to him on leaving Malaya: "To wish you good fortune and to tell you how much I appreciated your counsel in the executive council. You and I have not always agreed, but there is no harm in that. You politicians have tremendous responsibilities on your shoulders in the next few years. The happiness and peace of

mind of millions of people will depend on it for a long time. I think you know how fond I am of the people of this country, and I only hope and pray that the policies eventually decided upon will turn out to be for the ultimate good of the people" (Tunku 1986, p. 46).

6. F.G. Carnell in an article on constitutional reform and elections in Malaya (*Pacific Affairs*, vol. 27, 1955) as cited in Ratnam (1965, p. 185).

7. See Chapter 1 for a discussion of path-dependence theory and concepts.

8. See Means (1976, pp. 162–64) for more detailed accounts of these events.

9. The PMIP had participated in the UMNO–MCA sponsored national convention but did not agree with the concessions made to the MCA regarding citizenship and voting rights for non-Malays. In the 1955 election it contested 121 seats in the predominantly Malay constituencies to the north and east of Malaya. These areas remain as strongholds of PMIP's successor, PAS.

10. This is the term that has been used in analysing the 2008 general election and also in Chapter 9. See Ooi, Saravanamuttu and Lee (2008) and Saravanamuttu (2012).

11. See Chapter 1.

4

THE PATH-DEPENDENT RISE AND DEMISE OF THE ALLIANCE, 1959–69

This chapter will present and interpret the results of the elections of 1959, 1964 and 1969 and show the success of Alliance consociational electoral politics until its collapse in 1969. The Alliance, which saw its birth as a coalition of three ethnic parties in 1955, was able throughout this period to capitalize on its power-sharing arrangements and overcome most of its political opponents until its near defeat in 1969. As shown in the previous chapter, it had tasted success in the 1952 Kuala Lumpur municipal elections and thereafter won every national election from 1955 to 1969. However, the Alliance was unable to maintain its two-thirds control of parliamentary seats in 1969, a year which saw the outbreak of racial riots in Kuala Lumpur. By the beginning of the period, its major opponents, the IMP and Party Negara, were already assigned to history. Then, the parliamentary Left, led by the Socialist Front, mounted a concerted challenge as the main parliamentary opposition, until it chose to opt out of the electoral process, not least of all because of its own internal ethnic divide. It was left to the Malay-based PMIP to become the Alliance's major opponent.

Up until 1969, a path dependence of mediated communal, though elite-managed, consociational consensus was fully established by the Alliance, which remained the dominant ruling coalition throughout this first period of electoral politics after Independence from the British. A particular trajectory of politics may be said to be path-dependent when it exhibits not only immediate returns in political and economic gains but when it also establishes or reinforces institutional arrangements and structures that help to sustain and accelerate such gains.[1] The maintenance of such a system was clearly premised on political investment in institutional arrangements, which largely kept the peace, orchestrated by ethnic elites who dominated their respective parties. Most importantly, attaining the necessary and sufficient conditions of mediated communalism, as expounded in Chapter 1, made for the ruling coalition's electoral longevity. This book posits that such path dependence was indeed generated by the early success of the Alliance in the 1950s and 1960s and reconstituted highly successfully under the Barisan Nasional (National Front) alliance in the 1970s through to the late 1990s. However, a major rupture of this path-dependent success did occur in the 1969 election, as this chapter will demonstrate.

As shown in the previous chapter, originally formed as a coalition between UMNO and the MCA, the Alliance incorporated the MIC into its ranks for the 1955 national election under the self-governance framework before Independence. In this election its competitor, the PMIP, took only one seat out of fifty-two. However, by 1959 the PMIP was able to capture the states of Kelantan and Terengganu, showing that the Alliance's consociation of ethnic power sharing was vulnerable to the Islamic vote, particularly in the Malay heartland in the East Coast states of the Peninsula. The Alliance was less challenged on the West Coast and was able to maintain a strong level of federal strength through its consociation model of power sharing with non-Malay parties. Non-ethnically constituted parties such as Parti Rakyat and the Labour Party were able to make inroads into municipal or local-level politics, but failed at the state and federal levels. In 1964 the Socialist Front (SF) — comprising the Labour Party and Parti Rakyat — was only able to take two parliamentary seats, even though it was also a form of consociation between the Chinese-supported urban-based Labour Party and the more rural and Malay-based Parti Rakyat.

In the 1955 election the Alliance had won as much as 79.6 per cent of the vote (Ratnam and Milne 1967, p. 13). Malay voters helped return many MCA and MIC candidates, but by 1959 the Alliance's popular vote fell to 51.8 per cent, with the PMIP doing particularly well in Kelantan and Terengganu, winning respectively 68.3 per cent and 47.6 per cent of the vote. In Penang the SF took 38.2 per cent of the popular vote. The character of Malaya's first-past-the-post system still delivered more than a two-thirds majority of seats to the Alliance, i.e., 74 out of 104 seats. In its best post-Independence electoral outing in 1964, the Alliance took 89 seats by winning 58.5 per cent of the vote (see Table 4.1).

It would be germane to compare in greater detail the 1959 and 1964 elections in terms of a path-dependent development of the Alliance's power-sharing formula. By 1959 the electoral demographics had changed dramatically from the 84.2 per cent Malay electorate of 1955 to the following: 56.8 per cent Malay, 35.6 per cent Chinese, 7.4 per cent Indian and 0.2 per cent others — out of 2,144,000 voters (see Table 4.2). As shown in Table 4.3, the Alliance was able to capture 51.5 per cent of the popular vote, with the PMIP taking 21.2 per cent and the SF 13 per cent (the respective numbers for these parties were 58.5, 14.6 and 16.1 per cent in the 1964 election). The ethnic power-sharing model of the Alliance was challenged on

Table 4.1
Alliance and Malay Voters, 1964

Percentage of Malay electors	Votes won (%) 20–39.9	Votes won (%) 40–59.9	Votes won (%) 50–59.9	Votes won (%) 60–79.9	Votes won (%) 80–99.9	Seats
0–19	4	4	—	—	—	8
20–39.9	—	6	9	12	—	27
40–59.9	—	—	3	16	2	21
60–79.9	—	—	2	14	3	19
80–99.9	5	5	6	10	1	27
Total	9	15	20	52	5	102

Source: Ratnam and Milne 1967, p. 372.

two fronts; namely, the more exclusively Malay-nationalist-Islamist discourse of the PMIP and the national-socialist ethnic power-sharing model of the SF. The stable majority of the popular vote won by the Alliance, indeed its marked increase in 1964, indicated that the Malaysian electorate — now comprising significant numbers of Chinese and Indians — bought into the Alliance formula of mediated communalism, notwithstanding that a sizeable proportion of voters, mostly in the Malay heartland of the East Coast, supported the PMIP, while a sizeable number of urban mostly Chinese voters were supporters of the SF.

What Von Vorys calls the "vertical mobilization" of the ethnic vote by the "horizontal solidarity" of Alliance power sharing remained a powerful political tool in both these elections. The formation of Malaysia and the resultant Indonesian Confrontation boosted the Alliance vote even further in 1964. However, another trend had become clearly visible, even by 1964; namely, that the non-Malay partners in the Alliance — the MCA and the MIC — were increasingly winning seats because of Malay support, and that the Chinese electorate, for example, had begun to shift its vote to urban-based parties like Labour, the United Democratic Party (UDP) and the People's Progressive Party (PPP):

> Thus behind the façade of political stability signs of strain could be perceived. The coalition of English educated administrators (and politicians) and the Malay school teachers and other more communalist elements in UMNO — in fact, the intermediate leaders who were responsible for Malay mass-support for UMNO — was in peril. Fissures were developing among English educated Chinese, while the masses of Chinese voters temporarily supportive of MCA were rapidly becoming alienated. (Von Vorys 1976, p. 145)

While Von Vorys sees the above as communal trending, one could argue contrariwise, that urbanization had meant a shift away from more overtly communal parties like UMNO, the MCA and the MIC. Even in the 1950s and 1960s, the Alliance and its partners depended heavily on its large and more rural constituencies for victory. The opposition parties have traditionally relied on more urban and more populated constituencies. This trend continued till the present and proved particularly devastating for the Barisan Nasional (BN), the successor of the Alliance in 2008.

Ratnam and Milne (1967) undertook a major study of the 1964 parliamentary election and it would be instructive to draw further on some of their findings to illustrate the successful consociational model of the Alliance. As pointed out by the two authors (and as shown in Table 4.1), the Alliance did best in the mixed seats:

> The most striking way of stating this point is to look at seats where the Malays made up between 40 per cent and 79.9 per cent of the electors. *In none of these 40 seats did the Alliance proportion of the vote fall below 50 per cent.* In the seats with fewer than 40 per cent Malay electors there were fourteen where the Alliance vote fell below 50 per cent: in ten of those with 80 per cent or more Malays the Alliance also failed to reach 50 per cent of the vote. (Ratnam and Milne 1967, p. 372, emphasis in the original)

Writing some forty-five years ago, the conclusion by Ratnam and Milne prefigures a major question of this current study: "It is sad, but probably true, that there is little immediate prospect that Malaysia will have an effective two-party system, organized on non-racial lines. If the Alliance retains its multi-racial appeal, it will constitute a dominant non-authoritarian party. If it loses that appeal, a two-party system may result, but it would most likely have a markedly racial basis." One should add that while such a two-party system would be "racial", it would also entail moderate, centripetal policies. With the benefit of hindsight, one could say that the Alliance model remained potent as long as it maintained a centripetal spin of policies to capture the middle ground of ethnic politics. The parties of the opposition, whether under the SF or PMIP umbrella, had no stratagem such as mediated communalism to win this ground. This development had to wait for a new chapter of opposition politics, when a coherent multiracial two-coalition politics emerged.

With this in mind, I will now look in greater detail at the outcomes of 1959 and 1964. There was also an election in Singapore in 1963, which will also be touched upon.

THE 1959 AND 1964 OUTCOMES

As noted by Ratnam (1965), in 1959 the most significant change in
the electoral system came by way of the huge increase in non-Malay
voters. In 1955 the 84 per cent preponderance of Malay voters was
now balanced by a significant presence of Chinese as well as Indians,
as shown in Table 4.2. The main reason for the change was the rise
in citizenship figures of non-Malays owing to the provision of the
1957 Constitution, making the electorate more reflective of the overall
population of Malaya, while at the same time swelling considerably
the proportion of urban voters.

In contrast to 1955 the Alliance faced a much more formidable
opposition, particularly from the PMIP and the newly constituted SF.
The PPP (People's Progressive Party) and Party Negara (PN) were the
other main opposition parties. There were 259 candidates contesting
104 seats, with the Alliance standing in all, the PMIP in 58
(all Malay), the SF in 38 (20 Chinese, 11 Malay, 7 Indian), the PPP in
19 (9 Chinese, 9 Indian, 1 Malay), and the PN in 10 (all Malay).

The overall results of the 1959 election are shown in Table 4.3,
indicating in no uncertain terms that in regard to the popular vote
and seats, the Alliance was already losing its *first mover advantage*
as a consociational pact, but it still managed to hold on — by my
extrapolation of the results — to a substantial number of communal
as well as mixed seats, while losing considerable ground to the PMIP

Table 4.2
Electorate, 1955 and 1959

	1955		1959	
	No.	%	No.	%
Malays	1,078,000	84.2	1,217,000	56.8
Chinese	143,000	11.2	764,000	35.6
Indians	50,000	3.9	159,000	7.4
Others	9,000	0.7	4,000	0.2
Total	1,280,000	100	2,144,000	100

Source: Ratnam 1965, pp. 187 and 200.

Table 4.3
General Election Results, 1959

	Seats	Overall percentages	In constituencies contested
Alliance	74	51.5	51.5
PMIP	13	21.2	36.2
SF	8	13.0	34.8
PPP	4	2.2	22.2
Party Negara	1	6.4	32.2
Malayan Party	1	0.9	41.5
Independents	3	4.8	20.4
Total	104	100	100

Source: Election Commission 1970.

in the Malay heartlands of Kelantan and Terengganu and to the SF in the more urban and Chinese constituencies.

The PMIP won its 13 seats in Kelantan (9) and Terengganu (4), the SF won its 8 seats in Selangor (5) and Penang (3), the PPP all its 4 seats in Perak and the PN its single seat in Terengganu. What is rather impressive about the performance of the opposition was the high percentage of votes won in the seats it contested, with the PMIP winning as much as 68.3 per cent of the popular vote in Kelantan (Ratnam 1965, p. 206). The seasoned Muslim intellectual and politician, Dr Burhanuddin Al-Helmy, who had previously headed the Malay Nationalist Party, led the PMIP in this election. Farish Noor (2004, p. 98) considers "Pak Doctor" (as Burhanuddin was affectionately known) as "the most progressive Islamist intellectual" of the times, but more than that he was able to turn PAS from being just a small badly organized provincial party into one with a national ideological platform and reach.[2]

But, according to Von Vorys (1976, pp. 147–48), the PMIP campaigned on issues which were largely communally oriented, such as that citizenship laws should be more stringent for non-Malays; the establishment of Islam as a state religion with more palpable benefits to Malays; Malay to be the sole official language; and the reservation of primary official posts such as chief ministers, governors and Cabinet positions to be reserved for Malays. On the opposite side of the spectrum was the SF campaign, which argued that too many privileges had been bestowed on Malays and stressed that class differences were the underlying cause of Malayan problems, such as the poverty of rural Malays. In a real sense the SF was also a consociational arrangement of left-wing non-Malay (mainly Chinese) and Malay leaders, constituted by the merging of the Labour Party and Parti Rakyat. The main personalities in the Front were the Labour Party's Lim Kean Siew and Tan Chee Khoon and Parti Rakyat's Ahmad Boestamam.[3] The PPP was led by two Ceylonese Tamil brothers, S.P. and D.R. Seenivasagam, who had established Ipoh as their base, with massive Chinese support. The fading PN was still headed by Onn Jaffar, who won its only seat in Terengganu. The PPP's campaign revolved on issues similar to those championed by the DAP (Democratic Action Party) of the future; namely, acceptance of Chinese and Tamil as official languages along with Malay as the national language; a call for equal citizenship based on *jus soli,* or rights of being born on the soil; and the implementation of immigration and education laws to be based on equality of communities.

Von Vorys infers that the Alliance, by taking most of the middle ground, was able to defeat its opponents: "Where the Malay communal challenge of the PMIP was particularly strong, the Alliance received heavy Chinese support. Where the Chinese (and Indian) communal challenge of the Socialist Front and PPP was intense, the Alliance could count on solid Malay support" (Von Vorys 1976, pp. 150–51). It is ironic that this situation has been reversed in latter-day politics, where the BN (the successor to the Alliance) lost this crucial middle ground to its nemesis, Pakatan Rakyat, in 2008 and 2013, as we shall see in the later chapters of the book.

The next general election on 25 April 1964 saw a different configuration of opposition political forces, with the establishment of the Federation of Malaysia on 16 September 1963. The formation of Malaysia also sparked Indonesia's "Confrontation", which gave the Alliance a distinct advantage while being detrimental to the fortunes of the SF and the PMIP because of their opposition to the formation of Malaysia. The SF's Ahmad Boestamam was detained on the ground that he had been associated with the Brunei uprising led by Azahari. There were also arrests of PMIP leaders, with Dr Burhanuddin found guilty by the EC of an offence with respect to the Companies Ordinance and legally barred from contesting (Ratnam and Milne 1967, p. 17). Two new parties entered the fray in 1964, the National Convention Party, initiated by the erstwhile Agriculture Minister Aziz Ishak, and the United Democratic Party, started by Lim Chong Eu. Aziz parted ways with UMNO after a spat with the Tunku and Lim quit the MCA over a number of disagreements with the Alliance. There were attempts by the opposition parties to come together to form a front, but the efforts turned to naught over disagreements on seat allocations and policy.

Another party that entered the political arena on the Peninsula was Singapore's People's Action Party (PAP) led by Lee Kuan Yew. This entry of the PAP famously created a complex set of issues and tensions for the Alliance, not least of all because of the PAP's shutting out of the Singapore Alliance of the MCA and UMNO in the 1963 Singapore state election (ibid., p. 24–26), which will be discussed further below.

A word needs to be said about the 1961 takeover of Terengganu by BN-UMNO through the defections of two PAS assemblymen. In a development remarkably similar to what occurred in Perak in 2009,[4] the PAS defections of 1961 allowed the Terengganu state government to be toppled in a no-confidence vote engineered by the then deputy prime minister Abdul Razak, the father of Najib Razak, who engineered the "Perak Coup" of 2009. The no-confidence vote was made possible by not just the two defections but also by three PAS abstentions.[5] In almost a facsimile of events presaging the Perak situation forty-eight years later, the Terengganu Sultan refused PAS's request for a snap election, just as the Perak Sultan in 2009 had also refused the PAS Menteri Besar's request to do the same. Means (1976) suggests that the toppling of PAS had much to do with money politics, i.e., the promise of federal funds for Terengganu's economic development.[6]

Ratnam and Milne (1967) have studied the issues that animated the 1964 electoral campaigns of the government and opposition parties in great detail, and we need only highlight the most significant of these issues and their impact on the electoral result. Looming large, as the single most prominent issue, was Indonesia's Confrontation against Malaysia. As Ratnam and Milne (ibid., p. 110) aver, the election virtually became a "referendum" for the Alliance government's handling of Indonesian aggression and its defence of Malaysia's national integrity. It was used as a battering ram against the SF and PMIP, both of which had close associations with Indonesia and were also concomitantly against the very formation of "Malaysia". According to Ratnam and Milne, the most damaging attack on the SF and PMIP came just two days before polling day, when a government White Paper "gave detailed accounts of how certain leaders of the SF and the PMIP had over a period of years actively participated in clandestine activities in cooperation with known Indonesian agents" (ibid., p. 114).[7]

The Alliance's path-dependent success was not just a function of the domestic impact of Confrontation but also of other significant domestic factors; namely, an electoral map that remained unchanged on the Peninisula, guaranteeing the Alliance's rural advantage and its urban success in mixed seats, plus its grip on and control of the press, radio and television.[8] Moreover, the Alliance's continuing national institutional strength and stability easily trumped that of PAS's regional strength and the newly assembled Socialist Front. The opposition parties got a thumping, including the PAP of Singapore, with its foray in the Peninsula earning only a single seat, in Bangsar, won by Devan Nair. PAS won a respectable 9 seats while the SF and the PPP won a miserable 2 seats each.

While the Peninsula delivered to the Alliance 104 seats in the new Parliament, another 55 seats were contributed by the three new states of Malaysia: Sarawak (24), Sabah (16) and Singapore (15). The seats were determined not in the April 1964 elections but by indirectly allocating them based on the results of previous state district-level and legislature elections and, in Singapore's case, based on its 1963 election. This arrangement gave the Alliance party a major advantage, even though it had to deal with opposition parties in the three new states of Sarawak, Sabah and Singapore. The ruling coalition did pick up a total of 17 seats in Sarawak. This allocation was determined in a complex and convoluted manner based on Sarawak's district or local-level elections held in June 1963, for a total of 429 seats.[9] These were, in effect, Sarawak's first democratic elections, as explained by Ratnam and Milne (1967), held to determine representatives to its tiered system of governance, with an apex state legislature, the *Council Negri*, which also included nominated members. Ratnam and Milne aver that Sarawak did not really have the capacity to handle true federal elections, due its long period of rule by the White Rajahs, who kept the state underdeveloped economically and politically. Voter registration was carried out for the first time in 1962, with all its attendant problems. At the end of the day, the Sarawak Alliance — comprising Pesaka, the Sabah Chinese Association (SCA), BARJASA and SNAP — SUPP, PANAS and independents shared the spoils in the State Council in a political geography of rural–urban divide not unlike that of the Peninsula; that is, the Alliance capturing mainly rural seats and the SUPP and PANAS (urban-based political parties) taking the urban seats. The parliamentary seats allocated were 17 to the Sarawak Alliance, 3 each to the SUPP and PANAS, and 1 to an independent.

In Sabah the situation was even more complex, with local-level elections in December 1962, March to May 1963 and April 1964 being used to determine federal representation. Ultimately, 137 members were elected to the state legislature, and although the Sabah Alliance "institutional framework" was put into place to encompass pro-Malaysia parties, it was a poor facsimile of its Sarawak cousin. In effect this framework played second fiddle to strong political streams in local parties representing non-Muslims (UNKO) and Muslims (United Sabah National Organisation, or USNO), respectively. Notwithstanding this, the Sabah Alliance framework produced the following distribution of parliamentary seats: USNO 6, SCA 4, UNKO 5, and PM 1 (Milne and Mauzy 1978, p. 6). Eventually, most of these parties would come under the fold of the Alliance's successor, the Barisan Nasional. In terms of path-dependence, despite the complex local situations of Sarawak and Sabah, a nascent consociational politics began to take shape even in the early 1960s, and the Alliance clearly had *first mover advantage* by setting up state-level versions of its formula in Sarawak and Sabah. The 1964 election provided the necessary impetus and platform for the Alliance to make these moves, which has benefited its successor the BN till this day.

In Singapore an election held in September 1963, just before the formation of Malaysia, proved to be both controversial and most difficult for the PAP. Most controversially, many of the party's left-wing leaders were put in "cold storage" on 2 February in the eponymous "Operation Cold Store", which saw the detention of 111 left-wing politicians, journalists, unionists and students.[10] The election was won by the PAP, polling 47 per cent of the vote, which enabled it to claim 37 out of 51 seats, thus defeating the main opposition party Barisan Sosialis and its electoral partner Parti Rakyat (these two parties combined took 34.7 per cent of the vote). The Singapore Alliance achieved 8.3 per cent of the vote but took no seats.[11] The calling of the election for 21 September (with nomination day on 12 September), four days before the formal date for the formation of Malaysia, was forced upon the PAP government, and was at the same time an obvious ploy by Singapore's premier Lee Kuan Yew to endorse his government's "Malaysia" decision. The move also helped Lee defeat the left-wing faction of his party led by Lim Chin Siong, forcing it to form the Barisan Sosialis splinter party. One of the members of this faction resigned for Lim to contest in a by-election, but the government — which became one seat short of a majority because of the split — called for the general election instead. Just prior to this, Operation Cold Store had put Lim Chin Siong, Lee's political nemesis in the PAP, behind bars. Lee probably surmised that had the PAP lost the election to the Barisan Sosialis, the federal government in Kuala Lumpur would deal one way or another with an allegedly communist-influenced ruling party. Under the trying circumstances, Lee was understandably displeased that the PAP also had to face a federal-backed Singapore Alliance in the 1963 election. It was therefore not surprising that the PAP's participation in the 1964 federal election also aggravated tension between the Malaysian Alliance and the Singapore ruling party. [12] The fractious politics between the PAP, UMNO and the MCA eventually led to Singapore's expulsion from Malaysia, but not before events had sparked racial riots in Singapore in July and September of 1964.

The Singapore riots were virtually a prelude to the May 1969 riots in Kuala Lumpur.[13] The riots occurred at the peak of acrimonious politicking between Malayan and Singaporean politicians. An estimated 20,000[14] Malays and Muslims from some seventy-three organizations had assembled for the traditional parade in the heart of the city on the occasion of Prophet Mohamed's birthday. Inflammatory speeches by leaders of the Singapore UMNO preceded the riots. Things got out of hand as the procession went through the city and groups of Malays broke ranks and clashed with riot policemen and subsequently were seen attacking Chinese civilians. This sparked Chinese retaliatory attacks on Malays. By midnight, 220 incidents had been reported, 178 people had been injured — 32 of whom were admitted to hospital — and 4 had been killed. Some houses were also razed. A second riot broke out on 2 September the same year; after eleven days, 13 people were left dead and 106 injured. The police made some 1,439 arrests.[15] Lee Kuan Yew has in his first book of memoirs (1998) blamed UMNO for the riots. Given this sequence of events, it was not surprising that Singapore's exit from Malaysia would follow. In an oft-narrated story, the Tunku, lying in a hospital bed in London being treated for shingles, would unilaterally decide that the island state should be expelled from the Malaysian federation, and the date eventually chosen was 9 August 1965. Lee Kuan Yew dubbed the separation a *talak tiga*, meaning a divorce that is virtually irreconcilable.[16]

THE 1969 COLLAPSE OF THE ALLIANCE

The line-up of political parties for the 1969 general election was different from that of previous elections, with the boycott of this election by the Labour Party, which considered elections in Malaysia to be a "sham". The rationale for this was the arrest of a number of prominent Labour Party workers accused of colluding with the Malayan Communist Party.[17] The exit of the Labour Party and the hiatus it created for the Left was in some ways filled by two new major parties. The PAP had departed from Malaysia but in its place was the newly minted DAP, registered on 18 March 1966.[18] Another new political party, Parti Gerakan Rakyat (Gerakan), inaugurated on 24 March 1968, could definitely be said to have taken up some of the slack left by the Labour Party, while its SF partner Parti Rakyat remained in contention, albeit with a leadership change.[19] A third new minor party was the Negri Sembilan–based United Malayan Chinese Organisation (UMCO), which articulated Chinese communal interests (Rudner 1970, p. 4).

The Alliance by no means looked like a party under threat on the eve of the election, which was held on 10 May. Senior partner UMNO claimed a membership of over 340,000, and its organizational structure at the grass roots remained in place. The MCA under Tan Siew Sin saw its membership climb from 137,120 in 1965 to 208,534 by 1969, while the MIC was probably the Alliance's weakest link, with 75,000 paid-up members. Citing his own pet theory, Von Vorys avers that the "inter-communal Directorate" of the Tunku, Tun Razak, Tun Tan and Tun Sambanthan had further cemented its bonds and was "strengthened by a generous distribution of patronage" (1976, p. 252).

Therefore, the results of the 1969 election came as a major shock for all concerned. From the election results presented in Table 4.4, the Alliance getting about *45 per cent* of the popular vote proved to be

Table 4.4
Election Results (Parliamentary), 1964 and 1969

	1964		1969		
	Vote (%)	Seats won	Vote (%)	Contested seats only (%)	Seats won
PARTIES					
Alliance	58.5	89	44.9	45.8	74
SF	16.1	2	—	—	—
PMIP (PAS)	14.6	9	20.9	37.2	12
UDP	4.3	2	—	—	—
PPP	3.4	1	3.4	55.9	4
PAP	2.0	1	—	—	—
DAP	—	—	11.9	53.4	13
GERAKAN	—	—	7.5	54.5	8
SUPP	—	—	3.0	36.0	5
SNAP	—	—	2.7	28.7	9
USNO	—	—	0.6	72.7	13
Sabah Chinese Association (SCA)	—	—	0.8	71.2	3
PESAKA	—	—	1.3	22.5	2
PR	—	—	1.1	18.7	0
PN	0.4	0	—	—	—
United Malaysian Chinese Organisation (UMCO)	—	—	0.1	2.9	0
Independents	0.7	0	1.8	15.3	1
TOTAL	100.0	104	100.0	100.0	144

Source: Election Commission 1970, pp. 115, 121 and Appendix G.

the factor that ultimately brought about its de facto collapse. [20] The Alliance not only lost the popular vote but, on the first count, had won only 66 seats, which was 7 short of a majority. However, thanks to a further 10 seats won uncontested by its Sabah Alliance party, USNO, the Alliance was in fact able to command a parliamentary majority.[21] The ruling coalition was able to eventually capture some 74 of the 144 parliamentary total, which was significantly less than the all-important two-thirds majority it had commanded since 1955.[22] Moreover, the Alliance lost the popular vote in a majority of state-level contests, as will be discussed further below.

After the suspension of the election, the two East Malaysian states were later due to hold polls; Sabah on 25 May and Sarawak on 7 June. USNO and the SCA later delivered the remaining 6 seats to give the Alliance a clean sweep in the state. Both these parties constituted the "Sabah Alliance" and were state-level coalition partners of the national Alliance but remained loosely independent at the federal level. As there were no state elections in 1969, the configuration of seats won by the Sabah parties in the 1967 election remained intact.[23] In Sarawak the parties in contention were the Sarawak Alliance, which won 7 seats, the SUPP with 5, Party Pesaka 2, and SNAP 9, with a single seat going to an independent.[24] The election for the Melaka Selatan constituency, which was suspended, saw the Alliance win this seat in January 1971.[25] Such is the character of Malaysia's first-past-the-post system and its skewed distribution of seats that the Alliance, by winning just 45 per cent of the vote, was able to eventually command a strong majority of seats in Parliament. It is without doubt that the Malaysian electoral system clearly confers generous *manufactured majorities* to the ruling coalition and allows it to apparently "steal" elections, as pointed out in Chapter 2.

The state-level contests proved equally difficult for the ruling coalition, which for the first time lost control of two states — Kelantan and Penang — where it could only garner 47.5 and 34.6 per cent of the popular vote, respectively, and very nearly lost Selangor and Perak, capturing only 41.6 and 43. 6 per cent, respectively.[26] What is even more surprising, and not pointed out by most studies of the 1969 results, is that the Alliance also lost the popular vote in Terengganu, Negeri Sembilan and Malacca, as shown in Table 4.5. In effect the Alliance's consociational model of electoral politics had failed badly in delivering

Table 4.5
State Election Results, 1969 (Seats and Percentage)

	Perlis	Kedah	Kelantan	T'gganu	Penang	Perak	Pahang	Selangor	N. S'bilan	Malacca	Johor	Sabah*	S'wak	Total
Alliance	11 (53.5)	14 (53.1)	11 (47.5)	13 (49.3)	4 (34.6)	19 (43.6)	20 (55.1)	14 (41.6)	16 (46.2)	15 (48.1)	30 (65.0)	—	15 (25.4)	182
PMIP (PAS)	1 (43.8)	8 (41.3)	19 (52.2)	11 (49.4)	1 (7.0)	0 (18.5)	2 (16.8)	0 (9.6)	0 (10.6)	0 (17.0)	0 (6.5)		—	40
PPP		—			0 (0.4)	12 (18.8)	—			—			—	12
DAP					3 (8.4)	6 (9.5)	0 (1.7)	9 (31.1)	8 (36.4)	4 (12.7)	1 (12.5)			31
GERAKAN					16 (46.8)	2 (3.8)	1 (2.0)	4 (16.5)		1 (4.4)	0 (1.9)			26
Partai Rakyat	0 (2.6)		—	0 (0.7)	1 (1.2)		2 (1.6)		0 (0.5)	0 (16.0)	0 (0.6)	—		—
SUPP													12 (28.8)	12
SNAP													12 (24.4)	12
PEKASA													8 (12.7)	8
USNO	—											—		—
Sabah Chinese Association (SCA)	—											—		—
Independents	—						1	1			1		1	4
TOTAL	12	24	30	24	24	40	24	28	24	20	32	(32)	48	282

Source: Election Commission 1970, pp. 115 and 118.
Note: * No state elections were held in Sabah in 1969; elections were held in 1967 and 1971 for 32 seats.

the desired results in 1969. I should point out it was not just the loss of non-Malay votes that cost the Alliance its near defeat, but it was also due to inroads made by PAS into the constituencies on the East Coast and in northern Malay-majority states — taking away votes that would otherwise have been UMNO's. Thus, without doubt, one of the crucial conditions for the Alliance's mediated communalism, discussed in Chapter 2, had been undercut; namely, sufficient support from the Malays for the ruling coalition.

MALAYSIAN MALAYSIA

After Singapore's exit from Malaysia and the end of Confrontation in 1965, domestic politics and ethnic tensions continued to roil. We should not forget that in the same year that riots broke out in Singapore, 1964, Bukit Mertajam in Penang witnessed communal clashes on 21 July in which two people were killed and several injured. These clashes may well have been linked to the Singapore riots (Vasil 1972, p. 13). As most political commentators have noted, the PAP's and Lee Kuan Yew's entry into Malaysia left an indelible mark on the Malaysian political landscape. While aiming to debunk the MCA as UMNO's Chinese-based Alliance partner, Lee prematurely also offered to Malaysians his version of "democratic socialism", which promised a "Malaysian Malaysia". This strategy was doomed to fail given the then strength of the Alliance's consociation and, as noted by Von Vorys, the willingness of the Tunku to stay with his Chinese and Indian allies *per aspera ad astra* (i.e., through thick and thin; Von Vorys 1976, p. 166). Lee's failure to win over Malay support despite or because of his comprehensive defeat of the Alliance in the 1963 Singapore election was fuelled by Malay opponents such as Syed Albar Jabar, Secretary General of UMNO, and Ali Ahmad his assistant, who were known to be "ultras" with respect to Malay rights. Ironically, these same ultras had sealed a relationship with the MCA to neutralize the PAP with great success in the 1964 election. However, the concept of "Malaysian Malaysia" propounded by Lee in 1965[27] was destined to haunt the MCA, arguably till the present day. After the PAP's failure to make an impact on the 1964 election, the party tried to galvanize the opposition parties through the so-called Malaysian Solidarity National Conference held in Singapore on 9 May 1965. It attempted to enlist the support of the PPP, UDP and other groups in Sabah and Sarawak, and proposed the following "fundamental principles" of the Malaysian Malaysia concept:

- Malaysia should be a democratic society where legitimate differences of views should be permitted and where individuals and political parties should have full freedom to persuade its citizens by constitutional means to their particular point of view.
- Malaysia being a multiracial and multicultural society must show respect and tolerance for legitimate diversity, provided these do not weaken Malaysian unity or hamper loyalty to Malaysia.
- Malaysia was conceived as belonging to Malaysians as a whole and not to any particular community or race. (Vasil 1972, p. 13)

Soon after the convention, Singapore was expelled from Malaysia, but the idea was pursued with even greater vigour by the DAP, led essentially by peninsular Malaysians, although Devan Nair, the PAP Member of Parliament who remained as its representative, stayed on in the Peninsula as the party's (DAP) founder.

Suggestions that the DAP was a clone of the PAP are probably only half true. The bulk of its leadership, including former chairman Chen Man Hin, its secretary-generals such as Lim Kit Siang and Fan Yew Teng and party supremo Karpal Singh, were domiciled in the Peninsula, and many leaders were subsequently critical of the PAP and its authoritarian politics in Singapore. [28] The new party's guiding principles were made in the "Setapak Declaration" of 29 July 1967, which sought "the ideal of free, democratic and socialist Malaysia, based on the principles of racial equality, and social and economic justice ... founded on the institutions of parliamentary democracy" (Vasil 1972, p. 16). As Vasil notes, the DAP differed from the PAP on a number of questions and was more strident with regards to certain issues — such as the classification of citizens into bumiputera and non-bumiputera — and on language, culture and education rights of non-Malays. The party argued that the Malaysian Constitution guaranteed the free use of the Chinese and Tamil languages and was committed to making them official state languages, including their use for education. In its election manifesto it charged that the government committed racial discrimination, while denying that the party itself was anti-Malay.

The other new party, post-1969, was the Gerakan. It comprised a constellation of prominent personalities, such as Lim Chong Yew (formerly of UDP), Tan Chee Khoon (formerly Labour) and Labour leaders such as V. David, V. Veerappen and Tan Phock Kim. It also had the support of intellectual heavyweights like Professor Syed Hussein Alatas and Professor Wang Gungwu and was the party of left-leaning English-educated moderates. Thus, its stances on major issues were only marginally different from those of the DAP, except for its stance of not calling for Chinese and Tamil language secondary schools. While it may have equivocated on the question of bumiputera rights, it did put the accent on economic policies for the benefit of workers and peasants, maintaining an overall stance on non-discrimination of every kind, and particularly with respect to women (Von Vorys 1976, p. 269). Another party, the PPP, being mainly Perak-based, seemed merely to latch on to the stances of the other parties and the theme of a "Malaysian Malaysia" as the antithesis of a Malay Malaysia (ibid., p. 271). The Parti Rakyat in its manifesto predictably rejected communalism and called for class solidarity. In typical rhetorical fashion, it called for the destruction of Anglo-American neo-colonial systems, a new national and progressive economic system and a democratic and progressive culture.

The PMIP was the only opposition party that could be said to be on the opposite pole to the other opposition parties. Roundly rejecting a Malaysian Malaysia was implied in its advocacy of Malay-nationalist cum Islamic agendas. In practice, in these early years, it was more the PMIP's championing of nationalist qua Malay rights (rather than narrowly Islamic rights) that won it support. In 1969 it targeted the Alliance's failure in racial harmony, which it argued was only "skin deep". Second, it held, rightly or wrongly, that under the Alliance government, 90 per cent of wealth was in the hands of non-Malays. It thereby offered constitutional provisions to ensure native rights and social justice in line with Islam, the nationalization of industries, land reform in the interest of farmers, and one education system with Islam as a compulsory subject (Von Vorys 1976, p. 271–72). In effect, the latter-day UMNO practically supplanted these policies from PAS with the New Economic Policy (NEP). From this perspective the demands of the young Turks battling the Tunku within UMNO were hardly original, and it explains why the NEP was so important for UMNO to recapture Malay votes won by PAS in the 1969 election.

ELECTORAL PACT

The idea of an electoral pact among the opposition parties followed from the Alliance victory in the Serdang Baru state by-election of 28 December 1968 in Selangor. The seat, previously held by Parti Rakyat, was contested by DAP and Gerakan, but saw the Alliance candidate win by a mere 607 votes in a three-cornered fight. The combined votes of the two opposition parties of 5,928 and 1,330 easily exceeded that of the ruling party. Lim Kit Siang was the DAP candidate and Tan Han Swee stood for Gerakan.[29] The DAP then called for an electoral pact and Syed Hussein Alatas, president of Gerakan, invited the opposition parties for a meeting on 12 January 1969 (Drummond and Hawkins 1970, p. 321). A third meeting at Gerakan secretary general Tan Chee Khoon's house saw an agreement among five parties (Gerakan, Partai Rakyat, the DAP, SUPP and SNAP) to work towards an electoral pact. In the event, only the DAP and Gerakan announced such a pact, on 21 February 1969, with the DAP's Goh Hock Guan waxing emotional on the significance of the Serdang-influenced decision: "The experience we have got from this election had been bitter enough and I believe we will never again fight among ourselves and allow the Alliance to sit on our corpses" (ibid., p. 322). Vasil argues that a major premise of the electoral pact was the effort to deny the Alliance a two-thirds majority in Parliament so as to prevent the ruling coalition from freely curtailing fundamental rights and liberties through constitutional amendments (Vasil 1972, p. 21). The political differences of the opposition parties stymied any formal electoral pact. The PPP was basically a Perak-based party and the Gerakan was also primarily based in Penang and had a more moderate position vis-à-vis Malay rights issues, while the DAP had more national ambitions and was more stridently a champion of non-Malay rights and Chinese education matters. In the event, the arrangement that was decided on was for each party to enter into separate bilateral arrangements as opposed to a tripartite pact. Clearly, these early attempts to form an opposition alliance were weak and there was a mortal consociational flaw owing to the PMIP's non-involvement because of its strident Malay-Muslim rights agenda. As such, no path dependence — neither institutional nor ideological — was created at this early stage of opposition collaboration. Furthermore, it wasn't long before a party like the Gerakan, and even the PMIP, were persuaded to join the new grand coalition of the Barisan Nasional engineered by Tun Razak by the early 1970s.[30]

LOSING THE MIDDLE GROUND

UMNO may have been buoyed by the fact that in 1968 it had won three by-elections, including that in Serdang discussed above. UMNO also won in Segamat Utara — a constituency with only 40 per cent Malays — and in Tampoi, both state constituencies of Johor. However, it lost the parliamentary constituency of Bachok to the PMIP. On the other hand, the MCA may have had reason for concern given the onslaught of the non-Malay-based opposition parties. Among the issues that would have put the MCA on the defensive was the passing of the controversial National Language Bill in 1967 and the related setting up of Universiti Kebangsaan (National University) with Malay as the medium of instruction. These moves may have been helpful to UMNO, but not to the MCA or MIC. At about this time the Chinese educationists, in support of the DAP, were already calling for the setting up of the Mandarin-medium Merdeka University. The MCA, for its part, initiated the Tunku Abdul Rahman College as a sop to the Chinese educationists. Perhaps the founding of the Penang University (later Universiti Sains Malaysia) by the Tunku government in 1969 was to assuage non-Malay sentiments on the contentious issue of access to university education.

The passing of the National Language Bill may have in the end proved detrimental, not just to the MCA and MIC, but also to UMNO because of the demands of Malay nationalists like Syed Nasir Ismail, who led the Barisan Bertindak Bahasa Kebangsaan (National Language Action Front). Syed Nasir and his group, citing Article 152 of the Constitution, wanted Malay to be the sole official language, while junking English altogether and ignoring the call for Mandarin and

Tamil to be officially recognized. This notwithstanding, the non-Malay efforts to secure liberal use of these languages after the implementation of the National Language Act on 1 September 1969 was successful and affirmed in Parliament. Moreover, "the Yang Di Pertuan Agong could permit the use of English for such official purposes as it deemed fit" (Vasil 1972, p. 15). The Alliance was thus put on the back foot with respect to the demands of UMNO extremists and lost considerable Malay ground by the time of the election because of this issue.[31] The Alliance was also confronted with serious divisions in Sarawak with the split between Party Pesaka, representing mainly Iban interests, and Party Bumiputera, representing other natives and Malays (Drummond and Hawkins 1970, p. 323).

The Tunku seemed to be in denial that the Alliance was facing difficulties and still referred to himself as "the happiest Prime Minister in the world" in his Preface to the Alliance manifesto.[32] The forty-eight-page manifesto, dubbed "A Better Deal for All", tried to celebrate the government's achievements, which in actual fact were not inconsiderable. An objective reading of it shows that it was comprehensive enough, stressing the need for political stability in creating a democracy and a liberal and tolerant society. It showed with ample statistics the economic progress of the country and its rural development, stressed the need for strong defence and security, and detailed why it was necessary to have a foreign policy aligned to non-Communist states. A section called "The Racial Nemesis" reprimanded opposition parties for playing on racial emotions, suggesting that "each and every one of these parties is in the control of its craven core of racial bigots". It emphasized instead the Alliance's efforts to create a single Malaysian-centred consciousness in a multiracial country.[33]

There was considerable attention paid to economics, with the government targeting an increase of per capita income from $1,000 to $1,500 by 1985 at a growth rate of six per cent. The plan was for a diversification of the economy in agriculture, with particular emphasis on rubber research and increasing palm oil production. The section on industrialization included the plan to maintain long-term growth at 10 per cent annually and for industry to contribute 25 per cent of GDP by 1985.[34] In campaign speeches the Tunku also stressed that the British left Malaya with a small rich class and a large poor sector, but that the Alliance in twelve years of rule had created a large middle class (Drummond and Hawkins 1970, p. 323).

When the results of the election were announced on 11 May, it almost seemed like the Alliance had lost the election, even though it had won a clear majority of seats on the Peninsula. The most humiliating defeats were as follows: the minister of information and broadcasting Senu Abdul Rahman losing to the PMIP candidate in Kedah; minister of commerce and industries and deputy president of the MCA Lim Swee Aun losing his Larut Selatan Perak seat to an unknown Gerakan candidate; the MCA's Ng Kam Poh, minister of social welfare, losing in Teluk Anson; and UMNO's rising firebrand politician Mahathir Mohamed losing the Kubang Pasu seat in Kedah to PAS's Yusof Rawa. Moreover, leaders of the Alliance — including the Tunku, Abdul Razak, Tan Siew Sin, Khaw Khai Boh, Khir Johari, V.T. Sambanthan and V. Manickavasagam — all suffered heavy reductions in their winning majorities. The MIC president Sambanthan scraped through with a mere 146 votes in his hometown constituency of Sungei Siput, Perak (Vasil 1972, p. 36).

The sombre mood created by these outcomes was enhanced by the fact that Penang was lost comprehensively to the Gerakan, Kelantan remained in PMIP control, the Selangor state assembly was hung with the Alliance and opposition parties each winning 14 seats, and in Perak the Alliance fell 2 seats short of a majority. But eventually, in both Selangor and Perak, post-election manoeuvring helped the Alliance retain control of these states. The MCA's egregious defeat — where it was virtually vanquished in the more urban states of Penang, Perak and Selangor — signalled what I would consider to be the collapse of the Alliance party's strategy of mediated communalism. While its consociational pact held, its ethnic leaders had become ineffective in commanding the middle ground of politics with its usually efficient pooling of ethnic votes. While non-Malay votes were greatly undercut by the opposition, a more crucial factor perhaps was a precipitous loss of Malay votes. There was no doubt that UMNO lost massive ground, but it was still able to hold on to a proportion of its Malay base, giving away 37.2 per cent of votes to seats it contested against the PMIP. The MIC, like the MCA, was likely to have lost a majority of the Indian vote, although this is hard to assess.[35] The MCA was quick to admit defeat when MCA president Tan Siew Sin announced the party's opting out of government. Having lost 20 of 33 contested parliamentary seats, he was merely recognizing the fact that the MCA had lost its mandate as the legitimate representative of the Chinese community as a component of the Alliance.[36] Although the MCA later rejoined the new caretaker Cabinet, the situation thus created of the perceived collapse of the ruling coalition was ready made for the possible outbreak of ethnic violence.

THE 13 MAY RIOTS

There is much by way of folklore and conspiracy theories about the 13 May outbreak of riots in the capital city of Kuala Lumpur, and the literature about the event is considerably large.[37] In this section I will attempt a rough historiography of the event, with a view to understanding why it signified a failure of the Alliance formula and why particular interpretations of this event impelled the rise of a new ruling elite that prolonged a reconstituted path-dependent consociational politics. Only corroborated and known events and incidents will be cited. I will exclude evocative and sensitive incidents which may have been reported but have no proper corroboration. It certainly remains a huge task to fully triangulate this tragic event of Malaysian history, and many of the facts will remain buried for years to come despite copious material on the subject. Among the major writings regarding the event are *The May 13 Tragedy: A Report* (NOC 1969; hereafter, The NOC Report); Tunku Abdul Rahman (1969); Slimming (1969); Gagliano (1971); Goh (1971); Von Vorys (1976); Comber (1983); and Kua (2007). There are textbooks, biographies and other writings that also give various accounts of the event; too many to cite here. I consider two accounts to be the default narratives of the incidents, even though they provide different interpretations of why the violence started. Slimming's account (1969, pp. 25–65) is very detailed and spliced with anecdotes of Malay brutality and barbarism. Von Vory's account in Chapter 13 of his book (1976, pp. 308–38) runs through antecedent events and then provides an almost hour-by-hour depiction of incidents. The problem with Slimming's narrative is that he alludes to anecdotes and stories as told to him by individuals (victims and others), but without attribution, and thus may suffer the taint of being apocryphal. While Von Vorys conveys a positive role of Menteri Besar Harun Idris in trying to stall the onset of the riots, Slimming sees Harun to be a major perpetrator of the violence. Gagliano's summary of events (1971, pp. 15–19) is another useful source of information.[38]

Based on existing work, a number of political perspectives and academic renderings on the events can now be constructed. In his preface to the NOC Report on the tragedy, Tun Abdul Razak alluded to three causes; namely, communism, communalism and the secret societies.[39] The subtext of this view is that the Malays did not initiate the rioting, but that a series of spontaneous incidents sparked the bloodshed. We could refer to this perspective as that of the ruling elite and also as the orthodox and official position on the events. The strong underlying theme of this official view is that 13 May represented a communist conspiracy to destabilize the Malaysian regime. This thesis is greatly elaborated on in the NOC Report and in the book by the Tunku. Scholarly writers for the most part tend to dismiss such a pristinely conspiratorial interpretation of 13 May. Most scholars would consider the deleterious effect of communalism or its racially charged politics to be the major factor behind 13 May. The communalism thesis constitutes the standard view conveyed by academic analysts such as Vasil, Gagliano, Ratnam and Milne and Von Vorys, whom I have already cited. More journalistic interpretations of the events, such as that held by Slimming (1969), see them as a series of incidents caused by self-serving Malay politicians who enlisted Malay mobs to carry out a pogrom on the Chinese and other non-Malays. The alternative UMNO interpretation, held by its Young Turks of that time — Mahathir Mohamed, Musa Hitam and Tengku Razaleigh — was that the events reflected the government's fundamental failure to address the problem of Malay economic advancement or, its obverse, Malay rural poverty. Such a view has been popularized by the controversial 2013 film *Tanda Putera*, which also largely purveys the orthodox and mainstream interpretation of the event while further implying that non-Malays were initial perpetrators of the violence sparking a Malay reaction.[40] More recently there has emerged a "revisionist" view, emanating largely from the political Left and elaborated by Kua Kia Soong (2007), that the event was a de facto political coup against the Tunku government, effected by the UMNO racial supremacists and/or "state capitalists". Kua uses declassified materials from the National

Archives of the United Kingdom to substantiate his claim, essentially drawing from the reports of foreign missions present in Kuala Lumpur at the time of the May riots.

Naturally, there will be various shades of interpretation among the different perspectives of the event. Most importantly, the orthodox view latterly included the perspective of the post-1969 UMNO new ruling elite led by Tun Razak and Tun Ismail, who crafted a new Malay-dominant consociational formula of electoral politics in the post–13 May era. Tun Ismail's off-the-cuff statement on TV that "Democracy is dead" was later explained by him that he saw it as the new government's duty to resurrect it (Ooi 2006, pp. 192–93). He later told a Danish journalist that "we cannot yet practise democracy in the manner of Denmark or England", but that the government intended to retain democratic principles and parliamentary rule (ibid., p. 218). Moreover, he was steadfast against what he saw as the move by the UMNO "ultras" to establish "the wild and fantastic theory of absolute domination of one race over the other communities".[41]

CONCLUSION

This chapter began with an analysis of the Alliance's path-dependent electoral successes, which I argue are premised on the execution of a consociational strategy of mediated communalism aimed at gaining an optimal number of ethnic-majority as well as mixed seats in elections for the ruling coalition. As long as constituent ethnic parties were able to deliver ethnic support, the strategy worked well and conferred path-dependent success to the Alliance. However, this approach snapped because of a huge haemorrhaging in 1969 of UMNO's non-Malay — especially Chinese — vote and to a significant extent also its Malay vote. The new-found success of UMNO's nemesis the PMIP fed on the Alliance's weakness in capturing the Malay vote during this election due to the ruling group's perceived ineffective policies for the Malays. The Alliance lost precious ground at both extreme ends of the ethnic voting continuum. Non-Malay assertiveness and Malay political and economic anxieties were arguably the main factors propelling the failure of the Alliance's strategy of mediated communalism when its non-Malay partners, the MCA and MIC, failed to pool enough ethnic votes to the ruling coalition. Viewing this from the opposition's perspective, in 1969 it benefited from a major *overdetermination* of ethnic issues of language and cultural rights. While the opposition parties were able to capitalize on these issues and to erode Alliance support, they were still incapable of capturing a sufficient amount of the middle ground. Primarily mobilizing and winning voters at the ethnic extremities, the opposition thus allowed the structural biases of the electoral system to confer the margin of victory to the Alliance.

Notes

1. For such an argument see Chapter 1 and, in particular, Pierson (2000, pp. 252–23).
2. See Farish Noor (2004, pp. 97–191) for a detailed narrative and analysis of Dr Burhanuddin's leadership in PAS from 1956 to 1969.
3. "Ahmad Boestamam" was Abdullah Sani bin Raja Kechil's *nom de guerre*. It was thought that he wanted it to bear a resemblance to the name of Subhas Chandra Bose, the Indian nationalist whom he admired.
4. See Chapter 8 for the narrative on the "Perak coup".
5. For details of this episode, see Farish Noor (2004, pp. 159–60).
6. In the Perak takeover orchestrated by then deputy premier Najib Razak, it was heavily rumoured that considerable sums of money had changed hands to facilitate three lawmakers (two PKR and one DAP) to defect from the Pakatan coalition. For a detailed account of the Perak constitutional crisis of 2009, see Quay (2010). See also Chapter 8.
7. The fact that the leadership and the whole country were engaged in coping with the exigencies of this consuming political development during 1964 proved a major disadvantage to the opposition. Parties like the SF and PMIP were hard put to explain why they would take a conciliatory stance against an aggressive neighbour, which was the predominant popular perception. For the impact of Indonesia's Confrontation on Malaysia from a foreign policy perspective, see Saravanamuttu (2010, pp. 87–93).
8. Interestingly though, in those days the opposition parties were given a fair shake of radio broadcasting time in Malay, English, Chinese and Tamil. Each speaker was given thirteen minutes per broadcast and the opposition parties had equal broadcasting time to the Alliance (Ratnam and Milne 1967, p. 214–17). However, the airing of a series of twenty ministerial broadcasts several weeks before the election was an obvious ploy by the government to take an incumbent's advantage over its opponents (ibid., p. 223).

9. Ratnam and Milne (1967, pp. 266–95) provide a detailed narrative of these elections and how the seventeen parliamentary seats were determined.

10. See the book on Operation Cold Store edited by Poh, Tan and Hong (2013) which provides first-person accounts of the event, conveying what is considered a revisionist history of Singapore, which the editors argue was one in which "the left wing will be an integral part of and on its own terms" (p. 12). See, especially, the lead article by historian Wade, who suggests that the operation was to ensure that "the British policy of Greater Malaysia was realized, and that the PAP was able to achieve domination in the political sphere in Singapore" (p. 68). The idea that the formation of Malaysia was part of a British "grand design" based on the "Ulster Model" for Singapore has been documented by Tan Tai Yong (2008).

11. For a detailed analysis of this election, see Starner (1967, pp. 312–58). See also the website <http://www.singapore-elections.com> for full details of the contests and the background of the controversies surrounding the election, which virtually became a second referendum for Singapore joining Malaysia.

12. See Milne and Mauzy (1978, pp. 67–76) for a rendering of these tensions leading to Singapore's exit from Malaysia.

13. See Lau (1998, pp. 161–210) for a detailed rendition of the events of the Singapore riots. On the events leading to Singapore's exit from Malaysia, see Saravanamuttu (2010, Chapter 10).

14. Lee Kuan Yew mentions a figure of 25,000 (Lee 1998).

15. I have drawn from Lau (1998, pp. 161–210) for this account because of its detailed rendition of events.

16. See the chapter "Talak, Talak, Talak", in Lee Kuan Yew's memoirs (Lee 1998, pp. 14–15).

17. See Drummond and Hawkins (1970, pp. 320–21) who, however, point out that an arrested party member Sim Kok Chye admitted that the party had passed a motion on 24 September 1967 which called on members to abandon the parliamentary struggle and wage a Maoist "mass struggle". One should also recall that Labour Party leaders implicated in the Penang hartal riots of 1967, including Lim Kean Siew, had also been detained and that actions detrimental to the party were well in place by a stridently anti-communist and authoritarian government.

18. The DAP website states that the party was formed in October 1965 but had its registration approved only on 18 March 1966. See <http://dapmalaysia.org/en/about-us/our-history/> (accessed 25 March 2014).

19. According to Von Vorys (1976, p. 263), Parti Rakyat, which had replaced its leader Ahmad Boestamam, was now led by a collective of Young Turks

with links to urban workers of Penang, Malay fisher folk of Terengganu and Pahang, and university students from Kuala Lumpur. Its new president was Kassim Ahmad, who hailed from Penang.

20. There has been considerable confusion, due to the suspension of the election, over what percentage was actually won by the Alliance. I have presented the official results of the Election Commission in Table 4.4. It appears that the Alliance fared much poorer than even assumed by most, as one should exclude the votes of the Sabah Alliance that was not part of the parliamentary coalition. The figure most cited is 48.4 per cent, from the results as presented in the *Straits Times* immediately after the election on 10 May, as indicated by Ratnam and Milne (1970, p. 203) and Drummond and Hawkins (1970, p. 329). Other authors who more or less use this same figure are Crouch (1996, p. 74), Vasil (1972, p. 36), Von Vorys (1976, p. 297), and Mauzy (1983, p. 36). Nohlen et al. (2001, p. 155) cite the figure of 44.9 per cent, which excludes 24,609 votes from Melaka Selatan, where the election was not carried out on 10 May due to the death of a candidate.

21. The Sabah Alliance remained independent at the state level while throwing in its lot with the ruling Alliance in Parliament, as did the SCA. Both these parties took all the 16 parliamentary seats in Sabah, hence providing the ruling coalition with its first East Malaysian "fixed deposit", a metaphor that that has now become cliché as reference to the state's continuous support of the BN.

22. It is important to note that eventually the Alliance was able to secure its two-thirds majority when Parliament was restored after the twenty-two-month rule by the caretaker National Operations Council (NOC). The seats to make up the two-thirds majority came out of the maneuvering and complex politicking in Sarawak during the 1970 election and after. The Sarawak Alliance comprised three parties: Party Pesaka, Party Bumiputra, and the SCA. The opposition parties were the SUPP and SNAP. Because of feuding, the three Alliance parties campaigned separately without using the Alliance symbol, with Pesaka remaining somewhat ambivalent at being formally part of the national Alliance but finally did join. When the SUPP decided to let its MPs throw in their lot with them (after one of its MPs, Ong Kee Hui, was appointed a federal minister), the Alliance got its two-thirds majority in Parliament just as NOC rule ended. For details, see Vasil (1972, pp. 52–55) and Leigh (1974, p. 145).

23. The 1967 state election was Sabah's first direct state-level election. The results were as follows: USNO 14, UPKO 12, SCA 5, independents 1. In the complex politicking among these parties, UPKO opted out of the Sabah Alliance. In the subsequent 1971 election, the Alliance candidates

of USNO (28) and SCA (4) were all returned unopposed when 10
Independents were disqualified for filling their forms incorrectly! See
Milne and Mauzy (1978, pp. 164–67).

24. See Report on 1969 Election (EC 1972, p. 45).

25. This complicated situation was the result of the death of one of the
candidates before the 10 May election. As the by-election could not be held
on 31 May due to the 13 May riots, it was pushed back to 31 January
1971. See Report on 1969 Election (EC 1972, p. 46).

26. There were suggestions immediately after the hung results that Selangor and
Perak could hold fresh elections, even with the prospect of the opposition
parties attempting to band together to form non-Alliance governments.
PPP president S.P. Seenivasagam announced that his party, which took
12 seats, would seek the support of the DAP (6) and Gerakan (2) to
form the government without the PMIP's single seat. UMNO held the
other 19 seats (*Straits Times*, 13 May 1969).

27. The speeches by Lee on "Malaysian Malaysia" can be found at this
Singapore government source: <http://eresources.nlb.gov.sg/history/
events/86267d39-af24-45be-a49d-3c7e2906d61d> (accessed 26 May 2015).

28. One of the most critical among these was the late Fan Yew Teng, who
advocated the removal of the PAP from the Socialist International because
of its swing to the right and its authoritarian politics (Devan Nair 1976).

29. It was Kit Siang's first political outing and he provided a valuable lesson
for his party. See <http://malaysiafactbook.com/Chronology:Democratic
ActionParty> (accessed 25 March 2014).

30. The narrative of the formation of the BN and its new consociational
rationale will be discussed in the next chapter.

31. Vasil notes that large sections of the Malay community considered the
Tunku's concessions to non-Malays as an act of betrayal. Syed Nasir's
group held demonstrations against the Act, complete with the burning
of an effigy of the Tunku, but the bill was passed by 95 votes *for* to 11
against (9 PMIP, 1 PPP and 1 DAP) in the Dewan Rakyat on 3 March
1967. As the Tunku himself admitted during the reading of the bill in
1967: "I learn, however, that there has been suspicion among the Malays
that I and my friends and leaders in the UMNO and the Alliance have
failed to carry out our promises and that we have relegated the Malay
language to a secondary position instead of making it the official language
of the country. They also suggest that we have sold the Malays down the
drain." *Straits Times*, 3 March 1967, as cited in Vasil (1972, p. 15).

32. The Tunku's exact phraseology was: "I have always described myself as the
happiest Prime Minister in the world. This is because I enjoy the support
of the people, and with it this country has progressed so well and so fast

since Merdeka that it has become a 'shining star' in the Asian horizon."
Alliance Manifesto (1969, p. 1).

33. Alliance Manifesto (1969, pp. 10–11).

34. Ibid., pp. 15–29.

35. Ratnam and Milne (1970, pp. 219–20) provide what could be considered a contrarian view of the manner the ethnic voting may have gone for the Alliance. Using a complex methodology of assessing this, they suggest that the Malay vote for the Alliance may have declined by 13 per cent compared to 1964, while its non-Malay vote dropped by 7.9 per cent.

36. While the MCA decided to pull out of the Cabinet, it continued to remain with the Alliance. See *Straits Times*, 14 May 1969.

37. The major oeuvres on 13 May by way of books, monographs and academic articles are cited in this chapter. I was a journalist working for the *Straits Times* (before it became the *New Straits Times*) at that time and have my own evaluation of the tragedy, having witnessed and heard my fair share of accounts, anecdotes and narratives of the event.

38. A well-known journalist of the *Far Eastern Economic Review* also carried stories on 13 May; see Reece (1969). My own recollection of 13 May is unfortunately marred by the fact that on the evening of that day I had returned to my home in Petaling Jaya from the *Straits Times* office before the riots started. My colleagues, who were at the office till late, slept overnight there and in the morning helped Leslie Hoffman (later Tan Sri), the then group editor, to distribute the newspaper on the streets. We journalists were later issued with curfew passes. On the evening of 13 May I received a phone call from my friend, a lawyer, Louis Cheah, who warned me not to go to town and meet him for a badminton session at the Selangor Assembly Hall. As it turned out, Cheah and his family had to flee from their home in Jalan Hale, which was torched. I later went to see Cheah, who had taken refuge in Merdeka Stadium, set up to house non-Malay victims of the riots. The whole stadium ground was tented-up as a refugee camp. On the eve of polling I personally witnessed the highly charged funeral rally of the Labour Party worker in the vicinity of Petaling Street.

39. See NOC Report (1969, p. iv).

40. The DAP, among many others, objected to the film (directed by Suhaimi Baba; commissioned by the government at the cost of RM4.8m) because of this interpretation of the events and depiction of incidents, particularly the alleged act of a young Lim Kit Siang urinating on the Selangor flagpole in the Menteri Besar Harun Idris's house, the venue for the large gathering of Malays on 13 May who were to take part in UMNO's victory procession. The film's screening was postponed for months till August

2013 and was not shown in Penang. In the end it was a box office flop. Closed-door viewings had been held prior to its public screening; one such viewing was in February to Felda settlers. Opposition leaders charged that this was the government's veiled attempt to fish for Malay votes before the May 2013 general election. Having watched the publicly screened version of the film myself, there appeared to be no scene depicting Lim Kit Siang; however, there was verbal allusion to a Chinese person urinating on the Selangor flagpole.

41. See Gagliano (1970, p. 29). Tun Ismail apparently also tried to make a case for the expulsion of Mahathir from UMNO but was unable to prevail on Tun Razak. Ismail did succeed in blocking two attempts to re-admit Mahathir to the party. This information is attributed to Tengku Razaleigh; see Ooi (2006, p. 206).

5

THE NATIONAL FRONT'S RISE IN THE ELECTIONS OF 1974 AND 1978

In hindsight, the 13 May 1969 racial riots were a predictable outcome of stark inter-communal conflicts born out of anxieties over what the nation-state could hold by way of benefits for the Malay/bumiputera majority on the one hand and for the non-bumiputera minorities on the other. Without doubt the Alliance's model of mediating communalism had failed in a very real sense with the occurrence of the 13 May tragedy. However, in path-dependence terms the 1969 crisis was only a temporary setback in how communalism had been poorly mediated or managed through the consociational arrangements of the Alliance. This was so because, the situation was one which had no reasonable alternative or counter-coalition to the failing Alliance. Much was lost, but not everything for the ruling coalition. What was needed was not a replacement of the consociation; rather, its reconstitution. In the end this was achieved in a heavy-handed fashion through the establishment of a new ruling coalition. In the words of Von Vorys, the outbreak of the riots led to a "democracy without consensus" that structured this next phase of politics. Thus, investment in political arrangements swung to the other extreme. Indeed, the structuring of politics moved in the direction of non-democratic political engineering, executed by the second Malaysian prime minister Tun Abdul Razak.

In this second phase of Malaysian politics, one saw how Malay supremacy became both the discursive trope and the primary institutional tool of the dominant Malay political party. UMNO refurbished its role by patently dominating wide aspects of Malaysian political life through the implementation of its New Economic Policy (NEP) which would be designed to raise the socio-economic status of Malays and other bumiputera and by so doing ensure Malay primacy in electoral politics. Basically, this reconstitution meant that UMNO had to wrest back some Malay votes from PAS, while its non-Malay partners had to win back support lost to the new "non-communal" parties; primarily the DAP and Gerakan. The challenge for UMNO, after having assumed leadership, *primus inter pares*, was to reconstitute a new coalition, one which would have a bigger partnership base, which was to be inclusive, not just ethnically but also regionally. This super-coalition, with UMNO firmly and unequivocally dominant, was the Barisan Nasional (BN, the National Front). In effect the new approach was geared to success at the polls with a maximum not minimum winning coalition[1] and should be seen as a modification — though not an insignificant one — of the old mode of mediating communalism. In other words, in terms of the thesis advanced in this book, it was an attempt to continue the ruling coalition's path-dependent success in elections. The difference between the pre- and post-1969 consociation was that, by the latter period, UMNO was to be given full rein to secure a more fully manufactured, Malay-bumiputera majority, and this entailed bringing PAS into the equation.

In tandem with the rise of the BN, the framing of Malaysian politics in the post-1969 political climate under the NEP saw the entrenchment of the new discursive device of *Ketuanan Melayu* ("Malay supremacy", or "Malay overlordship"), which invariably impacted heavily on democratic electoral politics. While the ruling coalition successfully expanded its base and became the more encompassing National Front, electoral democracy was clearly hamstrung by a highly proscribed form of politics which placed a premium on the generation of bumiputera institutions more than on maintaining the more pristine power-sharing consociational arrangements among ethnic-based parties. While UMNO was able to capitalize on the increasing returns to its

NEP-driven policies, its non-Malay partners began to lose political ground. A Malay-first politics was euphemized under the economic thrusts of the NEP primarily as affirmative action for the bumiputera, but in practice this created the basis for a strong Malay politics under the dominance of UMNO. Admittedly, this sort of politics did have the immediate salutary effect of constituting a highly stable if authoritarian political order anchored around the BN governments and ensured a path-dependent success for a long period of time, starting from the 1974 and 1978 general elections. In these two contests the necessary and sufficient conditions for the BN's path-dependent success were restored; namely, majority Malay votes for UMNO, strong Malay leadership of the coalition, a unified BN coalition with no equally matched coalition contenders, return of non-Malay support to other BN partner parties, and the entrenchment of institutions and structures of advantage to incumbents. As before, the challenge of mediating communalism in this new post-1969 phase would be to soften the most extreme demands by partners in the coalition by gravitating them towards win-win or variable sum outcomes rather than allow bargaining to reach zero-sum conclusions. But this new phase became riskier for BN's path-dependent success, as UMNO was to gradually assume increasing dictatorial authority in the BN, thus diluting both the consociational spirit of the pact as well as upsetting the fine balance of a mediated communalism.

In this chapter I will give particular focus to the general elections held in 1974 and 1978, as these were the two successive elections held after the disrupted 1969 poll. The chapter will be analysing only these two elections because they were also held before the start of the Mahathir years, from 1982 till 2002. The latter period deserves its own treatment.

Malay supremacy came along with the notion that the BN, with UMNO in charge, could never afford to lose its two-thirds majority of seats in Parliament or, for that matter, the control of any state government. With that in mind, the BN leadership went out of its way to court the Islamic party, PAS, and brought it under its wing from 1974 till 1978. In this period there was significant investment in a plethora of institutions created for the bumiputera, a term used to refer to Malays and other indigenous groups, namely from the East Malaysian states of Sabah and Sarawak. Conferring bumiputera status on East Malaysian indigenous groups entitled them to the rights, privileges and other affirmative action stipulations contained in the NEP. This strategy was successful in bringing a wide array of political parties from Sabah and Sarawak into the BN coalition.

NEP AND THE MANUFACTURED MALAY/BUMIPUTERA MAJORITY

When the NEP was launched, its stated primary objective was to achieve national unity through a twofold mechanism: by reducing poverty regardless of race; and by restructuring society so as to correct economic imbalances and diminish, or even eliminate, the identification of race with economic function. National unity, according to the government, could only be attained once interethnic economic parity had been achieved, specifically by targeting the group most in need: the bumiputera.

In an important study of the NEP after its formal termination in 1990, Faaland, Parkinson and Rais (1990) provided a clear narrative of the social, political and economic rationales for the policy.[2] The 13 May 1969 episode was the catalyst for the government to introduce the NEP and its ideological tool, the Rukunegara (National Principles), the latter basically crafted by Ghazali Shafie, who was then minister of home affairs. The NEP and the Rukunegara stressed the imperative of national unity and the equitable sharing of wealth in the creation of a just and liberal society. However, as explained by Faaland and his co-authors, two broad "schools of thought" representing clear philosophical perspectives informed the manner by which the NEP was to be implemented. Both schools of thought had the benefit of foreign consultants. According to Faaland, the Economic Planning Unit (EPU), which advocated a "return to normalcy", had the support of foreign owners, bankers and experts from most of the international agencies. The Department of National Unity (DNU) received advice from Harvard University's Advisory Service and its Harvard-based economists, including Faaland.[3]

The first school of thought was promoted by the EPU and is termed the "EPU School" by Faaland, while the second is dubbed the "DNU School". The EPU approach emphasized economic growth and drew its inspiration from an orthodox school of economic thought that stresses balanced budgets and rejects the use of policy instruments such as "deficit financing". According to this approach, growth was to come first and distribution would follow through a "trickle-down effect". Tan Siew Sin, the Malaysian icon of financial discipline and the country's first finance minister, was partial to this type of thinking (Faaland, Parkinson and Rais 1990, pp. 29–30). While conservative in approach, the EPU school of thought could be said to have erred on the side of caution, and its major recommendations clearly had no overt policy of targeting any specific ethnic group. The DNU school advocated a diametrically opposite policy and had the backing of another iconic figure, Ghazali Shafie. It stressed the problem of lopsided economic distribution and called for the correcting of ethnic imbalances in three key areas: income, employment and ownership of capital. The ideas for such ethnically based affirmative action were contained in the document, *Problems of Racial Economic Imbalance and National Unity* (1970), agreed to by the Economic Committee of the National Consultative Council (Faaland, Parkinson and Rais 1990, p. 26). The DNU school had adopted a horizontal inequalities approach to resolving the inequities exposed by the 13 May incident. In tangible terms, the goals of the NEP were to be attained by reducing the poverty level to 15 per cent and by increasing bumiputera corporate equity ownership to 30 per cent by 1990. The three areas targeted by programmes related to the NEP were public higher education, government employment, private sector employment and equity ownership.

The initial primary concern of the NEP was to provide poor children with quality education. The NEP created educational structures which significantly opened doors for bumiputera access to special residential schools, public universities and various tertiary institutions. Young bumiputera were plucked out of rural areas, sent to well-equipped residential schools and then provided preferential access to tertiary education. A quota system was implemented to increase the number of bumiputera places in local universities and a scholarship scheme was created to allow large numbers of bumiputera students to pursue their professional degrees abroad. The outcomes were laudable. The early beneficiaries of such quality education from an early stage of their lives have now emerged as the new middle class with a still growing presence as a community with entrepreneurial capacity. The rise of this new Malay middle class was seen as the key success of the NEP.

PATH-DEPENDENT SUCCESSES, 1974 AND 1978

A considerable corpus of work exists on the formation of the BN and its electoral success in the 1974 and 1978 general elections, before Mahathir held the helm in the 1980s and 1990s. Major studies of the emergence of the BN and its electoral successes in this period include Pillay (1974), Milne and Mauzy (1978), Crouch, Lee and Ong (1980), Mauzy (1983), Means (1991), and Crouch (1996). Without doubt, the creation of the BN under the guiding hand of Abdul Razak Hussein, Malaysia's second prime minster, was pivotal to the resounding success of the ruling coalition in the two elections after its formation. The determination with which Razak pushed and manoeuvred the political circumstances to create the BN has been analysed in the studies cited above, and it will not be necessary to rehash the details. The BN could be thought of as a "revved up" version of the Alliance, although some would argue that it had a different *raison d'être*, a different structure, and not to say a different symbol of the *dacing* to apparently signify justice and balance (Means 1991, p. 30). At baseline I would argue that the BN was still premised on the Alliance formula of consociation but with UMNO's de facto veto power much more evident than that of its partners, thereby giving the lie to its own symbol. All said, Razak worked the ground very hard on the Malay and non-Malay sides of the political terrain and, most importantly, brought political parties from East Malaysia under the BN umbrella. This, as time would tell, was the real political coup, less so Razak's tireless efforts at bringing PAS into the fold. By 1970 a Sarawak state-level coalition had been formed.[4] For Razak, arguably the most "troublesome" opponents of the time emanated from the non-Malays on the West Coast of the Peninsula. The DAP was probably a lost cause for him so he trained his efforts on Gerakan, which had comprehensively won Penang in 1969, and the PPP in Perak. By 1972 Razak had worked out coalition arrangements with these two parties and by 1973 PAS had also acceded. With the Sabah Alliance coming on board the BN was officially registered as a confederation of parties in June, two months before the August 1974 general election.

1974

The outcome of the 1974 election, which was held on 24 August, was said to be a "stupendous triumph" for the BN (Pillay 1974, p. 2). On polling day itself, 48 parliamentary and 43 BN state candidates won their seats unopposed (Mauzy 1983, p. 87). The coalition won 86 per cent of parliamentary seats (135 out of 154) and swept into power in all states. The details of this landslide victory for the BN are shown in Table 5.1, which provides the results for both parliamentary and state-level outcomes.

Table 5.1
Parliamentary and State Election Results, 1974

	Parliament	%	No. of seats contested	No. of state seats won	Seats before election
Barisan Nasional					
UMNO	61	—	61	—	52
MCA	19	—	23	—	15
Gerakan	5	—	8	—	2
MIC	4	—	4	—	3
PAS	14	—	14	—	10
PPP	1	—	4	—	4
BN Sarawak	15	—	24	—	14
BN Sabah	16	—	16	—	16
Total BN	**135**	**60.7**	**154**	**313**	**119**
Opposition					
DAP	9	18.3	46	23	9
Pekemas	1	5.1	36	1	5
SNAP	9	5.1	24	18	7
Kita	0	0.3	4	0	3
PSRM	0	4.0	21	0	0
PBRM	0	0.1	—	0	—
Bisamah	0	0.03	—	0	—
Independents	0	4.7	38	5	1
Total Opposition	**19**	**37.6**	**169**	**47**	**25**

Source: Means 1991, p. 34.
Note: Percentages may not add up to 100% due to rounding and the absence of spoilt votes.

What can one say of the 1974 outcome? Was this merely the masterstroke of a pragmatic new leadership of the country led by Tun Abdul Razak? Did it generate a new path-dependence based on a new model of consociationalism which guaranteed electoral success, or were there other factors at play? Lest it be forgotten, the first-past-the-post electoral system was still well in place. Moreover, by the time of the election the legal regime had proscribed debating and discussing "sensitive issues" such as the position of the Malays and the rulers with the 1971 constitutional amendments to the Sedition Act. How important a factor was ethnicity during this election as well as other cleavages such as class and religion? The large overhang and context of this election was no doubt the May 1969 riots and the introduction of the NEP under National Operations Council rule. Did this and related factors affect the 1974 electoral results? Let me try to answer these questions by briefly examining the election campaign and the reasons why the opposition parties failed to develop their own path of success. I will also touch on student activism which burst on to the scene in late 1974, soon after the election.

The amendments to the British 1948 Sedition Act clearly made it difficult for the opposition parties to effectively mount their campaigns. Restricted by this, as noted by Milne and Mauzy (1978, p. 197), campaigning centred around the state of the economy, the implementation of the NEP, inflation and the personalities of the candidates. The BN's manifesto focused on explaining the aims of the Front and the government's progress in the economy and foreign policy, in particular Malaysia's initiative in setting up diplomatic relations with the People's Republic of China in May 1974. Much was made of this in the Gerakan and PPP campaigns in Penang and Perak. As an observer of the electoral campaign in Penang, I can vouch that a large number of posters of the historic Abdul Razak–Mao Tse Tung handshake were brandished all over George Town.[5] The DAP's campaign appeared to target the non-Malay parties in the BN fold, particularly the Gerakan and the PPP in their capitulation ("political surrender") to the BN model of a one-party state. Pillay (1974) notes in particular the DAP's campaign theme of the "betrayal" of the Chinese by non-Malay parties while it had held steadfast in championing causes such as Chinese vernacular education. The incumbent chief minister of

Penang Lim Chong Eu countered the DAP's challenge by arguing that that if the opposition took over the state its economic development would falter, along with a whispering campaign that suggested that if Gerakan lost, Penang would not have a Chinese chief minister (Pillay 1974, p. 10). Ethnicity no doubt remained as an important trope of elections. Pekemas, led by Tan Chee Koon, which was essentially a splinter party of Gerakan, campaigned on principles of "democratic socialism", calling for free university education and a national social security system, which surprisingly seemed to cut little ice with the electorate.

Parti Sosialis Rakyat Malaysia's (PSRM) foray into Terengganu — fielding 28 state and 8 parliamentary candidates, including 3 national leaders — turned out to be a failure partly because the BN in its campaign played on a poem by PSRM president Kassim Ahmad that had used the phrase "God is dead" (Pillay 1974, p. 14). More pointedly perhaps, the party's socialist analysis of Malaysian socio-economic woes failed to penetrate the Malay heartland, which could be said to be bound more by ethnic and Islamic-based affiliations than those of class. That said, PSRM managed to win some 30.7 per cent of the popular vote in Terengganu (Crouch 1980, p. 8). The primarily Iban-based Sarawak National Party (SNAP) provided the main challenge to the BN in East Malaysia, with its slogan of "Sarawak for the Sarawakians" and its campaign on the issues of nepotism, corruption and the wastage of public money (Milne and Mauzy 1978, pp. 199–200). There was hardly a contest in Sabah, with only one opposition candidate, from Pekemas, managing to file his nomination papers without technical rejection, as Mauzy (1983, p. 91) puts it, "having escaped the hazards of bribery and intimidation".

We turn now briefly to a political development that the success of the BN in 1974 may have masked, namely the high level of discontent among detractors of the government, especially among students, intellectuals and the emerging civil society. This dissatisfaction with government policies — with respect to Malay poverty in places like Baling, Kedah — was amply illustrated by the outbreak of student and academic activism and demonstrations soon after the general election on the campuses of the University of Malaya in Kuala Lumpur, Universiti Kebangsaan Malaysia in Bangi and Universiti Sains

Malaysia in Penang, resulting in a large number of detentions by the government. Among those arrested were such rather well-known political figures as Anwar Ibrahim, Syed Hussin Ali, Hishamuddin Rais and Gurdial Singh Nijar. University lecturers such as Tengku Shamsul Bahrin and Lim Mah Hui were also detained for good measure. The largest demonstration was on the Selangor Club grounds (a.k.a. Dataran Merdeka) on 3 December 1974, held after the general election (Means 1991, pp. 35–38). What is less well known is that there were also massive demonstrations in Baling itself, mostly by rubber smallholders and their supporters. On 19 November 1974 a thousand people began their protests and more then twelve thousand people from the town and surrounding areas joined them three days later (Weiss 2011, pp. 157–58).[6]

The main issue raised by the students and political activists was the failure of the NEP to eradicate poverty, particularly in areas such as Baling in Kedah and among squatters in Johor. These issues were championed by University Malaya's student union, the National Union of Muslim Students and the Malay Language Society. Mahathir Mohamed, who was then education minister, took a hard stance against staff and student activism and pushed for new guidelines to curb such activity on campuses, which later led to the beefing up of the University and University Colleges Act.[7]

These events failed to stem the comprehensive electoral success of the BN in the 1974 general election, which could be explained by its historical trajectory following the May 1969 riots and the post-trauma political landscape where a new mode of power sharing based on the strong hand of UMNO had become emplaced. UMNO became dominant by astutely extending its consociational model to new partners on both the Peninsula and on Sabah and Sarawak and, as noted by Crouch (1980, p. 6), allowed for more than one political party to represent one community (the inclusion of PAS and Gerakan being the prime examples). This could be seen as a *consociation-plus* model. In the post-trauma environment of Malaysian politics of the 1970s, there appeared to be a willingness on the part of most non-Malay parties to accept the new realities and accede to the strong hand of UMNO and Razak's leadership in it (Mauzy 1983). But, as noted by Crouch, political parties joined the BN on its terms and when these terms were breached they would be forced out (Crouch 1996, p. 34). Thus, the model of the BN's success was ironically the valorization of Malay supremacy masked by a sophisticatedly engineered power sharing under the guiding baton of the pragmatic Tun Abdul Razak. The NEP and its political facet, the Rukunegara, provided the overall framing for Razak's political engineering, which one could well argue also generated path-dependent electoral successes following 1974, and ensured the BN of its customary control of a two-thirds majority of parliamentary constituencies. The break in this electoral stranglehold of the BN only occurred thirty-fours years later in the 2008 general election. I now turn to an analysis of the outcome of the 1978 election.

1978

The unexpected death of Tun Razak in January 1976 from leukaemia, a medical condition which was a closely guarded secret,[8] led to the rise of Hussein Onn as Malaysia's third prime minister. From the outset, the Onn administration was plagued with a mounting set of issues and problems. These included the internal bickering and factionalism in UMNO which led to the arrests of two prominent Razak appointees and then the jailing of former Menteri Besar of Selangor, Harun Idris, for corruption; the Kelantan crisis which led to the snap state election of 1978 and PAS's departure from the BN; the Chinese unity movement led by MCA Young Turks; and the Merdeka University issue. We will deal briefly with these developments as the backdrop to the 1978 general election, which was held more than a year ahead of schedule.

The politicking within UMNO had already commenced while Razak was still alive, with what some commentators have called the "old guard" being unhappy with many of Razak's appointments to the Cabinet.[9] Tun Mustapha of Sabah who had initially demurred joining the Sabah Alliance was a key person in this internal politics, allegedly with the support of Tunku Abdul Rahman and later in cahoots with Harun Idris. One of the allegations of the old guard was that Razak had surrounded himself with "socialists". Thus, soon after Razak's death, home minister Ghazali Shafie obliged Harun and company by detaining UMNO leftists. Ghazali himself had strong anti-communist leanings and was also frustrated that Hussein Onn had chosen Mahathir to be the deputy premier when he probably thought he was the more suitable candidate.[10] The managing editor of the *New Straits Times*, Abdul Samad Ismail, and his alleged "accomplice" from another Malaysian daily, were arrested on charges of the purported promotion of communism through the media. This was followed by the arrests of two "Razak boys" (Thambipillai 1989, p. 88), deputy minister of labour and manpower Abdullah Majid and deputy minister for science, technology and environment Abdullah Ahmad, who were detained for several months and only released after they confessed to "Soviet connections".[11] Hussein Onn later decided to pursue the corruption charge against Harun Idris which began during Razak's time as premier. This was a case of criminal breach of trust related to his sponsoring of the world heavyweight fight between Muhammad Ali and Joe Bugner in Kuala Lumpur in 1975. Harun Idris was removed as the Selangor Menteri Besar due to his corruption charge, but was offered an ambassorship by Hussein Onn, which he demurred. Harun was found guilty and sentenced to two years jail, which effectively ended his political career, although his associates continued to be significant in UMNO.

Meanwhile, UMNO's internal problems were overtaken by the crisis in Kelantan which had developed since the 1974 election (Means 1991, pp. 61–64; Kamlin 1980, pp. 37–68). This arose from continuing PAS–UMNO rivalry and the unhappiness of PAS members — led by Mohamad Asri Muda, the party's president — with the Menteri Besar Mohamed Nasir. The latter was a PAS appointee who had annoyed Asri by freezing logging concessions, which allegedly were previously enjoyed by Asri's family and friends. Land policy was the most contentious issue; when the Menteri Besar froze logging on land concessions in 1977 — alleging corrupt practices — this led to the call for his resignation from the Asri camp. In turn the Menteri Besar orchestrated demonstrations, one as large 80,000 people, to support his move. A non-confidence vote in the state assembly saw it being carried by twenty PAS votes against thirteen of UMNO's. In the event, after much politicking at the state and federal levels, the government imposed "emergency rule" over Kelantan, which lasted some three months, before Hussein Onn called a snap state election set for 11 March 1978. Meanwhile, Asri Muda had announced that PAS would leave the BN coalition on 17 December 1977.[12] Following this, Mohamed Nasir set up a new party — Barisan Jemaah Islamiah Se-Malaysia, or Berjasa — which then had an electoral pact with UMNO to contest in the snap election. Restrictions were imposed on large rallies and the *ceramah* (small discussion group) format was introduced to give UMNO, with its financial and organizational resources, a decided advantage. When the results were announced, PAS had captured only a miserable two seats, with the popular vote recorded as follows: BN 36.7 per cent, PAS 32.7 per cent, Berjasa 27 per cent (Means 1991, p. 63). An analyst of the 1978 election attributes "serious miscalculations, ventures in self-delusion, and grave errors of judgement" in PAS's failure in surviving as a "distinct and autonomous political party of the Malays" (Kamlin 1980, p. 57). In years to come PAS proved that it could become an "autonomous political party of the Malays" distinct from UMNO. But the 1978 debacle implied that PAS's own path-dependent condition for electoral success had to be largely premised on its ability to contest as a coalition rather than as a stand-alone party.

Another political development that the Hussein Onn government had to face before the 1978 general election was what had been dubbed as the "Chinese Unity Movement". In fact the movement had started in the early 1970s, with prime movers such as the MCA and the Gerakan Young Turks — Alex Lee, Tan Tiong Hong and Lim Keng Yaik — calling for more attention to Chinese rights in the face of the NEP. While the direct challenge of these individuals was snuffed out, many of the ideas became mainstream as part of the MCA and Gerakan political discourse. One major concern of the Chinese-based parties was the passing of the Industrial Coordination Act (ICA) in April 1975, which targeted an NEP goal of a 30 per cent Malay employment quota as well as equity participation in private sector companies. Such legislation was alarming to Chinese businesses, particularly the smaller entities which would have problems even complying with the quota requirements of bumiputera employment, let alone bumiputera equity. The ICA was virtually scuttled by the 2000s after much acrimonious contestation, but probably more so because of its ineffectual implementation during the era of the privatization policies under Mahathir.[13] The other issue that exercised non-Malay political parties was the rejection of the Merdeka University proposed by the United Chinese School Committees Association and the United Chinese School Teachers Association (Dong Jiao Zong). The idea of a Chinese-medium tertiary institution flowed naturally from the fact that Malaysia allowed for Chinese vernacular education (i.e., "mother tongue" education) up to the secondary level through Independent Chinese schools. It was at the peril of losing Chinese support that Chinese-based political parties failed to support the Merdeka University, which UMNO opposed. The Chinese-based parties continued to push for its implementation after 1978 until the Federal Court in 1982 ruled that the project to have a Chinese-medium university in Malaysia was contrary to the Constitution.[14]

Thus the new premier clearly still had a lot on his hands when he called for a general election to be held on 8 July 1978. Nomination day was set for 21 June, leaving sixteen days for campaigning, but the government had put a ban on all public rallies just two days before thus forcing political parties to use *ceramah* and door-to-door campaigns as the main methods of canvassing for votes (Kassim 1979, p. 37; Means 1991, p. 66). The results of the election, held in all states except Kelantan, Sabah and Sarawak, are shown in Table 5.2.

The BN clearly lost a significant proportion of its popular vote, partially due to the migration of PAS back to the opposition, but by 1978 it had SNAP, a Sarawak party, on its side. On polling day the BN had already taken 9 federal and 17 state seats unopposed. PAS suffered badly, contesting 89 seats and winning a mere 5, with its president describing their situation as recovering from "giddiness" caused by the Kelantan crisis (Abdullah 1980, p. 69). It won no state seats in Terengganu but took 7 in Kedah. By all accounts it was a dismal performance, but the Islamic party still managed to garner half a million votes, and many of its losses were by narrow margins. Its nemesis in Kelantan, Berjasa, also lost out in the end as its application to join the BN was rejected. The DAP were the main gainers on the non-Malay side of the spectrum, winning seats at the expense of the MCA and Gerakan, increasing its parliamentary representation from 9 to 16 and garnering some 18.5 per cent of the popular vote. The election of 1978 may be said to have established the DAP as the main

Table 5.2
Parliamentary and State Election Results, 1978

	Parliament	%	No. of state seats won[c]
Barisan Nasional			
UMNO	70	—	175
MCA	17	—	43
Gerakan	4	—	12
MIC	3	—	9
PPP	0	—	1
BN Sarawak	23	—	—
BN Sabah	13	—	—
Total BN	130	55.3	239
Opposition			
PAS[a]	5	14.9	9
DAP	16	18.5	25
SAPO	1	0.3	—
Pekemas	0	0.7	—
SNAP[b]	—	—	—
Independents	2	0.2	2[d]
Total Opposition	23	44.7	36
TOTAL	154	—	351

Source: Means 1991, p. 68.
Notes: Percentages may not add up to 100% due to rounding and the absence of spoilt votes.
[a]PAS was in the BN in 1975 and was an opposition party in 1978.
[b]SNAP was an opposition party in 1974 and was in the BN in 1978.
[c]For the 10 Peninsular states holding elections.
[d]One Independent joined the BN after the outcome.

opposition party until the *reformasi* era. A major critique of the party remained that it basically won its seats on the strength of Chinese support, and not cross-ethnic voting or multi-ethnic vote pooling, nor based on its own ideology of a "Malaysian Malaysia". It won votes in championing the race-based grievances of the Merdeka University and on the unfairness of the ICA.[15] Thus, parties like the DAP and its supporters saw their platform as one that was geared against the "racial polarization" that had been perpetrated by UMNO, although this was paradoxically valorized through the DAP's championing of the non-Malay cause. At this stage of the game the DAP and other opposition parties saw no gain in orchestrating consociational arrangements of their own against the BN. The BN, meanwhile, had consolidated its hegemonic multi-ethnic vote-pooling model, with some haemorrhaging on the part of the MCA, but balanced with the inclusion of important new vote-bearing partners from Sabah and Sarawak. As noted sharply by Kassim (1979, p. 102), the success of this reconstituted "Alliance" had UMNO firmly as the leading force of BN: "The triumvirate in the old Alliance has been replaced by the UMNO supremo in Barisan." The 1978 result was an affirmation that the new model of consociational politics crafted by Razak, which saw an enlarged and more ethnically and regionally inclusive BN with UMNO as its unequivocal leader, had cohered well and was able to deliver desired outcomes under the post-1969 reconfiguration of electoral politics.

CONCLUSION

In concluding this chapter, one could surmise that the first phase of electoral politics post-1969 saw the rise of Malay political primacy, witnessed through the outcomes of the 1974 and 1978 general elections. During this period the consociational politics was modified to make UMNO an unchallenged hegemonic political party. Affirmative action for Malays and bumiputera, through the implementation of the NEP, was a successful strategy in manufacturing a majority Malay consensus on the Peninsula for UMNO, along with the capture of a majority of bumiputera votes for its partner parties in East Malaysia.

The 1974 election showed the spectacular recovery of the UMNO-led multiparty coalition, with almost all quarters giving their stamp of approval to the new consociational arrangement. Nevertheless, by the time of the 1978 election, minority positions and rights, such as those of Chinese educationists and the business class, began to be somewhat eroded, leading to near zero-sum outcomes for some of the BN's non-bumiputera partners. In the 1978 election the MCA became a casualty of this imbalance in communal mediation, though it was not quite sufficient to upset the path-dependent success of the BN. Nevertheless, any imbalance could potentially be risky for the BN's continued strategy of mediated communalism crucial to its electoral success.

The next chapter will deal exclusively with electoral politics under the premiership of Mahathir Mohamad. There were five general elections under his term. The astuteness of Mahathir in leading the BN to resounding success in four of these elections cannot be doubted. However, there were other new factors that determined the BN's path-dependent success. This time the mediation of communalism involved more than just finely balancing the demands of each partner so as to prevent zero-sum outcomes. Instead, a new mediated communalism would ensure the maximum returns (largely economic) to all partners, thus preventing any one party from going to the extremities of the ethnic continuum. Maximizing the returns for all parties — whether Malay, other bumiputera, Chinese or other minorities — necessarily involved enlarging the largesse, notably of the party coffers. With such largesse it was possible to expand the electoral game of positive gains for all BN parties. I postulate here that the Mahathir years were a logical extension of the onset of wealth accumulation for the BN parties started in the Razak period. The route to that massive accumulation of wealth was party capitalism.

Notes

1. See Chapter 1 for a brief discussion of Riker's concept of minimal or minimum winning coalitions.
2. I draw on the introductory chapter to the book on the NEP (Gomez and Saravanamuttu 2013) for important portions of this section.
3. Faaland was attached to the DNU in 1969 and 1970, as he himself states, and was clearly deeply involved in all the discussions about the NEP.
4. For a meticulous account of the many moves in East and West Malaysia made to potential coalition political parties in response to Razak's overtures — including the necessary adjustments made within existing coalition partners, such as the MCA and MIC — see Mauzy 1983, pp. 74–86 and Milne and Mauzy 1978, pp. 173–91.
5. As noted in Saravanamuttu (2010, pp. 125–26), Malaysia was the first Southeast Asian country to establish diplomatic ties with the PRC

("Communist China"), with Premier Razak and Chairman Mao agreeing to a policy of "non-interference" in each other's internal affairs and China and Malaysia accepting the principle of *jus soli* (right of soil) as the basis of its dealings with overseas Chinese, including the 200,000-odd stateless Chinese domiciled in Malaysia. China also acknowledged its formal severing of ties with the Malayan Communist Party. This was obviously a major political coup for Razak and must have won the BN considerable support among the Chinese population.

6. Weiss's narrative of the student protests, both in relation to the Johor and Baling situations (pp.155–63), is the most complete I have read and provides some interesting vignettes. One such story was that Anwar Ibrahim (by then leader of ABIM, the Islamic Youth Movement) and Ibrahim Ali (then president of the students' union of ITM) were both taken away along with many others in an FRU truck, but students blocked the truck and "liberated" the pair. Anwar was later rearrested when he tried to bail out detained students (p. 159). It is ironic that Anwar and Ibrahim were later on different sides of the political divide, because they became close friends in Kamunting, the detention centre where they stayed in the same block: Block 8. Syed Hussin Ali, sociology professor and later president of PSRM and deputy president of PKR, who also befriended Anwar in Kamunting, was then secretary of the University of Malaya's Staff Union, and was detained for nearly six years after the Baling incident. According to Syed Hussin, Anwar was released three months before him in 1975. See S.H. Ali, 1966, p. v and <http://www.thenutgraph.com/the-making-of-ibrahim-ali/> (accessed 28 April 2015).

7. For an account of how the act was beefed up following this event, see Weiss (2011, pp. 193–97).

8. Tun Dr Ismail, deputy prime minister under Tun Razak, and possibly his closest political associate and confidante, kept that secret. Ooi writes that Razak's condition was known at the end of 1969 to only Ismail, a couple of Ismail's friends, and the medical staff involved (Ooi 2006, p. 4). Razak's illness was to be kept under wraps and Ismail was expected to step into Razak's shoes should the former pass on. Little did Razak expect that Ismail would die before him (see Ooi 2006, *passim*). Some of this narrative is shown in the rather poorly made but controversial film directed by Suhaimi Baba, "Tanda Putera", released in 2013.

9. For this narrative, see, in particular, Crouch (1980) and Means (1991).

10. According to Milne and Mauzy (1991, pp. 27–28), Hussein Onn had prevaricated over the choice of Ghazali, Ghafar, Razaleigh or Mahathir until the night before his announcement. Mahathir himself was surprised by Onn's choice. It was rather well known that Ghazali had aspirations

to be deputy premier but was rejected by the UMNO party rank and file and the Young Turks because he had not risen from the party ranks but was recruited into politics as a senior civil servant from the Ministry of Foreign Affairs.

11. Mahathir himself has commented on these arrests in his memoirs (Mahathir 2011, pp. 323–24). He notes that Ghazali Shafie "did not stop at trying to associate me with alleged communists" (p. 324) and also that had he not been deputy premier he might have been taken into detention (p. 323). Thanks to Mahathir's revelation we can now easily surmise that the charges were trumped up, although the leftist leanings of the individuals were known. Samad Said was a founding member of the People's Action Party (PAP) of Singapore who escaped the PAP's crackdown on leftists in the government's infamous Operation Cold Store of 1963. Samad was the editor of *Berita Harian* in Kuala Lumpur which shared premises with the *Straits Times* in Jalan Riong in the 1960s. The late Abdullah Majid, a former member of the Singapore University Socialist Club, was clearly an important adviser to Tun Razak on relations with the Third World and on Malaysia's establishing of diplomatic ties with the PRC. Abdullah Ahmad is the prominent Kelantan politician and former MP of Kok Lanas and later editor-in-chief of the *New Straits Times*. He was a prominent spokesperson for Tun Razak at the time of his arrest by Ghazali Shafie. Abdullah has written a book on the Tunku's foreign policy based on his master's thesis (Abdullah Ahmad 1985) and it was well know that there was no love lost between him and "King Ghaz".

12. Farish Noor (2004, p. 280) writes that when Hussein Onn tabled the motion for the Emergency Act in Kelantan under Article 150 of the Constitution, he said he was not "playing politics", to the guffaws of the opposition bench.

13. When the ICA was implemented it was in practice aimed at foreign companies and was handled by the Malaysian Industrial Authority (MIDA), which issued manufacturing licences. Only companies with more than RM2.5 million in capital and employing more than seventy-five employees were subjected to the Act.

14. The Dong Jiao Zong formed a company, Merdeka University Bhd, and submitted a petition to the Yang di-Pertuan Agong for an incorporation order for the Merdeka University under the Universities and University Colleges Act, 1971, but the petition was rejected. Merdeka University Bhd then went on to challenge the decision in court, but the Federal Court held that the university, if established as a public authority, with the use of Mandarin as medium of instruction, could be prohibited under Article 152 of the Constitution at the discretion of the executive and

restrained by various education and language legislations. This effectively killed the project. <http://www.malaysiakini.com/letters/34746 (accessed 26 April 2015).

15. In a contrarian vein, Ong (1980) suggested that the party was not as strong as it seemed and was plagued with internal problems, which saw the resignation of important leaders such as Fan Yew Teng.

6

MEDIATING COMMUNALISM THROUGH PARTY CAPITALISM
The Elections of 1982, 1985, 1990 and 1995

Following a coronary bypass in February 1981, Hussein Onn resigned as prime minister, after serving only four years in the job. From then on Malaysia's longest-serving premier till date, Mahathir Mohamad, stepped into the breach. In July 1981 the new team of Mahathir and Musa, or the "2-M", took the helm of UMNO and the reins of the government of Malaysia. These same two people were earlier considered by Tunku Abdul Rahman to be "ultras", or extremists within UMNO, and were expelled from the party for a time.[1] Much has been written about Mahathir, including books by himself, which this chapter will draw on as may be relevant to electoral politics under his long tenure of twenty-two years as premier. Although Mahathir's premiership lasted from 1982 till 2003, this chapter will only cover four general elections held under his term. The last general election during the Mahathir years was in 1999 — a pivotal election deserving of a more extensive treatment. Thus, following this chapter I will devote the next to the

Reformasi Movement and the 1999 election, thought by many to be a transformative moment of Malaysian history.

MAHATHIR AT THE HELM

From the outset I would like to stress that while it is hard to avoid the fact that Mahathir dominated and to a great extent "personalized" UMNO and Malaysian politics (Hwang 2003), this politics was embedded within the discursive and institutional constraints that we have already foregrounded in this book. These constraints are the electoral system and the consociational imperatives of power sharing politics in a multi-ethnic society, overlaid with the often unforgiving constraints of Malay and Islamic politics, which any leader of Malaysia could only eschew at his peril. Furthermore, as we will show in political economy terms, Mahathir was also functioning within the parameters of the country's interventionist developmental state and capitalist system, which he cleverly turned to UMNO's advantage through the practice of "party capitalism". However, this same factor of party capitalism, with its corollary of corruption and pork-barrel politics, has become UMNO's bane and the potential source of its political decline. We will return to these points in fuller fashion; the analysis in this chapter will cover the first four elections of Mahathir's tenure.

In this period, especially from the 1980s onward, Malaysia began to manifest the phenomenon commonly known as "money politics". In Malaysia, money politics in the form of preferential economic policies to favoured political parties and their supporters has greatly affected the process as well as the outcome of elections and helped incumbent political parties remain firmly in power at the national and state level. I will examine the impact of such money politics by invoking the concept of "party capitalism" (Fields 1998; Kahn 1992; Ng 2001, 2013; Saravanamuttu 2007) to dissect the character and persistence of such money politics. Malaysia is a prime example of how political parties are directly involved in business wherein capitalist practices have become a function of political agendas (Gomez 1990, 1994, 1999). UMNO, under the leadership of Mahathir Mohamad, took party capitalism to its zenith in the 1990s, and the BN's landslide victory in the 1995 election perhaps marked the high point of this type of politics.[2] As with the economic notion of "boom and bust", the 1995 election also symbolized the beginnings of diminishing returns for the ruling coalition. The financial meltdown of 1997–98 occurred in tandem with this decline. The limits to money politics and its deleterious impact on the BN's political fortunes will be analysed more fully in the next chapter.

During Mahathir's tenure the primary focus of the NEP, particularly from the early 1980s, was on business. Initially, public enterprises — now referred to as GLCs, or government-linked companies — were established to acquire corporate equity on behalf of bumiputera. A key mechanism to enable bumiputera to obtain 30 per cent of corporate equity was through preferential distribution of discounted blocs of stock in publicly listed companies. Following active state intervention through public enterprises and trust agencies to acquire primarily foreign corporate assets,[3] these government institutions had emerged as major owners of corporate equity by the early 1980s. By this time bumiputera equity ownership, according to government figures, had increased by more than 10 percentage points, to 12.5 per cent. The government would subsequently decide, following the appointment of Mahathir Mohamad as prime minister (1981–2003), to nurture bumiputera capitalists through preferential treatment involving government contracts and cheap loans. Mahathir often justified this on the grounds that parity could only be said to be achieved once there was an equal number of Malay and Chinese millionaires.

The key mechanisms employed by Mahathir to cultivate Malay enterprise were the Bumiputera Commercial and Industrial Community policy and privatization, a method he used to transfer ownership and control of public enterprises to private entrepreneurs. Mahathir's choice of the beneficiaries of privatized projects was based on the concept of "picking winners", influenced as he was by the South Korean model of development. In this development plan, known as the developmental state model, the role of a (strong) state was central to the South Korean government's successful strategy of using selective patronage to create privately owned conglomerates such as Samsung and Hyundai (Amsden 1989). Mahathir had used this model as his template while promoting the creation of large internationally recognized Malaysian conglomerates that would help rapidly industrialize the economy. However, this avenue of distributing government-created concessions, or rents, led to serious allegations of political patronage and rent-seeking behaviour of cronies, the so-called "winners", who happened to be well connected.[4] Privatization also allowed the ruling class to indirectly control private equity without the need to account to the public for contentious business transactions. What is indisputable is that a "new rich" rose rapidly during the late 1980s and the first half of the 1990s, during a period when industrializing Southeast Asian countries registered high growth rates.

In 1990, as the NEP came to an end, many of the policy's stated goals had been met. A massive reduction in poverty was registered among the beneficiaries targeted by the NEP. Absolute poverty among Malays was reduced from 64.8 per cent in 1970 to 20.4 per cent by 1990. Corporate equity owned by individual bumiputera and trust agencies in 1990 amounted to 19 per cent, well short of the targeted 30 per cent, but still an impressive improvement from the 1.5 per cent ownership figure attributed to this community in 1969. I will return to a discussion of the NEP in the next chapter and link it to the rise of the Malay middle class, which could be argued provided the conditions for the schism in Malay politics sparking the politics of the Reformasi Movement.

For now, suffice it to say that with its early implementation the governments of Abdul Razak and subsequently Mahathir Mohamad were seen, contrary to that of the Tunku, as establishing a Malay-first politics which brought about major dividends for UMNO over the next three decades. Because the NEP was framed within the DNU concept of national unity and its two-pronged approach of eradicating poverty irrespective of race and uplifting bumiputera, it was largely palatable to the non-Malay coalition partners of UMNO. Institutionally, the NEP contributed greatly to the path-dependent success of the Barisan Nasional, while preserving in smaller measure the Alliance's consociational approach. I will also show in this chapter that, along with the implementation of the NEP during the Mahathir era, the new discourse and practice of large-scale money politics became the order of the day underpinned and undertaken by political parties, primarily UMNO and its BN coalition partners. Following the pioneering work of Karl Fields, I use the term "party capitalism" (Fields 1995, 2002) to characterize politics under Mahathir. The analysis of party capitalism and its imputed impact on Malaysian electoral politics will be one of the main foci of this chapter.

USES AND PERILS OF PARTY CAPITALISM

The concept of "party capitalism" is derived from Karl Fields's work on Taiwan, which was seen as a classic developmental state.[5] Taiwan under the Kuomintang (KMT) party was also known as a "party-state", that is, one that saw a blurring of the distinction between the party and state since the two seemed to be fused as a single entity. The KMT had a Leninist-authoritarian party structure, but not a Marxist ideology. The "KMT Inc." discourse was a way for the party to penetrate, control and own the economy. Central to the party state was the practice of authoritarian corporatism: "In organizational life the individual obeys the organization and the minority obeys the majority. Prior to a decision there is free discussion. After a decision has been made it must be obeyed in full. Thus is realized organized democracy and disciplined liberty."[6] By the end of the 1990s, estimates of the party holdings ranged as high as 50 per cent of all company assets, with annual earnings of up to 30 per cent of Taiwan's GNP. This comprised 150 party-invested enterprises, with estimates of assets ranging from NT$112 billion to NT$500 billion. According to Fields, the manifestation of party capitalism can be categorized into six types of activities which can derive benefits and pose as burdens for the party involved. These include profit sourcing, patronage outlets, propaganda organs, development agents, market regulators and corporate emissaries. Taiwan's party capitalism could be applied almost exactly to Malaysia's party system under Mahathir. However, one important difference is that the KMT actually chose to register its corporate holdings under the party in 1994 (Fields 2002, p. 123), but Malaysian political parties have never done so. To put it plainly, under Mahathir, deliberately or otherwise, the premier's policies and penchant for using the political party to achieve his economic goals led to an unprecedented level of party-driven businesses carried out by rent seekers practically hand picked by the political leadership.

Although a more complex case to that of Taiwan, particularly with its ethnic mix, Malaysia could definitely be seen as a prime example of party capitalism. In his public discourse Mahathir was careful to avoid any suggestion that UMNO was the target of his policies and ideas; he would invariably cast the policies in terms of national objectives. Alternatively, one could say he cleverly dovetailed national goals with that of his party. Mahathir famously initiated the "Malaysia Incorporated" concept very soon after assuming leadership in the 1980s, and his model was that of "Japan Incorporated".[7] This policy came together with the "Look East Policy", which put on a pedestal the East Asian models of capitalist development.[8] Since it was not "politically correct" for Mahathir to emulate the Chinese-populated Taiwan, he regularly cited Japan and South Korea as his examples of economic success.[9] As suggested earlier, Mahathir's national policies began to increasingly dovetail with those of his own political party, which was also used as an instrument to realize his economic ideas and ideals. The work of Terence Gomez and K.S. Jomo has documented how party finance and business was melded with the corporate sector.[10] One could trace the emergence of party capitalism and also tie it to the birth of the NEP in 1971. The terms "state capitalism" and "bureaucratic capitalism" were concepts used earlier, but in the Mahathir era state capitalism morphed into full-blown party capitalism (Ng 2001; Kahn 1996). Party capitalism in the Malaysian case denotes ownership and control of the economy by political parties such as UMNO, the MCA and MIC. It also connotes linkages of parties to noted business tycoons, or "cronies", many of whom are engaged in rent-seeking enterprises condoned by the state.

It was during the middle of Mahathir's tenure that the contours of a "party-state" were realized through the notion of "Malaysia Incorporated", much like in Taiwan. Mahathir ushered in a national privatization policy and programmes such as the development of heavy industries (such as the Perwaja steel mill), the creation of the Bumiputera Commercial and Industrial Community and the privatization of many state enterprises. The bulk of these projects were under the aegis of the ruling coalition of parties, which controlled the federal as well as state-level funds. UMNO and UMNO-related individuals were said to hold directorships in more than a hundred companies with assets valued at RM4 billion by 1990, including companies such as Fleet

Holdings, Hatibudi, Halimantan, Koperasi Usaha Bersatu (KUBB), and the like. After April 1990, all the UMNO-sponsored companies, except KUBB, came under the Renong group (Ng 2001).

Thus, there is ample evidence to illustrate various dimensions of party capitalism and its corollary of "money politics" or, more specifically, rent-seeking economic behaviour during Mahathir's tenure. Readers should refer to the important work of Gomez and Jomo cited earlier, and more recently that of Barry Wain,[11] which show the extent to which UMNO (and also its partners the MCA and MIC) had deeply participated in business and politics, using the political party to engage in corporate holdings and entanglements whether directly or through proxies. The amassing of such private holdings were a product of the BN's political hegemony, which in turn propelled its path-dependent electoral successes, particularly given its almost bottomless access to electoral funding. Drawing on the work by Wain, Gomez, Gale and others, I will now proceed to show the nexus between business and politics during Mahathir's tenure.

Mahathir's closest economic ally for most of his tenure was lawyer-businessman Daim Zaiunuddin, who served twice as finance minister (1984–91 and 1998–2001). For most of Mahathir's tenure Daim was also UMNO's treasurer. Politically and economically, Mahathir and Daim, who both hailed from Kedah, were like two peas in a pod. Mahathir said of Daim that "he knows the nitty gritty, the way to carry out (a mandate), for example, if I say privatization, his job is to find the means.... he showed how it should be done and all that." (Wain 2009, p. 90). With Daim at his side, Mahathir plunged UMNO deep into the corporate world, turning the party into a vast conglomerate with investments spanning practically all facets of the economy. To quote Wain:

> The mandatory 30 percent of share allocation for bumiputera during a company's public listing, or restructuring, was usually channelled to UMNO-owned or linked corporate entities and other political allies. With privatization, too, UMNO was used as a vehicle to transfer government holdings to private or semi-private ownership, mostly for the benefit of the same clique. With UMNO as active corporate player, the party at times was in competition or collaboration with state-owned agencies and private companies. Some valuable state assets passed into UMNO hands. The fusion — often confusion — of party, state and private roles went far beyond the government–corporate cooperation implied in the Malaysia Inc. concept. (Wain 2009, p. 124)

Gomez points out that by the mid-1990s, Malaysia's leading corporations included firms that were controlled by UMNO-linked bumiputera, almost all of them with some connection with Mahathir, Daim and Anwar Ibrahim (who had become finance minister):

> The bumiputera in control of major firms included Halim Said, Tajudin Ramli, Wan Azmi Wan Hamzah, Rashid Hussain, Shamsuddin Abdul Kadir, Azman Hashim, Ahmad Sebi Abu Bakar, Ishak Ismail, Mirzan Mahathir, Mokhzani Mahathir, Amin Shah Omar Shah and Yaya Ahmad ... [and a] number of non-Malay businessmen who were also well-connected quickly developed huge enterprises with government patronage. These businessmen included Vincent Tan Chee Yioun, T.K. Lim, Ting Pik Khiing Lee Kim Yew, Tong Kooi Ong and T. Ananda Krishna. (Gomez 2004, p. 161)[12]

Gomez elucidates further that Daim Zainuddin, whose personal assets were thought to amount to a billion ringgit in 1992, was regarded as the most powerful figure in the Malaysian corporate scene in the Mahathir years. Moreover, his closest business associates — Halim Saad, Wan Azmi Wan Hamzah and Tajudin Ramli — had emerged as major corporate figures. Halim in particular was acknowledged as a "trustee" of UMNO's vast corporate assets, and allegedly controlled these assets through the conglomerate Renong (Gomez p. 163).

Wain suggests that when UMNO was declared illegal in 1988 and the new UMNO was born, in theory, the old UMNO assets were placed under a government agent; in practice, he alleges, some of these assets may have been transferred to the "UMNO Political Fund".[13] He further suggests that only Mahathir and Daim had knowledge of the details of this fund, and that "millions of members remained in the dark about the party's multi-million dollar enterprises, even though the assets theoretically belong[ed] to them" (Wain 2009, p. 125).[14] How this political fund was used is anybody's guess, but we can surmise that it could well have been used in electoral contests whether within UMNO or at the national level. Interestingly, Mahathir himself had decried the use of "money politics", declaring in 1984 that if the trend continued, millionaires would lead UMNO. Securing the nomination as division head in UMNO entailed huge expenditure, and even more so if one wanted to contest a post in the party hierarchy. Ghafar Baba revealed that one aspirant spent RM600,000 to secure such a post (Wain 2009,

p. 143).[15] With his almost absolute control of the Malaysian "party state", Mahathir plunged the country into a number of economic scandals, such as the disastrous attempt to corner the tin market, the BMF scandal, the Forex debacle and the failed Perwaja steel mill.[16] These scandals have been touched on in many books and articles, but Wain provides us with detailed narratives that reveal some new shocking facts too complex to relate fully here. Here is how he summarizes the losses to Malaysia:

> In fact, based on incomplete public information, RM15 billion was a conservative estimate of Perwaja's losses. Similarly, Bank Bumiputera dropped at least RM10 billion. Bank Negara's foreign exchange forays drained perhaps RM23 billion from Malaysia's reserves. The cost of trying to push up the price of tin seemed paltry by comparison, maybe RM1 billion. The total, RM50 billion or so, could have easily doubled if a professional accounting had been made, factoring in all invisibles, from unrecorded write-offs to blatant embezzlement and opportunity costs. (Wain 2009, p. 177)[17]

The involvement of the MCA in business is also well documented. The setting up of Multi Purpose Holdings Bhd (MPHB) by its former leader Tan Koon Swan succeeded in mobilizing capital from small Chinese businesses and ordinary Chinese investors turning MPHB into one of the biggest corporations in Malaysia. However, all came to nought for Tan after the recession of the mid-1980s and the infamous Pan Electric Industries bankruptcy which saw Tan's conviction in Singapore for corruption in 1985. Tan was also charged for bailing out the failing MPHB with Pan Electric money to the tune of RM23 million (Gomez 1994, p. 209). The MIC's involvement in business was through MAIKA Holdings, which was an attempt to expand Indian corporate wealth following the example of MPHB. Some 66,000 shareholders composed of Indians from the middle and lower classes contributed to MAIKA to raise as much as RM125 million in the mid-1980s, despite the recession at the time. The corporation invested heavily in GLCs such as Malaysian Airlines System, Malaysian International Shipping Corporation, Edaran Otomobil Nasional Bhd and Telekom Malaysia, apparently posting high profits for many years. However, by the end of 2002, probably due to mismanagement and the bleeding of funds to party cronies, MAIKA accumulated losses of RM71.7 million (Ramakrishnan 2010).

THE ELECTIONS OF 1982 AND 1986

This section will detail the results of the elections under Mahathir's tenure and then go on to examine the main issues of the campaigns and compare the outcomes for patterns and differences. In undertaking this narrative I shall seek to elucidate how, and to what extent, the BN's (and UMNO's) path-dependent electoral successes were generated, what institutional and policy discourses and practices valorized "increasing returns" and what factors caused negative effects on electoral performance. I will pay close attention to the various themes surfacing during the Mahathir era and how they provide the overarching contest for electoral performance. As noted by Wain (2009), one could hardly escape the impression that during the Mahathir era, general elections were "used" for his larger agenda. As I shall show below, the 1986 election was but a prelude to the real political contest in the 1987 UMNO elections, which saw an internecine battle between Team A and Team B of UMNO. It became commonplace for political pundits to suggest that UMNO elections were more important than general elections. As I shall show in a later chapter, the outcomes of general elections can also adversely affect the fortunes of UMNO politicians. Table 6.1 shows the parliamentary outcomes of the four elections before 1999. The 1999 results will be examined in the next chapter, as that election marked the first to be held after the Reformasi Movement.

By the time of the 1982 general election, politicking for UMNO's peninsular partners had stabilized with Lee San Choon at the helm of the MCA, Lim Chong Eu firmly in control of Gerakan in Penang, and the MIC under the leadership of Samy Vellu. On Borneo, SNAP had been brought into the BN fold and the Sabah Alliance continued to look formidable. It was within UMNO that political regeneration was brewing. The Young Turks led by Mahathir had to galvanize a new team of candidates, which political scientist Gordon Means has noted was a virtual shift to a "second generation" of professionals and often those with a business background (Means 1991, p. 87). In this mix came Anwar Ibrahim, the prominent leader of ABIM, already by then a firebrand political activist noted for his critiques of government policies. Mahathir must have recognized Anwar's talents, for on the eve of the 1982 election he announced that Anwar was joining UMNO and that he would be given a position of responsibility in his government (ibid., p. 88).[18] The election was called for 22 April, allowing fifteen days for campaigning, with BN mounting its campaign on the slogan of "Bersih, Cekap dan Amanah" (Clean, Efficient and Trustworthy) under the tag team of Mahathir and Musa, the 2-M government. The opposition parties campaigned on their usual themes, but were greatly hampered by the Sedition Act, which outlawed the airing of "sensitive issues", as noted earlier. When the votes were counted, although the BN had breached the 60 per cent threshold of the popular vote by half a per cent, in terms of the distribution of seats this did not make much of a difference. UMNO took 70 of the 73 seats it contested and the MCA won a record 24 out of 28 seats contested, basically at the expense of the DAP, whose chairman Chen Man Hin was defeated by the MCA's new leader Lee San Choon by 23,258 to 22,413 votes. PAS won a mere 5 seats, retaining about the same level of the popular vote as before, and not having really recovered from its Kelantan crisis of 1974 (ibid., p. 90). However, more importantly, due to the change of party leadership, PAS was now dominated by the ulama faction and directed more towards fundamentalist Islam after the Iranian Revolution and the setting up of the Islamic state. Post-election, Anwar was put in charge of Islamic affairs as minister under the Prime Minister's Department. Musa Hitam took over the Home Ministry, Ghazali Shafie was tasked to handle foreign affairs and Tengku Razaleigh Hamzah assumed the duties of finance minister. But despite having all these UMNO heavyweights within the Cabinet, it was evident that it was Mahathir who was firmly in charge of Malaysia.

The 1986 election was held with a year to spare on 2–3 August. This period is best signified by Mahathir's newly adopted discourse of accelerating the project of modernity for the Malays, amplified in his second book, *The Challenge* (1986). As aptly put by Hilly,

> from the "discourse of dilemma" in the 1970s to the "challenge of modernity" in the 1980s, Mahathir had sought to promote a reformist, growth driven agenda conducive to modern Islamic thinking; one that would give impetus to Bumiputera competitiveness and lift the Malays out of their "dependent" socio-economic condition. (2002, p. 50)

This new perspective, as further explained by Hilly (2001, pp. 50–51), overtook Mahathir's somewhat pessimistic vision about the Malays in

The Malay Dilemma (1970), which was written when his own political fortunes were in the doldrums. Khoo (1995, pp. 24–48) provides a thorough dissection of the two Mahathir books, contrasting the "aggressive and accusatory polemic" of *The Malay Dilemma*, which called for a "constructive protection" of the Malays as the "definitive race", with the second book's call for a new system of ethics and values that the Malays needed to adopt in lieu of Western imitation in the face of the economic challenges of the time. The second book also drew on the idea of progressive Islam.[19] As we shall see further below, Mahathir had to fight tooth and nail to have his vision accepted by the UMNO power bloc in the first major crisis of his tenure, commonly referred to as the struggle between Team A and Team B. By February of 1986, six months before the general election, Musa Hitam had already resigned as deputy premier when he was accused of disloyalty to Mahathir. Nevertheless, he retained his position as deputy president of UMNO.[20] But we are ahead of our narrative.

The results of the 1986 election were to be as expected, even though it delivered an "ambiguous mandate", as argued by Means (1991, p. 153). What prompted Mahathir to call it one year in advance was the economic recession that Malaysia encountered at that time. However, all manner of state apparatuses were mustered to help the BN, including the EC's 1984 re-delimitation and gerrymandering of electoral boundaries, which seem to have affected PAS's performance in particular. Among the more novel tactics was the use of an international public relations firm to promote the BN candidates and to denigrate the opposition figures with political cartoons (Saravanamuttu 1989, p. 237). Consequently, UMNO added another 13 seats to its 1982 tally, which was an indication of the closing of ranks and the lack of politicking up until the holding of the general election. In path-dependent and consociational terms, the various coalition partners held their ground, but the MCA lost terrain to the DAP in their perpetual struggle for the Chinese vote. The DAP amassed 24 seats and more than 20 per cent of the popular vote, making it the biggest party in the opposition. PAS lost further ground and took only one parliamentary seat. The MIC and Gerakan more or less held their ground, while the Borneo parties delivered their massive dividends of 36 seats as the BN's "fixed deposit" states. The new party, Hamim, led by the erstwhile PAS leader Asri Muda, delivered 1 seat, but its admission into the

BN caused the withdrawal of Berjasa. It is of interest to note that soon after the holding of the general election, Abdullah Ahmad (whom I have mentioned earlier) famously made his speech in Singapore about the necessity for "Malay dominance". In a talk delivered to the Singapore Institute of International Affairs on 30 August 1986, Abdullah argued that Malay supremacy or Malay dominance was born out of a sacrosanct social contract among the three main ethnic groups — the Malays, the Chinese and the Indians — that even preceded Malaya's Independence (Das 1987). This was the type of discourse that was bitterly challenged by the DAP and which clearly won the party unstinting support among the non-Malays.

I will now move on to discuss the schism between UMNO's Team A and Team B and touch on the resultant "collateral damage" in terms of the establishment of a new authoritarianism aimed at silencing detractors in the legitimate opposition, as well as the newly emerging voices in civil society. This collateral damage extended to the judiciary, as we shall also see. The literature on this phase of the Mahathir era is extensive, and we cannot do justice in the space available here to analyse fully the larger social implications of the crackdown on political dissent during Operasi Lalang (Operation Weeding Out), which was executed in October 1987 and saw 106 opposition party members and social activists arrested and detained under the ISA (see Appendix 6A). We will return to these socio-political developments in the conclusion of the chapter, but for now we turn our focus instead to the highly explosive and divisive UMNO party politics of 1987, which evidently masked its earlier highly commendable outing in the 1986 election.

The "Battle Royal" (A.B. Shamsul 1988) that ensued at the April 1987 UMNO General Assembly was more than just *sandiwara* (Malay theatre), as most people had come to expect of UMNO party caucuses. This time, as Khoo (1992) suggests, it may have had something to do with the "Grand Vision" of Mahathir to push for an accelerated modernizing of the Malays and Malaysia, and thus it was necessary for him to remove the Old Guard from the party that may have opposed his grand plan. For their part, Mahathir's opponents clearly had a different vision and were possibly opposed to Mahathir's authoritarian style of leadership. Tengku Razaleigh was the leader of Team B; he and Musa (we have already mentioned his resignation) had become allies. Khoo illuminates the possible differences between the two visions by referencing the writing of Malek Merican (a senior banker), who characterized Team A as wanting to push aggressively for the fulfilment of the 30 per cent equity target of bumiputera share in the corporate economy, while Team B felt such an aggressive push could lead to stagnation of the economy (Khoo 1992, p. 69).[21] In Shamsul's (1988, pp. 176–84) depiction of the struggle, it was a winner-takes-all contest, but even so, with immense internal hemorrhaging (*menang jadi arang, kalah jadi abu*, "winner turns to charcoal, loser turns to ash", he explains). But win Mahathir did, defeating Razaleigh by 43 votes (761 to 718). And so too did Ghafar Baba, his deputy, beating Musa Hitam (739 to 699). But Anwar Ibrahim, only thirty-eight-years old then, was the new rising star of UMNO, making his mark by taking the third vice presidency behind Wan Mohktar Ahmad and Abdullah Badawi. Anwar had relinquished his UMNO Youth chief's position to contest one of the three vice president positions, clearly with Mahathir's concurrence. The only heavyweight in Team B to win a high post was Abdullah Badawi, along with only 9 positions out of 25 in the Supreme Council. The 1987 UMNO elections also had far-reaching implications for the political economy of the party and, by extrapolation, the country. As explained by Shamsul, Mahathir's "shareholders" had defeated Tun Razak's "technocrats", and with it Mahathir's notion of "Malaysia Incorporated" was well on the road to implementation (Ibid., p. 186).

Political developments came thick and fast in the aftermath of the UMNO crisis, bringing Malaysia to the brink of ethnic breakdown in what could be said to have ushered in one of the most undemocratic phases of its history. Some of the effects of government action from this time remain with the country to this day. Thus, the years 1986–88 saw a host of imponderable and improbable events, marked by UMNO's de-registration and the birth of "UMNO Baru", along with the earlier-mentioned passing of amendments to the Official Secrets Act and the Printing and Publishing Act, the massive crackdown on the opposition codenamed Operasi Lalang, the withdrawal of the licences of three newspapers, and the assault on the Judiciary, which resulted in the sacking of the chief justice. A summary of the major events of this period is provided at the end of this chapter in Appendix C.

Table 6.1
Parliamentary Election Results, 1982–95

Malaysia	1982 Seats	1982 % votes	1986 Seats	1986 % votes	1990 Seats	1990 % votes	1995 Seats	1995 % votes
BN	132	60.5	148	57.3	127	53.4	162	65.1
PAS	5	14.5	1	15.5	7	6.7	7	7.3
DAP	9	19.6	24	21.1	20	17.6	9	12.1
Semangat 46					8	15.1	6	10.2
PBS					14	2.3	8	3.3
Others	8	5.4	4	6.1	4	4.9	0	2.0
Total	**154**		**177**		**180**		**192**	
Peninsula only								
BN	103	61.3	112	58.1	99	55.3	123	
UMNO	70		83		70		79	
MCA	24		17		18		30	
MIC	4		6		6		7	
Gerakan	5		5		5		7	
Others	0		1		0		0	
PAS	5	16.4	1	17.5	7	7.8	7	7.2
DAP	6	20.3	19	21.4	18	18.0	8	12.0
Semangat 46					8	17.5	6	10.4
Others	0	2.0	0	3.0	0	1.4	0	2.0
Total	**114**		**132**		**132**		**144**	

Source: Crouch 1996, p.75; Tan 2001, pp. 10–40.

I will move on now to examine the next two general elections, of 1990 and 1995, as well as the by-elections that preceded 1990.

THE ELECTIONS OF 1990 AND 1995

In terms of its impact on general elections, the post UMNO crisis period paradoxically saw the consolidation of power by Mahathir as undisputed leader of the country, rising to the pinnacle of his power by the time of the 1995 election. This would be the period of "Late

Mahathirism" according to Hilly (2001). This consolidation of power was achieved with a series of Team A versus Team B proxy contests in by-elections prior to the 1990 general election.[22]

The first such by-election was held in March 1988 for a state assembly seat in Johor, Tanjong Puteri, owing to the death of its incumbent. It was the first test for UMNO Baru, the newly constituted UMNO under Mahathir. In the event, after three recounts, the UMNO candidate Mohamed Yunos Sulaiman won by a wafer-thin 31 votes, defeating his PSRM challenger Abdul Razak Ahmad. The result showed that the new UMNO was still reeling from the 1987 crisis, although no Team B candidate stood. In the next by-election, in August — for the Johor Baru urban parliamentary constituency — the new party of Semangat 46 (Spirit of 46), registered by Team B, showed its hand by putting back into contention Shahrir Samad who had been purged by Mahathir after the 1987 crisis. Musa Hitam and the Johor UMNO were strongly behind their hometown candidate, while Tengku Razaleigh and other Semangat 46 leaders also joined the campaign trail. Shahrir recaptured his seat, increasing his margin from 2,335 to 12,595 in a three-cornered fight, despite the fact that his poster campaign was overwhelmed 20–1 by the BN. According to one analysis of this by-election, Shahrir, who garnered 64 per cent of the popular vote, may have taken some 70 per cent of the Malay vote and even more from the Chinese (Hari and Suresh 1989, p. 518).[23] Then, a week later, came the third by-election — of Parit Raja, a Johor state seat which was thought to be a barometer of the rural Malay vote. In the event, the BN/UMNO won by a narrow margin of only 413 votes in a multi-cornered fight. The real test for the Mahathir government came on 28 January 1989 in the Ampang Jaya constituency situated in the periphery of Kuala Lumpur. The by-election was caused by the resignation of the incumbent. This parliamentary seat had been held by the BN's MCA, although the proportion of voters stood at 67 per cent Malay, 27 per cent Chinese and 5 per cent Indian. The MCA's candidate Ong Tee Kiat was pitted against UMNO's old guard and the Semangat 46 candidate Harun Idris. Despite his gravitas as former Menteri Besar of Selangor and a campaign that stressed the Mahathir government's corruption and patronage politics, the MCA's Ong romped home with 54 per cent of the popular vote against Harun's

44 per cent. This was a crushing defeat for Semangat 46 and the result re-established Mahathir's hegemony as still the putative leader of the three major communities in Malaysia. Although Mahathir had a heart attack which required a five-way bypass in January of 1989, Harun's defeat at Ampang Jaya by a BN novice politician meant that Mahathir was now firmly at the "epicentre" of Malaysian politics (Wain 2009, p. 77).

Given the resolution of the UMNO split and crisis and the evidence that Mahathir had overcome its most deleterious impacts, it was logical that he would soon want to seek a new mandate. Polling day was set for 21 October 1990 with 180 parliamentary seats up for contest — 48 in the Borneo states. By the time of the election, Semangat 46 had formed two electoral pacts: Angkatan Perpaduan Ummah (APU), or "Muslim Unity Movement", with PAS and the other two smaller Muslim parties, Berjasa and Hamim; and Gagasan Rakyat (People's Concept) with the DAP, the PRM (formerly PSRM) and a small splinter group of the MIC (Crouch 1996, p. 123). The reason for the split alliances was that the DAP was unable to accept the PAS's goal of establishing an "Islamic state". PAS, for their part, declared that it "has never and will not work with the DAP as long as it remains a secular party" (ibid.). The stated goal of the two pacts was to deny the BN its two-thirds majority in parliament. But, as is shown in Table 6.1, the BN again scored a significant victory, taking 127 seats — 7 more than needed for the two-thirds majority — while garnering some 53.4 per cent of the popular vote. However, UMNO lost 8 seats to Semangat 46 and 14 to the PBS of Sabah, which had left the BN just two days before polling.

The most important outcomes for the opposition occurred in the states of Kelantan and Penang. With the APU pact it was able to win all parliamentary and state seats in Kelantan. This was a colossal thumping for the Mahathir government, indicating that votes in the Malay heartland of the East Coast had decidedly swung in favour of his nemesis Tengku Razaleigh's Semangat 46 and PAS. In Penang the DAP came close to defeating the BN, winning 14 of the 33 state seats (Khong 1991, p. 38), with Gerakan's leader and chief minister Lim Chong Eu falling victim to DAP supremo Lim Kit Siang. However, DAP's Gagasan Rakyat partners Semangat 46 and PRM failed to win any seats, and the opposition was three seats short of taking the state.

The 1990 election re-established the path-dependent success of the BN, despite the concerted challenge from the opposition, which included a breakaway party from UMNO. Even as two opposition pacts sought to establish similar power-sharing arrangements as the BN, their institutional weakness and lack of cohesion saw them easily trumped by the BN. That said, in the run-up to the election the government went a great distance to make concessions to the Chinese electorate on the question of vernacular education after the debacle of the Merdeka University project. The new education minister Anwar Ibrahim promised that the government was committed to the preservation of clause 21(2) of the Education Act, which if amended would allow Malay to replace Mandarin as the medium of instruction in schools. In fact Anwar promised that that particular section of the act would be abolished. Most importantly, before the election the Mahathir government had set up the National Economic Consultative Council (NECC), which had a series of meetings in 1988 to discuss the implementation of the NEP goals. These meetings involved fifty members of political parties — including opposition parties — others from the business community, trade unions, farmers, fishermen and members of civil society.[24] This attempt at inclusivity possibly won the BN much needed support from the Chinese on the eve of the election.

The 9th general election was held on 24 April 1995. There were now 192 seats, compared to 180 after the re-delineation exercise carried out by the Election Commission between October 1992 and August 1993. In the new delineation, Sarawak was given the largest number of parliamentary seats of 27, followed by Perak with 23 and Johor and Sabah with 20 each. The other states received seats as follows: Selangor 17, Kedah 15, Kelantan 14, Terengganu 8, Negeri Semilan 7, Malacca 5 and Perlis 3. The Federal Territories of Kuala Lumpur and Labuan were allotted 11 seats and 1 seat, respectively. On polling day the BN won 11 seats uncontested and eventually garnered 162 seats — almost 85 per cent of the total. The BN's popular vote breached 65 per cent, the highest in its history, while the opposition's 35 per cent of the vote won it a miserable 21 seats, with each of the opposition parties' tallies reduced to single digits (see Table 6.2). The BN's only

Table 6.2
Results of 1995 State Elections

	BN	DAP	S46	PAS	Total
Johor	40				40
Kedah	34			2	36
Kelantan	7		12	24	43
Malaka	22	3			25
N. Sembilan	30	2			32
Pahang	37	1			38
Penang	32	1			33
Perlis	15				15
Perak	51	1			52
Selangor	45	3			48
Terengganu	25			7	32
Total	338	11	12	33	394

Source: Chin 1996, p. 406

defeat was in Kelantan, where it picked up 7 seats and where the PAS–S46 coalition held firm. Elsewhere this arrangement collapsed, as we shall see below. The 9th general election turned out to be Mahathir's finest hour, but what were the reasons for his rise from hated villain to his ineffable status as Malaysia's quintessential politician?

The first observation is the resurgence of the Malaysian economy, with its 8 per cent growth after the recession-ridden 1980s, accomplished, some would contend, by the economic liberalization polices implemented by the Mahathir government in the 1990s (Balasubramaniam 1995, p. 1363). The strong economy allowed for a generous "election budget" in October the previous year, where income and other taxes were reduced or cut and civil servants received a one-month bonus (Chin 1996, p. 396). The BN's slogan of "Vision, Justice and Efficiency" was premised on the government's Wawasan 2020 (Vision 2020) of the New Development Policy (NDP), which in theory replaced the NEP and promised a doubling of incomes every year to propel Malaysia to become a "Developed Country" by 2020. Even though the UMNO

Assembly of 1993 had seen Anwar's "Vision Team" defeat Ghafar Baba as deputy president and Anwar's political ascendance in winning that post, by the time of the 1995 election Mahathir was able to persuade a demoralized Ghafar to campaign for the party. The non-Malay BN peninsular partners had more or less overcome their internal feuds, and in Sarawak — with PBDS back in the BN fold of PBB, SUPP and SNAP — it was unassailable, causing the DAP to win only a single seat. Only the PBS in Sabah provided a challenge. The state election in 1994 saw a narrow win for the PBS, but the government collapsed due to defections and the state was taken over by the BN. These actions were seen as treachery by most of the native Kadazan-Dusuns, thus allowing their symbolic leader (*Huguan Siou*) Joseph Pairin to lead the PBS to take 8 out of 12 parliamentary seats in 1995. Penang saw the collapse of the DAP's attempt to take over the state, with Lim Kit Siang himself defeated by the future chief minister Koh Tsu Koon. Terengganu similarly saw the humiliating defeat of the opposition, with PAS holding on to one seat and S46 being totally wiped out. By 1993 PAS had promulgated the controversial *hudud* (Islamic criminal law) legislation in Kelantan, but this seemingly had little effect on winning Muslim votes in Terengganu or across the country in general. As summarized by Chin (1996, p. 408), the most important factor explaining the BN's stellar performance in 1995 was its capture of the middle ground, the lack of issues exploitable by the opposition and the latter's poor organization and lack of cohesion.

CONCLUSION

UMNO's continued hegemony, Mahathir's autocratic and authoritarian style, along with his purging of opponents to achieve his "grand vision" of economic modernism for Malays and Malaysians, actually led to less attention being focused on Malay political supremacy. Instead, much energy was devoted to the use of the political party as a critical vehicle to attain economic goals. Party capitalism gave rise to economic cronyism and rent seeking, which benefited the upper echelons of the bourgeoisie and the would-be bourgeois class of Malays and non-Malays. Paradoxically, this was the means that ensured "increasing returns" and political dividends for UMNO and other BN political parties, or perhaps one should say for their leaders and their cronies. This elite-based political economy of party capitalism succeeded in stabilizing ethnic relations since the economic spoils saw some level of ethnic distribution with a significant number of non-bumiputera also becoming business cronies. They in turn were forced to lubricate electoral politics through their financial support of BN political parties. Needless to say there was little "trickle-down effect" to the political masses who were usually content to receive political doles and instantaneous development projects just prior to elections. However, the mixing of business and politics had its perils for the national economy, as we have noted above, and possibly for the political longevity of the ruling coalition as well, as we shall see in the next chapter. It led to a major revolt against the Mahathir leadership, causing a further splintering of the Malay bloc. A unified Malay bloc and a low level of complaints from the non-Malays had always been the factors behind the path-dependent electoral successes of the BN. As was shown in the 1995 electoral outcome, these two factors were the main levers that not only lifted Mahathir's status to that of an "uncrowned king" of Malaysia (Wain 2009) but had kept alive the BN's consociational model of politics, by mediating communalism through a fine balancing act of preventing coalition partners from gravitating to the (religious and racial) extremes and ensuring optimal returns to each player on the team, without zero-sum outcomes or losses for any specific partner. This seemed like executing a near-impossible strategy, which was nevertheless realized through the largesse of party capitalism and the tried and tested deployment of a stratagem of mediated communalism. The success of mediated communalism now depended on the use of money politics to lubricate the party machine. The most important driver of this path-dependent success for the BN was a powerful and rich UMNO helmed by an unassailable Malay leadership in the form of the singular and formidable figure of Mahathir Mohamad. However, this rosy situation nearly came to an end with the onset of *reformasi* in the late 1990s. The next chapter will analyse this final phase of the Mahathir years.

APPENDIX 6A: MAJOR POLITICAL EVENTS, 1986–88

1986

In November the government introduced amendments to the 1972 Official Secrets Act (OSA) to the effect of the imposition of a mandatory one-year jail term (to a maximum of fourteen years) and with fines of up to RM10,000 on anyone revealing official materials obtained from government sources. The National Union of Journalists (NUJ) collected 36,000 signatures to petition against the amendments. A plethora of human rights, consumer and environmental NGOs — such as Aliran, CAP and EPSM — opposed the amendments, along with the DAP and PAS.

1987

On 21 May sixteen people in Singapore are arrested under the ISA in Operation Spectrum. The so-called "Marxist Conspiracy" was allegedly masterminded by Tan Wah Piow, a former law student in political exile in the UK, studying at Oxford University, and spearheaded by Vincent Cheng, a full-time Catholic lay worker with the Justice and Peace Commission of Singapore. By the end of the year, six more arrests were made, bringing the total to twenty-two. Some writers have suggested a strong connection between this action by the Singapore government and Malaysia's Operasi Lalang in targeting leftists (Jomo 1988).

In early October the appointment of a hundred non-Mandarin speaking senior assistants to vernacular Chinese primary schools sparked a storm of protest. On 11 October the MCA, DAP and Gerakan joined a protest organized by Dong Jiao Zong (Chinese educationists) in a two-thousand-strong gathering at the Thian Hou Temple in Kuala Lumpur.

On 18 October an AWOL Malay soldier with an M16 rifle killed one person and wounded two others in a rampage in the Chow Kit Road area in Kuala Lumpur.

A rally of ten thousand was organized on 17 October by UMNO at the TPCA stadium to criticize Chinese politicians on their stand on the senior assistants issue. The police cancelled another mass rally to celebrate UMNO's 41st anniversary scheduled for 1 November at the Merdeka Stadium, with an expected attendance of half a million UMNO supporters.

On 27 October the police began its detention of 106 people under the ISA and revoked the publishing licences of two dailies, *The Star* and the *Sin Chew Jit Poh*, and two weeklies, *The Sunday Star* and *Watan*. Among those arrested were the DAP's Lim Kit Siang and Karpal Singh, the MCA's Chan Kit Chee, PAS's Ibrahim Ali and Halim Arshat, Dong Jiao Zong's Lim Fong Seng, and civil activists Chandra Muzaffar and Kua Kia Soong. Initial arrests saw 37 from political parties, 23 from social movements and 37 other individuals (Saravanamuttu 1987, p. 68). Those arrested included human rights activists, trade unionists, environmentalists, Chinese educational activists, academics and Muslim converts to Christianity. Most were released after the sixty-day remand period, but 33 were forced to serve a two-year detention and were adopted as prisoners of conscience by Amnesty International.

During the December 1987 sitting of Parliament, amendments were made to two acts giving them more bite. With the changes, the Printing Presses and Publishing Act required all periodicals and newspapers to apply for new licences annually rather than simply to renew them, while amendments to the Police Act made it almost impossible to hold any public meeting without police permission. Contravening these acts could see offenders receiving jail terms or stiff fines.

1988

On 4 February, Justice Harun Hashim of the Kuala Lumpur High Court ruled that UMNO was an illegal political party because it had thirty unregistered branches. The case was the result of twelve UMNO members earlier pressing charges that the 24 April 1987 UMNO elections were faulty or rigged. As a result of the court ruling, Razaleigh, backed by the Tunku and Hussein Onn, attempted to form a new party called "UMNO Malaysia", but this action was rejected by the Registrar of Societies, which instead allowed (with no reason given) the formation of "UMNO Baru" (New UMNO) by Mahathir and his supporters.

Razaleigh and his group were later allowed (only on 3 June 1989) to register Semangat 46 after their first choice of name "UMNO 46" was turned down.

On 31 May the Lord President of the Supreme Court, Tun Mohamed Salleh Abas, was suspended, allegedly for dabbling in politics. Later, on 6 July, five Supreme Court judges who were supportive of him were also suspended.

Tan Sri Hamid Omar, appointed as Acting Lord President, sat along with two retired judges from Singapore and Sri Lanka in a Tribunal constituted by the government to hear proceedings on the impeachment of Tun Salleh Abas as head of Malaysia's Supreme Court. Salleh Abas was accused of meddling in politics in fixing a full panel of Supreme Court judges to hear the appeal against UMNO Baru's registration. The tribunal held its hearings in camera and found Salleh Abas guilty of misconduct. On 8 August he was dismissed as Lord President (Crouch 1991, pp. 14–141).

Notes

1. Mahathir was particularly bitter after he lost his seat in the 1969 general election and carried out a campaign to discredit the Tunku through an infamous *surat layang* (poison pen letter) in which he alluded to the Tunku's association with poker-playing Chinese cronies, but mostly attacked him for being responsible for the 13 May riots and called for his resignation because "the Malays hated him" (Wain 2009, p. 26 and Von Vorys 1976, pp. 372–74). Musa Hitam decided to take a break from politics and went to complete a master's degree at Sussex University, UK (Means 1991, p. 84).

2. Malaysia's sixth premier Najib Razak, who was embroiled in a major financial scandal at the time of writing, could well have surpassed Mahathir in terms of the sums of money involved in alleged malfeasance, although Najib's actions may not be "party capitalism" per se as it is not clear what the funds secured were used for. Certainly, a good sum was alleged to have been used for the general election of 2013, but large sums were alleged to have gone to personal accounts and companies of individuals and foreign entities (see Chapter 10).

3. See Gale (1981) for an in-depth analysis of the development of these public enterprises during the first decade of the NEP. See also his study of the MCA-linked Multi-Purpose Holdings (Gale 1985).

4. See Gomez (1990, 1991, 1994, 1999, 2002) for comprehensive reviews of the distribution of rents to well-connected businessmen. Also see particularly Chapter 5 of Gomez and Jomo (1997, pp. 117–65), which provides details and case studies of the rise of the new Malay and non-Malay capitalists under Mahathir.

5. See Fields's major work (1995). See also Saravanamuttu (2009) for a brief exposition of party capitalism in Malaysia. The parallels between UMNO and the Kuomintang (KMT) are amazingly stark, especially when one reads Fields (2002) on how the KMT's corrupt politics caused the first electoral turnover in March 2000 after fifty years of KMT rule with the election of the Democratic Progressive Party's (DPP) Chen Shui Bian as president. Ironically, Chen was jailed for bribery subsequently and the KMT was back in power since 2008, but again lost the presidency in 2016.

6. As elucidated by Fields (1995), this stipulation is found in Article 4 of the KMT's 1988 party charter.

7. Japan is also a prime example of the melding of business and politics. See, for example, the work of Langdon (1967). Mahathir was likely to have been influenced by such books as Chalmers Johnson's *MITI and the Japanese Miracle* (1982) and Ezra Vogel's *Japan as Number One* (1979).

8. It wasn't that Mahathir had it easy with the introduction of these policies. There was a torrent of criticism about looking to Japan as a model. The Chinese business community was probably uneasy about this. Many had not forgotten Japan's cruel occupation of Malaya during World War II, while intellectuals saw the copying of Japan as choosing a model of economic development that was deeply flawed. See Jomo (1989) for a collection of critiques on the Look East Policy.

9. See Saravanamutu (2010, pp. 186–89). The other model Mahathir couldn't or wouldn't cite was of course Singapore. For an exposition of "Malaysia Incorporated" as a corporatist economic model and strategy, see Jomo (2014).

10. The book most relevant as documentation of party capitalism — although the concept is not used by the authors — is *Malaysia's Political Economy: Politics, Patronage and Politics* by Gomez and Jomo (1997). Political economist Terence Gomez, as noted earlier, produced the most extensive work on the subject; see, particularly, Gomez (1990, 1994, 2004).

11. The late Barry Wain (formerly editor of the *Asian Wall Street Journal*) was writer-in-residence at ISEAS before his untimely death in February 2013. His book on Mahathir illuminates the many aspects of "party capitalism" that have been mentioned here (although he does not use the term).

12. Observers of the Malaysian scene will immediately recognize these names as individuals at the commanding heights of the economy, in businesses

ranging from banking, airlines, heavy industry, shipping, telecommunications to media. Two of the individuals mentioned, Mirzan and Mokhzani, are Mahathir's sons. Halim Saad, Wan Azmi and Tajudin Ramli were known to be "Daim's boys". For case studies of some of these individuals, see Gomez and Jomo (1997, *passim*, and especially pp. 138–65).

13. In 2015, Mahathir, in his efforts to bring down Najib Razak for his egregious personal accumulation of money for elections (see Chapter 10), confirmed that such an UMNO political fund existed. Mahathir claimed that he used only about RM10 million for each election and that the UMNO slush fund was controlled by three trustees, two having to agree to any use of the money. He also revealed that when he left office in 2003, there was some RM200 million in cash and RM1.2 billion in assets and all of this was handed over to his successor Abdullah Badawi. See <http://www.freemalaysiatoday.com/category/nation/2015/08/03/mahathir-no-huge-election-funds-in-my-personal-account/> (accessed 9 September 2015).

14. Rumour had it that "the loot" that Team A got from the old UMNO's deregistration ranged from RM5 to 6 billion (Wain 2009, p. 131).

15. In an interview with Encik Tawfik Tun Ismail at The Curve, Kota Damansara, on 23 February 2013, the son of Tun Ismail — who is a former UMNO MP of Pontian, Johor — he told me that money politics had become rife in Mahathir's tenure. He intimated that he had been unable to nominate a candidate for the Pontian division because of the heavy use of money for other candidates. He said he was concerned that UMNO "had become like a religious organization" where a circle of persons undemocratically re-elect themselves instead of being the "political confederation" that it used to be.

16. Perwaja Holdings Bhd had defaulted on its loans and has been listed as a PN17 company (company in financial distress) since November 2013. Since 2009, losses ballooned to RM1.2 billion for the eighteen months ending 30 June 2014, and its operations in Kemaman were suspended in August 2013. *The Edge*, 5 May 2015, p. 9.

17. Mahathir claimed that the sum he lost could not have exceeded RM10 billion. After the publication of Wain's book he had reserved the right to take the author to court but in the end he never did. See <http://www.thestar.com.my/story/?file=%2F2009%2F12%2F25%2Fnation%2F20091225141245&sec=nation> (accessed 4 April 2015) and <http://www.themalaysianinsider.com/malaysia/article/dr-m-says-barry-wain-can-say-what-he-wants> (accessed 4 April 2015).

18. A senior Singapore diplomat who served in Malaysia at that time intimated to me how he witnessed the inexorable ascendancy of Anwar, whom he

admired not just for his oratory ability and charisma but also for his ability to galvanize political support. Anwar had used ABIM to set up a secretariat for 115 NGOs in their campaign against the Societies Act amendments in 1981. The amendments sought to make it difficult or impossible for NGOs to challenge or criticize public policies unless they were registered as "political" entities and not just "friendly" associations (Saravanamuttu 1989, p. 246). It was soon after this high point of Anwar's social activism that he joined the Mahathir government.

19. Mahathir's own revisiting of his ideas is somewhat brief (Mahathir 2011, pp. 229–54). He does say that Tun Razak told the drafting panel of the NEP to read *The Malay Dilemma* and broadly that he still has not abandoned the original ideas therein, but the Malays today face yet another presumably deeper dilemma: "Telan mati mak, luah mati bapak" (If you swallow your mother dies, if you spit, your father dies), namely: to persist with the NEP would obstruct self-reliance but to take it away would weaken their political position. I read on but found neither a proposed resolution to this new dilemma nor a rehashing of *The Challenge* in Mahathir's memoirs.

20. Musa Hitam who said he had "irreconcilable differences" with Mahathir was apparently accused of being "disloyal", which Musa said was "a terrible blow to my dignity and credibility" (Wain 2009, p. 62). It is not clear whether Musa's handling (as acting premier) of the Memali incident of 19 November 1985 which resulted in the deaths of 14 Muslims of a radical sect and 4 policemen had anything to do with his resignation, but as the late K. Das (1986) suggested, the whole event had become the point of departure for a critique of the Mahathirian style of leadership. Das surmised that Mahathir was at the nadir of his popularity, among Malaysians of all stripes. Apparently the editors of the *New Straits Times* had spiked a cartoon by the well-loved cartoonist Lat. The cartoonist drew four men on camels crossing the desert calling plaintively, "Musa, Musa" as they espied a set of lonely footprints in front of them (Das 1986, p. 122). Many people today would love to see that cartoon!

21. Malek also identified "militant" and "moderate" wings within Group A, with the former wanting the 30 per cent target to be achieved quickly, at least by 1990, and even raised, while the other wing was content with a more flexible timeline. See Khoo 2002, pp. 69–71, who also suggests that an earlier assessment based on a consultancy of UMNO politics (1977) may have been wrong about Razaleigh being the more aggressive NEP advocate.

22. I draw from the narrative provided by Means (1991, pp. 243–48).

23. The authors used a triangulation method of assessing this through the voter turnout (65.1 per cent), a 10 per cent swing against the BN and an estimate of the Indian vote, thus calculating that Shahrir's Chinese vote was about 80 per cent and Malay vote 70 per cent.

24. Intellectuals who participated in the NECC included such names as Professor Ungku Aziz, Professor Syed Hussein Alatas, P.G. Lim, Chandra Muzaffar (president of Aliran), K.S. Jomo (University of Malaya lecturer and social critic), Lim Teck Ghee (also from the University of Malaya and "MCA think tank") and many others. See Means (1991, p. 266).

7

REFORMASI AND NEW POLITICS
Constituting an Alternative Coalition
in the 1999 General Election

By the time of Malaysia's 10th general election of 1999, there had
been two major ruptures in the hegemonic Malay bloc led by UMNO,
which I have already discussed in previous chapters. The first was the
Tunku's departure from politics after the 13 May riots and the rise of
UMNO's young second echelon of leaders who counted among them
the irrepressible Mahathir Mohamad, while the second was the 1987
crisis causing the UMNO split and the formation of two new parties, a
New UMNO party (UMNO Baru) and the Spirit of 46 party (Semangat
46). This chapter will deal with the third rupture of the Malay bloc
caused by the imbroglio around Anwar Ibrahim that erupted in 1998
after his removal from UMNO and as deputy premier. It is interesting
to note that all three of these ruptures involved Mahathir. There was
great anticipation after this third major rupture, especially in intellectual
circles, that such a major crack in the hegemonic edifice of UMNO
would augur a real change in Malaysian politics, and much hope was
thus placed on a regime change of sorts to be brought about after the

1999 general election. Malaysia had arrived, as it were, at a crucial political crossroads with the eruption of the Reformasi Movement after Anwar's sacking and what many saw as his unjust incarceration on the charge of sodomy. In terms of the larger framing of Malaysian politics, it also seemed an opportune time for social activists to work towards debunking the debilitating model of ethnically overdetermined politics. Indeed, as noted in the previous chapter, the New Economic Policy (NEP, 1971–90) had been brought to a close with the implementation of the National Development Policy (NDP, 1990–2000). The latter, along with the Vision 2020 policy, generated much anticipation that multi-ethnic *new politics* would take centre stage, especially when the government's stated principal goal was the creation of a *Bangsa Malaysia* (Malaysian nation).[1]

However, as also noted in the previous chapter, the BN's electoral strategy remained one of mediated communalism, allowing for path-dependent success in the elections of 1990 and 1995 in spite of the major split within the UMNO ruling bloc in 1987. It was thus entirely possible that the BN would ride over the Anwar crisis just as it had over the Team A–Team B split of 1987 by continuing its time-tested strategy. Moreover, the BN's brand of politics appeared to have been consolidated, with its largest ever haul of the popular vote in the 1995 election. In fact in 1994 in Sabah an UMNO-led coalition displaced the multi-ethnic Parti Bersatu Sabah (PBS), which had been in power since 1985. In Sarawak the Parti Bansa Dayak Sarawak (PBDS), which had constituted the principal opposition party in the state since 1987, returned to the BN Sarawak fold in 1994.[2] An Islamic movement, the Darul Arqam — a source of threat for UMNO, with its rural influence, independent source of income and rapid growth of Malay followers in the early 1990s — was swiftly dismantled in 1995 after its leader was arrested under the Internal Security Act (ISA). And in 1996 Semangat 46 dissolved itself and its leaders rejoined UMNO. The familiar "consociational" ethnic pattern of politics had persisted. Meanwhile, the country had experienced uninterrupted economic growth (Loh 2000a). The BN's hegemony and, concomitantly, Mahathir's grip on power seemed assured until the breaking of the Asian financial crisis, which by chance also coincided with the Anwar affair.

With hindsight, one could say that there were two possible scenarios that could follow from the Anwar crisis. The first was that its political and economic ramifications might have brought about a genuine change in electoral politics with the rise and stabilization of a new alternative alliance of political forces pitted against the old regime of the BN. Given the severe crisis faced by UMNO, the new alternative coalition could have used this to its advantage. The second scenario was that the BN's proven electoral formula of success and path-dependent strength of its established multi-ethnic institutions and grass-roots support would still carry the day. We know the answer to the question as to which scenario prevailed, though in November 1999 this was far from clear to those observing the political imbroglio of the time. Thus, it would be germane to delve into the political developments on the eve of the 1999 election since these developments generated a new path dependence of oppositional politics based on alternative multi-ethnic support which over a longer period of time would yield substantive electoral dividends for parties opposed to the BN.

Following the unceremonious dismissal of Anwar Ibrahim as deputy prime minister and his sensational political trial for "corruption" and sexual misdemeanour,[3] Malays became instantly divided, sparking the Reformasi Movement and the birth of a new political party. The National Justice Party (or Parti Keadilan Nasional, PKN),[4] launched in 1999 to embody the aspirations and ideals of Anwar and his supporters, immediately attracted many Malays and non-Malays disaffected by the excesses of the Mahathir regime. Islamists and democrats also pounced on the opportunity to throw their lot behind the Reformasi Movement, which had the ultimate object of unseating the increasingly unpopular Mahathir from office. Social activists and their NGOs also got into the fray, openly espousing *reformasi* ideals.

The political ferment that followed was truly exceptional in that it saw the first serious grass-roots challenge to UMNO within the Malay community, and, as we have noted, the third crack in the edifice of Malay hegemony. The challenge of S46, led by Tengku Razaleigh Hamzah in the late-1980s, hardly affected politics in the same populist fashion. Most importantly, *reformasi* had led to the participation of many new forces of civil society in political developments and electoral politics quite unlike what had occurred in the past. The political mobilization from the Reformasi Movement was initially housed under two umbrella organizations called Gagasan and Gerak.

Later, with the formation of a new party, set up by Anwar's supporters, the PKN, it was logical for PAS and the DAP to join forces with the PKN to bring about the birth of the Barisan Alternatif (BA, or Alternative Front), with the support of large sections of civil society already galvanized under Gagasan and Gerak. The emergence of the BA as an alternative power-sharing mode was itself a major event, given that it was an amalgamation of all the significant opposition political parties on the Peninsula, and to a lesser degree of parties from Sarawak.[5]

The prime minister was forced by statutory strictures to call for a general election before August 2000 against the backdrop of these unfavourable developments for the BN. Despite his prevarication about various plausible election dates, most pundits knew that with the economic recovery of 1999 he was unlikely to drag the decision into 2000. With Parliament dissolved on 11 November, and a hung budget, the Election Commission went ahead to set 29 November as polling day. Before we analyse the 1999 electoral outcome, it will be necessary to discuss two antecedent socio-political developments — the new Malay middle class and the crisis of party capitalism — that had spurred the rise of *new politics* and the Reformasi Movement.

NEW MALAY MIDDLE CLASS

Hardly any discussion of Malaysian politics, post-1969, can ignore the centrality of the NEP as the dominant discourse. In the 1970s and 80s the implementation of the NEP proceeded virtually unchallenged save for a few opposition voices such as those of the DAP or the PSRM which stressed equity for the needy regardless of ethnic background. The DAP found its natural constituency in the disaffected Chinese working and middle classes and won its laurels as the main opposition party in Parliament. The acquiescence by other non-Malay parties to the NEP agenda meant that "consociational" inter-ethnic politics through mediated communalism was always the order of the day for the BN. After the famous victory of the newly formed BN in 1974, politics of the NEP ruled the roost, and not until after 1987, when the UMNO split occurred, was there any hint of the prospect of some change. The opposition forces performed well in 1990, having formed a two-part coalition model to that of the BN's, but because of this imperfect alternative the BN consequently consolidated its hegemony in the landslide victory of the 1995 general election. This victory came at a period of high economic growth, coinciding with the introduction of the NDP and the strategy of deregulating the economy and privatizing the public sector. Few people expected that the various thrusts of the NEP, which allowed for bumiputera affirmative action, would be sidelined in the NDP or any successor policy.

In hindsight, the NEP had turned out to be less detrimental to non-Malay constituencies than had been anticipated. This was particularly so since various amendments had been introduced to NEP-derived policies, among others the Industrial Coordination Act had been greatly softened as noted earlier. The NEP over time arguably had the twin effects of creating a nascent bumiputera commercial and industrial community (BCIC) and a Malay middle class.[6] By the end of the 1980s, with NEP thrusts firmly in place, bumiputera had come to control some twenty per cent of the corporate sector, and Malaysia had become the developing world's sixth largest exporter of manufactures.

It was in this climate of the success of the government's social engineering that Mahathir launched the NDP and Vision 2020 policy. It was timely for Mahathir to announce his vision for a doubling of Malaysia's GDP every ten years, that is from RM115 billion in 1990 to RM920 billion by 2020, at an average growth rate of 7 per cent per annum. The main economic features of the NDP were:

a. A diversified and balanced economy with a mature and widely based industrial sector, a modern and mature agricultural sector and an efficient and productive and equally mature services sector.

b. An economy that is technologically proficient, fully able to adapt, innovate and invent, moving in the direction of higher levels of technology, and driven by brain-power, skills, diligence, knowledge, escalating productivity.

c. An economy that is self-reliant, sustained by exemplary work ethic, quest for excellence, characterized by low inflation and that is subjected to the full discipline and rigor of market forces.

(Mahathir 1991, pp. 8–9)

Until 1997, many of these goals did not seem overly flamboyant. The NDP stressed growth rather than just ethnic wealth redistribution, and Mahathir introduced a slew of economic policies guaranteed to assuage non-Malay opinion while seeming to not threaten Malay political pre-eminence. These policies were at the same time in tune with the neo-liberal thrust of globalism and dovetailed well with Malaysia's trajectory of industrial growth under the NDP. The policies introduced included deregulation, privatization and a general liberalization of education allowing for the burgeoning of myriad private colleges and twinning university programmes. This satisfied the countless non-Malay students who were denied tertiary education because of the tight quota system practised by public universities.

I would also argue that the NDP was consonant with the evolving character of Malay politics and the rise of a new Malay middle class. As had been argued in a number of articles about middle class politics (Saravanamuttu 1992, 2001, 2003, 2009, 2013), what ultimately provided the conditions for a definitive step in the direction of Malay reformist politics was the rise of the urban-based middle class Malays. The Reformasi Movement was the needed catalyst to activate a major behavioural shift in Malay politics among large sections or significant fractions of the Malay middle class. By the late 1990s a new trajectory in Malay politics had seemingly emerged which was not averse to social reforms that ran counter to any explicit race-based agendas. This can be shown through a path-dependent development of Malay reform politics. Thus, while it may be true that UMNO-oriented politics, anchored on Malay supremacy and NEP-driven policies, had for decades generated increasing returns for the ruling BN coalition through manufacturing Malay-bumiputera majority consensus, by the late 1990s this was beginning to run its course. Moreover, party capitalism as the source of UMNO's wealth, which had superseded the older route of Malay-bumiputera mobility through the NEP, was already fraying by the time of the Asian financial crisis. The dichotomy of the Malay-bumiputera "shareholders" (beneficiaries of "party capitalism") versus "technocrats" (those benefitting from the NEP per se) had become too apparent, with the new Malay middle class becoming more complex and too diverse to be easy pickings for UMNO politicians. A large section of the Malay community saw Anwar's sacking as patently unfair, and this precipitated the eruption of their open anger towards UMNO. Mahathir's obsession of creating a new class of wealthy Malays may also have had its unintended nemesis, that of a countervailing class of reform-minded, democratically oriented Malays. This rupture in UMNO-dominated Malay politics ushered in a significant dip in political returns to the BN as one of the conditions in its path-dependent success, that of Malay majority support, appeared to diminish.

The construction of a Malay middle class does not imply a monolithic entity; indeed, class fractions obviously exist within the Malay middle class, which is itself a subset of a larger Malaysian middle class. Recent survey research shows this to be the case.[7] However, as part of the new Malaysian middle class and as bearers of status, skills and professional qualifications, we can infer that the Malay middle class as a whole would have shared social and political inclinations which were pertinent to *reformasi* ideas and ideals. It is further suggested that class may have become as significant as ethnicity as a political cleavage of Malay politics by the time of the *reformasi* years (Weiss 2006). My calculations showed that in 1988 the middle class comprised about 36 per cent of the total workforce, or some 2.2 million people. The middle class would have grown to about 45.2 per cent of the working population by 1998. By 1998 bumiputera formed the majority in all categories of the middle class except for the managerial and sales categories.

The various studies I undertook showed that reform-minded Malay middle class actors were already much in evidence by the 1990s. I will provide more analysis on the impact of the Malay middle class on electoral politics in the later section of this chapter. For now, let us turn to party capitalism and the crisis it sparked in the late Mahathir years.

PARTY CAPITALISM IN CRISIS

The élan of BN politics with its apogee of the 1995 elections was dealt a severe blow by the 1997 financial crisis, from which it failed to recover sufficiently by the time of the 1999 election. However, as alluded to above, the cleverly orchestrated economic recovery of 1999 did provide the necessary window of opportunity for the BN government to seal a quick electoral win by the end of that year. This was achieved only after considerable social and economic upheaval in the preceding two years. The impact of the financial crisis on Malaysia can be summarized by the facts and figures presented below:

1. The Ringgit depreciated from RM2.52 vis-à-vis the USD on 1 July 1997 to RM3.53 by end of the same month, before reaching an all-time low of RM4.88 in early January 1998. It was subsequently fixed at RM3.80 on 2 September 1998 along with the introduction of other capital controls.

2. The KLSE [Kuala Lumpur Stock Exchange] Composite Index fell by 73% and market capitalization decreased by 74% between 1 July 1997 and 2 September 1998. In the banking sector, NPLs (non-performing loans) rose to 11.4% by August 1998.

3. Real output of the economy contracted at an unprecedented rate of 6.7% in 1998. The inflation rate rose 5.3% and the rate of unemployment to 3.9%. The federal government account registered a deficit for the first time since 1993.

4. External debt also increased although the current account saw a surplus because of reduced domestic demand causing a drop in imports.

(Mid-Term Review of the Seventh Plan 1999)

The Malaysian government's initial response to the crisis — and especially Mahathir's own response — was one of denial. Several direct steps were then taken to insulate the domestic interest rate from capital mobility. The offshore, over-the-counter CLOB (Central Limit Order Book) in Singapore was stopped to prevent illegal short selling of Malaysian shares. The step was also taken of banning the short selling of a hundred blue-chip stocks to shore up share prices. This was followed by the announcement of capital controls on 1 September 1998.[8]

Although most of the capital controls were later removed, the Malaysian ringgit was pegged at a fixed rate to the U.S. dollar (RM3.8 to US$1) for the next seven years. The Mahathir government claimed that the various measures introduced made the difference in Malaysia's economic performance compared with the other crisis-stricken East Asian economies. With this action, and in tandem with various other fiscal and monetary measures, Malaysia avoided an IMF rescue package. By the middle of 1999 the Malaysian authorities were already trumpeting that the recovery was more than evident, with the stock market showing signs of new life, indicated by the KLSE-CI breaching 800 points by August after a low of about 260 points at the nadir of the crisis. By August, regular monthly surpluses in the current account had also boosted Malaysia's international reserves to US$31 billion, good for seven months of imports. Although 1998 saw a decline in GDP of minus 6.7 per cent, growth recovered in subsequent years to as much as 8.5 per cent by 2000, even as global economic conditions again brought growth to a near standstill at 0.4 per cent in 2001.[9]

An important measure to deal with the meltdown was the setting up of an asset management corporation (Danaharta) in March 1998 to undertake restructuring and re-capitalization of the banking system. A "special purpose vehicle", Danamodal was also set up to mop up NPLs and generally to source funding for re-capitalization of companies and to improve liquidity. Malaysia's central bank, the Bank Negara, which supervized both bodies, continued to restructure the banking sector and to cushion debt-ridden companies by keeping interest rates low and by injecting liquidity through measures like issuing bonds. Such economic recovery as was achieved was carefully crafted to insulate certain corporations and corporate figures from suffering the adverse effects of the financial meltdown. The Mahathir government was able to draw for this purpose on its various "cash cows" such as the national oil corporation, Petronas, the Employees' Provident Fund and the Muslim Pilgrimage Fund (Tabung Haji).

Petronas's most controversial acquisition occurred at the high point of the crisis, namely a RM1.8 billion controlling stake in Malaysian International Shipping Corp (MISC), the country's largest shipper. However, this move was merely a precursor to MISC's buy-up of Konsortium Perkapalan, the ailing shipping firm of Mirzan Mahathir, the prime minister's eldest son. MISC paid Konsortium Perkapalan RM836 million in cash and also assumed RM1.2 billion ringgit of its debt. At the same time, Petronas raised its stake in MISC to 62 per cent to allow it to undertake the Konsortium acquisition. In August 1999 the oil company also bought a 27.2 per cent stake in national carmaker Perusahaan Otomobil Nasional Bhd, Proton, at a cost of

RM1 billion (*New Straits Times*, 7 August 1999). Proton was burdened with heavy debts, although its distribution and sales arm, Edaran Otomobil Nasional, had been reaping profits.[10] Anwar, who was still finance minister, was said to have objected strongly to these moves, but Mahathir's will prevailed.

To a great extent these bailouts were actions of damage control to deal with the excesses of party capitalism of the Mahathir period, which was now clearly in a deep crisis. The financial meltdown dealt a near-lethal blow to this party-driven structuration of business and politics and effectively temporarily put to rest Mahathir's "grand vision" (Khoo 1992) for the Malays and for Malaysia. While handled rather well on one level, the measures taken to cope with the meltdown failed to address the fundamental problems that had been unmasked; namely, gnawing cronyism deep within the economy. In fire fighting the meltdown, the Mahathir government had clearly protected favoured businessmen and companies from collapse, thereby giving further life to policies that had largely been responsible for the financial crisis in the first place. A classic illustration of this would be the problems associated with the national airline, MAS. Parcelled out in boom times in 1994 to UMNO-linked private ownership, it was repossessed by the government in early 2001 with a debt of RM2.7 billion, but with executive chairman Tajuddin Ramli disposing his 29 per cent stake to the government at a premium share price of RM8. The market price of MAS shares at the time was RM3.68. In a restructuring exercise in early 2002, it was revealed that the MAS debt had ballooned to RM9.2 billion. The commercial crime division of the Malaysian police then investigated Tajuddin Ramli for alleged irregularities to do with cargo operations involving a German-based handler controlled by the erstwhile chairman. After a court case that dragged on for years, Tajuddin Ramli was eventually let off the hook by Danaharta and his liabilities absolved, but not before he took the opportunity to say that Mahathir and Daim had directed him to purchase MAS, obviously in the interests of the ruling party.[11]

The 1997 financial crisis also brought to a head differences between Mahathir and his deputy Anwar Ibrahim, particularly over how the crisis should have been managed. Anwar, who was then finance minister, severely cut government expenditure and allowed interest rates to float upwards. Privatized "mega projects" like the Bakun HEP

Project, a linear city perched over one of Kuala Lumpur's rivers, a railway linking the central station to Kuala Lumpur International Airport in Sepang, a highway connecting Peninsular Malaysia's hill resorts, and the like, were shelved. Calls to bail out Malaysian companies facing bankruptcies were also rejected by Anwar. But Mahathir considered these measures advocated by Anwar to be no different from the IMF's response to the crisis, and took the view that the crisis was not a result of domestic shortcomings. Worse, Anwar, by refusing to assist the bumiputera corporations, was allowing the gains secured under the NEP, specifically, the BCIC, to come unstuck. Jomo (2001) has advanced the argument that while Anwar approved tighter fiscal and monetary measures in late 1997 in line with IMF recommendations, by June 1998 he had increased public spending, especially to provide for credit and investment in food and agriculture, and also sought to increase liquidity and banking margins.[12] In contrast to Anwar's actions, a different set of policies focusing attention on how to deal with foreign manipulation of the Malaysian economy on the one hand and on bailing out Malaysian corporations via restructuring, debt relief and access to new credit on the other were proposed by the National Economic Action Council, headed by former finance minister Daim Zainuddin.

In June 1998, when the UMNO Youth leader[13] associated with Anwar launched an attack on cronyism and nepotism at the UMNO annual general assembly, Mahathir hit back openly at Anwar and his supporters. Anwar's position in government became untenable and he was ousted on 2 September, the same day the government had pegged the ringgit to the U.S. dollar and introduced capital controls.

NEW POLITICS

Anwar's sacking from government, expulsion from UMNO, subsequent arrest, prosecution, sentencing of six years' imprisonment and his black eye, caused from a beating by the Inspector-General of Police while in detention, galvanized opposition supporters into a mass movement of NGOs and political parties, earning the moniker of the "Rainbow Coalition" (Khoo 2000, p. 174). The eruption of public rallies and street demonstrations in support of Anwar occurred with the participation of

Malaysia's urban middle class actors as well as civil society activists across a wide spectrum of Malaysian society and led to the emergence of what I have termed *new politics.*

A stated in Chapter 1, the term *new politics* denotes a new modality of engagement rather than an outcome of electoral changes. This new modality denotes an ongoing participatory politics of civil engagement in the public sphere with the objective of valorizing democratic values, human rights, and transparency and accountability of governance over ethnic distributive justice. Importantly, the folklore associated with this *new politics* sparked by the Reformasi Movement has been well documented by writers from the ranks of civil society.[14] As already noted in the introduction to this book, this is the key concept used to explain Malaysia's trajectory of democratization. While historically *new politics* was the offshoot of the Reformasi Movement, it remains as an ongoing process of civil society to achieve comprehensive human rights. However, it does not supersede the stratagem of mediating communalism deployed by political parties or even by NGOs engaged in the electoral process.

Anwar's treatment and the regime's apparent abuse of power were widely criticized in publications, cassettes, videos and numerous websites. The demands of the movement quickly moved beyond concern for Anwar's well-being to issues such as "rule of law", "participatory democracy" and "justice for all" (including for opposition DAP youth leader and Member of Parliament Lim Guan Eng who had been imprisoned while championing the plight of a minor alleged to have been raped by a high-ranking UMNO leader and chief minister of a state). It also called for the repeal of coercive laws like the ISA, for "accountability" and "transparency" in decision-making so as to put an end to "corruption, cronyism and nepotism", and ultimately for Mahathir's resignation. The leaders of the Reformasi Movement first formed ADIL, and, subsequently, the Parti KeADILan Negara (PKN), led by Dr Wan Azizah Ismail, Anwar's wife.

As noted earlier, already cooperating with one another and with various NGOs under the two umbrella organizations Gagasan and Gerak, the PKN and three other opposition parties — PAS, the DAP and the small multi-ethnic socialist-inclined Parti Rakyat Malaysia — formed a new opposition coalition, the Barisan Alternatif (BA) in mid-1999, in anticipation of the elections due by mid-2000. This is not to suggest that the opposition parties had no problems in terms of becoming ideologically compromised by collaborating under the aegis of the BA.

Despite joining the BA, many in PAS continued to maintain a literalist-fundamentalist notion of Islam, and understood the party's goals in terms of furthering Islamic laws, working ultimately towards an Islamic state. This same constituency within PAS would likely reject democracy as a Western imperialist legacy and an extension of secularism, and would tend to be narrow in outlook in contrast to the perspective of Islamic universalism advocated by its more progressive wing. This moderate group, who believed Islam to be fully compatible with democracy, was largely responsible for steering PAS towards support for Anwar's plight and the formation of the BA. In all likelihood it was this group which supported the issues of justice and democracy that the BA highlighted in the run-up to the 1999 polls. Thus, while maintaining its Islamic credentials, important elements within PAS nonetheless supported the democratic momentum.

The DAP, while advocating the deepening of democracy, was plagued by internal schisms, which did not help its image. In 1998–99 several party stalwarts and their supporters who accused Lim Kit Siang and the other DAP national leaders of authoritarianism and nepotism were suspended or expelled. In fact many within the party evidently disagreed with the leadership's decision to cooperate with PAS on the grounds of ideological incompatibility. Even members who had remained within the party after the formation of the BA continually took issue with PAS over the stringent application of Islamic tenets vis-à-vis women, for instance (Tan and Ng 2003). The BA was also beleaguered by internal differences within the newly formed PKN. Erstwhile UMNO leaders and supporters who were now in the party not surprisingly displayed evidence of UMNO-styled exclusivist ethnic politics. For instance, some leaders reportedly disagreed with the BA's proposals towards greater cultural and educational liberalization.

All of this notwithstanding, initially it did seem that the formation of the BA was not merely a "marriage of convenience" among incompatibles. The fact was that there were sufficient numbers of leaders and members of the four major opposition parties subscribing to the new democratic discourse. And through a process of protracted debate and a spirit of give and take, they succeeded in reaching agreement on the allocation of electoral seats, the contents of a joint manifesto "For a Just Malaysia", and even on a "people friendly" alternative budget which would aim to jump-start the economy by increasing public spending for social programmes. It was also significant that the BA component parties cooperated, facilitating an effective joint electoral campaign as evidenced by the presence of other BA leaders and campaign workers in the constituencies contested by any respective BA party. In many cases "joint committees" involving the different BA parties were organized. The BA's cooperative efforts were greatly assisted by the BN's reluctance to conduct the elections earlier. The longer the delay the more time the BA parties had to promote cooperation, not only at different levels — national, state and local — but also over a widening spectrum of issues contained in the "Joint Manifesto" and the alternative budget. It was this apparently deeper and wider character of cooperation that differentiated the BA from previous "electoral pacts" among opposition parties.

Apart from these efforts by the opposition parties, many other independent groups also emerged and made their voices heard as the 1999 elections approached. Although it appeared that they were critical of the BN government and its policies, these new groups and NGOs were probably also addressing their concerns to the BA coalition that was seeking to rule the country. These groups and their espoused campaigns were as follows:

- The "Women's Agenda for Change", which demanded that the laws be enforced to protect women's rights and that these rights be furthered through new legislation;
- The "Citizens Health Initiative", which mobilized Malaysians from all walks of life to oppose the corporatization of the general hospitals and other health services;
- The "People are the Boss", involving Chinese youths who reminded people of the original meaning of democracy and demanded transparency and accountability apart from rule of law;
- The "17-Point" Election Appeals (*Suqiu*), which focused on issues of justice and democracy rather than specific Chinese issues, yet was endorsed by more than two thousand Chinese associations;

- Informal groups of students enrolled in public and private universities and colleges who called for a review of the Universities and University Colleges Act and other coercive laws, and for the formation of an independent Malaysian Students Council;
- Election Watch, or Pemantau, organized by Budi, a new NGO, which rallied forty-odd NGOs to monitor the electoral campaign and subsequently prepared a report of its findings;
- More than fifty thousand signatories of a petition demanding a monthly wage scheme and better working conditions for plantation workers, several busloads of whom converged on Parliament's doorstep to deliver the petition;
- A coalition of NGOs, principally Indian-based, that called for an enquiry into the killing of eighteen Indians (including a pregnant woman) whom the police had suspected were criminals;
- An unprecedented march through the streets of Kuala Lumpur in December 1998 by some three hundred lawyers in support of a colleague who had been found guilty of "contempt of court" for remarks uttered while defending Anwar Ibrahim in court;
- The anti–Bakun Dam coalition formed several years earlier, which now protested the continued resettlement of natives, although the Bakun HEP project had been shelved;
- Another coalition of NGOs protesting the proposed construction of the Selangor Dam which threatened destruction of some pristine forests and required eviction of the Orang Asli (indigenous people) from their traditional settlements;
- A mass campaign led by the consumer organizations to encourage parliamentarians to pass the Consumers Protection Act;
- Artists who parodied the unfolding events and protested against injustices in their compositions and songs, artwork and installations, performances and skits, in verse and in one instance an entire novel;
- Many groups of ordinary Malaysians who had bought into housing development projects which were now stalled on account of the economic crisis protested collectively against the developers and pressured the government to look into their plight.

Taken together these developments showed that Malaysia was in considerable political ferment. Arguably, one could also link the post-1997/98 impulse towards democracy to the burgeoning popular movement of the mid-1980s, which similarly called for "rule of law", "participatory democracy", "accountability", "social justice", et cetera, during an earlier period of economic recession. That momentum was nipped in the bud when more than a hundred activists from opposition parties, trade unions and NGOs were arrested under the ISA during Operasi Lalang in October 1987, which I have already touched on in the last chapter. Indeed, some of these demands for social justice and democracy had been foreshadowed in the struggles of the radical wings of the Independence movement in the 1940s and 1950s, and by the leftist opposition of the 1960s.

What was particularly evident was that the Reformasi Movement brought significant numbers of the Malay middle classes into its ranks. Reflexively supportive of the BN government in times past, many middle-class Malays now considered the BN government, or perhaps more pointedly the Mahathir government, to be *zalim* (repressive), *tidak adil* (unjust), and involved in "cronyism and nepotism". No doubt their change in attitude and involvement in *reformasi* had much to do with the unjust treatment of Anwar, but this change and involvement also moved beyond concern solely for Anwar's plight. And because these Malays had contact with the grass roots through organizations such as ABIM (Angkatan Belia Islam Malaysia, or Malaysian Youth Islamic Movement) and JIM (Jemaah Islah Malaysia), the movement drew in considerable support from the poorer Malays in urban areas and, to some extent, the rural areas. Perhaps because of such popular support and the democratic ferment generally, expectations ran high for the prospects of a change of government at the November 1999 polls.

OUTCOME OF THE 1999 GENERAL ELECTION[15]

Overview of Results

First, remarkably, almost every constituency registered straight fights between the BN and the BA, avoiding the splitting of votes which in the past had benefited the ruling coalition: "Unlike the often hastily patched and intra-opposition bickering that followed the 'electoral pacts' in the past, the opposition demonstrated a remarkable degree of cooperation and resilience in mapping out a united electoral strategy aimed at denying the ruling Barisan Nasional (BN) a two-thirds parliamentary majority" (Hari Singh 2000, p. 33). This also meant that voters were in theory able to make their choices based on the merits of the two sets of manifestos proffered by the two coalitions, as in the normal practice of matured two-party political systems. However, from the outset there was no suggestion that the BA hoped they could form the government. Instead, its campaign was based on the battle cry of denying the BN its customary two-thirds of seats in Parliament.

The common manifesto of the BA was an unprecedented achievement, as the opposition parties in previous elections had never collectively done this. The BA released its manifesto *Towards a Just Malaysia* on 24 October. Anwar's black eye became a symbol of the BN's injustice. The BA also emphasized the unfair jailing of the DAP's Lim Guan Eng for sedition for his efforts to help an underage girl who allegedly was raped by UMNO's erstwhile chief minister Rahim Thambi Chik. The differences between the DAP and PAS over the "Islamic State" were glossed over, with the emphasis on the imperative for dialogue between Muslims and non-Muslims and overcoming the bane of "Malay dominance". A "people's budget" was presented with the emphasis on helping the poor and on the need to assist SMEs, but the BA's campaign was aimed particularly at the cronyism, corruption and the wasteful "mega projects" of the government (Khoo 1999). The BN, for its part, argued for "peace and stability". It put out an unprecedented amount of pro-BN material in all the government-owned or linked newspapers. Mustafa Anuar notes that a survey of English Language dailies found that about 50 per cent of reports on the BN were favourable compared to only 1.6 per cent favourable to the BA (Anuar 2003, p. 55). On the first day of the campaign, 21 November, there were five full-page advertisements in the English and vernacular dailies against the BA, with headlines such as "Don't Let Violence Triumph", "Don't Let Hatred Win", "Don't Let Anarchy Rule", and "Don't let Mob Rule Lead Us" (ibid., p. 60).

But, arguably, the most damaging disadvantage that the BA suffered was the fact that more than 680,000 voters had been disenfranchised.

Table 7.1
Parliamentary Results of the 1999 General Election

	Votes	% votes	Seats	% seats	1995/99
Barisan Nasional (BN)	3,748,511	56.5	147 (+1)[a]	76.6	−19
United Malays National Organisation (UMNO)	—	—	71	37.0	−22
Malaysian Chinese Association (MCA)	—	—	29	15.1	—
Malaysian Indian Congress (MIC)	—	—	7	3.7	—
Parti Gerakan Rakyat Malaysia (Gerakan)	—	—	6	3.1	—
Sarawak Parties			(28)	14.6	
Partai Pesaka Bumiputera Bersatu (PBB)	—	—	10	—	—
Sarawak United People's Party (SUPP)			7	—	—
Sarawak National Party (SNAP)			4	—	—
Parti Bansa Dayak Sarawak (PBDS)			6	—	—
BN Direct			1	—	—
Sabah Parties (other than UMNO)[b]			(6)	3.1	—
Parti Angkatan Keadilan Rakyat (UPKO)			3	—	—
Parti Maju Sabah (SAPP)			2	—	—
Parti Liberal Demokratik Sabah (LDP)			1	—	—
Barisan Alternatif (BA)	2,691,172	40.1	42	21.8	+26
Parti Islam Se-Malaysia (PAS)	994,279	15.0	27	14.1	+19
Democratic Action Party DAP)	830,870	12.5	10	5.2	+1
Parti Keadilan Nasional (PKN)	773,679	11.7	5	2.6	+5
Parti Rakyat Malaysia (PRM)	68,990	1.0	0	0.0	—
State Reform Party	23,354	0.4	0	0.0	—
Other Parties					
Parti Bersatu Sabah (PBS)[c]	143,342	2.2	3	1.6	−5
BERJASA	409	0.0	0	0.0	—
Parti Angkatan Keadilan Insan Malaysia (AKIM)	274	0.0	0	0.0	—
Independents	39,385	0.6	0	0.0	−1
Overall total	6,631,094	100	193	100	

Sources: Configured from Malaysia Factbook <http://malaysiafactbook.com/Malaysian_general_election> (accessed 12 May 2015); <http://warkah.com/elections-for-1999/> (accessed 15 May 2015); Zakaria (1999, pp. 9–10); Weiss 2000, p. 417.
[a] Labuan seat added minus percentage.
[b] UMNO won 11 seats in Sabah.
[c] PBS could not complete the seats negotiation with the BA in Sabah.

From April to May 1999, the Election Commission had carried out a voter registration exercise which had netted 681,120 eligible voters, about three times more than in previous exercises. But the Election Commission ruled that it would only use the roll of registered voters up till January 1999, citing lack of preparation time. It was reasonable to expect that the majority of new voters would have been young, newly eligible voters, who were likely supporters of the Reformasi Movement (Khoo 1999, p. 178; Weiss 2000, p. 421).[16]

In the event, the BN with 56.5 per cent of the vote was able to *manufacture* a two-thirds majority of 76.6 per cent of seats,[17] while the BA garnered a significant 40 per cent of the vote (if the PBS vote was included this would be almost 43 per cent), showing a performance of the opposition quite similar to the 1990 outcome when the BN won 53.4 per cent of the vote.[18] The BN made clean sweeps of parliamentary seats in six states: Sarawak (28 seats), Johor (20), Selangor (17), Pahang (11), Negeri Sembilan (7) and Perlis (3), and recording overwhelming state victories in Perak, winning 20 out of 23 seats (2 to PAS and 1 to the DAP); Sabah, with 17 out of 20 seats (3 to PBS); and Malacca, with 4 out of 5 seats (1 to DAP).

The BN's marginal victories came in Penang, where it won 6 out of 11 seats (4 to DAP and 1 to PKN), and Kuala Lumpur, with 6 out of 10 seats (4 to DAP). However, the BN also suffered significant losses in Kedah, gaining only 7 out of 15 seats (8 to PAS); Kelantan, with just 1 out of 14 (10 to PAS, 3 to PKN; the only BN victory being Tengku Razaleigh's in Gua Musang), and losing all 8 seats in Terengganu to the BA (7 to PAS, 1 to PKN).[19]

Malay Swing to the BA

What was most important for the opposition coalition was the comprehensive takeover of the state of Kelantan (41/43) and the capture of Terengganu (28/32), basically through the stellar performance of the PAS. Four UMNO cabinet ministers lost their seats: Mustapha Mohamad, second finance minister; Megat Junid Megat Ayub, domestic and consumer affairs minister; Annuar Musa, rural development minister; and Hamid Othman, minister in charge of religious affairs in the Office of the Prime Minister. Additionally, six deputy ministers also lost: Tengku Mahmud Mansor, deputy agriculture minister; Idris Jusoh, deputy entrepreneur development minister; and Abu Bakar Daud, deputy science, technology, and environment minister. Of particular interest was Najib Razak's narrow victory in Pekan, with a margin of only 241 votes. A study of the Malay vote by Maznah Mohamad (2003) showed with great clarity the precipitous decline of the Malay vote for UMNO, largely because of the Anwar factor, and that the main beneficiary of this was PAS. Taking the 58 Malay-majority seats with two-thirds or more in Malay voter composition, the author shows that UMNO votes declined in all of these 58 constituencies. The biggest declines occurred in Negri Sembilan (−31 per cent), Selangor (−31 per cent) and Penang (−25 per cent). Of these 58 seats, PAS and PKN took 31 wins, while UMNO managed only 27. Even in Johor, where UMNO won all the seats, its vote share dropped by 11 per cent (ibid., p. 73).

Non-Malay Swing to the BN

In contrast to the Malay vote which swung definitively in favour of the BA, the non-Malay vote swung in the opposite direction, leading to some shocking defeats of DAP stalwarts such as Lim Kit Siang, Karpal Singh and Chen Man Hin. Had it not been for such a pro-BN swing on the part of non-Malays, the ruling coalition may have lost its two-thirds majority (Loh 2003, p. 259). However, despite the BN winning 15 of the 24 Chinese-majority seats, in terms of the overall popular vote, one estimate of the Chinese vote suggests that the DAP still outscored the BN to the tune of 51.3 per cent to 46.5 per cent (Ng 2003, p. 91). The swing factor had a disproportionate effect in Malaysia's first-past-the-post system, which clearly favoured parties like the MCA and Gerakan. In a study of the 67 per cent Chinese-majority seat of Bayan Baru in Penang (Saravanamuttu 2003), the author came to the conclusion that *reformasi* had little to no impact on the non-Malay voter. The BN candidate won in all 23 polling districts of the constituency, even though voters in a 95 per cent Chinese polling district had a significant 47 per cent support for the DAP's Malay candidate against his BN Chinese opponent.[20]

Sarawak and Sabah as "Fixed Deposits"

It is not clear when the term "fixed deposits" first came to be used to characterize the consistent support of voters on the island of Borneo for the BN. The 1999 result was further testimony of this, delivering 42 out of 45 seats contested to the BN. Francis Loh has shown in various studies (1992, 1996, 1997, 2002) how these two states have come to be within the BN's ambit over a period of time owing to the nature of federal–state relations, the discourse and practice of "developmentalism" and through the use of money politics. Suffice it to note here that in 1999 all these elements were at play to ensure the overwhelming performance of the BN parties in Sarawak and Sabah. Money was of great importance to the BN's victories in Sabah, just as it was the PBS's lack of funds which led to its poor performance, along with its failure to endorse the BA's joint manifesto and negotiate the allocation of seats before polling day. In Sarawak, Chin (2003) has highlighted the complexities and the primacy of Melanau-Malay politics there. But it was mostly the BN's deep pockets and development promises, coupled with the DAP's association with the Islamic politics of PAS, that delivered the hundred per cent BN wins. The fixed deposits became even more profitable soon after the 1999 election, when first, in September 2001, BN Sarawak won 60 out of 62 seats in the state election and, second, when the exhausted PBS returned to the fold of the BN in early 2002. This meant that by that year the BN controlled 49 parliamentary seats of the Borneo states, accounting for more than a quarter of all federal seats (Loh 2003, p. 271).

Impact of Social Movements and Social Media

Women's issues also featured prominently in the BA campaign, not only due to the high profile of Anwar's wife, Wan Azizah Wan Ismail, the president of PKN contesting, but because the Women's Agenda for Change (WAC) and Women's Candidacy Initiative (WCI) were given much prominence by civil society (Tan and Ng 2003, pp. 108–26; Weiss 2000, pp. 423–24). The WAC, which had the backing of seventy-six NGOs and political parties, spelled out the actions to be taken to rectify gender imbalance and biases. After much debate, searching and negotiation, the WCI chose NGO activist Zaitun Kassim to run in the elections. Zaitun stood as an independent in the parliamentary constituency of Selayang in Selangor under a DAP ticket, received considerable mainstream media attention and polled 26,000 votes, substantially reducing her BN opponent's majority.

Along with Zaitun, many other social activists inspired by *reformasi* took to direct political engagement, such as Sivarasa Rasiah and Tian Chua (both from the human rights group Suaram), Irene Fernandez (Tenaganita), Chandra Muzaffar (Movement for a Just World), Zainur Zakariah (Bar Council), Jeyakumar Devaraj (workers' advocate and PSM member), and Fan Yew Teng (former DAP politician who led Cenpeace). While all these candidates lost, their defeats were by narrow margins. In subsequent years Sivarasa and Tian Chua have become Members of Parliament and prominent politicians in the PKR. Controversial university professor, Shahnon Ahmad, author of *Shit*, a scatological novel against UMNO, contested and won, along with a number of candidates from ABIM. The BA's campaigns often relied on the campaigning of NGO activists in Suara Rakyat Malaysia (Suaram), the All Women's Action Society (AWAM), Pusat Komunikasi Masyarakat, JIM, and other Islamic groups. A number of respected academics and professionals participated in BA *ceramah*, including economist K.S. Jomo, sociologist Kua Kia Soong, and lawyer Chandra Kanagasabai (Weiss 2000, p. 424).

CONCLUDING POINTS

In retrospect it would be fair to say that the BN would not have retained its two-thirds hold of Parliament had it not been for the non-Malay swing of votes in its favour, indicated among other things by the poor performance of the DAP. The PKN and the Anwaritas performed credibly given the late baptism of fire in many of their cases. There was no path dependence yet for this newly formed party and Malay disaffection was basically mopped up by PAS. A better result for the BA would have required not only a split in UMNO but sustained strategic and tactical cooperation among the BA parties, including the ability to reach the lower classes. Activism among the middle class multi-ethnic elements of civil society was an insufficient condition to deliver the necessary votes, in contrast to the tried and tested (path-dependent) multi-ethnic consociational politics of the BN. Clearly, the BA's inchoate stratagem of mediated communalism, while innovative, was still untested, and a large portion of the electorate remained sceptical of its effectiveness. In the event, the political ferment of the Reformasi Movement proved inadequate for a major electoral change. The existing political culture anchored to the political stability provided by the BN — whether on the basis of ethnicism or developmentalism — still had a deep hegemonic hold over most Malaysian voters.

As to whether PAS made gains because the Malays were split in their inclination to Islamization, this was not clearly evident. There were other considerations that gave PAS its electoral advantage this time around. Thus, Funston writes:

> PAS made gains not because it represented fundamentalism, but by identifying with the mood for change, establishing its first ever coalition with the non-Muslim DAP, putting up attractive, professional candidates, and demonstrating a record of moderate and clean government during its years of rule in Kelantan state. (Funston 2000, p. 56)

Furthermore, the Malay votes that were transferred from UMNO to PAS were the highest only in the most urbanized states of Selangor, Penang and Negri Sembilan, all of which did not have much history of strong voter support for PAS. In these three states UMNO lost between 25 and 31 per cent of votes in Malay-majority seats. As the *reformasi* protest movement was concentrated in these areas, it is likely that these were the voters who shifted their support from the BN to the BA (Maznah Mohamad 2003, pp. 71–73).

More importantly it may have been the deleterious and negative impact of party capitalism that caused Malays to shun UMNO in favour of PAS. Hari Singh (2000, p. 35), in his assessment of the 1999 outcome, suggests that:

> The ordinary Malay now began to compare his lot with the palatial residences and executive jets owned by the UMNOputras. The perception that emerged was that no longer were the Malays being "robbed" by the Chinese, but by the UMNO elites. The majority of Malays now viewed "corporatization", "privatization", and "industrialization" as state-legitimization of corruption, cronyism and nepotism. This aspect

became more salient following the revelation of business deals by Datuk Seri Anwar Ibrahim, who also emerged as the rallying point as well as the ideological bridge among the opposition.

In an important work on authoritarian stability and breakdowns, Thomas Pepinsky examines the cases of Indonesia and Malaysia (Pepinsky 2009). He devotes a chapter to the *reformasi* period with an analysis of the 1999 election in Malaysia and offers an explanation for why Mahathir's government was able to overcome the destabilizing developments I have discussed in this chapter. Pepinsky suggests the following:

> [I] argue that this political stability is the product of the regime's adjustment policies, which fulfilled the demands of each of its political supporters, poor Malays and the new Malay business class. Capital controls enabled expansionary policies, fulfilling the demands of fixed capital and the Malay masses. The effect of this radical adjustment measure for Malaysia's political opposition was striking. Having received their preferred adjustment policies, the regime's coalition of supporters had no incentive to withdraw support. So Malaysia's regime survived the crisis, despite the BN's most significant political challenge since the racial riots of 1969. (Pepinsky 2009, p. 192)

He offers four hypotheses for why this was the case; namely, that the crisis was not serious enough to unseat the BN (mild crisis); that the ruling coalition maintained a coherent ideology of governance (Mahathirism versus anarchy); that the regime's institutional structure was able to contain the opposition (party system); and that the coalition's policy adjustments satisfied the electorate (coalition unity). The use of two descriptors — "mild crisis" and "Mahathirism versus anarchy" — purportedly propounded by BN supporters, is clearly inaccurate. The crisis was no doubt milder compared to Indonesia, but the contraction of Malaysia's economy by 7 per cent was much worse (as Pepinsky himself notes) and moreover I have described earlier the huge policy adjustments that needed to be made to address what was at the time Malaysia's worst economic crisis. Second, the alternative to Mahathirism was hardly "anarchy"; it was a political reformism that continues till today.[21] However, I would largely agree with Pepinsky's analysis but modify it to argue that along with the important economic adjustments was the

BN's continued deployment of mediated communalism. This was the strategic factor that was particularly effective in electioneering as the fading ideology of Mahathirism became increasingly discredited. It was mediated communalism that held the coalition together, coupled with the BN's institutional strength and path-dependent success, which is implied in Pepinsky's third hypothesis. Finally, it cannot be denied that Mahathir's introduction of capital controls contained, if belatedly, the effects of the financial crisis and stemmed the crisis of party capitalism on the eve of the 1999 general election.

Thus, while the Reformasi Movement augured for the possibility of a sustained alternative power-sharing model for Malaysia, the outcome of the 1999 election was ultimately explainable. Despite the stridency of protests against UMNO, the BN was still able to secure its two-thirds majority in Parliament. Many dubbed it a pyrrhic victory, as massive resources and money had been poured into the election to mitigate the negative fallout among the Malays of Anwar's imprisonment, while the rest of the electorate remained lukewarm to the political implications of the election itself. Perhaps for the ordinary voter there was still little recognition that the BA represented a realistic alternative to the BN, despite the latter's extreme negative image. But largely because Malaysia's electoral system provided an advantage to the incumbent, the goal of denying it its customary two-thirds majority was also off-target.

The BN was still fulfilling the sufficient conditions for its path-dependent success. While a substantial number of Malay voters did shift their preference away from the BN, the BA did not really fulfil its role as an equal, alternative model of consociation to the BN. No real path dependence of significant overall or balanced success was created for the BA, with PAS essentially becoming a disproportionate beneficiary of the victimization of Anwar. In fact it was the presence of PAS as a partner party within the BA that cost the DAP its Chinese support. It was thus no surprise that the opposition coalition did not endure for long. In the aftermath of the elections the DAP, which had fared disappointingly, pulled out of the BA in August 2000. It cited as its reason for withdrawal a greater concern on the part of PAS to promote the realization of the Islamic state rather than the more inclusive agenda contained in the Joint Manifesto. At the end of the day the lack of institutional strength and an underdeveloped strategy of mediated communalism brought the short-lived BA experiment to a close.

Notes

1. Unofficially the NEP had been held in abeyance since 1987 after a new set of economic deregulation and privatization policies were introduced to promote economic recovery following the recession of the mid-1980s. The NDP, which replaced the NEP, restated the twin objectives of poverty eradication and restructuring within the context of economic growth. However, no specific time frame had been set for achieving, for instance, the goal of at least 30 per cent of corporate equity for the bumiputera, greater attention being given to the qualitative aspects of bumiputera participation instead. Continuing the strategy adopted in 1987, the private sector was identified as the engine of growth for the duration of the NDP. In the early 1990s the controversial Industrial Coordination Act and Industrial Investment Act were amended yet again to encourage local Chinese and foreign investors to participate more fully in investment activities.

2. The party was dissolved for the first time in 2003 and then again in 2004 as a result of a leadership crisis. See Chin (1996).

3. The political character of the trial was never in doubt. The so-called "Sodomy II" trial of Anwar (spanning 2010 to 2015) was virtually a carbon copy of the first. For an account of the first Anwar trial, see Marican's book, *Anwar on Trial* (2009).

4. The PKN was later merged with Parti Rakyat Malaysia and subsequently changed its name to Parti Keadilan Rakyat (PKR, People's Justice Party).

5. In Sarawak the opposition parties came together in a loose alliance known as the Sarawak Alternative Front (SAF) (Chin 2003, p. 219).

6. On the rise of the BCIC, see Gomez and Jomo (1997); on the emergence and politics of the Malay middle class, see Saravanamuttu (1992, 2002 and 2012).

7. There is no space to delve into these surveys here. See, for example, the many interesting surveys carried out by the Merdeka Centre <http://www.merdeka.org/>. Two that indicate the cleavages of a Malay middle class are "Malaysian Voter Values Survey 2010: Political Typology" and "Malaysian Political Values Survey 2010 Public Opinion Poll".

8. The move by Mahathir supposedly carried the legitimacy of a proposal by MIT professor (and later Nobel laureate) Paul Krugman who had argued in an article in *Fortune* magazine in 1998 that such capital controls

could give crisis-ridden Asian economies an opportunity to resume growth. Krugman subsequently wrote an "Open Letter to Prime Minister Mahathir" arguing that capital controls only provided "breathing room for economic recovery" and were no substitute to reforming non-performing economies. The professor was later invited to a ninety-minute dialogue with the prime minster and to a corporate who's who in Kuala Lumpur but maintained after the meeting that Mahathir could only claim "partial vindication for his economic heresies" (see *The Unofficial Paul Krugman Archive* <http://www.pkarchive.org/>).

9. See *The Star*, 30 October 1999.

10. Apart from bailouts, Petronas had also been in the forefront of acquisitions and projects of particular interest to the prime minister. It bankrolled the US$800 million (RM4 billion) Petronas Twin Towers in Kuala Lumpur, the tallest buildings in the world at the time they were built. Even more incredible was Petronas's financial backing for Malaysia's new RM22 billion administrative centre known as Putrajaya, situated twenty-five kilometres from Kuala Lumpur. Putrajaya houses the prime minister's magnificent office and palatial residence and all the major ministries (Saravanamuttu 2003, pp. 8–9).

11. See *Asian Wall Street Journal*, 20 Feburary 2002 and <http://www.themalaysianinsider.com/malaysia/article/putrajaya-directs-glcs-danaharta-to-drop-all-claims-against-tajuddin-ramli> (accessed 11 May 2015).

12. Jomo (2001) states further: "With an estimated 25–30 billion Malaysian ringgit in Singapore, the Malaysian monetary authorities could not expect to altogether prevent interest rates from rising with the much higher interest rates available in the republic", a situation which Anwar was acutely aware of. "While Anwar was undoubtedly more inclined to cater to 'market sentiments', his post-September 1998 demonisation by Mahathirists as an IMF stooge and agent of the West is certainly not supported by his economic policy record" (p. xxv).

13. It is of some irony that the same person, Ahmad Zahid Hamidi, who used to be a close associate of Anwar, is the current (2016) deputy prime minister in the Najib Razak government.

14. See in particular what has become a classic piece of writing by Sabri Zain detailing as a participant observer the events associated with *refomasi* (Sabri Zain 2000).

15. The analysis draws from Loh and Saravanamuttu (2003). Other studies of this election include Zakaria (2000), Funston (2000), Weiss, (2000) and Khoo (2000). Funston's piece attempts an analysis of how Malay electoral behaviour had changed because of the Anwar episode and how the BN still managed to overcome this (see especially p. 53ff), while Weiss's

survey discusses whether "real" political change had occurred in Malaysia, concluding that communalism still ran deep (p. 435). Zakaria's effort is essentially a "preliminary" analysis of the results and trends. Khoo (2000) recognizes that "disenchantment with BN has grown" but cautiously concludes that "no one can predict yet whether this sentiment will subside ... or threaten UMNO's ability to remain in power" (p. 311). See also ANFREL and FORUM-ASIA (2000, pp. 59–60), a report prepared by thirteen international observers, principally from Asia, on the conduct of the general elections, which it concludes "is defeated by the current system of law and politics" that is biased against the opposition. The report contains various proposals on how to "level the playing field" so that "the promise of free and fair elections for the people of Malaysia may be fulfilled".

16. Funston (2000, p. 360) suggests an alternative idea; namely that since this batch of voters had been scheduled for inclusion in February 2000, the date of the election was deliberately fixed for November 1999 to avoid enfranchising them if the election were held in the year 2000.

17. For the notion of "manufactured majorities" expounded by Rae, see Chapter 2.

18. See Chapter 2 for the earlier discussion of disproportionate representation and malapportionment in the Malaysian electoral system. This is discussed further in Chapter 8 about the outcome of the 13th general election.

19. See Nathan (2000, pp. 26–28).

20. The Parliamentary seat was won by the BN's Wong Kam Hoong with 57.6 per cent of the vote, beating his opponent Zulkifli Mohd Noor of the DAP, who took 42.4 per cent of the vote. In a pre-election sample survey, 36.6 per cent of respondents had never heard of "Barisan Alternatif" and 81 per cent had no idea who would be prime minster if the BA won the election (Saravanamuttu 2003, p. 192).

21. Citing interviews, Pepinsky also alluded to "Mahathir's intelligence and devotion to the Malaysian people" and, in contrast, "Anwar proved himself to be a power-hungry politician rather than a committed reformist" (p. 195). Most Malaysian analysts would consider such views to be biased in the extreme.

8

THE OPPOSITION'S BREAKTHROUGH
The Leap from 2004 to 2008

The decline of Mahathir's political leadership appeared to have come as a consequence of the Anwar Ibrahim saga. Although Mahathir was able to lead the Barisan Nasional (BN) to an electoral victory in November 1999, a legitimacy crisis occurred during his tenure. The Anwar saga exposed the dangers and deleterious consequences of party capitalism. Moreover, the emergence of the BA, the alternative coalition, and a host of civil society organizations banding around the *reformasi* banner and calling for his scalp, clearly left a mortal scar on the Malay leader (Hwang 2003, p. 331). As I have suggested in the previous chapter, UMNO may in fact have lost the Malay vote in 1999; the fact was there was a precipitous slippage to PAS. In September 2000 Mahathir experienced his first international snub when the Islamic Society of North America withdrew its invitation to him to be the keynote speaker at one of its meetings (Maznah 2001, p. 219). On the domestic front another electoral blow came in the Lunas by-election of 29 November 2000. Although this was a mixed constituency in

Mahathir's home state, Kedah, it was a People's Justice Party (PKR) candidate who defeated the BN man by 530 votes, showing that UMNO had still not recovered from the poor showing of the last election (Maznah 2001, p. 220). Some relief came to Mahathir only in September 2001 when it became evident that the DAP was in an unhappy marriage with the PAS in the alternative front and quit participating in it.

The woes of party capitalism were far from over, even though Mahathir had apparently steered Malaysia to economic recovery. I have already alluded to the bailouts of Malay businessmen such as Mirzan Mahathir and Tajuddin Ramli. The governmental buyback of Malaysian Airlines, headed by Tajuddin, further eroded Mahathir's credibility. So too did the bailout of alleged UMNO proxy (and Daim's protégé) Halim Saad's Timedotcom by the use of state pension funds (Salazar 2004, p. 288). In fact, Halim's loss-laden flagship, the Renong conglomerate, which had debts totalling RM13 billion, was subjected to a restructuring that saw the removal of its chairman. By June 2001 Daim Zainuddin had resigned from the government, indicating there was a rift among UMNO elites in how to deal with fallen Malay corporate figures. As Salazar (2004, p. 291) suggests, it appeared that the re-nationalization and corporate restructuring of highly leveraged conglomerates was fuelled by political factionalism, in particular the growing disagreement between Mahathir and Daim, rather than by economic logic. Mahathir at the 55th UMNO General Assembly in June went on an attack against money politics and corruption at the same time lambasting the Malays yet again for their complacent attitudes (Nathan 2002, p. 170). Against the backdrop of all his travails, Mahathir in September 2001 pronounced the *non sequitur* that Malaysia was already an "Islamic State". But such a declaration at the same time was an acknowledgement by Mahathir that his strongest and most persistent critics were the Islamists of PAS. Here then was perhaps a last-ditch effort to reinvigorate the Malay agenda for UMNO and simultaneously attempt to undercut the growing clout of PAS. At the 2002 UMNO General Assembly, Mahathir made the announcement of his intention to resign on 22 June. It may have been unexpected and baffling at that point of time, but in retrospect it was hardly possible for Mahathir to hang on, given that the UMNO legitimacy crisis had been exposed by events harking back to the Anwar imbroglio.

Abdullah Badawi assumed the reins of government on 31 October 2003. Before long he was rolling back a number of Mahathir's policies and decisions, in particular, mega projects, while at the same time the new premier also initiated an anti-corruption drive and various efforts at government reform. Even within a month of becoming the prime minister, Abdullah Badawi (known by his moniker "Pak Lah") started to, as one journalist put it, "tinker with" Mahathirist policies and decisions (Netto 2004). Most prominently, he placed the new anti-corruption thrust at the fore of his government and promised to correct the low efficiency and ineptness of various branches of the government service. He made it clear that he would put a hold on mega projects, most visible of which was his immediate scuttling of a RM14.5 billion double-track railway line awarded to Gamuda and the Malaysian Mining Corporation. This despite the fact Mahathir had given the project the green light just prior to his retirement. The project was particularly controversial because it involved business tycoon Mokhtar Al-Bhukary whose growing business empire led to much speculation that he had strong political patrons.

At the ideational level Abdullah introduced a much softer style of dealing with the outside world, through a modernist and moderate Islamic approach coined by his government as "Islam Hadhari", or "civilizational Islam". The ten purported principles of Islam Hadhari, the mantra in numerous speeches by Abdullah and his spokespersons, were: faith and piety in the Almighty; a just and trustworthy government; a free and independent people; the vigorous pursuit and mastery of knowledge; balanced and comprehensive economic development; a good quality of life for the people; protection of the rights of minority groups and women; cultural and moral integrity; safeguarding natural resources and the environment; and strong defence capabilities (Saravanamuttu 2010, pp. 239–41).

BN'S LANDSLIDE WIN IN 2004

The Islam Hadhari concept was also used to optimum effect in the campaign for the general election of March 2004 to upstage PAS. The transition from Mahathir had the desired effect for the BN. It resulted in a landslide electoral victory where the coalition not only captured more than 90 per cent of parliamentary seats but also dealt a serious blow to PAS as well as the PKR. PAS failed to retain control of Terengganu and nearly lost its base in Kelantan. PKR, which by now had an effective merger with Parti Rakyat Malaysia, was only barely able to retain the seat held by its president, Wan Azizah Ismail, the wife of the jailed Anwar Ibrahim. In short, the BN's victory dealt blows to both the political Islam of PAS and to the Reformasi Movement.

As noted in Chapter 2, a re-delineation exercise had been completed in 2003 that saw the over-weightage of Malay seats on the Peninsula reduced. As a result of this, more mixed seats were created. Of the total 219 parliamentary seats, there were 26 new constituencies, of which 21 were in the Peninsula and 5 were in Sabah. Malay majority seats accounted for 13 of the new seats; Chinese majority seats accounted for 2 of them. Of the 13 new Malay-majority seats, only 3 had 80 per cent or more Malay voters; 18 constituencies were of the mixed variety (Moten and Mokhtar 2006, p. 321).

This re-delineation exercise, with its larger number of mixed seats, contributed to the BN's huge victory, because Pak Lah's anti-corruption drive, moderate image and willingness to debunk "Mahathirism" won him the middle ground. Political analysts have observed that he in fact stole *reformasi's* thunder by adopting its agenda. Pak Lah's BN looked formidable against an emasculated BA comprising only PKR and PAS, with its bland slogan of "prosperity for all". Islam became a central issue of the campaign with *Islam Hadhari* taking centre stage along with Pak Lah's stance of moderation in ethnic relations against PAS's "Islam for all". The DAP stood apart from this arguing against the form of any "Islamic state". According to Khadijah Khalid (2007, p. 150), Islam was less a factor in the BN's victory than was Pak Lah's strategy to regain the rural vote, which he did by placing emphasis on agricultural policies after years of neglect under Mahathir. On polling day the BN had already won 17 parliamentary seats and 11 state seats uncontested, and when the results were announced it spectacularly claimed 90.4 per cent of all contested parliamentary seats, although its 64 per cent of the popular vote was one percentage short of the 1995 result. The opposition collected a miserable 19 seats (DAP 12; PAS 6; PKN 1). Tables 8.1 and 8.2 show the parliamentary results and party vote percentages of seats contested.

Table 8.1
Parliamentary Results, 2004 Election

State	BN	Non-BN	Total
Perlis	3		3
Kedah	14	1	15
Kelantan	9	5	14
Terengganu	8		8
Penang	8	4	13
Perak	21	3	24
Pahang	14		14
Selangor	22		22
N. Sembilan	8		8
Melaka	6		6
Johor	26		26
Sarawak	27	1	28
Sabah	24	1	25
Kuala Lumpur	7	4	11
Labuan	1		1
Putrajaya	1		1
Total	199	20	219

Source: Abdul Rashid Moten and Tunku Mohar Mokhtar 2006, p. 331.

Table 8.2
Distribution of Seats and Votes by Parties, 2004 Election

	Total seats	Total votes	Percentage of valid votes
BN	181	4,434,203	63.93
PAS	7*	1,057,853	15.25
PKN	1	621,330	8.96
DAP	12	688,630	9.93
Independent	1	133,976	1.93

Source: Balasubramaniam 2005, p. 46
* PAS was originally declared to have won the Pasir Mas Kelantan seat but this was later reversed by the Election Commission.

Flushed with his landslide electoral victory, Pak Lah perhaps felt more confident in pushing forward with his own plans. Most controversially, on 11 April 2006 Abdullah cancelled the "crooked (or scenic) half-bridge" project of Mahathir, which was to build a bridge on the Malaysian side over the Singapore–Malaysia causeway. This bridge would allow for ships to pass under it and access the South China Sea without passing though the Singapore port. Another significant event related to the mismanagement of mega projects to occur during Pak Lah's tenure was the much-publicized trial of Eric Chia, the erstwhile chief executive officer of Perwaja Steel, for criminal breach of trust involving some RM76.4 million.[1] Although it must be said that the Anti Corruption Agency (ACA) had begun its investigations of Perwaja Steel much earlier on, the new prime minister now promised that some eighteen or so high-profile ACA cases would be pursued during his tenure. The Abdullah government also set up a Royal Commission to explore reforming the police. Headed by a former chief justice, Mohamed Dzaiddin Abdullah, the commission managed to produce a preliminary report in August 2004 which found that corrupt practices had involved officers and personnel "at all levels" (New *Straits Times,* 10 August 2004). However, after the final report was completed in May 2005, few of the twenty-four recommendations of the commission were implemented, including the most important one of setting up an Independent Police Complaints and Misconduct Commission.[2]

Thus it seems clear that while the general change over the first two years of Pak Lah's ascension to power boosted his image and reputation, the subsequent slide in the lack of implementation of some stated polices, such as his anti-corruption plan, the mounting concerns of non-Malay constituencies over policies related to questions of Islam, the international publicity of a murder trial of a Mongolian model, implicating persons in high places (including Najib Razak, then deputy prime minister), and other negative events dogged an increasingly defensive Pak Lah government. By April 2006 Mahathir had also begun to fire a salvo of shots at Abdullah's policies. Indeed, by the middle of 2007 there were rumblings that a snap election could be held to stem the mounting dissatisfaction with Pak Lah's leadership, or lack if it.

Furthermore, under Pak Lah, old-style ethnically divisive (even racist) UMNO money politics reared its head. Mahathir himself bitterly complained of his failure to be elected to be a delegate in his old constituency to attend the UMNO General Assembly in November 2006. He openly accused Pak Lah's supporters of bribing the divisional delegates. In the run-up to the UMNO General Assembly, Abdullah nominated Najib Abdul Razak as his deputy after months of speculation, and the pair secured virtually all the nominations of the party divisions. Abdullah lost one nomination to the lame challenge of Tengku Razaleigh Hamzah, who managed to receive the sole vote from his own division. During the Assembly proceedings, UMNO Youth leader Hishamuddin Hussein Onn spectacularly whipped out a *keris* (Malay dagger) to berate his audience about the virtue of *ketuanan Melayu* (Malay supremacy). More was to come by way of incendiary racist statements made against the Chinese by other delegates, all of which was telecast live for the first time for all Malaysians to witness.

On 31 March 2006 Pak Lah unveiled the Ninth Malaysia Plan, which would see expenditure in excess of RM200 billion between 2007 and 2012. The plan itself drew flak from the Centre for Public Policy (CPP) of the Asian Strategy and Leadership Institute (ASLI). The CPP claimed that the NEP target of 30 per cent ownership of the economy had been surpassed, leading to a series of public debates which ultimately led to the resignation of CPP director Lim Teck Ghee (Ooi 2007, p. 187–88).

Even more controversial were the contestations and court decisions regarding conversions in or out of Islam (apostasy) that have led to acrimonious public debates and even street demonstrations.[3] Matters came to a head when in January 2006 all ten of Pak Lah's non-Muslim cabinet ministers signed a memorandum requesting that Article 121 (1A), which gives jurisdiction of Islamic matters to shariah courts, be reviewed. Pak Lah managed to prevail on his ministers to withdraw their memorandum (Ooi 2007, p. 185). The prime minister also deemed it fit to step in to halt the "Article 11" forums organized by a coalition of NGOs to discuss the federal constitution and protection under the law on questions of religion. On two occasions when Article 11 forums were held, one in Penang and the other in Johor Baru, Muslims held demonstrations to protest the group's alleged "hidden agenda" to revive the moribund Inter Faith Council, which incidentally was scuttled by the government. In Penang protesters heckled the panellists, who included speakers such as Shad Saleem Faruqi, professor of constitutional law at UiTM; Imtiaz Malik, president of the human rights body HAKAM; and Zaid Ibrahim, Kota Bharu Member of Parliament. The police who appeared on the scene forced the forum to end early, without all the scheduled speakers having had their say. The forum in Johor was similarly brought to a close early, but all the speakers were able to deliver their presentations.

On the heels of the Article 11 forums was a reported gathering of ten thousand Muslims at the Masjid Wilayah on 24 July 2006. Among the personalities who spoke at the forum — titled "The Syariah and Current Issues" — were former Bar Council presidents Sulaiman Abdullah and Zainur Zakaria, Perak mufti Harussani Zakaria, constitutional expert Abdul Aziz Bari, and Muslim Youth Movement of Malaysia president Yusri Mohamad. Other speakers included shariah lawyer Kamar Ainiah Kamaruzaman, former Penang mufti Sheikh Azmi Ahmad, and forum chairperson Azmi Abdul Hamid, who headed the Malay-advocacy group Teras. The speakers called on the government to strengthen the country's Islamic institutions and not weaken them.[4]

More controversies peppered the Abdullah administration as he moved into the fourth and fifth years of his stewardship. The "Bersih" coalition of political parties and NGOs calling for clean elections on 10 November reportedly saw forty thousand people taking to the streets, and the HINDRAF rally of some thirty thousand Indians came close on its heels on 25 November 2007. Abdullah took the heavy-handed action of detaining five HINDRAF leaders under the draconian Internal Security Act, which he did not appear to relish. Some of these developments were truly remarkable in exposing the mendacity, incompetence and corruption of the government, its leaders, political cronies and institutions. Abdullah himself was embroiled in charges of nepotism. Amongst the more damning revelations were those related to the judiciary, albeit acts implemented during the Mahathir era. The V.K. Lingam video recording impelled Abdullah himself to call for a Royal Commission to ascertain the extent of judge-fixing and case-fixing by the eponymous lawyer named in the scandal. The hearings revealed the alleged writing of judgments by the same defence lawyer for the presiding judge.

More than ever before, as the prime minister himself pointed out, the government needed a fresh mandate. There could even be a more mundane factor that caused the early calling of this general election, namely the emergence of new blood or a generational shift in the BN. Many untested, younger UMNO and BN politicians were anxiously waiting in the wings to rise in the hierarchy and to seek their baptism of fire. Among them were Abdullah's son-in-law, the fast-rising Khairy Jamaluddin, as well as the son of the receding Gerakan Party leader, Lim Si Pin. The Malaysian Chinese Association (MCA) also needed to jettison some so-called "Team A" members, although one of them, former health minister Chua Soi Lek, conveniently disqualified himself after a widely distributed sex video led to his resignation. And, in the tiny northern state of Perlis, two UMNO ministers were evidently on the chopping block. There were also political trimming exercises to be undertaken within the Malaysian Indian Congress (MIC), in its desperate attempt to retain the Indian vote. A whole year ahead of the mandatory five years, Abdullah announced that he would call for a general election. The date was set for 8 March 2008. Much of the reasoning revolved around two factors — the economy and Anwar Ibrahim. The economic situation seemed destined to deteriorate, with the American economy likely to go into recession with its potential knock-on effects on Malaysia. Anwar Ibrahim, former deputy premier, now de facto leader of the opposition PKR, would have been eligible to contest by mid-April, five years after his release from jail on charges for which he was cleared in 2004. It was entirely credible that the Abdullah Badawi government would have agonized that an elected Anwar as a Member of Parliament would have meant trouble.

THE RUPTURE OF 8 MARCH

Against the backdrop of Abdullah's fading popularity, Parliament and state assemblies, with the exception of Sarawak, were dissolved on 13 February 2008. The Election Commission called for nominations on 24 February for the 12th general election of Malaysia to be held on 8 March 2008. An unusually long period of thirteen days was given for campaigning, and some 222 parliamentary seats were in contention along with 505 state seats. Two days before election day, Malaysian analysts (including this one) speaking at an ISEAS seminar were not prepared to concede that the BN would lose its two-thirds majority in Parliament, let alone four more state governments.[5]

The outcome of 2008 has been dubbed a "political tsunami" that some have argued brought about a tectonic shift (Saravanamuttu 2008) to the Malaysian political landscape. Another hyperbole used was "a perfect storm".[6] But as political analyst Khoo notes more accurately:

> The metaphors may be excessive. A true tsunami, say, would have swept the BN out of office. A perfect storm would not have bypassed Sabah and Sarawak. (*Aliran Monthly* 28, no. 2, p. 6)

This notwithstanding, the three major ethnic communities — Malays, Chinese and Indians — and almost all the Peninsular states[7] swung decisively in the direction of opposition parties, as shown in Table 8.3,

Table 8.3
Results of Parliamentary Election, 2008

Party	Votes	%	Seat	%
Barisan Nasional	4,090,670	50.14	140	63.1
UMNO	2,381,725	29.19	79	35.6
MCA	849,108	10.41	15	6.8
MIC	179,422	2.20	3	1.4
Gerakan	184,548	2.26	2	0.9
Others	495,867	6.08	41	18.5
Pakatan Rakyat	3,786,399	46.41	82	36.9
DAP	1,107,960	13.58	28	12.6
PAS	1,140,676	13.98	23	10.4
PKR	1,509,080	18.50	31	14.0
Others	28,683	0.35	0	0
Independents	63,960	0.78	0	0
Spoilt Votes	175,011	2.14	—	—
Unreturned votes	41,564	0.51	—	—
Total	8,159,043	100	222	100

Source: Computed from Election Commission data.

and deprived the ruling coalition of its all-important two-thirds majority in Parliament, thus dealing a heavy blow to its ethnic power-sharing formula. The 8 March general election created enduring political outcomes which surpassed the 1969 watershed general election that triggered the outbreak of riots in Kuala Lumpur on 13 May.[8] The 2008 series of opposition election rallies throughout the campaign was oddly reminiscent of May 1969, but they perhaps eclipsed the 1969 campaign by the sheer numbers that attended the rallies throughout the country.[9] One large rally in Penang saw some fifty thousand in attendance; clearly unprecedented.[10]

The outcome of the general election of 8 March 2008 dealt a devastating blow to the BN government. It altered significantly the political parameters of electoral politics and constituted or at least contributed to a reconfiguration of the political landscape in Malaysia (Saravanamuttu 2008, 2009; Ooi, Saravanamuttu and Lee 2008).[11] In terms of electoral politics it may be suggested that 8 March created a de facto two-party (or two coalition) system, if one considers not just the parliamentary level but also the state level of contests. In path-dependence terms the political moment of 8 March created an incipient two-party system in Malaysia, which was reinforced by the results of the by-elections that followed and was consolidated by the outcome of the 2013 general election.

Factors driving Malaysia's new politics are a function of its political transformations since arguably the 1980s and certainly after Anwar Ibrahim's sacking and incarceration in 1998. While ethnicity remains a crucial variable in Malaysian politics, cross-ethnic voting represents the driver of Malaysia's new politics. Citizens across the board are now more informed of universal issues such as corruption and minority rights, and the opposition alliance has been able to capitalize on these new sensibilities by offering an alternative political institutional format to that of the ruling coalition. Going beyond the older consociational arrangements of ethnic power sharing, the Pakatan Rakyat — PR, or People's Alliance, the electoral pact of the PKR, DAP and PAS, which was yet to be formalized as a formal coalition then — relied on political mobilization and institutions that valorized good governance, economic welfare and human rights in the tradition of delivering "political goods".[12]

The event saw the ruling BN government lose its two-thirds share of seats in Parliament which it had held since Malaysia became independent in 1957. The opposition parties, later formalized as the Pakatan Rakyat,[13] won a total of 82 out of the 222 seats up for contest. The BN barely won 50 per cent of the 7.9 million ballots cast, demonstrating that the electorate was virtually split down the middle. Furthermore, five state governments fell to opposition hands, unprecedented in Malaysian history. One could argue that the BN had lost is *first mover advantage* as the only successful coalition able to mediate communalism within its consociational institutional arrangements. UMNO under Abdullah Badawi failed to mitigate the rising Islamic stridency of Muslims which resulted in the haemorrhaging of non-Muslim voters for the BN. The convergence of rights-based civil society movements, the HINDRAF movement and the discontent of a liberal urbanized middle class created a tectonic shift of voting preference against BN parties. Significantly too, the BN was not able to check the formation of a coherent opposition pact which was able to capitalize on the mounting grievances of citizens. The PR was thus able to articulate these grievances within its own consociational model with its centripetal spin towards more moderate and less communal stances and policies at the onset of the 2008 election. This cost the BN its two-thirds command of parliamentary seats.

Several important points should be made about considering March 2008 as an historical rupture and the beginning of a new trajectory of path dependence in Malaysian politics. It is important to note that the event may not be of the order of a "critical juncture" of the sort alluded to by Collier and Collier (2002), namely that it produces a distinctly new legacy by ending an old one, such as demolishing an *ancien régime*. Secondly, the critical junctures identified by the Colliers in Latin America spanned periods of nine to twenty-three years (ibid., p. 32). March 2008 was only about ten years after the antecedent event of *reformasi* in 1998, which was followed by the 1999 general election.

What then are the salient facts of the 2008 outcome? The BN government arguably suffered its worst defeat in history, with a loss of its two-thirds majority of seats. The BN government also just about lost the popular vote in Peninsular Malaysia, including the loss of four state governments, while one continued to be in opposition hands. There was a vote swing away from the BN government in every state on the Peninsula (see Table 9.3 in the next chapter). Table 8.4, based on estimates, shows that Chinese and Indian voters clearly preferred the opposition parties, while Malays still had a preference, albeit a reduced one, for the BN parties. The most significant swing came from Indians, who evidently abandoned the ethnically constituted MIC. The Chinese voters also swung palpably in the direction of ostensibly non-Chinese parties, leaving the MCA with its poorest showing since 1969.

Most significantly, Malaysia edged towards a formal parliamentary two-party system, and in fact instituted a two-party system at the state-level of governance, given that the opposition alliance won five state governments.[14] Some of the most salient outcomes of 8 March could be said to be the following:

- The BN got barely half (50.1 per cent) of the 7.9 million ballots cast nationwide and lost the popular vote on the Peninsula, garnering only 49 per cent of ballots.
- The BN lost its two-thirds majority in Parliament, winning 140 federal sets and 307 state seats. The opposition took 82 and 307, respectively.
- The BN lost the state governments of Selangor, Penang, Perak and Kedah, while Kelantan remained in opposition hands. (Its worst performances of the past were when the BN failed to capture two state governments — Kelantan and Terengganu in 1959 and 1999, respectively.)

Table 8.4
The Malay, Chinese and Indian Vote for the BN

	1995	1999	2004	2008	Change, 2004–8
Malay	69%	53%	63%	58%	5%
Chinese	56%	62%	65%	35%	30%
Indian	96%	75%	82%	47%	35%

Source: Straits Times, 11 March 2008.

One of the more significant aspects of 2008 in contrast to previous general elections was the comprehensive vote swing of all major ethnic communities away from the BN parties. Political scientist-turned politician Ong Kian Ming had estimated that some 30 to 35 per cent of non-Malay voters swung to the opposition parties compared with the popular vote in the previous election of 2004. Although the overall corresponding swing for Malays was only about 5 per cent, Ong argued the following:

> It is important to highlight that these vote swings are not uniformly distributed. For example, the Malay vote swing in the West Coast states, especially in Penang, Selangor and Kuala Lumpur was higher than the estimated 5% and was closer to 10% or even higher in certain constituencies like Balik Pulau, Gombak and Lembah Pantai. It would not have been possible for the opposition, PKR in these cases, to win without a sizeable swing in the Malay vote. (Ong 2008)

Nationwide, in mixed seats where the electorate formed 40–60 per cent of Malay voters, the BN won 28 seats and the opposition 26 seats, showing that the alternative Pakatan had become a veritable contender to the BN and in some sense was emulating the BN's model of electoral success.[15] It could well be argued that cross-ethnic voting accounted for a significant number of Pakatan victories and, had the pattern of cross-ethnic voting which occurred in Klang Valley been replicated in states like Pahang, Malacca, Negeri Sembilan and Johor, the BN government might have been toppled on 8 March.[16]

TWIN COALITION PARTY SYSTEM

The rupture of the old political trajectory and my positing of a new path dependence rests on the fact that Malaysia may have become a genuine two-party system at the state level due to the stunning victories of the PR coalition as shown in Figure 8.1. In fact some analysts have pointed out that the sixth "state" to fall was the federal territory of Kuala Lumpur, where all but 1 out of 12 parliamentary seats went to the PR.[17] Anwar further reinforced the 8 March outcome by sweeping the Permatang Pauh by-election on 26 August with a majority of well over fifteen thousand votes and was subsequently officially anointed as Leader of the Opposition in Parliament.

Figure 8.1
Malaysian Election 2008: Distribution of Seats Won in Each State Legislature

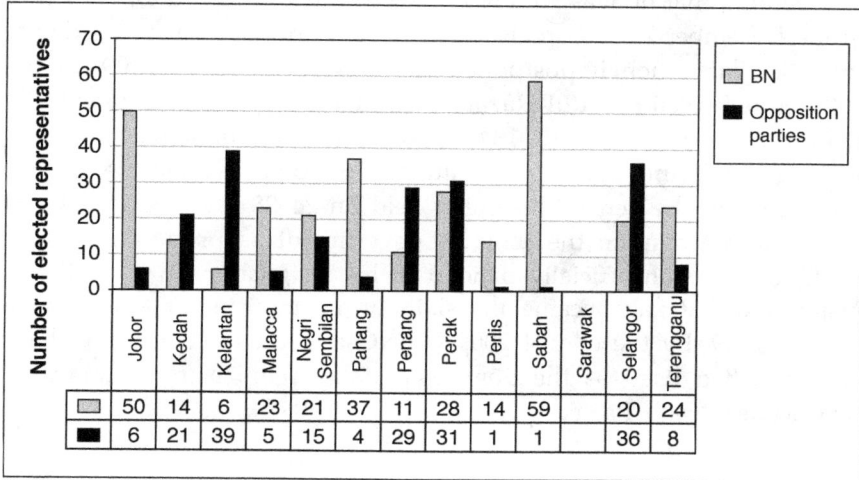

	Johor	Kedah	Kelantan	Malacca	Negri Sembilan	Pahang	Penang	Perak	Perlis	Sabah	Sarawak	Selangor	Terengganu
BN	50	14	6	23	21	37	11	28	14	59		20	24
Opposition parties	6	21	39	5	15	4	29	31	1	1		36	8

First, it must be stressed that the main change in the political landscape in terms of a nascent, two-party (or two-coalition) system has been at the state level, where the PR initially commanded five governments; namely, Selangor, Penang, Perak, Kedah and Kelantan.[18] In these states the BN found itself in the unfamiliar role of opposition, except in Kelantan where this had been the case for about two decades. One could argue that Malaysian democracy had arrived at a new threshold and that citizens now had the opportunity to judge four alternative state governments and choose to re-elect or reject them the next time around. As such, the formalization of the PR as an alternative coalition to the National Front was fait accompli by 2008. Unlike its predecessor, the Alternative Front (Barisan Alternative) of 1998–99, the PR governmental presence seemed to be guaranteed for a good length of time by virtue of it assuming state-level power. By late 2009 the PR had announced a common political manifesto and agreed to a common logo, but its registration was stymied due to the requirement of approval from the Registrar of Societies.

After the BN's disastrous showing at the hustings of 2008, Mahathir and Tengku Razaleigh persistently called for Pak Lah to step down as president of UMNO. Abdullah managed to resist these calls until his own minister Muhyiddin Yassin also threw down the gauntlet in early May, stating that he was willing to contest one of the two top positions in the December UMNO polls.[19] UMNO provided a face-saving device for Abdullah when it postponed the UMNO polls till 2009. Before 2008 ended, Najib Abdul Razak, Abdullah's deputy, had practically won the presidency with 134 nominations out of a possible 191, making him prime-minister-in-waiting. He would assume the UMNO presidency at the general assembly held on 24–28 March 2009 and by the same act assume the reins of government as prime-minister-in-waiting. Abdullah officially handed in his resignation on 2 April and Najib Abdul Razak became the sixth prime minister of Malaysia on 3 April 2009. By the end of 2009 UMNO appeared ostensibly to have re-established itself as the dominant Malay political force under its new leader, Najib Razak.

ETHNIC AND CROSS-ETHNIC VOTING ON 8 MARCH

The new trajectory of politics should be understood in its behavioural dimensions as a change in the character of ethnic mobilization and voting during the 2008 election. This trend could be continued if the Pakatan forces capitalize on voters' changed political behaviour and invest in efforts and processes to enhance it. In trying to comprehend this potential, the nature of ethnic voting patterns in 2008 deserve further analysis. As can be seen from the results of previous elections, even minor swings in the popular vote can produce significant changes in seats in the first-past-the-post electoral system of Malaysia, but the comprehensive character of the BN's slippage in 2008 cannot be denied. The 2008 election is comparable to the 1969 result when the Alliance lost the popular vote across the nation. In 2008 the BN barely scraped through, but showed an even poorer performance in terms of the percentage of parliamentary seats secured.

The scatter plots in Figures 8.2 to 8.4 show the ethnic proportionality of the parliamentary seats won by the main parties in Peninsular Malaysia. As we are using the data provided by the Election Commission, the parties of the ruling coalition have been collapsed

Figure 8.2
Percentage of Malay Voters for Each Seat Won by Political Parties, 2008

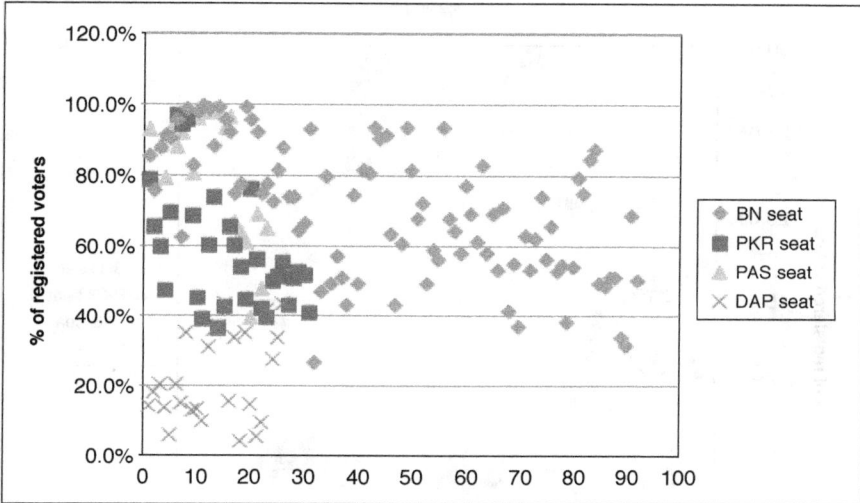

Figure 8.3
Percentage of Chinese Voters by Seats Won, 2008

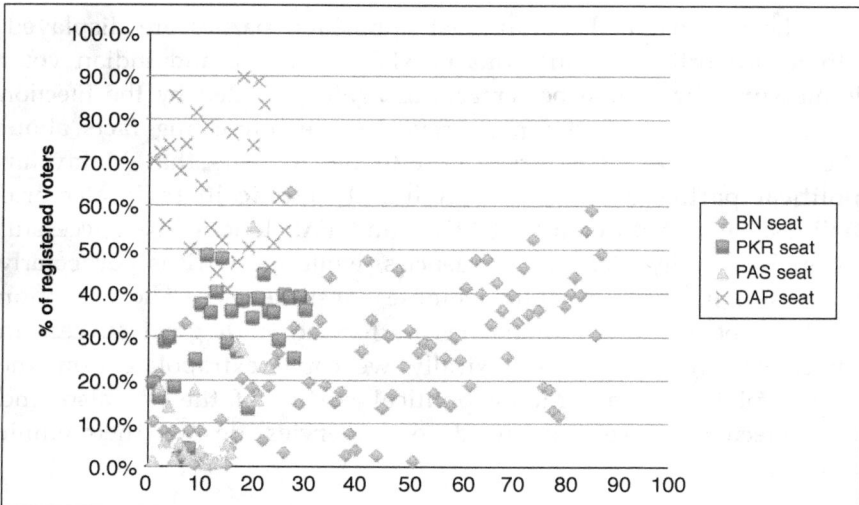

Figure 8.4
Percentage of Registered Indian Voters by Seats Won, 2008

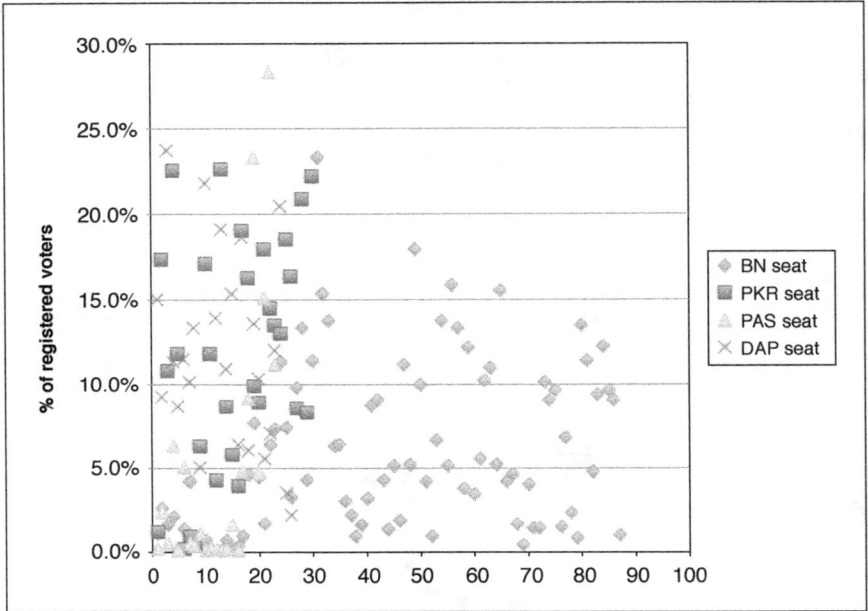

into the BN, while the individual opposition parties are displayed. Ethnic proportionality in terms of Malay, Chinese and Indian votes is measured by simple percentage, as again provided by the Election Commission. Our scatter plots reveal some interesting facts about the 2008 election. The first point to be made is that Malaysian political parties are still predominantly ethnic in their electoral politics; or, put differently, UMNO and PAS tend to be successful in predominantly Malay constituencies, while the DAP is particularly successful in predominantly Chinese constituencies. The exception tends to be the PKR, which has performed with great success in mixed constituencies. Paradoxically, we could extrapolate from the scatter plots that non-Malay political parties of the BN also find their electoral success in mixed constituencies, despite their ethnic orientation.[20]

In the first scatter plot (Figure 8.2) we can clearly see the PAS and DAP at the two extreme ends of the Malay racial continuum — PAS winning in high-density Malay constituencies, while the DAP takes low-density Malay seats. The PKR plays the perfect role of winning the mixed seats and thereby holding the PR coalition together. The second scatter plot (Figure 8.3) shows the obverse position vis-à-vis Chinese high-density constituencies. The PKR coalition again holds the middle ground. When looking at the BN's performance, which unfortunately is not decomposed into those of its component parties, it can still be deduced that UMNO won the high-density Malay constituencies. A much larger proportion of high- to middle-density Malay constituencies were won by the BN, suggesting that its component parties can also do well in Malay majority constituencies. A clear rejection of the BN parties in high-density Chinese constituencies is indicated in the second scatter plot, and implied in the first.

Turning to the Indian vote as shown in the third scatter plot (Figure 8.4), the first thing to note is that the PKR had performed very well along with the DAP with two PAS outliers seemingly securing high Indian votes. Since there are no real high-density Indian constituencies — with 30 per cent as the uppermost limit — one could extrapolate that winning seats above the 15 per cent margin is a good indicator of Indian support. This being the case, the BN parties fared poorly in securing the Indian vote, with barely four wins in that category.

The main point to be made here is that the PKR, acting as a multi-ethnic political party and offering a slew of multi-ethnic candidates, succeeded in gaining the middle ground. Its partners, the DAP and PAS, continued to hold their own on predominantly Chinese and Malay terrain. The new Pakatan arrangement clearly dented the BN's advantage of winning mixed constituencies — the earlier domain of the BN's MCA, Gerakan and MIC. I would argue that a new path dependence has been created in the mixed electoral constituencies favouring the PKR. This argument will be developed below in the voting-pattern analysis for Kuala Lumpur and Selangor, with the presence of Malay-weighted and Chinese-weighted mixed seats.

CROSS-ETHNIC VOTING IN KUALA LUMPUR AND SELANGOR[21]

As can be seen in Table 8.5, the BN received a severe thrashing in Kuala Lumpur in 2008. UMNO candidates only won two seats, while Gerakan and the MCA were shut out completely. The UMNO candidate, who won in the predominantly Malay constituency of Putrajaya where civil servants constituted the electorate, saw the PAS candidate winning some 12.7 per cent more votes than in 2004. All but one of the mixed seats fell to Pakatan. This is explained by a massive swing of Malay, Chinese and Indian votes to the DAP, PKR and even PAS. In total, Pakatan won 61.6 per cent of the vote in Kuala Lumpur and most significantly won all the mixed constituencies except for Setiawangsa. The top-performing Teresa Kok of the DAP won a 19.4 per cent swing of votes in Seputeh, garnering a stunning 36,500 votes, which was 82 per cent of the total. Perhaps the most significant result, however, came in the mixed constituency of Lembah Pantai, where Nurul Izzah, Anwar Ibrahim's daughter, up-ended three-term incumbent and women's minister Shahrizat Abdul Jalil.

Table 8.5
Ethnic Composition and Seats Won in Kuala Lumpur, Putrajaya, 2004 and 2008

	Malay %	Chinese %	Indian %	2004	2008
Kepong	4.1	89.5	6.0	DAP	DAP
Batu	42.9	39.6	16.3	Gerakan	PKR
Wangsa Maju	51.1	39.0	8.5	UMNO	PKR
Segambut	34.9	50.4	13.6	Gerakan	DAP
Setiawangsa	56.4	31.3	10.0	UMNO	UMNO
Titiwangsa	65.0	22.9	11.1	UMNO	PAS
Bukit Bintang	14.7	73.9	10.3	DAP	DAP
Lembah Pantai	52.8	25.3	20.8	UMNO	PKR
Seputeh	5.4	88.9	5.5	DAP	DAP
Cheras	9.3	83.3	7.0	DAP	DAP
Bandar Tun Razak	51.7	39.1	8.3	MCA	PKR
Putrajaya	93.5	1.5	4.2	UMNO	UMNO

Source: Adapted from Ooi, Saravanamuttu and Lee 2008, p. 93.

The 22.2 per cent change in voter swing saw Nurul win by a 2,895 majority, an impressive result for a rookie candidate by any measure. As pointed out by Lee (2008, p. 101), Nurul's win came from the sizeable Chinese and Indian votes, since these communities make up 25.3 and 20.8 per cent of the constituency, respectively.

We now turn to the Selangor results. Selangor registered the largest vote swing of about 21 per cent for Pakatan in both the parliamentary and state contests, winning the coalition some 55 per cent of the total vote. Most impressively, Pakatan won 18 of the 22 parliamentary seats and left the BN with only 3 out of the 18 mixed constituency seats. The DAP and Pakatan swept the 4 constituencies where Chinese voters made up the majority or largest plurality; namely, in Petaling Jaya Utara, Klang, Serdang and Petaling Jaya Selatan. The DAP also won in the mixed seat of Puchong, which had a Malay plurality. PAS candidates defeated their UMNO counterparts in other mixed Malay plurality seats in Shah Alam, Kuala Selangor and Hulu Langat. It is clear from the above results that Pakatan won most of the middle ground in Selangor. This extends the argument for a new path-dependent development of voting behaviour favouring the PR in mixed constituencies in general.

BY-ELECTIONS AFTER 8 MARCH

It will be argued in this section that the path dependence created on 8 March was further reinforced by the results of by-elections held after the general election. There were an unprecedented sixteen by-elections held after the 2008 general election and, remarkably, it was all square for the two coalitions.[22] This section will attempt to briefly review and analyse the results of some of these by-elections and related political developments. On 26 August 2008, as noted above, Anwar Ibrahim won a landslide victory in his old parliamentary constituency of Permatang Puah after his wife Wan Azizah stepped down to let him contest the seat. While this was largely predictable, Anwar's political comeback meant that Pakatan as a coalition was further strengthened with the return of its leader. The second by-election came in Kuala Terengganu on 17 January 2009 with the death of UMNO's deputy education minister Razali Ismail. The PAS candidate,

Abdul Wahid Endut, won 51 per cent of the vote with a comfortable margin of 2,631 votes. This was a major blow to the faltering UMNO leader Abdullah Badawi and his deputy Najib who was responsible for the campaign. Abdullah turned out to be a major casualty of the 8 March political tsunami, with the Kuala Terengannu result propelling his departure from the political stage.

Then came the triple by-elections of 7 April 2009 in Bukit Gantang, Perak; Bukit Selamabu, Kedah; and Batang Air, Sarawak — all state seats. The Batang Air result —which saw a convincing BN win with some 66 per cent of the vote from the mostly Iban population — confirmed that the overall 8 March trend did not really penetrate into East Malaysia. However, the outcome in Perak and Kedah proved the opposite. As I have argued elsewhere (Saravanamuttu 2009d), the new political dynamics were reinforced by the double whammy defeats delivered to the BN in the two "bukits".

Bukit Gantang was the more significant of the two Peninsular by-elections, a parliamentary constituency with an electorate of 55,471 voters lying on the outskirts of Taiping town. A former stronghold of UMNO, it slipped into PAS's grip with the 8 March general election, the Islamic party capturing a credible majority of 1,566 votes. The death of the PAS assemblyman forced the 7 April outcome which saw the charismatic Nizar Jamaluddin take on UMNO's local boy, Ismail Safian. In the event, Nizar, the deposed Menteri Besar of Perak, took the seat with an increased majority of 2,789 — this despite the fact, PAS would admit, that he lost the Malay vote. An analysis by PAS showed that Nizar may have won only 43 per cent of the Malay vote. The results showed that the more rural areas of Trong gave UMNO a majority of votes, while the more urbanized regions around Sepang, Bukit Gantang proper and Kuala Sepetang gave Nizar sizeable majorities. It was a moral victory for Nizar, who was ousted in the Perak Coup orchestrated by UMNO, to be explained below.

The former Menteri Besar won the seat by capturing a sizable portion of the Malay vote, but in Malaysian politics today this is a necessary but not sufficient condition for success. Nizar also had to win the non-Malay vote by a good margin; and he did. Thus the non-Malay electorate have become kingmakers whenever the Malay vote is evenly split. It was clear that Nizar had swept the non-Malay — mostly Chinese — vote to the tune of something like 80 per cent. At the DAP contribution dinner at Simpang, Bukit Gantang, on 5 April, Nizar arrived to speak to the tumultuous roar of approval of thousands of Chinese supporters.[23] A field trip to Kuala Sepatang (formerly Port Weld), gave me the distinct impression that the Chinese fishing community seemed totally supportive of this man, who in his short tenure as Menteri Besar had legalized TOL (Temporary Occupational Licensed) land to Chinese farmers and other tenants.

Nizar had called the by-election a "referendum" on the BN government, particularly the action of new premier Najib Razak in seizing power from the Pakatan government in February 2009. The hung Perak Assembly saw Nizar mounting a legal challenge to newly minted UMNO Menteri Besar Zambry Abdul Kadir, but eventually the courts ruled in the BN's favour. The by-election result was seen not only as indictment of Najib Razak's action but also that of Sultan Raja Azlan Shah, who had speedily anointed Zambry as Menteri Besar without a vote of confidence in the assembly and had rejected Nizar's request to dissolve the assembly for fresh elections after three Pakatan members (one DAP and two PKR) hopped out of the coalition.

In the Bukit Selambau by-election, S. Manikumar of PKR won by a large majority of 2,403 votes, adding a thousand votes to the previous win. This happened despite a line-up of fifteen contenders, something unprecedented in Malaysian history. The PKR win was a major blow to Najib and, in particular, the MIC. Bukit Selambau, with 30 per cent of Indian voters, is a barometer of the MIC's popularity among Indians. The MIC's more experienced S. Ganesan lost to newcomer Manikumar, even though six other Indians — along with six Malays — were there to split the PKR vote. The campaign became acrimonious when MIC Youth kicked up a ruckus at a *ceramah* and the Federal Reserve Unit of the police had to intervene to stop the event early. To my mind the outcome showed that Anwar Ibrahim, who campaigned vigorously in the constituency, effectively deployed a multi-ethnic coalition mode of politics. Additionally, Indian voters prefer to support PKR candidates rather than those from the MIC. The corollary of this is that the BN lost an important plank of support among Indian voters. Furthermore, as shown above, the Chinese also evinced great support even for PAS candidates like Nizar. The Chinese party, MCA, was conspicuous by its absence in campaigning for both by-elections.

Three subsequent by-elections followed. On 14 July PAS retained the Kelantan seat of Manek Urai by a wafer-thin 65 votes. PAS was clearly on the back foot after the exposé and open altercations over "unity talks" with UMNO which implicated their top leadership. By 25 August PAS had regained its ground in Permatang Pasir in the state of Penang, defeating UMNO by capturing some 65 per cent of the 14,832 votes. The PAS candidate of Pakatan routed the UMNO candidate of the BN by 4,511 votes, just 882 shy of the previous victory on 8 March 2008. A drop in voter turnout from 82.6 to 73.1 per cent could account for this margin of difference. More interestingly, according to ground reports, PAS won in both Malay and non-Malay polling stations, and the Chinese areas evinced even more comprehensive support. It appeared then that Pakatan remained the choice for Malaysian voters after seven by-elections on the Peninsula. The other by-election on 31 May in the Penang state seat Penanti saw a no-contest on the part of UMNO and was easily retained by the PKR's Mansor Othman. Three independent candidates lost their deposits.

The BN finally stemmed the tide of by-election losses by a landslide victory in the state seat of Bagan Pinang on 11 October 2009, when former UMNO Negeri Sembilan supremo, Mohd Isa Abdul Samad, roundly defeated his PAS opponent by a majority of 5,435 votes. The Bagan Pinang outcome certainly gave the new prime minister Najib and his government a much needed boost, and pro-government commentators opined that it had stemmed the tide of the 8 March tsunami. What was interesting was the large non-Malay swing towards BN — in particular the Indian vote, which constituted some 21 per cent for that constituency.[24]

The Bagan Pinang result seemed to seal a north–south divide in Peninsular Malaysian politics. Put differently, the states south of Selangor appeared to remain firmly under the BN wing. Conditions in Penang, Kedah and Selangor had largely firmed up with Pakatan well in place. Kelantan on the East Coast remained terra firma for PAS. By the middle of 2010 it seemed that Malaysia's nascent two-party system would remain in place until the next general election. The Perak situation remained muddled until the Federal Court, with a full panel of five judges, unanimously ruled on 9 February 2010 that the UMNO leader Zamry Abdul Kadir was the rightful Menteri Besar. This legal nicety completed Najib's well-executed Perak Coup.[25]

An important contest came on 25 April 2010 by way of the tenth by-election for the parliamentary seat of Hulu Selangor, which was a two-way contest between the MIC (BN) and the PKR (Pakatan). In 2008 the seat had been won by the PKR's candidate by a whisker-thin margin of 198 votes. The new Pakatan heavyweight, Zaid Ibrahim, the former UMNO minister, was clearly affected by money politics and character assassination tactics. The seven thousand FELDA dwellers in the constituency were targeted with a RM1,000 handout and the promise of another RM49,000 should the BN win, while a Chinese school was promised RM3 million after the by-election. To compound the PKR's problems, there were suggestions of internal differences in Zaid's choice as a candidate. In the event, the BN candidate, the MIC's P. Kamalanathan, defeated the PKR's Zaid Ibrahim by 1,725 votes. The BN's win was still a far cry from their 14,483 majority of 2004.

A famous victory for Pakatan came in the parliamentary constituency of Sibu in Sarawak on 16 May. Taking up the cudgels for Pakatan, the DAP candidate Wong Ho Leng defeated his SUPP (Sarawak United Peoples Party) opponent Robert Lau by a 398 vote margin in this predominantly Foochow–Chinese seat (Chinese 66.7 per cent, Iban 22 per cent, Melanau/Malay 10.5 per cent). While slim, the Pakatan victory demonstrated a serious erosion of Chinese and possibly even of Iban support for the BN in its stronghold state of Sarawak. Most importantly, the trajectory of DAP electoral strength in Chinese-dominant constituencies had stabilized two years after March 2008, and indeed had extended to East Malaysia through the 16 April 2011 Sarawak state election. Moreover, the Pakatan as a whole took some 41 per cent of the popular vote and established itself, for the first time, as the main opposition party in the state of Sarawak.[26] The outcome of the Sarawak state election showed that two-coalition electoral politics had found traction in this East Malaysian state, and that particularly Pakatan had made major inroads into the non-Bumiputera constituencies of Sarawak.

Let us now examine the Tenang by-election held on 30 January 2011, which saw the third consecutive by-election victory for the BN since the March 2008 general election.[27] This fourteenth by-election witnessed a resurgence of voter support for the ruling coalition, but it fell short of the five-thousand-vote majority the BN had expected.

UMNO took the seat by a majority of 3,707, some 1,200 more than
it achieved during 2008, with a voter turnout of 9,833, which is only
67 per cent of the electorate. Massive flooding in the constituency on
voting day accounted for the low turnout. Tenang practically exhibits
the Peninsular template of Malay–Chinese–Indian distribution
(49–38–12, and 1 per cent "others"). The UMNO candidate Azahar
Ibrahim swept more than 80 per cent of the Malay vote, while the
PAS challenger Normala Sudirman evidently won the Chinese vote.
She was able only to win a majority in the 95 per cent Chinese polling
area of Labis Tengah, but lost in Labis Timor and Labis Station,
which had lower Chinese percentages. DAP publicity chief Tony Pua
suggested that UMNO's Azahar Ibrahim received 83.3 per cent of the
Malay vote, up four percentage points from 2008. This was helped by
an 81 per cent showing of Malay voters. The Indian vote also went
to the BN, but the community had a low 40 per cent turnout. The
flood situation meant that more assistance was given to UMNO voters
to get to polling stations. The Tenang by-election result could be
predicted before voting day — only the margin of victory was at
issue. As such the interesting points to be made are about the different
styles and tactics taken at the by-election. The BN clearly optimized a
strategy of using its copious resources and electoral machinery to great
effect. The Pakatan on the other hand floundered under the weight of
the BN's power and monopoly of state resources, and had to rely on
its *ceramahs*.

What then was the political significance of the sixteen by-elections
in terms of path dependence for the opposition? *First*, the momentum
of 8 March 2008 establishing a two-party or dual-coalition party system
was clearly affirmed. Indeed, the symmetrical by-election results of
eight wins each seemed to reinforce the trend. Moreover, the Sarawak
state election of April 2011 exhibited a similar traction to the opposition
coalition politics, with the DAP's strength established in the urban areas
and the PKR and PAS making important inroads in rural and semi-
urban areas. The results of these by-elections also showed there was
little room in Sarawak for independents or third parties outside the
coalitions of the BN and Pakatan. *Second*, the BN formula for capturing
cross-ethnic votes became even less effective, while the opposite was
true for Pakatan's forces. *Third*, the Islamic party, PAS, despite some
internal hiccups, increasingly appeared to supersede UMNO as the

voice of the Malays and, furthermore, as the putative Malay voice to non-Malays. This last point comes with two caveats. First, that the process had been ongoing for many years on the East Coast. After 2008, West Coast states like Perak and Kedah increasingly imbibed such a trend. And second, that UMNO still retained strong support among the older generation of voters and among highly rural constituencies. Thus, after sixteen by-elections and one state election, three years into the post-2008 electoral environment there had been no sign that the ruling coalition was regaining its political strength.

CONCLUDING REMARKS

The political moment of 8 March basically had its antecedent in the Reformasi Movement of 1999 in partially disembedding established processes and behavioural characteristics of Malaysian politics. The Anwar episode of 1998–99 generated a post-Mahathirian politics which, coupled with the failure and ineptitude of the short-lived Abdullah Badawi government, created the conditions for the 8 March moment. However, I would not go as far as to argue that "[s]ince March 2008, Malaysia's political landscape has changed forever" (Chin and Wong 2009, p. 83), but that a new path dependence was palpable and reinforced by events, structures and processes generating "increasing returns" to the opposition, and that it promised a genuine political shift in the character of Malaysian politics. This may not have taken the form of a Gramscian moment of organic change (O' Shannassy 2009), but it did steer the political system away from what Pepinsky has termed "electoral authoritarianism" (Pepinsky 2009, p. 115). This same political scientist has also averred that 8 March was a "landmark event" with the suggestion that a sort of political liberalization was occurring.[28] Again, such a change would depend greatly on whether the incipient two-party system took firm root.

In my view March 2008 did indeed symbolize a moment of political crisis for the ruling coalition. In a real sense, UMNO and the BN faced a legitimacy crisis in which the former could no longer stand its ground firmly as a consociational party representing Malays and non-Malays. This legitimacy crisis also ran deep because of the egregious corruption and money politics of the political regime under the BN. Political parties such as UMNO, with its particular form of party capitalism, could evidently lose their legitimacy, just like similar ruling parties had in countries like Taiwan and Japan.[29] Whilst once it was its strength, it could well be argued that UMNO's cronyism became its Achilles heel. After 2008 the Malay vote was spilt almost evenly between UMNO and its two rivals PAS and PKR. PAS has increasingly assumed its role as the putative voice of the Malay-Muslims. The PKR on the other hand, since the 1999 election, has established the importance of its role in vote pooling through the manifestation of cross-ethnic voting in its favoured constituencies — constituencies that had in the past bestowed electoral hegemony to the BN.

Several necessary conditions in mediating communalism to its electoral advantage were lost by the BN. The first was UMNO's previous success at centripetalizing its own extremist racial and religious tendency towards moderation and centrist religious policies. This took a turn during Abdullah Badawi's era when UMNO was not able to rein in the more extremist and non-accommodative stances among some sections of the Islamic bureaucracy and civil society on inter-faith issues and controversies. This cost the BN its non-Malay support. The second condition was the prevention of an alternative but equally formidable coalition to compete with the BN. Despite Abdullah's strategy of calling for an early election to prevent Anwar from contesting, this was unsuccessful at preventing the three parties from entering into an electoral pact to contest seats in a more strategically distributive manner. The PKR contested in mixed constituencies, PAS in Malay-majority areas, while the DAP took on the traditional urban and Chinese-majority seats. Hence, while the BN did not lose the election outright, its formula for successfully mediating communalism had been shaken, if not overtaken, by the PR. One very important condition (among several) which saw the BN to victory, was its continuing ability to garner the majority vote from its Malay and bumiputera constituencies. The former was from its rural seats and the latter from the East Malaysian seats.

Finally, we return to the point made earlier that 8 March saw a culmination of *new politics* generated by the Reformasi Movement of the late 1990s. This was a politics which valorized participatory democracy and the engagement of civil society forces directly in the electoral process. It was also one which set reformist agendas aimed at eroding a power bloc embedded in a form of highly corrupt, party politics. The trajectory of *new politics*, while remaining ethnic in sensibility and political mobilization, nonetheless favoured cross-ethnic or multi-ethnic political coalitions aiming for a reformed political economy not anchored entirely on race.

Notes

1. Eric Chia was Mahathir's ill-fated choice to run the already troubled steel company that Mahathir started in the 1980s (see previous chapter). In the end, Eric Chia, after a three-year legal battle, was acquitted on 26 June 2007 because of insufficient evidence.
2. Many have accused the prime minister of not moving on this because of the objection of the upper echelons of the police force against its implementation.
3. There was a spate of such cases. Most famously was that of Lina Joy (alias Azlina Jalaini), a forty-three-year-old woman who was denied her conversion to Christianity when the Federal Court ruled on 29 May 2007 that the word "Islam" could not be removed from her identity card. In another case, in the last week of 2005, the body of thirty-six-year-old Moorthy was claimed by the Islamic religious authorities for burial after a shariah court ruled he had converted to Islam. Moorthy's wife challenged the decision in a civil court but to no avail.
4. See *Malaysiakini*, 24 July 2006. Among the resolutions passed were the following: the Federal Constitution and other laws be strengthened to stop attempts to use the courts to weaken the position of Islam; every threat to Islam signifies a threat to the dignity and position of the Malay Rulers who are the heads of Islam in every state and to the integrity of the Islamic institutions; efforts to overhaul and erode the position of Islam in the Constitution and national laws should be stopped; religious rights and freedoms should be understood in the framework of Islam, not according to individual inclinations; all state and federal legislative assemblies should pass enactments that prevent the propagation to Muslims of religions other than Islam, and these should be implemented immediately. An account of the failure of Pak Lah to contain Muslim pressure groups is found in Saravanamuttu (2010*b*, pp. 90–101).
5. Most pundits couldn't see the opposition winning more than 40 seats. At a pre-election seminar in ISEAS, two days before polling day, the

main speaker Dato' Michael Yeoh of the Malaysian think tank ASLI and other speakers were confident that the BN would retain its two-thirds majority.

6. See Stephen Gan's editorial in the Internet paper *Malaysiakini*, 19 March 2008.

7. The exceptions were Terengganu, Perlis and Pahang, but even these states swung in single digit percentage points. See Table 1.

8. In the 1969 general election the Alliance took only 44.9 per cent of the ballot, while the opposition captured a majority of the total vote. The Alliance lost its two-thirds majority in Parliament and the elections in Sarawak and Sabah were postponed. Both Perak and Selangor were also on the balance in terms of seats held; Perak virtually lost, but the opposition was split and had no electoral pact. See Chapter 4. For a broad discussion of the implications of 8 March in contrast to 1969, see Chapter 1 of Ooi, Saravanamuttu and Lee (2008).

9. This observation is based on personal experience as I was present in May 1969 as a journalist in Kuala Lumpur and I also observed the 2008 event in Kelantan and Penang.

10. See Ooi's "the Opposition's Year of Living Demonstratively" for an account of extraordinary events in Penang in Ooi, Saravanamuttu and Lee (2008, pp. 17–20).

11. The narrative of 8 March, its outcome and ramifications draw considerably on these earlier pieces of my writing, but further updating and analytical points have been added in this chapter.

12. For the notion of political goods, see the work of Pennock (1966). Some debate has ensued about the nature of political goods (cf. De Mesquita and Downs 2005), but I refer to the political goods identified by Pennock; namely, security, welfare, justice and liberty.

13. Also known as "People's Pact". I will also be using "Pakatan" to refer to the PR as this is commonly used by journalists and politicians.

14. Admittedly, this may not be absolutely correct going by standard political science concepts, which require "turnovers" of governments and also their consolidation by subsequent elections. In Malaysia's case this could apply to only Kelantan and Terengganu at the state level.

15. See Maznah Mohamad (2008, p. 446).

16. This is the conjecture advanced by Lee (Ooi et al. 2008, pp. 113–14).

17. See Lee's analysis of the Kuala Lumpur voting (Ooi et al. 2008, pp. 92–103).

18. Perak was lost to the BN after three Pakatan legislators crossed over in February 2009. Two were from the PKR and one was the deputy speaker from the DAP. See the discussion further below.

19. See *The Star* <http://thestar.com.my/news/story.asp?file=/2008/5/11/nation/21218890&sec=nation> (accessed 30 December 2008).

20. The scatter plots do not show the seats won by UMNO, the MCA, MIC and Gerakan or other component parties of the BN. I have made my inferences by examining the information on candidates' ethnicity given in the detailed results provided by the Election Commission.

21. I draw the data and analysis from the study by Lee (Chapter 3) in Ooi, Saravanamuttu and Lee (2008).

22. There was also the Sarawak state election held on 16 April 2011, the implications of which will be drawn in the concluding section.

23. I was there to witness the immense popularity of this man, who was greatly liked by Chinese and Indian voters.

24. The actual break-out of fights between UMNO and PAS supporters in the campaign period showed the intensity of intra-Malay politics, a phenomenon which I was able to witness for myself on my visit there towards the end of the campaign period. The rumour was also circulating that Mohd Isa had spent a great deal of money to fish for Indian votes.

25. See the *Star Online*, 9 February 2010 <http://thestar.com.my/news/story.asp?file=/2010/2/9/nation/20100209091318&sec=nation> (accessed 26/02/10). The decision has been criticized by civil groups and legal experts as having overturned a legal precedent that a vote of no-confidence is required if a head of government does tender his resignation. The judges ruled that the Perak Sultan's decision to appoint a new Menteri Besar was valid despite the lack of a no-confidence vote in the state assembly.

26. I was in Sarawak to observe some of the electoral campaigns and the mood in urban areas was decidedly pro-opposition, with typical massive attendances at PR rallies. The state election saw the BN winning 55 seats, with the PBB — Taib's party — winning all 35 seats contested, the PRS winning 8, the SPDP winning 6, and the SUPP 6. The BN more than retained its two-thirds majority, with the PR winning 15 seats in total, and 1 going to an independent. Within the BN coalition, SUPP crashed with the defeat of its leader George Chan and deputy Tiong Thai King and retained only 2 Chinese seats. Its nemesis was the DAP, which was the biggest winner on the opposition side, taking 12 of the 15 seats it contested. The PKR faired poorly in terms of seats, contesting 49 and winning only 3. However, Baru Bian, the land rights champion won his seat for the PKR in Ba'kelalan. So too another prominent land rights lawyer, the PKR's See Chee How, in Batu Lintang. One other seat in the Miri area (Senadin) was won by the BN by a mere 58 votes. While

PAS lost all 5 seats that it contested, it came within 391 votes of winning the predominantly Malay-Melanau seat of Beting Maro. See Saravanamuttu and Rusaslina (2011).

27. The BN went on to win two other by-elections on 6 March 2011 in Malacca; namely, in the state seats of Merlimau and Kerdau, previously held by UMNO.

28. The caveat, according to Pepinsky, was whether UMNO "hard-liners" (Najib) or "soft-liners" (Abdullah) had the upper hand in politics: "For the 2008 Malaysian elections to yield true liberalization, the BN's soft-liners must come to believe that liberalization holds the key to their political survival, while hard-liners must be contained" (Pepinsky 2009, p. 117). Going by this argument, Abdullah's fall and Najib's ascendancy must then have cast a gloomy shadow over Malaysian political liberalization.

29. See my analysis of party capitalism in Chapter 6.

9

ELECTORAL IMPASSE OF DUAL-COALITION POLITICS IN 2013

The 13th general election could be seen as failure for both grand coalitions of the BN and the PR. The BN failed to win as many seats as it did in 2008, indicating that its previously highly successful coalition politics and its strategy of mediated communalism was finally being seriously contested. For the PR, its failure to win the election in spite of its spectacular success in overtaking the BN for the share of the popular vote (of 51 per cent) was an indication that its consociational model was still unable to surpass that of the BN. In a sense, for the first time in Malaysia's history, there was an almost perfect competition between the two rival coalitions, leading to a sort of impasse in terms of electoral outcome.

For some the 13th general election could be interpreted as a "victory" of the people and civil society in that citizens' political efficacy had never been greater. There were record voter turnouts and civic engagement had surged to its most impressive level, even surpassing that prior to the previous general election. For the BN it was a pyrrhic exercise, given the massive resources expended and the less-than-satisfactory overall returns. Notably, a skewed electoral system, manipulation of voter rolls, unethical electoral practices and outright fraud continue to stymie the movement towards a critical break for a change in the electoral system. It could, however, be hypothesized that the progressive change in electoral dynamics, while affecting ethnic relations marginally, seems to have broken new ground, symbolized by a shift in the national popular vote to the PR for the first time. Against this is the resurgence of the deeply embedded political discourse of Malay supremacy, which is reflexively reinforced by a pivotal Islamic discourse and practice among the Muslim population.

What was evident was that the path dependence of the *twin-coalition system* of the BN and PR was affirmed as the system remained firmly on track. More remarkably, no third parties won any seats at the parliamentary level. Most third-party and independent candidates lost badly at both the state and federal levels — many forfeiting their deposits — indicating that the electorate had by and large accepted the incipient two-coalition system. Whether this path dependence will develop further depends on the opposition's capacity to continue to develop its institutional structures and its strategies to reap increasing returns.[1] As the next chapter shows, the opposition coalition disbanded in mid-2015, showing that the substantial differences between two of the constituent parties (PAS and the DAP) could not be resolved, and that institutional mechanisms of conflict resolution were weak or absent in the PR.

When comparing the outcomes of 2008 and 2013, not much seemed to have changed by way of broad voting patterns. The impressive gain in the popular vote by the PR made a new technical break, but with little substantial meaning; that is, it was only a signifier without a signified. In fact, as I have suggested, the rupture or critical conjuncture in electoral politics occurred in 2008, which should be taken as historically more path-breaking than what occurred in 2013.[2] For the more sanguine among the opposition watchers, the electoral breach could come by the 14th general election but detractors might argue that internal party dissent coupled with the absence of Anwar Ibrahim could prove to be insurmountable obstacles to such an outcome.

UNPRECEDENTED CAMPAIGN[3]

Given the anticipation of a plausible opposition victory for the first time, 2013 witnessed one of the most, if not *the* most, participatory, exciting and vibrant campaigns in Malaysian electoral history. The BN conducted a presidential-style campaign to counter the PR's people-centric approach. The fifteen-day campaign period from 21 April till 4 May was the longest of the past seven general elections. That said, the issues raised on the PR campaign trail were anticipated as they had been brought up time and again over the past several years. However, this did not stem the avalanche of audiences to PR rallies throughout the country. The opposition coalition promised voters a Malaysia free of corruption and money politics, imbued with economic transparency and accountability, and democratic governance that implied instituting the electoral reforms advocated by the BERSIH movement. The PR manifesto, a populist one, offered, inter alia, free education up to the tertiary level, a minimum wage of RM1,100, affordable housing, cheaper cars, cheaper petrol and the incremental abolition of highway tolls. Targeting the oil-rich states, the PR promised a 20 per cent royalty instead of the current 5 per cent. In the Kuching Declaration of 16 September 2012 (made on Malaysia Day), along with "oil justice", the PR offered the Borneo states restoration of customary rights land and an equal partnership with Peninsular Malaysia.

In my visit to Sabah just before the campaign period, politicians from both sides of the divide never failed to remind me that Sabah and Sarawak joined Malaysia on equal terms with "Malaya".[4] As for the issues pertaining to the Indian minority — now greatly fragmented politically after the splintering of HINDRAF — the DAP's Gelang Patah Declaration of 31 March 2013 offered empowerment and citizenship to stateless individuals as well as other measures to deal with poverty and unemployment.

The BN manifesto was trotted out soon after Pakatan's, about two weeks before nomination day on 20 April. Najib offered a strong and stable government, moderation and power sharing, and continued "transformation" of the Malaysian economy. More blatantly, all the "1Malaysia" programmes were to be continued, including a third

BR1M — a cash handout programme of RM500 to Malaysians earning less than RM1,000 per month. Tagged on late in the day to its manifesto was also the lowering of car prices, which the PR alleged was a copy of their policy.

As I traversed the campaign trail on the west coast of the peninsula, two slogans — "Ini Kali Lah, Ubah" (This is the Time, Change) and "Wu Yue Wu, Huan Zheng Fu" (5th of May, Change the Government) — reverberated throughout the massive Pakatan rallies. These two clarion calls had replaced "Makkal Sakti", the HINDRAF battle cry constantly heard during the 2008 campaign. Thousands of Malaysians thronged the PR rallies to savour the rousing and entertaining speeches of Anwar Ibrahim and other prominent leaders of the PR parties. The atmosphere at these rallies was festive and celebratory. The BN could offer no real alternative, with hardly any rallies to talk of, though the free dinners in Penang did attract crowds. The expensive ploy of bringing the Korean sensation PSY (of the *Gangnam* hit song fame) to a Penang audience with Najib in attendance turned out to be a public relations disaster, as the crowd repeatedly rejected the premier's call to support the BN.[5] The PR in contrast expended little money to draw the crowds who swarmed to its entertaining *ceramahs*. The unprecedented seventy-thousand-strong PR rally at Sutera Mall in Johor and the hundred-thousand-strong rally at Padang Kota in Penang breached all records of rally attendances and evidently showed that PR supporters were hungry for a regime change.

FAILED QUEST

From a campaign perspective Pakatan gained massive ground, and yet it failed in its quest to take Putrajaya. Symbolic of this failure was PAS vice president Husam Musa's inability to wrest the seat of Putrajaya itself. We will focus mostly on the parliamentary contest in this section. The main reason the BN lost a great deal of ground in this election could be explained by the massive swing of urban votes to the PR. Another explanation for the swing towards PR could well be the youth vote, which I will touch on shortly with respect to a constituency in Selangor. What has been patently clear was that the

East–West divide evidently favoured the BN, with Sarawak and Sabah delivering 25 per cent of the BN's seats. These two states explain a great deal of the variance of the overall urban–rural electoral divide, which is discussed in some detail below.

Najib's knee-jerk response to the outcome of the 13th general election was to label it a "Chinese tsunami". Although clearly a political statement, it would not be wrong to suggest that large numbers of Chinese voters supported the PR. But for it to win big, even larger numbers of Malay as well as non-Malay-bumiputera votes were required, which the PR failed to obtain. The ethnic vote varies from state to state. For example, in 2013 a majority of Malays tended to throw their weight behind the BN in Kedah, when they had mostly swung in favour of PAS in 2008. (In an analytical section below, I show the percentage swings, positive and negative for the PR.) The Kedah vote contrasts starkly with the continued support the Malay voters gave to the PR via PAS in Kelantan. On the other hand there was a rise of Malay support for the BN in Terengganu, which it won by a mere two seats. The near decimation of the MCA and Gerakan, with the latter losing all seats it contested in Penang, and the low returns for the MIC revealed that Chinese and Indian voters had little appetite for these BN parties, which were supposed to represent their interests. Whether this is a testimony to growing multiracialism (as some even conferred victory to PAS candidates contesting in high non-Malay areas), or just a discretionary protest preference among these largely urban-based voters, would be hard to tell. But the DAP by fielding two winning Malay candidates showed that it was able to bandwagon on multiracial politics in the more urban areas.

THE 2013 RESULTS

One should first pose the question of what sort of "victory" the outcome of the 13th general election of 5 May 2013 represented for the BN and then ask whether it was truly a defeat for the PR. Without a doubt it was a poor victory for the BN, given the copious amount of money and resources expended in the campaign, and yet it won a lower majority of seats and lost the popular vote. Many have raised the point of how the BN could not be said to have really won the election, garnering as it did only 47 per cent of the popular vote while the PR went past 50 per cent, customarily thought to be a marker of victory in most contests (see Table 9.1). Malaysia's first-past-the-post system is notorious for immense distortions of voter choice, leading to what has been called "manufactured majorities" (Chapter 2) and "stolen elections".[6] In the 1969 election the Alliance won a simple majority in Parliament with about 45 per cent of the vote, taking 55 per cent of the 140 seats.[7] The 2013 outcome was rather similar. The BN won about 47 per cent of the popular vote but has garnered 60 per cent of the seats.

It has been pointed out by many analysts that the Malaysian electoral system has been gerrymandered to favour incumbents and constituencies apportioned to rural areas.[8] This has worked well for the BN, and the Alliance before it, in all general elections since Independence. The rationale for greater rural weighting was not initially thought to be unreasonable given that rural areas had scant access to resources and communication and deserved some form of affirmative action. However, the Electoral Commission has over time completely ignored a 15 per cent limit on weighting

Table 9.1
The Popular Vote in the 2013 General Election

Peninsular Malaysia	Total vote	Percentage
Pakatan Rakyat (PR)	5,035,611	53.29
Barisan Nasional (BN)	4,322,129	45.74
Others	89,986	0.95
Nationwide	**Total vote**	**Percentage**
Pakatan Rakyat (PR)	5,623,984	50.87
Barisan Nasional (BN)	5,237,699	47.38
Others	192,894	1.74

Source: Azlan Zamhari, Malaysiakini.

Figure 9.1
Parliamentary Constituencies, Ranked by Size 2008

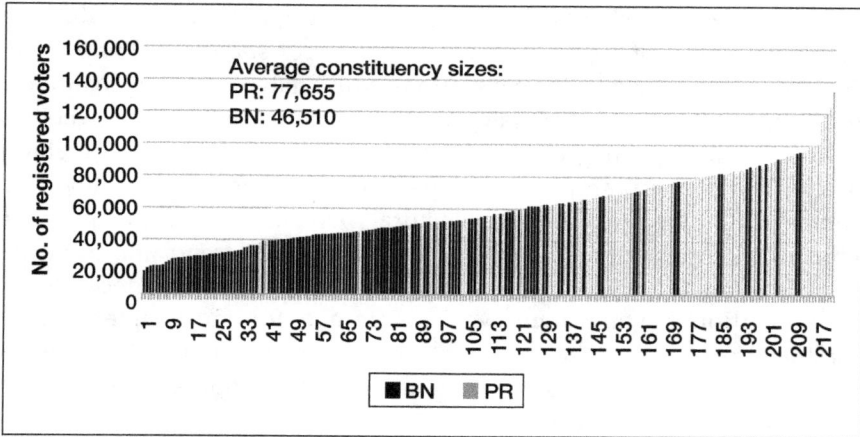

Source: EC data, 2013.

given to rural seats. This is the main reason for the current huge distortion in results. Figure 9.1 shows the extent of malapportionment in 2013.

As noted before, in 1969 and in the election in 2013, the Alliance and BN respectively failed to gain the popular vote but still retained power with a simple majority of seats. This anomaly is explained by the BN winning in predominantly rural and semi-rural areas (and with slimmer majorities) while the PR won convincingly in the urban areas, giving rise to what is now labelled a rural–urban divide in Malaysia's electoral politics. (I provide further analysis of this in a section below.) This is not to say that the PR did not win at all in rural areas, only that its wins were smaller, and the same goes for the BN in urban seats. The often-stated fact about such lopsidedness is that Sarawak and Sabah have been allocated 31 and 25 seats, respectively, counting for a quarter of the total parliamentary seats, and thus have been dubbed the "fixed deposits" for the BN. In this election the two states combined delivered 47 seats to the ruling coalition (see Table 9.2).

THE CONTEST FOR STATES

The sense of palpable failure to maintain the five state governments it won in 2008 was clearly felt by Pakatan supporters. The failure to maintain control of Kedah and the near miss of success in Perak were symbolic of this failure. In this section I will analyse the two coalitions, tracking the contest at the state level. An obvious question is whether Pakatan's slippage in peninsular states represents a re-strengthening of the BN's clout and its own path dependence at this level of contestation. Table 9.2 shows electoral percentages, or the popular vote, of the opposition since the 1995 election. The trend line from the table is shown as Figure 9.2. Without doubt, a clear path dependence of opposition advancement was maintained for most states except for the dip in 2004. That said, the opposition has only been able to rise above the crucial 50 per cent level of the popular vote in five states so far.

Table 9.2
2013 General Election Results by Parliamentary and State Seats Won

	Parliament			State		
	At stake	*BN*	*PR*	*At stake*	*BN*	*PR*
Perlis	3	3	0	15	13	2
Kedah	15	10	5	36	21	15
Penang	13	3	10	40	10	30
Perak	24	12	12	59	31	28
Kelantan	14	5	9	45	12	33
Terengganu	8	4	4	32	17	15
Pahang	14	10	4	42	30	12
Selangor	22	5	17	56	12	44
N.S.	8	5	3	36	22	14
Melaka	6	4	2	28	21	7
Johor	26	21	5	56	38	18
Sabah	25	22	3	60	48	12
Sarawak*	31	25	6	71	55	15
TOTAL	222	133	89	567	330	245

Source: Electoral Commission (*2011 state results).

Figure 9.2
Percentage of Opposition Vote Share by State and Election Year

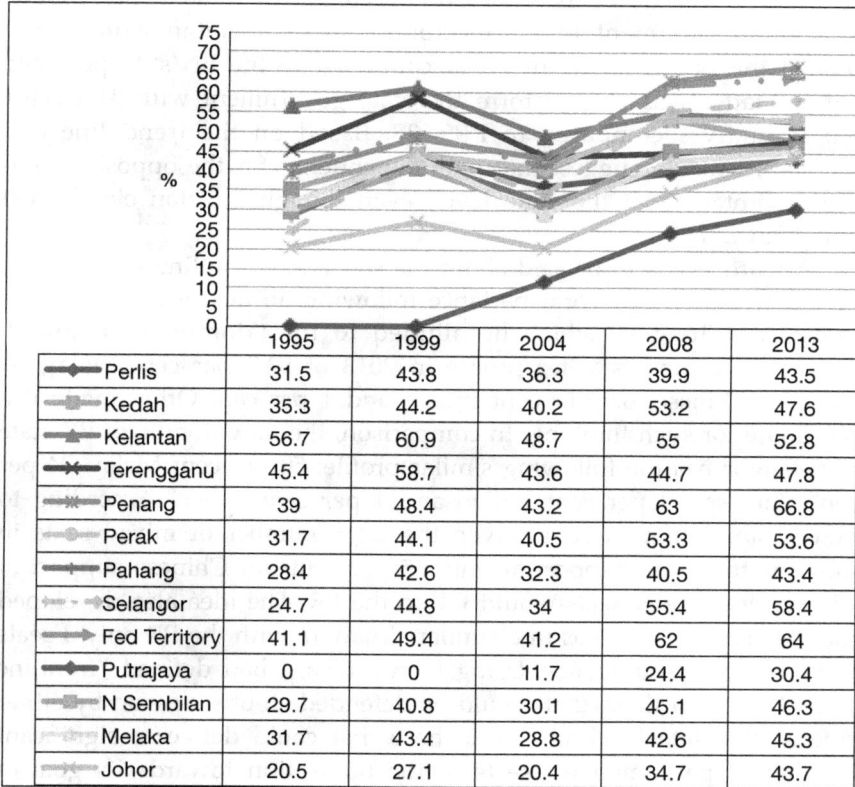

	1995	1999	2004	2008	2013
Perlis	31.5	43.8	36.3	39.9	43.5
Kedah	35.3	44.2	40.2	53.2	47.6
Kelantan	56.7	60.9	48.7	55	52.8
Terengganu	45.4	58.7	43.6	44.7	47.8
Penang	39	48.4	43.2	63	66.8
Perak	31.7	44.1	40.5	53.3	53.6
Pahang	28.4	42.6	32.3	40.5	43.4
Selangor	24.7	44.8	34	55.4	58.4
Fed Territory	41.1	49.4	41.2	62	64
Putrajaya	0	0	11.7	24.4	30.4
N Sembilan	29.7	40.8	30.1	45.1	46.3
Melaka	31.7	43.4	28.8	42.6	45.3
Johor	20.5	27.1	20.4	34.7	43.7

What was interesting in 2013 was that all states registered a positive improvement for the Pakatan over 2008, except for Kedah (not surprising) and Kelantan (somewhat unexpected). Of note is the opposition vote in Putrajaya, where PAS heavyweight Husam Musa, although losing, made the spectacular gain of six percentage points. Three other brief observations deserve to be made. First, Perlis and Terengannu, two Malay dominant states, registered a significant improvement of 3 or more percentage points. Second, Penang, Selangor and Kuala Lumpur seem destined to be Pakatan terrain, with the popular vote reaching 67, 58 and 64 per cent, respectively. These cases graphically illustrate that urbanization and modernization are broadly the main factors behind Pakatan's advance. Third, the Perak situation particularly illustrated the problem of malapportionment in the electoral system. Pakatan won 54 per cent of the popular vote in Perak compared to the BN's 45 per cent, but the latter was able to form the state government with 31 elected representatives compared to PR's 28. Based on the trend line and statistics, I would suggest that path dependence for the opposition has been maintained at the state level, even though Pakatan clearly lost Kedah in 2013.

A word needs to be said about the so-called "frontline states". This notion came into electoral parlance following an article by the DAP's Liew Chin Tong in which he alluded to the "dominoes in Johor" (Liew 2013). Johor's voter profile in 2013 of 53.2 per cent Malay, 39 per cent Chinese, 6.5 per cent Indian and 1 per cent Other made it a candidate for such thinking. In comparison, the now dominant PR state of Selangor has the following similar profile: 50 per cent Malay, 34 per cent Chinese, 14 per cent Indian and 1 per cent Other.[9] According to Liew's simulation exercise, given the large number of mixed seats in Johor, with Malay support at only 35 per cent but Chinese support at 75 per cent, 16 BN seats would fall to the PR. The idea also developed that Negri Sembilan was in a similar situation, with the PR only 3 seats short of state incumbency. Using Liew's idea, I had defined "frontline states" to mean those that would be defended stoutly or won by either side at the state level, and also those that could deliver a significant number of parliamentary seats to the opposition towards its goal of capturing the government. Let me focus particularly on the outcomes in Johor, Negri Sembilan, Sabah and Sarawak.

The PR made an unprecedented penetration of Johor, customarily touted as UMNO's and the MCA's bastion. From a standing of merely 1 parliamentary and 6 state seats, the PR has now secured 5 (out of 26) parliamentary and 18 (out of 56) state seats. In the *battle royale* of Gelang Patah, DAP veteran Lim Kit Siang resoundingly defeated Abdul Ghani Othman, the former Menteri Besar, by 14,762 votes in a mixed parliamentary constituency of over 106,864 electors. Thus, Johor no longer appears to be a safe haven for the BN. Many BN defeats came from MCA losses, while the PKR (Parti Keadilan Rakyat) picked up 1 parliamentary and 1 state seat and PAS took 4 state seats, an improvement of 3 from the previous outing. The DAP was Pakatan's major winner, securing 3 new parliamentary seats and 14 state seats, 10 more than before. Two significant defeats for the PR came by way of Salahuddin Ayub, a PAS vice president losing in Pulai, and Chua Jui Meng, a PKR vice president losing in Sagamat.[10] All said, UMNO stayed its ground in Johor and denied Pakatan parties the larger breakthrough that they had hoped for.

In Negri Sembilan the status quo was more or less maintained, with the PR holding on to 3 (out of 8) parliamentary seats but with 1 loss in the state, taking 14 out of 36 seats. This result put paid to the suggestion that Pakatan was en route to capturing state power and capable of taking an extra 4 seats from the outcome of 2008. In a similar situation in Perak, Pakatan was 3 short of reassuming the state power that it lost by crossovers in 2009. Oddly, while no major plan of capturing Terengganu was announced, Pakatan came within spitting distance, 2 seats short of the target, and winning about 48 per cent of the popular vote.

Table 9.3
Vote Percentages for Opposition Parliamentary Candidates, 1995–2013

State	1995	1999	2004	2008	2013	Change 2004–8	Change 2008–13
Perlis	31.5	43.8	36.3	39.9	43.5	+3.6	+3.6
Kedah	35.3	44.2	40.2	53.2	47.6	+13.0	−5.6
Kelantan	56.7	60.9	48.7	55.0	52.8	+6.3	−2.2
Terengganu	45.4	58.7	43.6	44.7	47.8	+1.1	+3.1
Penang	39.0	48.4	43.2	63.0	66.8	+19.8	+3.8
Perak	31.7	44.1	40.5	53.3	53.6	+12.8	+0.3
Pahang	28.4	42.6	32.3	40.5	43.4	+8.2	+2.9
Selangor	24.7	44.8	34.0	55.4	58.4	+21.4	+3
Kuala Lumpur	41.1	49.4	41.2	62.0	64.0	+20.8	+2
Putrajaya	—	—	11.7	24.4	30.4	+12.7	+6
N. Sembilan	29.7	40.8	30.1	45.1	46.3	+15.0	+1.2
Melaka	31.7	43.4	28.8	42.6	45.3	+13.8	+2.7
Johor	20.5	27.1	20.4	34.7	43.7	+14.3	+9

Source: Philip Khoo 2008, p. 4 and Election Commission, Malaysia, 2013.

In Sabah and Sarawak there were gains but no major breakthrough for the PR. In Sarawak, 6 parliamentary seats were captured, a modest gain, 5 delivered by the DAP and 1 by PKR. In Sabah the capture of 3 parliamentary seats by the PR was 2 more than before. As such, this was a poor performance, due mainly to multi-cornered contests in many seats. However, at the state level Pakatan's penetration could be said to be significant, with PKR winning 7 seats and the DAP 4.

All said, the PR's foray into the new frontline states and its defence of old terrain failed to yield the desired results. There was the loss of Kedah and the less-than-stellar performance in Negri Sembilan, and the lacklustre results in Sabah and Sarawak proved crucial in its failure to gain the seat of power in Putrajaya.

ETHNIC AND CROSS-ETHNIC VOTING PATTERNS IN 2008 AND 2013

In this section I will compare the ethnic character of voting as well as the level of cross-ethnic voting in the 2008 and 2013 elections. A major reason for the exercise is to explore and validate whether there has been path dependence from one election to the other, and if there is any indication of breakthroughs, especially in cross-ethnic voting. I will begin by examining the broad patterns of the ethnic vote and then move on to consider results of the largely mixed constituencies in the Kuala Lumpur Federal Territory.

Figures 9.3, 9.4 and 9.5 comprise three scatter plots showing parliamentary seats won in 2008 and 2013 by the main parties in Peninsular Malaysia in terms of the ethnic proportionality of seats. As noted before, based on data provided by the Election Commission, the parties of the ruling coalition are collapsed into the BN, while the three parties of the opposition are displayed. The first broad observation is that the scatter plots of the two outcomes reveal almost identical results and an almost identical pattern. Malaysian political parties are still predominantly ethnic in their electoral politics; and, as noted in the previous chapter, the Malay-based UMNO and PAS tend to be successful in majority Malay constituencies while the DAP scores in predominantly Chinese constituencies. The rising contender

Figure 9.3
Percentage of Malay Voters by Seats Won, 2013

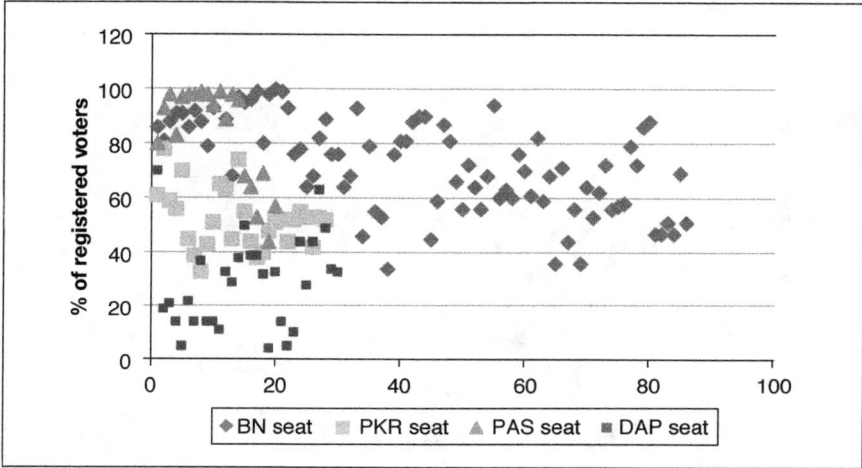

Figure 9.4
Percentage of Chinese Voters by Seats Won, 2013

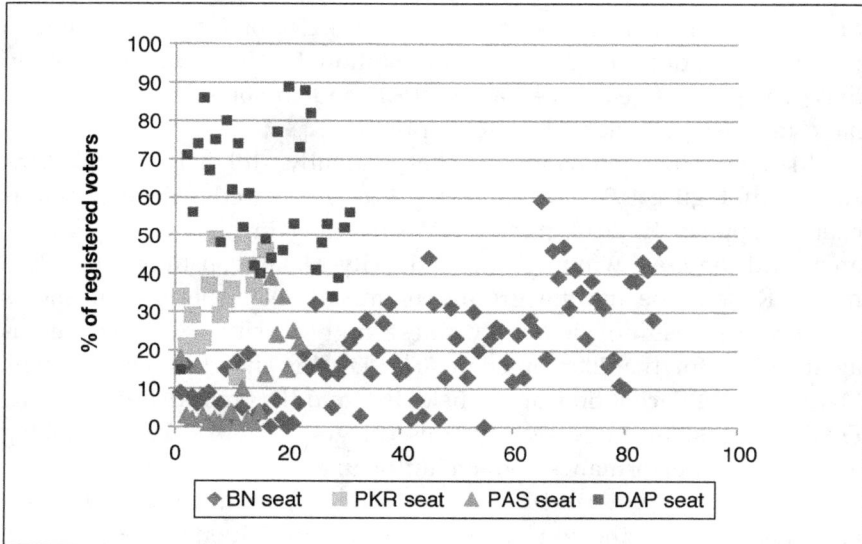

Figure 9.5
Percentage of Indian Voters by Seats Won, 2013

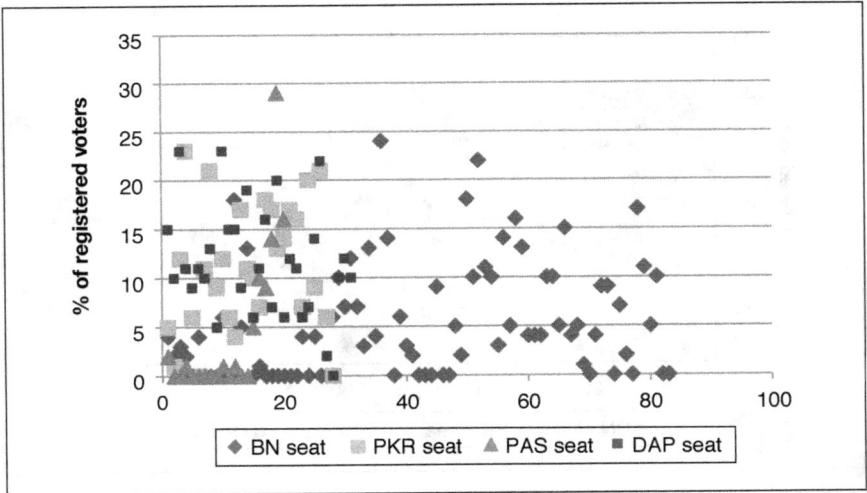

in mixed constituencies tends to be the PKR, which has performed with great success in the last two outings. We could extrapolate from the scatter plots that non-Malay political parties of the BN — like the MCA, Gerakan and MIC — also find some electoral success in mixed constituencies despite their ethnic orientation, but have faded visibly in these category of seats even as the PKR and to some extent the DAP have increasingly established their presence.

Malay voting behaviour in 2008 evidently still held for 2013, as shown in Figure 9.3. The modality that I stressed in the previous chapter applied in 2013; namely, PAS winning in high density Malay areas and the DAP winning in low density Malay constituencies while the PKR held the middle ground of mixed seats. Figure 9.4 shows the obverse position vis-à-vis Chinese high-density constituencies as again noted for the 2008 outcome. The DAP is the clear winner here. Overall, the PR coalition again held the middle ground but with the DAP taking some more seats in this category in 2013. When looking at the BN's performance, which unfortunately is not broken down into its component parties, it can still be deduced that UMNO continued to win the high-density Malay constituencies as in 2008, while the trend of BN rejection in high density Chinese areas also obtains.

The Indian vote as shown in Figure 9.5 exhibits similar modalities to 2008, with the PKR and DAP doing well but the two PAS outliers in 2008 now reduced to one. While the BN parties had fared poorly in securing the Indian vote in 2008, with barely four wins, their performance improved markedly to nearly seven wins in 2013 among Indians. The breakup of HINDRAF and the overall fragmentation of Indian political entities on the opposition side explain the MIC's credible performance in 2013. The PKR, acting as a multi-ethnic political party and putting up multi-ethnic candidates, continued to secure the Indian vote, with some marginal losses in the latest outing. Its partners, the DAP and PAS, continued to hold their own on predominantly Chinese and Malay terrain. The new PR arrangement had clearly dented the BN's advantage of winning mixed constituencies, which were the earlier domain of the BN parties such as the MCA, Gerakan and MIC. I would maintain through this comparison of outcomes that path dependence was created in the mixed electoral constituencies in 2008 and continued to hold in 2013. However, some erosion of the trend is duly noted among Indians. This argument will be extended below in the analysis of the Kuala Lumpur and Selangor voting pattern with respect to Malay-weighted and Chinese-weighted mixed seats.

CROSS-ETHNIC VOTING IN KUALA LUMPUR AND SELANGOR

Kuala Lumpur and urbanized Selangor turned out to be disaster zones for the BN in the last two electoral outings. Table 9.4 shows the Kuala Lumpur seats and voting outcomes for 2004, 2008 and 2013. Again, hardly anything had changed in 2013 except for the BN wresting Titiwangsa after the massive slide since 2004. UMNO candidates only won 3 seats, while its non-Malay partners completely lost presence. UMNO continued its win in the predominantly Malay constituency of Putrajaya, where civil servants constitute the majority of the electorate, but PAS picked up another 6 percentage points in 2013. All the mixed seats but 2 fell to Pakatan in 2013. Despite gaining 2 percentage points

Table 9.4
Ethnic Composition and Kuala Lumpur, Putrajaya Results

	Malay %	Chinese %	Indian %	2004	2008	2013
Kepong	4	89	6	DAP	DAP	DAP
Batu	44	38	16	GERAKAN	PKR	PKR
Wangsa Maju	52	40	7	UMNO	PKR	PKR
Segambut	33	53	12	GERAKAN	DAP	DAP
Setiawangsa	56	30	11	UMNO	UMNO	UMNO
Titiwangsa	68	20	10	UMNO	PAS	UMNO
Bukit Bintang	14	73	11	DAP	DAP	DAP
Lembah Pantai	55	23	20	UMNO	PKR	PKR
Seputeh	5	88	6	DAP	DAP	DAP
Cheras	10	82	7	DAP	DAP	DAP
Bandar Tun Razak	53	37	9	MCA	PKR	PKR
Putrajaya	94	0	3	UMNO	UMNO	UMNO

Source: Ooi, Saravanamuttu, Lee 2008 and Electoral Commission 2013.

in the popular vote to a noteworthy 64 per cent, 1 more seat fell to the BN in 2013. Most significantly, Pakatan won all the mixed constituencies, which had a high percentage of Malay voters, except for Setiawangsa and Titiwangsa. The top performing Teresa Kok of the DAP, who had won a 19.4 per cent swing of votes in Seputeh in 2008, continued her stellar performance in 2013 with a 51,552 majority, or about 72 per cent of the total vote.

One of the most serious challenges for Pakatan came in the mixed constituency of Lembah Pantai, where Nurul Izzah, Anwar Ibrahim's daughter, defeated three-term incumbent and women's minister Shahrizat Abdul Jalil in 2008. Riding the 21 per cent in voter swing in Kuala Lumpur, Nurul won by a 2,895 majority, an impressive result by any measure for a novice candidate. In 2013 she faced the formidable Raja Nong Chik, the Federal Territories and urban well-being minister who pulled no punches in trying to unseat her in a particularly acrimonious contestation marred by incidents. A major controversy revolved around the large number of new voters in Lembah Pantai, and on polling day Pakatan supporters blocked cars allegedly carrying a number of ballot boxes into the counting centre after polling was over.[11] In 2013 more than 16,000 new voters had registered in the 72,533-strong Lembah Pantai, which has a voter profile of 53 per cent Malay, 23 per cent Chinese, 20 per cent Indian and about 2 per cent Others. In the event, Nurul retained the seat with a majority of 1,847 votes.

In 2008, Selangor (together with Kuala Lumpur) registered the largest vote swing of about 21 per cent for Pakatan in both parliamentary and state contests, winning the coalition 55 per cent of the total vote. In 2013 Pakatan added another 3 percentage points to its popular vote in Selangor, making its tally 58 per cent of the popular vote, next in line to Kuala Lumpur (64 per cent) and Penang (67 per cent). Pakatan's hold on Selangor saw it winning 17 of the 22 parliamentary seats, 1 less than in 2008.

In 2013 (as in 2008) the DAP and Pakatan swept the four constituencies where Chinese made up the majority or largest number of voters; namely, in Petaling Jaya Utara, Klang, Serdang and Petaling Jaya Selatan. The DAP also won in the mixed seat of Puchong, which had the largest number of Malays. PAS candidates defeated their UMNO counterparts in the mixed Malay plurality constituencies of Shah Alam and Hulu Langat, but unexpectedly lost narrowly in Kuala Selangor this time around. The highly respected PAS standing committee member and head of PAS's research centre, Dr Dzulkefly Ahmad, lost to his UMNO opponent by a mere 460 votes in this constituency comprising some 64 per cent Malay, 13 per cent Chinese and 22 per cent Indian voters.[12]

It is clear from the above overall results that the PR continued to win the middle ground in Selangor. I would argue that the path-dependent trajectory of voting behaviour in mixed constituencies largely explains how Selangor has become a PR domain and the likelihood of its continued success in the future. The PR's success in Penang and Selangor — the states most urbanized, ethnically mixed and likely to have the largest concentration of middle class in the country — importantly indicates that political reforms through a turnover electoral system had only resonated well among a certain socio-economic section of the electorate. Hence, I would also posit that cross-communal and bridging political parties could only fare well when a plural society is also economically advanced.

THE RURAL–URBAN DIVIDE

Ever since 2008 there has been growing substantiation of the urban–rural divide in Malaysian electoral behaviour. This was even more evident in the 2013 outcome. This divide, generally coinciding with ethnicity, has always been a factor in Malaysian elections and has assumed a further new dimension with the inclusion of the rural constituencies of Sarawak and Sabah and the Electoral Commission's practice of giving rural weighting to such constituencies. Given rapid urbanization, the character of such rural weighting has been further exaggerated, making the BN even more dependent on the rural vote. The 2013 results show this to be the case in that without such rural weighting, electoral success would have in all probability eluded the BN.

According to Politweet (Malaysia), an independent online research facility,[13] the Malaysian electoral terrain in 2013 could be divided up in the manner shown in Table 9.5.

The definitions of rural, semi-urban and urban used were: *rural* = villages (kampungs)/small towns/farmland; *semi-urban* = larger towns and/or clusters of small towns, and may also include villages; *urban* = cities where a large proportion of the seat is covered by some form of urban development.[14] Politweet used this classification based on Google Maps satellite imagery, which it superimposed on the Electoral Commission's electoral maps. While not ideal, this seemed a creative manner of capturing crucial electoral data.[15]

Using these categories, Table 9.5 shows clear evidence of a putative rural–urban electoral divide manifested in BN and PR domains of success. The starkness of this political rural–urban divide is shown graphically in Figure 9.6.

As analysts have pointed out, the BN's electoral success has increasingly become dependent on its hold on rural constituencies, while it has effectively lost the urban vote. Its hold on Malay majority rural seats is particularly important, delivering 66 seats. In the final chapter of the book, drawing on the work of Maznah (2015) and Khor (2015), I will posit the idea that the large proportion of some 54 semi-rural FELDA seats has become a vote bank for

Table 9.5
Rural and Urban Seats, 2008

	Malay majority	Bumi Sabah majority	Bumi Sarawak majority	Chinese majority	Mixed	Total
Rural Seats (5,756,489 voters)	78	16	18	2	11	125
Semi-urban (3,952,432 voters)	27	3	1	12	11	54
Urban (3,559,081 voters)	14	—	—	16	13	43

Figure 9.6
BN–PR Electoral Divide

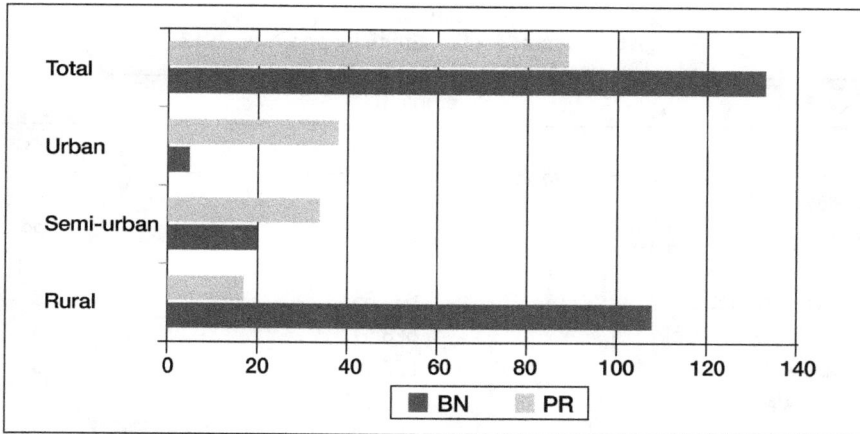

the BN. However, without the 33 East Malaysian rural seats, it is obvious that the BN would not have been able to secure Putrajaya. On the other hand, for Pakatan, electoral success would continue to elude it unless it can penetrate the rural constituencies, particularly of Sarawak and Sabah, which have become almost exclusive BN territories.

THE NEW VOTERS

There was much talk prior to the election that the large ballooning of the electorate with an additional 2.3 million presumed to be young voters would play a crucial role in affecting the 2013 outcome.[16] Voter breakdowns for 2013 are shown in Table 9.6.

In the discussion below I will analyse some of the 2013 *saluran* data from the parliamentary constituency of Klang in order to extrapolate on the voting choices of the new voters, much as was attempted by Loh.[17]

Klang is a 97,252-strong constituency of Selangor with a mixed voter profile of 32.9 per cent Malay, 45.8 per cent Chinese and 19.8 per cent Indian. There is a smattering of bumiputera from Sabah and Sarawak as well as some Orang Asli. As illustrated in Table 9.7, the overall results for Klang show that the PR's candidate Charles

Table 9.6
Registered Voter Profile, Ethnicity and Age, 2013

By ethnicity		
	Number	**%**
Malays	6.9 million	52.5
Chinese	3.8 million	29
Indian	953,478	7.1
Bumiputera Sabah	634,654	5
Bumiputera Sarawak	528,413	4
Orang Asli	69,703	0.5
Thai Malaysians	115,000	1
Total	13.29 million*	
By age group		
	Number	**%**
Under 40 years	*5.56 million*	*41.9*
30–39 years	*3.02 million*	*22.8*
21–29 years	*2.54 million*	*19.1*

Source: Straits Times, 5 April 2013.
* Numbers are approximations.

Table 9.7
Klang Result (P110), 2013

Overall	Teh Kim Poo (BN)	Charles A. Santiago (DAP)	Total (178 *saluran*)
Valid votes	29034	53719	82753
Percentage	35.09	64.91	100
New Voters			Total (37 *saluran*)
Valid votes	6485	12227	18712
Percentage	34.66	65.34	100

Santiago convincingly defeated the BN's Teh Kim Poo by gaining 65 per cent of the valid vote. To try to extrapolate whether new voters differed significantly in their choice, I added up all of the votes in the last stream (*saluran*) of each polling station — 37 in all, minus that of polling stations for postal voting and early voting and one station that had only one *saluran*. The last *saluran* would be the one in each polling station that would normally comprise the most recently registered voters. For example, one polling station in Klang had ten streams, thus one could assume that *saluran* number ten would comprise predominantly newly registered and presumably young voters who have recently come of voting age.[18]

The data appears to show very little to no significance in the manner "new voters" voted compared with those of other streams. Santiago's additional winning margin of about 0.4 per cent among the new voters is a rather insignificant statistic. Thus, from the evidence adduced from the Klang results, one is unable to draw any strong conclusion that new voters are any more pro-Pakatan or vice versa than their older counterparts. That said, further analysis would be necessary to determine in what sort of constituencies or regions the youth vote may have made a difference.

CONCLUSION

Malaysia's 13th general election proved to be a significant development in the onward trajectory of electoral democracy and provided evidence of path-dependent tracking of dual-coalition electoral politics. Having said this, in terms of political significance the 2008 outcome represented more of a critical juncture, as it led to the two-coalition situation. However, 2013 did mark a further progression with the breach of fifty per cent of the popular vote for the opposition, Such a breach, however, proved insufficient to capture federal power. Furthermore, when one examines political developments for 2013 at a deeper level, some indication may be discerned of what I have termed a consociational impasse between the BN and PR coalitions. Both sides appeared to have successfully exploited ethnic sensibilities and rural and urban voting inclinations to an optimal degree, given the structural constraints of each coalition and its partnerships. A rural–urban divide that appeared to be deeply embedded in Malaysia's current configuration of electoral politics aggravated this impasse. Gerrymandering and rural weighting had insured the BN against failing too badly, and the PR seemed to have maxed out its penetration of rural areas unless a new opposition alliance in the future could secure new partnerships with other political parties, particularly in Sabah and Sarawak. Even so, there would still be a preponderance of rural seats over urban seats, and this factor has to be addressed by any new coalition of forces in the future. It is predominantly in the latter that an alternative grand coalition with a vision of more democratization and intolerance for corrupt governance would have any chance of gaining a foothold. It is true that the 2013 electoral outcome did create a legitimacy crisis for a failing model of consociationalism long implemented by the BN. Its peninsular parties catering to non-Malays had begun to lose political relevance among their designated constituents of Chinese and Indian voters; possibly so too did the BN's original *raison d'être*. The opposition meanwhile failed to step into the breach fully because of its dismal capabilities in rural seats on the Peninsula and in a majority of seats in East Malaysia. The main obstacle structurally has been the contiguity of a large concentration of Malay voters with rural seats in the Peninsula and the contiguity of a large number of rural, indigenous voters with the most number of seats in East Malaysia. Malaysia's ethnically and regionally variegated and plural constituencies makes the issue of managing differences more complex than has been envisaged by ideal-type communal, consociational or centripetal model theories. In this and the foregoing chapters, I have tried to show the nuances involved in mediating the Malaysian form of communalized electoral politics.

Notes

1. See Chapter 1 for a discussion of these concepts.
2. The article that deals extensively with the notion of critical conjunctures is found in Saravanamuttu (2013*b*).
3. An earlier rendering of the events of the campaign trail is in Saravanamuttu (2013*a*).
4. In mid-April 2013 I had the opportunity to speak with Jeffrey Kitingan (STAR), Ansari Abdullah (ex-PKR), Salleh Said Keruak (UMNO), and others from opposition and BN parties, as well as non-politicians.
5. Malaysians lapped up YouTube videos showing the event of 11 February 2013, and this factor alone would have contributed significantly to the BN's dismal performance in Penang. I was present to witness the embarrassment of the prime minster and his entourage on stage when the crowd rebuffed his three calls to support the BN ("Are you ready for BN?"), while they earlier responded affirmatively with gusto to "Are you ready for PSY?" To add insult to injury, PSY failed to appear on stage with Najib, despite the many urgings of the MC. See Netto's piece for an account of the event <http://atimes.com/atimes/Southeast_Asia/SEA-01-140213.html> (accessed 18 October 2013).
6. See the recent work of Norris, Frank and Coma (2015) presenting cross-national studies of contentious elections throughout the world.
7. The general election was suspended in Sabah and Sarawak after the 13 May riots, but held later in June. Some of the Borneo parties later joined the BN, to boost its parliamentary majority to two-thirds of the seats.
8. See, for example, Lee Hock Guan (2013).
9. See Carolyn Hong, *The Sunday Times*, 17 February 2013.
10. In an interview on 1 May 2015 with Radziq Jalaluddin, campaign manager for Sallehudin Ayub, at the PAS headquarters at Johor Baru, his mood was distinctively upbeat. He said that the PAS vice president was well known among the Chinese voters and it was evident that Chinese support for PAS was strong. Salluddin lost by some 3,226 votes because of low Malay support, which was a disappointing but still credible result for him. In Johor I also had the opportunity to meet with Member of Parliament Liew Chin Tong who contested Kluang, a Malay majority seat, and won it by 7,359 votes. Liew leaving his safe seat of Bukit Bendera in Penang for this contest was part of the DAP Johor team's strategy to penetrate

this traditional stronghold of the BN/MCA and to build on the DAP's collaboration with PAS. I was able to meet with many Malay supporters of the PR at Liew's DAP Action Centre, showing that there was a high level of such collaboration.

11. There were numerous reports, including video footage, of the fracas on 5 May. See, for example <http://www.kinitv.com/channel/8/Nb4TyLW3Y VM?ModPagespeed=noscript> (accessed 3 October 2013).

12. When I spoke with the popular "Dr Dzul" just before the election at the PAS headquarters in Kuala Lumpur (on 25 March 2013), he appeared quietly confident of victory in the seat he wrested from UMNO in 2008 with a majority of 862 votes. Dr Dzul is noted for his moderate views and is thought to be part of the "Erdogan" wing of PAS and has naturally joined the Amanah splinter party of PAS.

13. As stated on its website, Politweet is a non-partisan research firm analysing interactions among Malaysians using social media. It has been monitoring politics and activism on Twitter since 2009 and expanded to include Facebook in December 2012 <http://www.politweet.org/site/aboutus.php> (accessed 1 October 2013).

14. I have slightly revised Poltitweet's language to make the categories clearer.

15. See <http://politweet.wordpress.com/2013/05/21/the-rural-urban-divide-in-malaysias-general-election/#more-321> (accessed 1 October 2013).

16. See, for example, the article, "Young Voters May Call the Shots in Malaysia Polls" by Yong Yen Nie in the *Straits Times*, 5 April 2013.

17. I would like to acknowledge my thanks to YB Charles Santiago for providing me with this data.

18. There will be the odd instance when older voters would have registered late.

10

TRANSITIONS OF COALITION POLITICS CIRCA 2016

Malaysia's electoral history, if one cared to examine it more minutely, has been strewn with liminal shifts of coalition politics from the 1950s onwards, as I have tried to show in preceding chapters of this book. That said, one major ruling coalition, the Alliance, dominated politics in the 1960s and its successor, the Barisan Nasional, from the 1970s till today. This two-stage movement of UMNO-crafted politics created a path dependence of electoral success that has been difficult to displace. On the other side of the ledger, oppositional coalitions since the 1950s have evinced poor sustenance owing to failures in crafting coalition strategies, particularly with the view to establishing an effective form of mediated communalism for electoral success. Importantly, in the 1960s the leftist coalition of the Socialist Front mounted a veritable challenge and then self-destructed, not without considerable help from repressive actions by the government. Minor electoral pacts followed, but it was only in the 1990s that one saw the formation of fairly well institutionalized opposition coalitions. One such attempt was the parallel formation of Angkatan Perpaduan Ummah and Gagasan Rakyat for the 1990 election, bringing together

Muslim and non-Muslim political parties into one electoral pact. A much more formalized coalition in the form of Barisan Alternatif (BA) was cobbled together for the 1999 election and, in 2008 and 2013, the most institutionalized opposition alliance, Pakatan Rakyat (PR), was formulated and remarkably held firm until 2015. This chapter delves into the events that brought an end to Pakatan and touches on how it reconstituted itself as events were unfolding up to early 2016. While the BN was also facing considerable internal strife and intra-party conflicts, there was still no suggestion at the point of writing that it would implode.

POLITICAL DEVELOPMENTS IN 2015

Much occurred on the political stage after the May 2013 general election. As tensions and politicking within the PR reached a crescendo in the middle of June 2015, this led to its formal disbandment. However, some reformulation of the opposition alliance was immediately manifest and its state-run governments appeared intact through coalitional adjustments. I will deal with this development further below, but let me first provide a brief narrative of the seven by-elections that took place after the 13th general election. One resulted from the untimely death of Karpal Singh, the veteran DAP (Democratic Action Party) politician, one other by the passing of the PAS Menteri Besar of Kedah and, more recently, the death of Rompin Member of Parliament Jamaluddin Jarjis in a helicopter crash. The seventh by-election was necessitated by the imprisonment of opposition leader Anwar Ibrahim. The by-elections were held in Kuala Besut (Terengannu state seat) on 24 July 2013; in Sungai Limau (Kedah state seat) on 19 October 2013; in Kajang (Selangor state seat) on 23 March 2014; in Bukit Gelugor (parliamentary seat in Penang) on 25 May 2014; in Teluk Intan (parliamentary seat in Perak) on 31 May 2014; in Rompin (parliamentary seat in Pahang) on 5 May 2015; and in Permatang Pauh (parliamentary seat in Penang) on 7 May 2015.

The Barisan Nasional (BN) retained the Kuala Besut seat, thus holding on to its thin two-seat majority in the state. This proved to be a little problematic later when the UMNO Menteri Besar and another member of the state assembly announced that they had resigned from the party in mid-May 2014, although they soon recanted their intention to do so.[1] The PAS candidate won easily in the Sungai Limau state seat, which the party had retained since 1995. The Kajang by-election was a complex move by the PKR (Parti Keadilan Rakyat) to initially provide its leader Anwar Ibrahim the opportunity to be in the Selangor state government, even to assume leadership of the state (see further below). In the event, Wan Azizah, his wife, stood in his place and won the seat with a reduced majority of 5,379 against the Malaysian Chinese Association's (MCA) Chew Mei Fun after Anwar was disqualified on technical grounds because of his court case. Bukit Gelugor proved to be a "shoo-in" for Karpal Singh's son, Ramkarpal, who won the seat with a majority of 41,242 votes. All three of his opponents lost their deposits.[2]

The Teluk Intan contest turned out to be the most interesting of the by-elections because of the DAP's young Malay female candidate. The DAP took a major risk by choosing the twenty-seven-year-old Dyana Sofya Mohd Daud, the political secretary to Lim Kit Siang, largely to test the waters of non-ethnic voting or, alternatively, for the DAP to build-up Malay support in Chinese-majority but mixed constituencies. Party strategists such as Tony Pua (who orchestrated the campaigning) and Ong Kian Meng were also trying to improve the DAP's image as a multiracial party. Dyana's looks, youthful image and composure generated a political reflexivity quite beyond the expectations of the party, giving it a considerable boost. In the event, she lost to the BN candidate, Mah Siew Keong, Gerakan's president, by only 238 votes. Voter turnout of 67 per cent was inadequate to swing a sufficiently large number of Chinese voters to her favour, and she lost a significant 15 per cent of Chinese votes to Mah. This fact could be explained by the lack of outstation voters, probably young, who did not or could not return to vote in this by-election. Dyana was able to pick up 3 per cent more of the Malay vote but saw a decline of 10 per cent of the Indian vote.[3]

In the Rompin by-election, UMNO's candidate Hassan Arifin won easily but saw a slippage of a 5 per cent margin against his PAS opponent, although voter turnout was a low 74 per cent compared with 86 per cent during 2013. The more significant by-election issue for the PR was whether Wan Azizah, who was chosen to stand in Anwar Ibrahim's constituency, could retain the seat and assume her role as leader of the opposition. She won the seat handsomely but with a reduced majority of 8,841 votes. Although the majority was down by 2,880 votes, this was probably due to a lower turnout (74.53 per cent compared to 88.3 per cent in 2013). Thus, in the middle of 2015, two years after the 2013 general election, judging purely by the results of by-elections, two-coalition politics appeared to remain on track.

However, major developments and politicking within the Pakatan alliance linked to developments in PAS and its growing spat with the DAP over *hudud* legislation led to the formal breakup of the opposition alliance in June 2015. Things started unravelling for the PR when PAS indicated its intention in April 2014 to again attempt to implement *hudud*, or Islamic criminal law, in Kelantan. PAS had planned to introduce enabling legislation for *hudud* through Parliament. The DAP had held all along that *hudud* was not part of the Pakatan common framework of policies, and as early as March 2015 had hinted at a possible breakup of the coalition if PAS was adamant about its *hudud* agenda. To aggravate matters, PAS sought the cooperation of the Najib government, which approved the setting up of a national-level technical committee, with participation of PAS, to study the long-term feasibility of *hudud*. However, much to the disappointment of PAS ulamas, the enabling legislation was not tabled in the parliamentary session ending June 2015.

Matters came to a head at the 61st PAS Muktamar (party congress), held from 3 to 6 June 2015. Abdul Hadi Awang retained the president's post easily despite a challenge from a relatively unknown opponent, and candidates of the ulama group won all major offices except for one. PAS moderates or "progressives" were soundly defeated; in particular, Mohamad (Mat) Sabu lost the deputy presidency to Tuan Ibrahim, and others like Husam Musa, Sallehudin Ayub, Dzulkifli Ahmad and Khalid Samad failed to retain or win any post. It was a devastating defeat for the "Erdogans" who had advocated strong Pakatan collaboration.[4] Worse was to come for the fate of the opposition coalition when the Ulama Council passed a motion to sever ties with the DAP. In the aftermath of these results and the action of the Ulama Council, the DAP's secretary general Lim Guan Eng announced on 16 June, after a meeting of the party's central committee, that the PR coalition was formally dead. Wan Azizah, president of PKR, after a meeting of the party top officials, also declared the next day (17 June) that the coalition did not function formally anymore, although collaboration of the political parties at the state level of government was to be continued. This was not necessarily the position of the DAP, which had taken quick action to dismiss PAS incumbents at the local council level as well as other PAS functionaries appointed by the state government. Paradoxically, the PAS president Hadi Awang maintained that the PR was still alive despite these developments.

Various political commentators and analysts immediately suggested that the disbanding of the PR did not mean the end of coalition politics for the opposition. Some opposition members were hopeful that the NGO, PasMa (Persatuan Ummah Sejahtera Malaysia), which was formed earlier as a splinter of PAS, led by Kedah lawmaker and former PAS commissioner for the state, Phahrolrazi Mohd Zawawi, could be the genesis of a new political party replacing PAS in the opposition coalition. Interestingly, its youth leader Sheikh Omar had opted to join the DAP, and his action followed the much publicized news of national literary laureate A. Samad Said, who was a co-chair of BERSIH, joining the DAP on 13 June 2015. The reconstitution of a new opposition coalition, possibly with a refurbished strategy of mediated communalism, was the implicit narrative for the opposition to maintain any level of future path-dependent electoral success. That said, the exit of PAS would clearly have an adverse effect on the opposition's politics, particularly if the Islamic party were to enter some form of collaboration with the ruling coalition. Following the earlier breakup of the BA after the 1999 general election, in the 2004 election the opposition posted one of its worst performances. However, there are three important differences between the developments of 2015 and those of 1999; first, in 2015 the PKR and DAP continued to run two major state governments — Selangor and Penang — second, a significant number of PAS political heavyweights opted to remain in the opposition coalition and moreover were prepared to leave PAS to form a splinter party. Third, the DAP left the BA in the earlier episode but now remains in Pakatan Harapan.

RECONSTITUTING PAKATAN

Without doubt 2015 turned out to be an *annus horribilis* for the PR. Anwar Ibrahim, Pakatan's symbolic leader, was incarcerated yet again in February at the point of time when his leadership was arguably most sorely needed. Coincidentally or not, relations within Pakatan deteriorated soon after the Pakatan parties opted in an almost facile manner to disband after many years of successful collaboration. What was worse was that Pakatan's breakup came at a time of internal dissension within the BN, and especially UMNO, over the 1Malaysia Development Berhad (1MDB) fiasco and Najib's highly beleaguered position in his own party (see further below). The BN's weakness was arguably at a high point with a split in the MIC[5] and the dismissal of its incumbent president. The Gerakan and MCA remained weak as well, but the BN, while fragmented, had somehow remained intact in the face of the Pakatan's unseemly implosion. Notwithstanding this, it cannot be denied that the Pakatan breakup had been in the making for months if not years given the irreconcilable differences between two of its major parties — PAS and the DAP. It will be useful for the reader to be apprised more fully of the sequence of events that brought about the collapse and, more crucially, the factors driving the breakup.[6]

The resolution passed at the 61st PAS Muktamar calling for PAS to cut ties with the DAP was sealed by the PAS Syurah Council confirming this on 11 July.[7] The DAP, for its part, acted in some haste to cut off the state appointments of PAS representatives at various levels of administration in Penang. What made it worse for Pakatan was the comprehensive defeat of the moderate group in the PAS elections as noted above. This group was the PAS backbone behind the PR coalition and its common agenda.

The PAS–DAP rift had its roots in the days when former DAP chairman, the late Karpal Singh, had famously stated that PAS's implementation of an Islamic state would be "over his dead body". As fate would have it, after Karpal's passing, PAS ulamas under Hadi Awang's leadership (including Hadi himself) persisted in pressing for *hudud*, or a shariah-based penal code, to be implemented in Kelantan by attempting to pass an enabling bill in Parliament with UMNO support. PAS went as far as to participate in a joint technical committee with UMNO set up for this purpose. UMNO members in Kelantan showed they were fully behind the *hudud* amendments passed unanimously in the state assembly on 19 March 2015.[8] This no doubt spurred Hadi's move to work further with UMNO on *hudud* at the national level. With such unilateral action on *hudud* policy on the part of PAS, the damage done to the festering relations with the DAP was irreparable.

Under Hadi Awang's leadership there was also an attempt to revive "unity talks" with UMNO. And, with the passing of spiritual leader Nik Abdul Aziz on 12 February 2015, his influence in stemming cooperation with UMNO and maintaining steadfast relations with Pakatan parties was evidently absent and sorely missed. There were suggestions that the PAS president Hadi Awang was again contemplating a "unity government" with UMNO in 2013 after the general election, an idea that had surfaced as far back as 2008, although Hadi denied this. Be that as it may, Hadi did clearly pursue his plan to canvass UMNO support for *hudud* legislation, as we have seen.

Another event that almost brought matters to a crisis earlier for Pakatan was the PKR's so-called "Kajang Move", orchestrated by the party supposedly to allow Anwar Ibrahim to take over leadership of Selangor.[9] This move was thought to be necessary due to the cumulative dissatisfaction with the actions and policies of PKR's incumbent Menteri Besar, Khalid Ibrahim, who, inter alia, had inked a controversial agreement with the BN government over the management of water resources in Selangor. As noted above, Anwar was disqualified for the Kajang contest and PKR president Wan Azizah Ismail duly won the seat. However, PAS objected to her becoming the Menteri Besar and after a convoluted sequence of events PKR deputy president Azmin Ali coyly emerged as the Menteri Besar with PAS support and the all-important approval of the Selangor Sultan. This development invariably created more friction within Pakatan and the situation in Selangor will remain somewhat dicey given that PAS's thirteen lawmakers could choose to withdraw from the coalition. At the point of writing, the PAS lawmakers seem content to remain as part of the ruling group, the current distribution of seats in the 56-seat state assembly being as follows: DAP 15, PAS 15, PKR 13.[10]

PAS's own internal conflict had been simmering for a long time and had already caused the formation of the splinter group PasMa led by Kedah politician Pharolrazi Zawawi, as noted above. This occurred not long after the disastrous outing by PAS in Kedah in the 13th general election. With the results of the 61st Mukthamar, which effectively disempowered its moderate or progressive leaders, it seemed inevitable that another new organization would be formed under the aegis of this group, with the prospect that eventually it would be an alternative Islamic party to PAS. This nascent political development came about by way of the formation of Gerakan Harapan Baru (GHB), led by former PAS deputy president Mohamad Sabu. Its interim committee members included former Selangor Menteri Besar Tan Sri Muhammad Muhammad Taib, former PAS secretary-general Kamaruddin Jaafar, former PAS vice-president Salahuddin Ayub, as well as the party's former senior leaders such as Khalid Samad, Mohammad Hatta Ramli and Mujahid Yusof Rawa. The group earlier indicated its plan in late July to take over the dormant political party KITA by 31 August 2013. An initial report was that the new party would be called Parti Amanah Negara (PAN, or National Trust Party).[11] It was further reported that some 413 PAS office bearers in Selangor had left PAS to join the splinter party.[12] At the end of August, coinciding with the anniversary of Merdeka (Independence), the GHB announced that because of difficulties for the group to take over the party KITA, it would instead use the defunct Worker's Party (Parti Pertubuhan Pekerja-Pekerja Malaysia) for this purpose and launch the newly formed party with a membership of 35,000 on 16 September, Malaysia Day. From jail, Anwar Ibrahim gave his blessings to the new party formed by GHB.[13]

All roads for the opposition pointed to the reinvention of a "new" Pakatan minus PAS. On 22 September 2015 the new coalition was launched and renamed "Pakatan Harapan" with the participation of PKR, the DAP and the new party, PAN. PAS was effectively excluded, so too the PSM (Parti Sosialis Rakyat), the latter complaining that it was not invited to the roundtable held to launch the new coalition.[14] Many have argued that the crafting of the new Pakatan, minus PAS, was a salutary development, as PAS under the dominance of the ulamas would not ensure the longevity of common, progressive Pakatan policies. However, the new coalition without PAS could fare poorly in the East Coast of Malaysia. It is conceivable that PAS could opt to join the BN as it has done in the past. Alternatively, there could be an electoral pact worked out with PAS for Muslim-majority seats, assuming the latter does not opt to join the BN. Given the opposition's axiomatic weakness in East Malaysia, it would also be imperative for the new Pakatan to continue to court coalition partners on that terrain and not just rely on existing Pakatan parties there. In her press conference after the Roundtable, PKR president Wan Azizah expressed the wish that political parties of East Malaysia could form a coalition of opposition forces in support of Pakatan Harapan in order to defeat the BN in the next election. She also announced that it was agreed that Anwar Ibrahim would be the prime minister should Pakatan win the next election. The first test for the new Pakatan would come by way of a Sarawak state election to be held on 7 May 2016.[15] Finally, it remained axiomatic that the major necessary and sufficient conditions for electoral success of a new opposition coalition, as argued throughout this book, is a continued strategy of mediated communalism anchored on a grand coalition of oppositional forces, effective and enlightened Malay leadership along with significant support of the Malay grass roots, majority support from Non-Malays and strong support from East Malaysian voters. Fulfilling these conditions will no doubt be a tall order for a reinvented Pakatan, which will have about two years to set their sights on potential success in the 14th general election.

Another gyration of opposition politics occurred when PAS formed an alliance with Ikatan (Parti Ikatan Bangsa Malaysia) on 16 March 2016. Most analysts saw this as a move by the PAS leadership to remain relevant, but it would likely have a spoiler effect on the new Pakatan as well as on the BN, as Ikatan is a splinter group of UMNO. Ikatan was formed by UMNO dissident and Kedah bigwig Abdul Kadir Sheikh Fadzir in 2015, with its logo showing an icon of the Tunku and the goal of promoting "Bangsa Malaysia" (Malaysian race). The move by PAS president Hadi Awang to forge such an alliance could well be a ploy to negotiate deals either with the BN or the Pakatan Harapan before the 14th general election. Hadi justified the move as consonant with the new softer approach by PAS along with its strategy to engage with the government rather than to simply oppose it.[16]

UMNO IN CRISIS

Unfolding events in 2015 and 2016 pointed to a plausible UMNO implosion given a serious unresolved crisis sparked by the prime minister himself. I will only touch on its impact on the BN coalition and UMNO. Up till the point of writing, a complex and convoluted web of developments was severely afflicting the party and its leadership. Most significantly, the prime minister Najib Razak was under the spotlight after revelations that a vast sum of money (about RM2.67 billion) had found its way into his private bank account in 2013, allegedly to fund the BN election campaign of that year. This led to unceasing intra-UMNO friction and a reshuffling of his Cabinet by the premier, including dropping his deputy. At the point of writing, the UMNO conflict remained unresolved, with rumblings occurring in divisional meetings, court cases filed, the detention of a dissident member, Khairuddin Abu Hassan, and with former premier Mahathir continuing to be Najib's unflinching critic, initiating a citizens' move for his resignation as prime minister.

As noted throughout this book, previous ruptures of the ruling Malay bloc have not seen a collapse of its grand coalition of communal parties; it has continued its reinvention of mediated communalism for electoral success. In the aftermath of the May 1969 incidents, UMNO remained intact despite a major internal rift between the old guard and the Young Turks. Under the baton of Tun Abdul Razak, the party orchestrated the new ruling coalition of the BN and has not looked back. A major split in the leadership in the mid-1980s saw the surfacing of the splinter group Semangat 46. Again, the ruling coalition held firm. Then came the sacking of Anwar Ibrahim, deputy leader and deputy premier, in 1998 leading to the Reformasi Movement, which we have dealt with at some length in this book. Again, the ruling BN has held firm until today, although it lost the popular vote in 2013 for the second time in its history (1969 being the first incidence).

The 2015 crisis for UMNO revolved around the 1MDB scandal and the debt owed by the government-sponsored fund of some RM42 billion. As a brainchild of Prime Minister Najib Razak, and given his role as chairman of its advisory board, as at September 2015 calls have continued from various quarters for his resignation. Compounding the crisis, in late July 2015 the prime minister in a reshuffle of his Cabinet sacked his deputy Muhhyiddin Yassin (also deputy president of UMNO) and others critical of his handling of the 1MDB scandal. Connected to this scandal was the allegation (and later admission) that a sum of US$700 million (about RM2.67 billion) found its way into Najib's personal account in AmBank through international transfers of funds.[17] Allegations were that some of this money was used in the campaign for the 13th general election and that large sums were also used to ensure the support of UMNO divisional heads for the UMNO chief. There appeared a host of reports and commentaries on the 1MDB scandal, particularly in the portal *Sarawak Report*. But the business media company the EDGE, which also carried out investigations of its own into 1MDB, saw two of its publications — *The Edge Financial Daily* and *The Edge Weekly* — slapped with a three-month suspension in July. Even more egregiously, the attorney general of Malaysia, Gani Patail, who put together a task force to investigate possible malfeasance with respect to 1MDB, was also summarily removed from his office in July.[18]

The repercussions of the 1MDB debacle further saw the banning and blocking of online portals in 2016, such as *Sarawak Report*, *Malaysia Chronicle* and the *Malaysian Insider*, which closed operations on 13 March 2016 citing commercial reasons.

In the continued unfolding of events at the point of writing, UMNO has remained intact despite the sacking of Muhyiddin, who had indicated that the prime minister was within his rights to choose his deputy. However, former president Mahathir, who relentlessly criticized Najib over the scandal and was among the first of UMNO leaders to call for Najib's resignation, seemed intent to get Najib to step down. In August the home minister and new deputy prime minister, Ahmad Zahid Hamidi, alleged that there was a plot to "topple the government" which supposedly involved a significant number of BN lawmakers agreeing to sign statutory declarations to effect a no-confidence vote in Parliament in collusion with the opposition. None of these allegations have been confirmed, but the developments prompted newly minted minister in the PMO, Azalina Othman, to moot the possibility of an "anti-hopping law".[19] The fracturing of UMNO politics did not abate on the eve of Independence Day, as Mahathir graced the BERSIH 4 rally twice. More ominous for Najib were the lawsuits by two UMNO members on his alleged malfeasance related to the 1MDB fiasco and the siphoning of money into his personal bank account. Former division head of Batu Kawan (Penang) Khairuddin Abu Hassan took up a lawsuit in Switzerland and filed reports in London and Singapore over the 1MDB scandal.[20] More sensationally, the UMNO member Anina Saadudin, who had delivered verbal lashings against Najib at the UMNO divisional meeting in Langkawi, filed a multi-million-dollar lawsuit in the Malaysian High Court against the UMNO president on 28 August for breaching the UMNO constitution and the Societies Act. She alleged the following:

1. He had refused to account to UMNO for the use of the RM2.67 billion;
2. He refused to allow UMNO to account for it in its financial years in 2013 and 2014;
3. He transferred out US$650 million to a bank account in Singapore which does not belong to UMNO;
4. He failed to ensure that the sum was accounted for in UMNO's financial statements;
5. He failed to inform or declare to the Supreme Council of the party that he had received the money;
6. He used a substantial part of the funds in violation of UMNO's constitution;
7. He utilized or retained part of it for his personal benefit;
8. He received the funds without having been appointed trustee by the Supreme Council for such purpose.[21]

These developments suggest that it was not only the opposition alliance that was encountering problems but also the ruling coalition, particularly UMNO, that was being rocked by internal dissent.[22] The trouble within UMNO had come to a head with the sacking of deputy prime minister Muhyddin Yassin in July 2015 and the removal of Mukhriz Mahathir as the Kedah Menteri Besar in February 2016. Dissent had continued to simmer in UMNO, but these two significant removals culminated in the Citizen's Declaration of 4 March 2016 initiated by Mahathir, which is recounted further below. The other important collateral damage of the crisis, as alluded to earlier, was the replacement of Attorney General Gani Patail (said to be sick) with former judge Mohamed Apandi in July at about the time of the Muhyiddin sacking. The new attorney general was fast to return a favour and in January 2016 cleared the prime minister of any malfeasance in receiving donations into his personal bank account.[23] Both the local online media and the international media, including major newspapers such as *The Wall Street Journal* and *The Guardian* and the Australian Broadcasting Corporation (ABC) have been in the forefront of exposés about the Malaysian prime minister's financial scandals and presumed malfeasance.[24]

NEW POLITICS AND BERSIH 4

The crisis afflicting the Najib government brought about the mammoth BERSIH 4 rally held in Kuala Lumpur on 29–30 August 2015. As mentioned in an earlier chapter, BERSIH 2.0 was formed in 2005 to press for the conduct of clean and fair elections and to advocate a set of related demands on institutional reform. Over the years BERSIH had become the umbrella organization of civil society to also make demands for clean and incorruptible governance. In 2015 BERSIH 4 proclaimed five demands as its objectives; namely, clean elections, clean government, right to dissent, strengthening parliamentary democracy and saving the economy.[25] The BERSIH movement, I have argued, grew out of the era of new politics sparked by the *reformasi* of the late 1990s. It is symbolic of the role of civil society in its constant resistance to authoritarian and repressive politics and in its efforts to expand the terrain of the public sphere for political activism.

Although there are disputes over the numbers that participated in BERSIH 4's thirty-four-hour rally, there is little doubt that it was the largest protest gathering in Malaysia to date, and coincidentally eclipsed the official Merdeka celebrations held the day after the rally ended.[26] Malaysian civil forces decided to celebrate Merdeka in their own way in a space that was contested physically and metaphorically — the Independence Square, or Dataran Merdeka. The Najib government cordoned off Dataran and deemed the rally to be illegal, but failed to prevent more than a hundred thousand Malaysians flooding the roads and vicinity surrounding Dataran. In a bizarre action on the eve of the rally (28 August), the Home Ministry actually gazetted legislation to make it illegal to don the yellow T-shirts with the BERSIH 4 logo. Its action, however, had little impact on the massive numbers of yellow-clad protesters in Kuala Lumpur, although twenty-two people were arrested in Malacca for some transgression or other. The BERSIH organizers who had met with the police umpteen times before the rally invoked the Peaceful Assembly Act of 2012 to justify holding it despite governmental disapproval.

The main issue that seemed to exercise political commentators and civil society activists about BERSIH 4 was the disproportionately small numbers of Malay protesters compared with non-Malays, particularly Chinese. Much punditry and numerous discussions addressed this issue in cyberspace and the mainstream media, but it was clear that the chief reason for the low turnout of Malays was the absence of PAS members and supporters. The PAS leadership had opted out of the rally and the GHP splinter group clearly could not muster a large number of supporters compared to the parent party. Previous BERSIH rallies on the other hand saw the full involvement of PAS. To put it plainly, the breakup of Pakatan Rakyat had a definite impact on the ethnic composition of the protestors. However, it cannot be denied that the BERSIH movement is in the first place an urban middle class phenomenon with much of it concentrated in the Klang valley with its predominantly highly politicized non-Malay citizenry. BERSIH rallies are not electoral politics per se, but their spontaneity as a new politics of protest continues from the *reformasi* agenda of reforming flawed democratic institutions. However, the more fractured character of Malay protest politics at the time of BERSIH 4 was in sharp contrast to that of the era of *reformasi*, and explains the lower enthusiasm in 2015 of Malays for BERSIH 4. Notwithstanding this, many organizers and leaders of the BERSIH agenda, including those who were on centre stage during the rally orchestrating the programme, were young Malay activists. The lesson of BERSIH 4 for the opposition could well be that the new alliance they hope to fashion in the future must factor in the uneven support for reform agendas among urban and rural voters, who also tend to coincide to a great extent with Malay and non-Malay constituencies.

THE RED SHIRTS RALLY

Dubbed as anti-BERSIH and as a Malay dignity gathering, but considered by observers to be basically a pro-Najib rally, a huge gathering of Malays wearing red shirts was held on 16 September 2015 in Kuala Lumpur.[27] It transpired that two groups were the main organizers; namely, Pesaka, the National Silat Federation, led by former Menteri Besar of Malacca Mohd Ali Rustam, and the UMNO division of Sungai Besar, Selangor led by its head Jamal Md Yunos. The organizers mustered some 250 NGOs to their cause and had expected a turnout of 300,000, many of whom would have been bussed in from other states, with generous funding from the government. The police had first allowed the rally but later declared it illegal as the organizers were persistent about occupying the predominantly Chinese commercial area of Bukit Bintang. On the day of the rally the police cordoned off major streets in Chinatown and the organizers were asked to gather their participants instead at Padang Merbok (near Parliament), away from the city centre. The organizers claimed that some 250,000 protesters showed up, but more objective estimates put the attendees at Padang Merbok at about 35,000 to 50,000, while much smaller numbers congregated at different venues in the city, notably Petaling Street, where the crowd broke through a police cordon and the Federal Reserve Unit was forced to deploy water cannons against protesters. Notably, former premier Mahathir and moderate Malay leaders, including former UMNO ministers such as Rafidah Aziz and Muhyiddin Yassin, did not support the rally. Rather disturbing to moderate-minded Malaysians were the racist posters and race-baiting remarks and speeches of participants, including the call for the abolition of Chinese vernacular schools. The Merdeka Centre carried a sample survey on the eve of the rally and found that only 24 per cent of Malays supported the rally, while 53 per cent were against it and 22 per cent were unsure about it.[28]

It could be argued that the Red Shirts rally brought Malaysia to a new high level of ethnic tension comparable to the events of 1987 — which also saw a rally of Malays at the TPCA stadium, which I have touched on in a previous chapter. Because of the lack of support from UMNO coalition partners for the event, and its openly anti-Chinese overtones, the MCA youth wing chief of Pasir Gudang condemned the Red Shirts event and called for the party to sever ties with Prime Minister Najib, who had supported holding the rally. Party president Liow Tiong Hai, while also condemning the race-baiting of the Red Shirts, insisted that the MCA would not leave the BN, arguing that it was vital for the MCA to remain in the government coalition to champion "multiculturalism".[29]

CITIZENS' DECLARATION 2016

One could hardly foresee the coming together of bitter political opponents in an event on 4 March 2016, which saw the launching of a "Citizens' Declaration" calling for the removal of the incumbent prime minster Najib Razak. The declaration was initiated by Mahathir Mohamad, the ninety-one-year-old former prime minister of Malaysia. The fact that Anwar Ibrahim, his former deputy in UMNO and government, endorsed the declaration from his jail cell made the event even more bizarre.[30] The coming together of opposition leaders and civil society actors with their long-time nemesis is surely a testament to the truism that there are only permanent interests and no permanent friends or enemies in politics. On the BN-UMNO side of the bench were Muhyiddin Yassin, Mukhriz Mahathir, Sanusi Junid and Ling Liong Sik, while the DAP's Lim Kit Siang, PKR's Azmin Ali and Amanah's Mat Sabu graced the other side of the bench. The primary participant from civil society in the Citizens' Declaration was BERSIH, while Aliran, along with other civil society organizations, was also an endorser of the declaration. Mahathir, in initiating the move, made it absolutely clear during the Q&A session that the primary goal of the Citizens' Declaration was the removal of Najib. Mahathir's son Mukhriz also said that he would not want a change of the BN government, despite his own dismissal by Najib. The fact that such an event had occurred epitomizes the extreme state of impasse in Malaysian politics at the time. Some observers of the "third sector" condemned the action by BERSIH and civil groups as "opportunism", while the opposition political party PSM also considered the move to be hasty and ill advised.[31] There was no mechanism in the declaration for what steps were to be taken to remove Najib. Liew Chin Tong provided interesting but rather fanciful scenarios of Najib being forced by this move to take more extreme self-defeating measures such as instituting emergency rule, or the possibility of the countervailing action of a coup in UMNO by Zahid Hamidi.[32]

POSTSCRIPT: THE SARAWAK ELECTION OF 2016

The 11th Sarawak state election was held on 7 May 2016 and saw a total of 226 candidates contesting for 80 seats — after 2 seats, Bukit Sari and Bukit Kota, were won uncontested by the BN — when nominations closed on 25 April. The BN contested 80 seats, the PKR 40, DAP 31, Amanah 13, PAS 11, Star 11, and PBDS Baru 5, along with 35 independent candidates. The outcome was a major endorsement of the state government and its new Menteri Besar Adenan Satem, who led the BN to win 72 of the 82 state assembly constituencies, constituting what political commentators call a "supermajority". This win saw the BN garner 87 per cent of the seats and 63.7 per cent of the popular vote — an 8.3 per cent increase in the margin of victory compared to 2011. The newly crafted Pakatan Harapan failed badly in its first test and won a mere 10 seats (DAP 7, PKR 3). Amanah failed to win any seats; so too did its nemesis PAS. The DAP and PKR were unable to strike an accord on not contesting with each other in 6 seats (Mambong, Simanggang, Murum, Mulu, Ngemah and Batu Kitang), which were all won by the BN.

This major success of the BN was attributed to the manner Adenan Satem was able to convince voters of his championing of local, state rights issues, in particular on oil royalty, Chinese education, the use of English as a medium of instruction and on religious conversion. Despite the regular presence of Prime Minster Najib Razak during the campaign period and the constant raising of big ticket issues such as the 1MDB scandal by the opposition, national-level questions hardly featured in the Sarawak election. The election was marred by a helicopter crash that saw the death of five people, including the deputy minister of plantation industries and commodities Noriah Kasnon and her husband, secretary general of her ministry Sundaran Annamalai, and Kuala Kangsar Member of Parliament Wan Mohammad Khairil Anuar Wan Ahmad. This event, however, had little bearing on the results.

Money politics and cronyism were clearly major factors contributing to the BN's success. The federal government made its customary handouts and promises of development projects amounting to billions of ringgit. And Adenan even directly fielded as candidates timber tycoons known to be well connected to the previous Menteri Besar Taib Mahmud. The barring of opposition peninsular politicians from campaigning was the worst ever recorded, with major opposition figures such as Tian Chua, Rafizi Ramli, Nurul Izzah, Anthony Loke, Liew Chin Tong, Hannah Yeoh and P. Ramasamy, as well as social activists such as Maria Chin, being denied entry into Sarawak. The absence of opposition notables no doubt was partly responsible for the poor turnout at election rallies. When polling was closed it was recorded that only 52 per cent of voters had cast their ballots, but later, at midnight, the Election Commission corrected the figure to a turnout rate of 70 per cent. Election watchdog BERSIH asked for an official explanation of the alleged discrepancy, but at the time of writing had received no response.

Political scientist Bridget Welsh, in a five-part analysis of the election, argued that in a contest of "strongmen versus pressure politics", the strongmen clearly won.[33] However, it was obvious that the major factor explaining the poor performance of the opposition was the swing of Chinese votes, which clearly affected the results in urban seats. The foray of the DAP into rural and semi-rural areas yielded no results whatsoever, although the PKR claimed it made some inroads in rural constituencies. The only solace for the new Pakatan opposition coalition was that no other opposition parties won seats in the election. From the perspective of this book, path dependence of two-coalition politics remained on track, even though a much weaker Pakatan was found to be somewhat rudderless and in disarray.

CONCLUDING REMARKS

Many analysts, including this one, would probably concede that despite attempts to steer Malaysian electoral politics away from its ethnic moorings, it has basically remained pivoted on ethnic mobilization, symbolized by the still successful if slightly frayed formula of crafting coalitions of racially constituted political parties. The growing literature on electoral politics in Malaysia has generally weighed in on the proposition that ethnicity or racial motivations have always driven Malaysian electoral politics, as I have shown in previous chapters of this book. However, I would maintain nonetheless that the reflexivity of a *new politics* begun in the *reformasi* period would likely continue to animate electoral politics for large sections of Malaysians for some time to come. While remaining anchored at the practical level on ethnic politics, *new politics* also prioritizes more universal goals of democracy and good governance and the impartiality of electoral systems. Following this, as I have argued, the impact of March 2008, which created a conjectural, new path-dependent politics, produced a changed trajectory of Malaysian politics, possibly for many decades to come.

However, as this chapter has shown, the opposition coalition of the Pakatan Rakyat had become defunct after two general elections. Remarkably though, its overall thrust or brand of coalition politics was vindicated by the formation of Pakatan Harapan in September 2015. As noted above, PAS would likely revert to its spoiler role to the two-coalition system, and the liminal character of opposition politics seems destined to remain for a time. Malaysian politics would likely continue to be deeply divided, but along lines that promise some level of two-coalition electoral politics, howsoever the two coalitions are reconstituted in the future. Third-party groups are unlikely to gain much traction. An alternative scenario would be the constituting of yet another cycle of domination by the BN "leviathan" and its authoritarian form of politics, which I discuss further in the concluding chapter. At the point of writing, the BN coalition has remained institutionally intact, although the frequency of the crises affecting its political parties also show something of a liminal state akin to that of the opposition. Some quick examples will serve to prove this point. The Sabah Progressive Party (SAPP) left the BN coalition on 17 September 2008, while Gerakan and even the MCA have continually sounded out their deep disaffection with UMNO politics. These two Chinese-based component parties are themselves in a state of political reinvention, spurning earlier suggestions of merger. After the 8 March result, one senior woman leader and her supporters left the MCA and joined Anwar's party. More significantly, former UMNO law minister Zaid Ibrahim and former MCA vice president Chua Jui Meng became members of the PKR. The most recent crisis for the MIC and the deposing of its president will likely continue the trend of internal haemorrhaging of BN parties. A newly reconstituted HINDRAF had also been persuaded by Najib to join the BN in 2013 and its leader P. Wyathamoorthy was given a full minister's post, but the group departed in no time at all (2014) after citing lack of progress on the question of Indian poverty. The suggestion by erstwhile Gerakan president Koh Tsu Koon to have direct membership in the BN and to turn it eventually into a multiracial party remains a long-term possibility, and was already a veiled critique of the present poor formula of racial power sharing and mediated communalism. The former leader of Sabah's native-based United Pasokmomogun Kadazandusun Murut Organization, Bernard Dompok, also expressed grave concern over the failure of the National Front government to deal with three urgent matters; namely, the unequal exchange of economic benefits to Sabah and its concomitant status as Malaysia's poorest state, the issue of religious freedom and the unresolved problem of the influx of more than one million illegal immigrants into Sabah.

Notes

1. For an analysis of the by-election, see <http://www.malaysia-chronicle.com/index.php?option=com_k2&view=item&id=293692:unprecedented-mania-despite-loss-dyana-broke-new-ground-daps-post-mortem-on-poll&Itemid=2#axzz33MCosF8n> and <http://anilnetto.com/malaysian-politics/malaysian-elections/teluk-intan-election-went-wrong-dyana-sofya/> (accessed 4 June 2014).

2. The 56 per cent turnout was among the lowest in elections due to the fact that the BN pulled out of the contest and Ramkarpal's opponents were not serious contenders. The candidate from Parti Cinta Malaysia, Huan Cheng Guan, garnered a near respectable 3,583 votes. The other two independent candidates, Mohamed Nabi Bux Mohd Nabi Abd Sathar (799 votes) and Abu Backer Sidek Mohd Zan (225 votes), provided much comic relief to the voters. See Netto <http://anilnetto.com/malaysian-politics/malaysian-elections/live-bukit-gelugor-election/> (accessed 4 June 2014).

3. For an analysis of the by-election, see <http://www.malaysia-chronicle.com/index.php?option=com_k2&view=item&id=293692:unprecedented-mania-despite-loss-dyana-broke-new-ground-daps-post-mortem-on-poll&Itemid=2#axzz33MCosF8n> and <http://anilnetto.com/malaysian-politics/malaysian-elections/teluk-intan-election-went-wrong-dyana-sofya/> (accessed 4 June 2014).

4. See <http://www.themalaysianinsider.com/malaysia/artibebecle/hadi-retains-pas-presidency> (accessed 30 July 2015).

5. The ouster of the incumbent president of the MIC, G. Palanivel, in June and its takeover by S. Subramanian was a protracted internal conflict which saw something of a closure after the prime minister himself dropped Palanivel from his reshuffled Cabinet of 28 July 2015.

6. Readers are referred to an Aliran newsletter examining the breakup <http://aliran.com/?wysija-page=1&controller=email&action=view&email_id=895&wysijap=subscriptions> (accessed 30 July 2015).

7. See <http://www.malaysiakini.com/news/304798> (accessed 30 July 2015).

8. See <http://www.thestar.com.my/News/Nation/2015/03/19/hudud-bill-passed/> (accessed 30 July 2015).

9. The move was the idea of Rafizi Ramli, secretary general of the party. And although endorsed by most members, it also led to a split between supporters of Rafizi and supporters of deputy leader Azmin. Although this internal schism of the party was never publicized, it was confirmed to me in private conversations with a PKR lawmaker.

10. See <http://www.themalaysianinsider.com/malaysia/article/with-too-much-to-lose-pas-unlikely-to-quit-selangor-posts> (accessed 30 July 2015). Two of the PAS assemblymen, known to be moderates, were supportive of Wan Azizah's appointment as Menteri Besar, and it would be possible to cobble together a PKR-led government without PAS support should the two choose to jump ship.

11. The obvious choice of 31 August was less important than an exodus of PAS rank-and-file to the new party. Should this occur, the PH could remain effective and continue to dominate the middle ground of Malay politics. See various reports: <http://www.themalaysianinsider.com/malaysia/article/gerakan-harapan-baru-party-to-be-formed-september-14-says-khalid-samad#sthash.5dUEI0i3.dpuf>; <http://aliran.com/e-newsletters/2015-e-newsletters/reinventing-pakatan-rakyat/http://www.malaysiakini.com/news/306928> (accessed 3 August 2015); <http://www.themalaysianinsider.com/malaysia/article/new-opposition-pact-must-learn-from-pakatans-mistakes-says-dap> (accessed 18 August 2015).

12. See the article by Shannon Teoh in the *Straits Times* <http://www.straitstimes.com/asia/se-asia/over-400-selangor-pas-members-quit-set-to-form-splinter-group?login=true> (accessed 20 August 2015).

13. See the news report by *Rakyat Post* and *Malay Mail* online <http://www.therakyatpost.com/news/2015/08/31/ghb-to-take-over-existing-party-rename-itself/> and <http://www.themalaymailonline.com/malaysia/article/harapan-baru-aims-for-35000-members-in-takeover-of-workers-party> (accessed 1 September 2015).

14. For such developments at the end of September 2015, I drew from a host of news stories and reports from *Malaysiakini*, the *Malaysian Insider* and the *Malay Mail Online*, making full citations rather tedious, for which I apologize.

15. On 7 August 2015, the Appeal Court endorsed the Election Commission's re-delineation of Sarawak state, increasing the number of constituencies from 71 to 82. This judgement reversed an earlier High Court decision which had ruled that the delineations contravened the 13th Schedule of the Malaysian Constitution. BERSIH considered the possibility to file an appeal at the Federal Court. See <http://www.themalaymailonline.com/malaysia/article/court-of-appeal-allows-ecs-notice-for-sarawak-redelineation> and <http://www.themalaymailonline.com/malaysia/article/ec-court-ruling-proves-sarawak-redelineation-was-lawful>.

16. See <http://www.themalaymailonline.com/malaysia/article/pas-and-ikatan-announce-alliance-but-unclear-of-direction315> (accessed 1 April 2016).

17. *The Wall Street Journal* in 2016 revised the figure to over US$1 billion. See <http://www.wsj.com/articles/deposits-in-malaysian-leaders-accounts-said-to-top-1-billion-1456790588> (accessed 1 April 2016).

18. My brief summary of this sequence of events is drawn from a host of media reports on the 1MDB scandal, such as Internet news portals *Malaysiakini*, the *Malaysian Insider* and *Malay Mail Online*. The original 1MDB expose was carried by *Sarawak Report*, which has also suffered the wrath of the Najib government and its webpage was blocked in Malaysia.

19. See a news report in which she calls for the amendment of Article 10 of the Constitution to make this possible <http://www.malaysiakini.com/news/308887> (accessed 10 August 2105).

20. Various news reports. See in particular <https://www.malaysiakini.com/news/309942> (accessed 2 September 2015).

21. See <http://www.freemalaysiatoday.com/category/nation/2015/08/28/sensational-us650m-suit-filed-for-umno-against-najib/> (accessed 2 September 2015).

22. At the point of writing, Khairuddin Abu Hassan, mentioned above, was prevented from leaving for the United States to assist in an FBI investigation of the property dealings and money laundering of individuals connected to 1MDB. He was detained for allegedly attempting to overthrow the government and later held under the Security Measures (Special Offences) Act, legislation that replaced Malaysia's infamous Internal Security Act (various news reports).

23. See <http://www.theguardian.com/world/2016/jan/26/malaysian-pm-najib-razak-cleared-corruption-gift-saudi-royals> (accessed 1 April 2016).

24. In a damning video broadcast of its "Four Corners" programme, the ABC even alluded to the gruesome murder of senior counsel Kevin Morais of the Attorney General's Chambers in September 2015 as possibly connected to the financial scandals involving 1MDB. See <http://www.abc.net.au/4corners/stories/2016/03/28/4431284.htm> (accessed 5 April 2016).

25. The online news portal *Malaysiakini* provided a live feed of the event held from 29 to 30 August for thirty-four hours until the stroke of midnight, which marked Malaysia's Independence Day. See more at the BERSIH 2.0 webpage <http://www.bersih.org> and the news reports — too many to cite here. I draw my narrative from the three major online news portals of *Malaysiakini*, the *Malaysian Insider* and the *Malay Mail Online*.

26. Estimates of the number of protesters over the two days range from the police's conservative 25,000 to BERSIH's 500,000. My own estimate, having been there during the two days, is that perhaps some 200,000 people would have populated the protest zones over the thirty-four hours, with numbers approximating 100,000 in the final hours approaching midnight of 30 August. Politweet, the independent social media research group, provided its own estimates based on its methodology of spatial analysis and social media measures, putting the overall turnout to be between 80,000 and 100,000. See <http://www.themalaymailonline.com/malaysia/article/so-how-many-people-were-in-kuala-lumpur-for-bersih-4> (accessed 2 September 2015).

27. Again, I draw from numerous news reports of the event found on Internet news portals.

28. See <http://www.themalaysianinsider.com/malaysia/article/more-than-50-malays-dont-support-red-shirt-rally-poll-shows> (accessed 25 September 2015).

29. See <http://www.themalaymailonline.com/malaysia/article/mca-says-wont-leave-bn-insists-pact-still-moderate> (accessed 25 September 2015).

30. See <http://aliran.com/media-statements/2016-media-statements/citizens-declaration-signals-split-ranks-umno-bn-elites/> (accessed 10 March 2016).

31. See <https://www.malaysiakini.com/news/332575; http://aliran.com/
    civil-society-voices/2016-civil-society-voices/saving-malaysia-reformism-
    opportunism/> (accessed 10 March 2016).
32. See <https://www.malaysiakini.com/news/332787>.
33. See <http://asiapacific.anu.edu.au/newmandala/2016/05/13/victory-
    and-insecurity-sarawak-results-and-trajectories/> (accessed 14 May
    2016).

11

CONCLUSION
The Desiderata of Ethnic Power Sharing

This book has presented readers with narratives on Malaysia's electoral politics spanning some sixty years. It has also attempted to explain why one major ruling coalition of parties has dominated elections since Independence. The book suggests that the ethnic power sharing model of the ruling coalition, the Barisan Nasional (BN) — and its predecessor, the Alliance — has been the main reason for such electoral successes for these six decades. Most importantly, the ruling coalition has been able to deploy a strategy of mediated communalism to achieve its electoral success. As noted in the introduction, there have been three phases in the employment of this dynamic strategy of mediated communalism, which is anchored on the consociational pact of a grand coalition of ethnic groups and centripetal stratagems of moderating extremist politics. The three periods are:

1. Emergent Mediated Communalism: 1950s to 1960s;
2. Corporatized Mediated Communalism: 1970s to late 1990s;
3. Contested Mediated Communalism: Late 1990s to 2013.

The book traces the beginnings of the Malaysian electoral system in Chapter 2, which contextualizes how mediated communalism found its salience through the institutionalization of electoral structures within a plural and ethnically divided society. In Chapter 3 the book explored the idea of the onset of an emergent strategy of mediated communalism from the 1950s to the late 1960s and showed how moderate policies of ethnic accommodation bestowed success to the Alliance in elections. Chapters 4 and 5 postulated the entrenchment of a new kind of mediated communalism via Malay primacy and party capitalism from the 1970s till the late 1990s. I have termed this the *corporatized* phase because of the extensive use of money politics dovetailing with the involvement of BN parties in business. While this particular phase of corporatized politics is clearly identifiable and represented its initial surfacing, there is little doubt that such a form continues to the present day. As noted in the previous chapter, the UMNO crisis of 2015 was partly the result of the use of massive sums of money in the 2013 general election, sourced through a complex web of local and international business entities established by the prime minister and UMNO president. Despite Malay dominance, corporatized politics was a highly successful strategy for the distribution of spoils to all BN parties, and the accommodation of non-Malay interests by the mid-1990s gave the BN its celebrated landslide electoral victory of 1995. Finally, Chapters 7 to 9 traced the origins of a contested mediated communalism of *new politics* spanning the period between the late 1990s till 2013. The slide in the BN's performance by the end of this final period showed how the rise of a cohesive alternative coalition, with its own form of mediated communalism, blunted and seriously challenged a weakening BN. Through these explorations the book was able to test the saliency of a distinct approach to ethnic power sharing and dominance through a process of mediated communalism, something that is unique to Malaysia, a social formation that has been both ethnically divided yet delicately integrated through its consociational institutions throughout its electoral history.

At this point in Malaysia's electoral history, constituting centripetal arrangements at different levels of engagement to generate bridging social capital among communal groups remains problematic so long as the electoral system remains anchored to its current first-past-the-post single-member plurality system with its large measure of rural weightage. The current system, as I have argued in Chapter 2, will tend to reproduce ethnic voting and ethnic allocations of seats. It does, however, encourage the pooling of ethnic votes as long as there are a significant number of mixed constituencies. Penultimate words need to be added here about institutional stability and flux and path dependence. The works of Pepinsky (2009) and Slater (2006, 2010), both of whom study Southeast Asian authoritarianism and democratization,[1] offer some explanations for the BN's political longevity. In analysing the crisis sparked by the Reformasi Movement, Pepinsky showed that the regime stayed intact largely because of policy adjustments, that the party system remained intact and the BN coalition maintained its unity (Pepinsky 2009, pp. 193–98).

Slater invokes the notion of the "authoritarian Leviathan", an idea that can be used to underscore the stability of authoritarian rule in Malaysia and its resistance to regime fragmentation.[2] His work stresses the durability of institutions such as single-party systems which are able to resist democratization processes (2006) and how, for example, "protection pacts" with primary constituencies of the regime — such as the middle class, state officials and ethnic elites — have been crucial to regime stability. In Malaysia's case, this is attributed to a "strong state" and ruling party. The extractive and coercive capacity of the BN Leviathan is stressed, and this accords well with my notion of party capitalism. Slater also emphasizes the importance of securing the support of the middle classes, suggesting that "The Malaysian case is noteworthy for the active support lent by urban middle classes to the authoritarian Leviathan *at its very inception*" (Slater 2010, p. 157; emphasis in the original). Yet another work premised on competitive authoritarianism posits two main factors — UMNO's organizational and coercive power minus the mitigating effects of external pressure (weak external linkages) — on the ruling regime's capability to check oppositional challenges (Levitksy and Way 2010, p. 318). However, in the post 2008 period the fact that the BN has increasingly lost ground among the urban middle classes, particularly over the last two general elections, suggests that the BN Leviathan is weakening.

The works cited in the preceding section point to important variables for analysing regime change in Malaysia, but, at the end of the day, Malaysia's unique multicultural social formation and its peculiar communal manifestation tend to call for even more specific political articulations to effect democratic political transition. The notion of mediated communalism propounded here suggests that the managerial model of the BN may have to be emulated rather than overcome by any alternative coalition. Thus, notions of conflict management and conflict resolution are still highly pertinent to effecting change in such severely divided and ethnically driven polities like Malaysia. I have stressed throughout the book, explicitly and implicitly, that bridging social capital and cross-ethnic associational life and political articulations have been the basis for the successful deployment of mediated communalism as a strategy of electoral success, reinforcing centripetal political arrangements. I will now focus on structural and intervening factors, though not insignificant variables beyond centripetalism and mediated communalism, that are especially pertinent to explaining electoral transition in Malaysia.

Throughout the book, by using path dependence theorizing to frame electoral politics, I have argued that the BN's (and the Alliance's) success has not just been the result of its first-mover advantage in using mediated communalism for pooling ethnic votes. As argued throughout the book, the ruling coalition's *manufactured majorities* have also been due to many structural elements, particularly the character of Malaysia's first-past-the-post system with its weightage in favour of rural constituencies, the use of money politics, machine politics and a biased media under its control. These have been the many customary advantages of incumbency. However, the landmark 2008 general election showed that the BN may have lost this advantage and its usually assured path-dependent success in elections. A new opposition coalition emerged in the shape of the PR, which was able to also muster its own grouping of ethnic parties and mount a strategy of mediated communalism, arguably as successfully as the BN. What was particularly important in this development was that the PR's mediated communalism was also the result of a *new politics* of a participatory multi-ethnic and multi-religious character that in several ways trumped the BN's old model of mediated communalism. The BN was denied its customary two-thirds majority of seats in Parliament and control of five state governments. The PR's path-dependent success continued into the 2013 general election when it captured more than 50 per cent of the popular vote, although it failed to capture federal power, partly

due to the problem of malapportionment of the Malaysian electoral
system, but also due to the fact that it was unable to win a large
enough proportion of the rural Malay vote and that of the non-Malay
bumiputera vote of East Malaysia. Figures 11.1 and 11.2 illustrate the
extent of the ruling coalition's domination of electoral politics over
sixty years. What is interesting to note is that the Alliance and the BN
consistently gained a disproportionate number of seats that did not
correspond to its vote share, while the opposition always collected a
much lower percentage of seats compared with the share of votes won.
Some of this statistical variance could be explained simply by the BN
having more candidates and often winning seats uncontested (which
are not added to percentages). However, by the late 1990s hardly any
seats were uncontested in elections. The two charts confirm earlier
observations in the book that because of the malapportioned distribution
of votes to seats (mainly to rural constituencies) in Malaysia's first-past-
the-post system, the opposition — with less capacity to access rural
bumiputera voters — has been systematically denied a fair proportion

Figure 11.1
Alliance/BN Vote Share and Seats

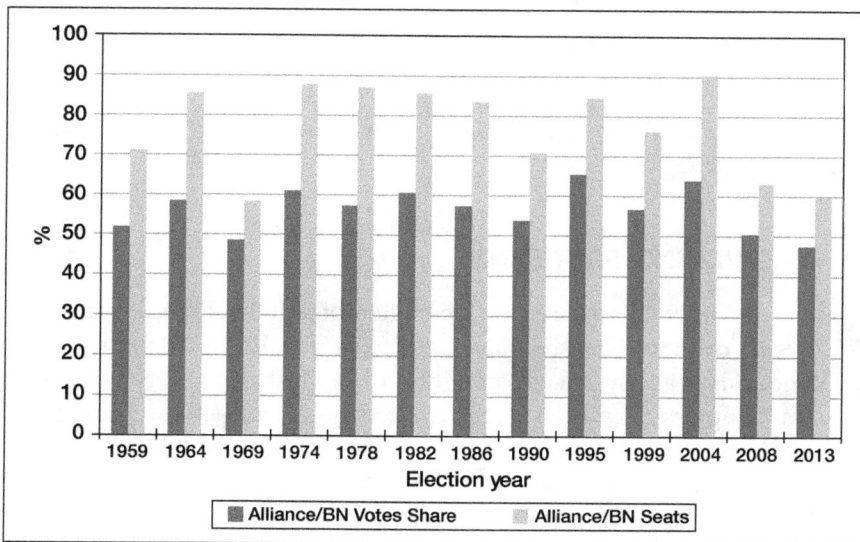

Figure 11.2
Opposition Vote Share and Seats

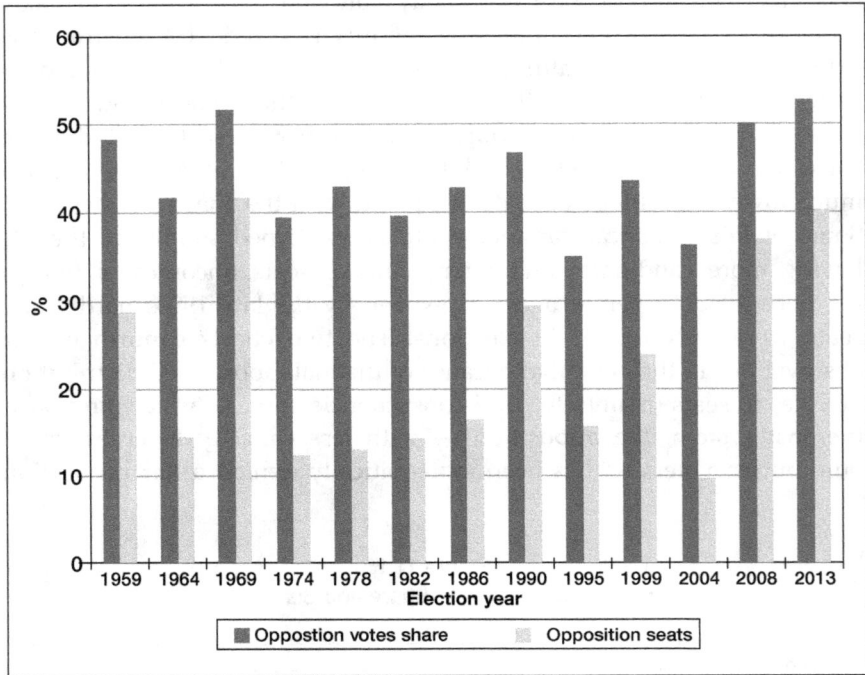

of seats in the Malaysian Parliament and elections more or less got
"stolen" by the incumbents.

ETHNIC VOTING PATTERNS

I move on now to discuss the character of ethnic voting patterns in
Malaysia, drawing on the latest electoral results. Malaysian voting
behaviour has always been thought to manifest ethnic voting trends,
and in Chapters 8 and 9 I demonstrated how cross-ethnic voting and
vote pooling have become evident in the opposition's successes. This
happened mainly in mixed urban constituencies, where results based
on the 2013 electoral outcome show that there was a strong ethnic
element in the character of support for the parties of the BN and PR.

However, I would add the caveat that ethnic voting behaviour is often a self-fulfilling prophecy in the sense that parties in the first place usually select candidates on the basis of ethnicity and voters seldom have the chance to choose candidates from another ethnic group outside their own. However, data in Figures 11.3 to 11.6 do not address this, but instead show how party candidates fare with voters of different ethnicities.

Figures 11.3 to 11.6 show BN and PR performances vis-à-vis percentages of Malay and Chinese voters and in terms of seats won by each party on the Peninsula. Sabah and Sarawak are excluded as the

Figure 11.3
BN & Malay Voters

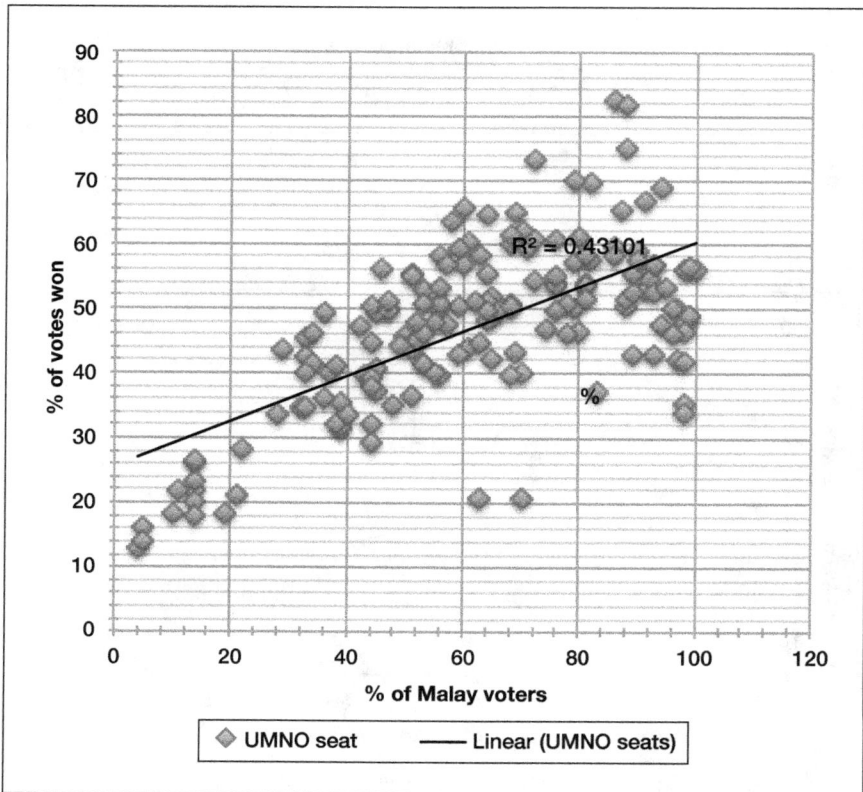

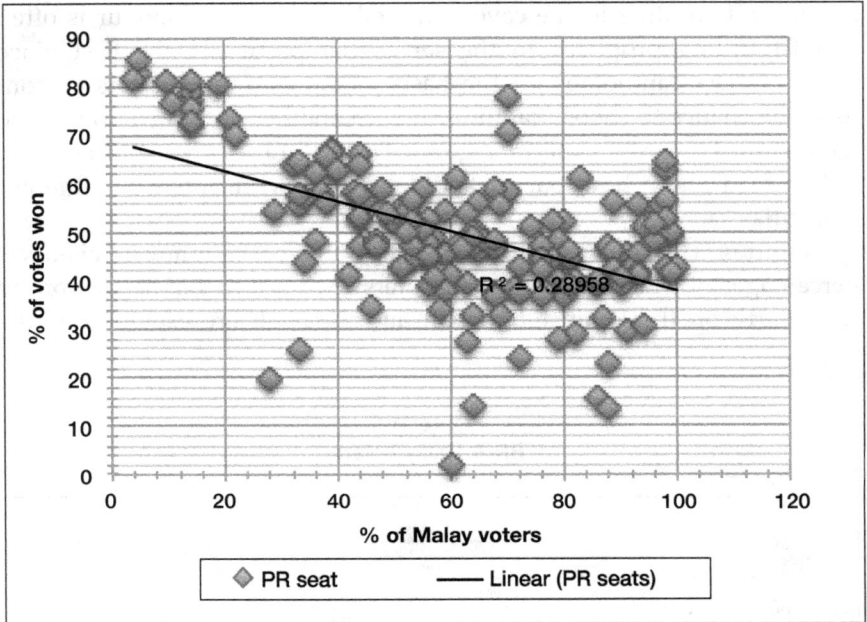

Figure 11.4
PR & Malay Voters

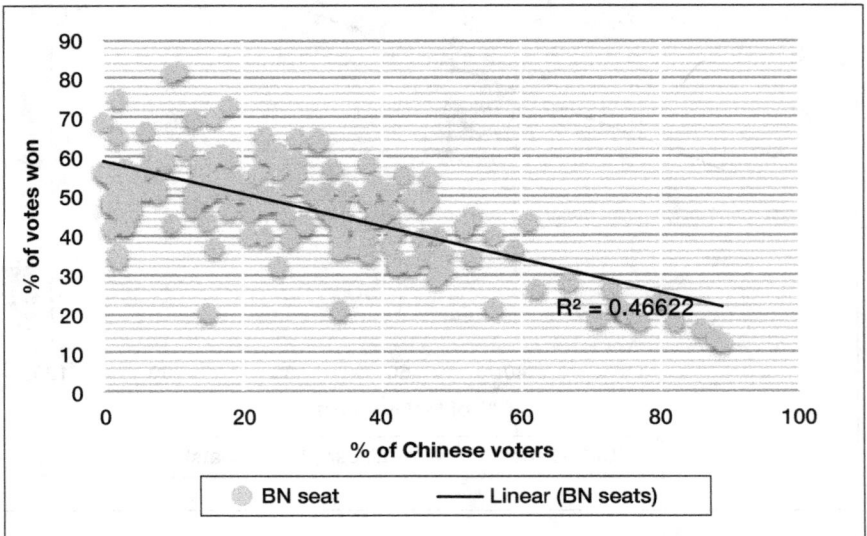

Figure 11.5
BN & Chinese Voters

Figure 11.6
PR & Chinese Voters

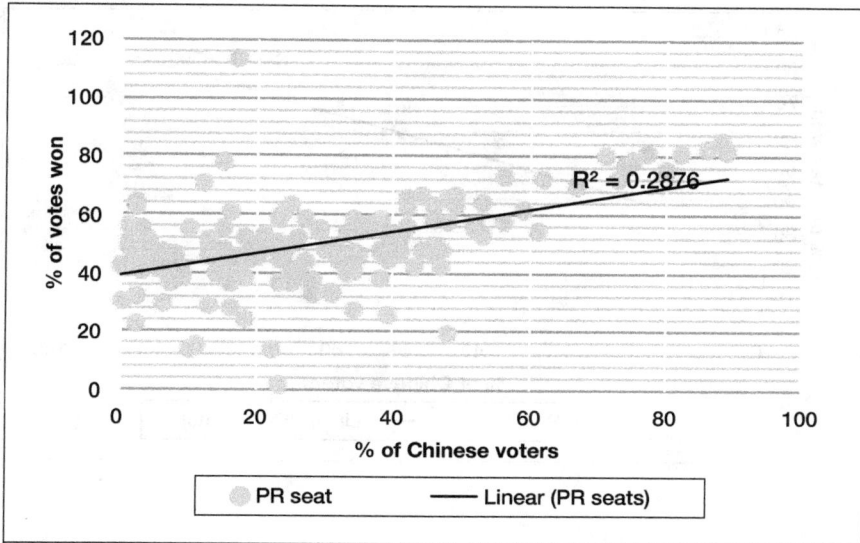

Election Commission provides only data for registered Malay, Chinese and Indian voters on the Peninsula. An additional chart (Figure 11.7) shows only the DAP's performance vis-à-vis Chinese voters. Figure 11.3 shows that the BN (mainly UMNO) captured a large number of seats in the upper zones of Malay-voter constituencies of above 50 per cent. The reverse is true for the PR, which performed only moderately for high Malay percentage constituencies. In the simple regression statistics shown, the BN's relationship to Malay voters is reasonably strong at 0.43, while the PR's line is negative at 0.21.

The result is reversed when it comes to Chinese voters, with the BN failing to secure seats with high Chinese percentages, coupled with a negative regression coefficient of 0.47. This in effect meant that the MCA failed to secure a significant or winning proportion of the Chinese vote in 2013. The PR on the other hand shows a positive regression line of 0.28 with respect to Chinese votes. The final chart showing the DAP's performance confirms that it is a major draw for the Chinese vote, with its positive steep regression line indicating a strong relationship with Chinese voters (0.59). Most studies of elections

Figure 11.7
DAP & Chinese Voters

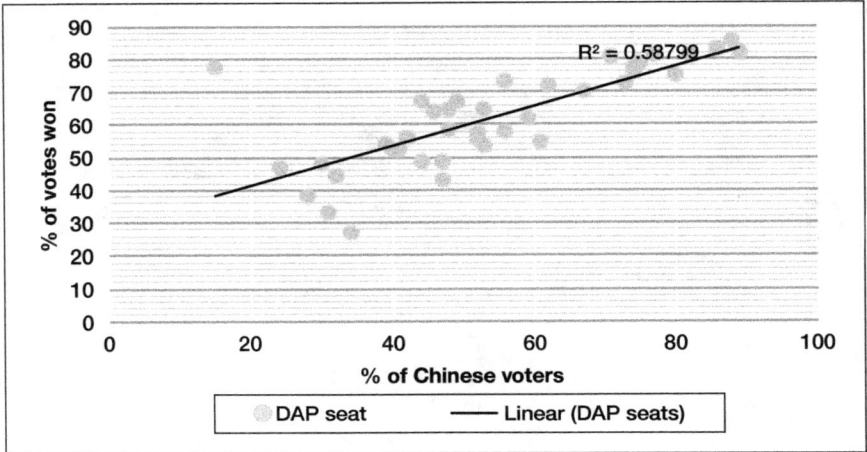

confirm that the DAP's performance has always been consistent on this score, but could swing by even double-digit percentage points in bad years. Any voter constituency with more than 80 per cent of Chinese voters is nevertheless a safe seat for the DAP (Ng 2003). From the current chart on the DAP, it is also evident that the DAP secured a significant number of seats in the mixed areas, i.e., in constituencies with Chinese percentages below 50 per cent. This seems to be a salutary effect of the DAP being part of the PR. However, the DAP is not known to contest for any seats with a composition of Chinese votes below 20 per cent. For the PR as a whole the relevant charts show that it wins the most significant number of seats in constituencies below the 50 per cent threshold of Chinese voters. A corollary of this fact is that the PR now wins most of the mixed seats.

Analysing the Malay Vote

As had been established throughout the book, one of the most crucial conditions of electoral success for Malaysia is to secure a majority of the vote among the hegemonic ethnic majority. Clearly this would be the Malay voters, who are concentrated in the Peninsula. Ironically, it is in Sabah where UMNO has established something of a consistent vote bank in terms of support from the *Muslim bumiputera*, in that this support has been unbroken there since UMNO's inception. Even if some years saw minor slippages of seats, UMNO has been winning the most number of parliamentary seats in Sabah in comparison to other contending parties in the state. It should also be noted that UMNO makes an exception for Sabah in that party membership is not strictly limited to Muslim bumiputera, but to all bumiputera within the state. But, overall, UMNO's winning of the majority of parliamentary seats has undoubtedly been somewhat predetermined by the gerrymandering and apportionment of more rural and Muslim-majority seats on the Peninsula.

It is obvious that winning the Malay vote is actually a complicated matter, especially for UMNO. Far from being monolithic or homogenous, the Malay bloc is increasingly more split and diverse in terms of voting preference. There is no real evidence to show that Malays vote on the basis of group rights, religion or cultural concerns. In fact, structural variables such as geographical residence (rural versus urban) or even developmental matters such as state-managed land schemes are the better predictor of voting patterns among Malays. As for a factor such as Islam or Islamization, that too has not appeared as the most convincing variable in contributing towards electoral gains. *The major observation to be made is that since the March 2008 watershed election, the proportion of the urban Malay vote won by the BN and PR are about equal.* In fact, the PR had made further headway among urban Malay voters in 2013, winning four seats more than the BN within this category. But the picture is reversed when it comes to rural seats. Turning to the 74 rural seats, UMNO/BN won 61 (3 by MCA candidates) or almost *82 per cent* of all Malay-majority rural seats. The PR coalition won only 13, or only *8 per cent* of these rural Malay-majority seats. The latter is, quite evidently, the PR's Achilles heel.

Let me now turn to the crucial importance of the so-called "FELDA seats", or constituencies which are located in Malaysia's biggest Malay land resettlement schemes under the federal agency FELDA (Federal Land Development Authority)[3]. Indeed, no understanding of the Malay vote is complete without taking this into account[4]. Drawing on the work of Maznah (2013), the fifty-four FELDA constituencies on the Peninsula have now been identified by mapping the distribution of FELDA plantations and smallholdings on to delineated parliamentary constituencies. When seats won by the BN and the PR in the 13th general election are superimposed on this map, the correlation between BN winning areas and FELDA constituencies becomes immediately visible[5] (see Map 11.1).

The map shows an almost perfect correlation between BN seats with the presence of FELDA schemes while, conversely, PR seats are conspicuous by their absence on these land schemes. FELDA constituencies are occupied by what Maznah (2015) has called "corporatized villages" whose economic livelihoods are linked to the now globalized and publicly listed corporate entity, Felda Global Ventures (FGV). In fact the FELDA resettlement schemes, which were initiated by Tun Razak in 1956, have been the basis of UMNO strength from the outset. The rollout of these schemes ended in 1990, but by this time there were already some 120,000 families located on them, constituting as many as 1.2 million voters by 2013 (Khor 2014, p. 95). FELDA settlers have been consistent BN supporters and are often showered with gifts and money prior to general elections. In 2013, of the 54 FELDA seats, the BN took 47 (87 per cent), while the PR only won 7. Thus, according to Maznah (2013), FELDA schemes could well be considered to be an UMNO vote bank, and the FELDA factor represents "UMNO's infrastructural advantage to mobilize, manufacture and capture the consent of the Malay settler-cum-voter". Further, "The dependency-patronage relations between UMNO and Felda voters played the biggest role in sustaining the Malay vote bank" (ibid., p. 154).

Thus, what is termed as the "rural middle class" (Khor 2003, p. 91) or the "captured rural-corporatized Malay vote" (Maznah 2013, p. 148) dovetails well with my notion of *corporatized mediated communalism* which has been deployed by UMNO since its venture into party capitalism. From a perspective of the political economy of the Malay vote, it is evident that capitalism and agricultural development are both packed into a potent concoction to ensure UMNO political longevity.

Map 11.1
Location of FELDA Settlements and Seats Won by the BN and PR, 2013

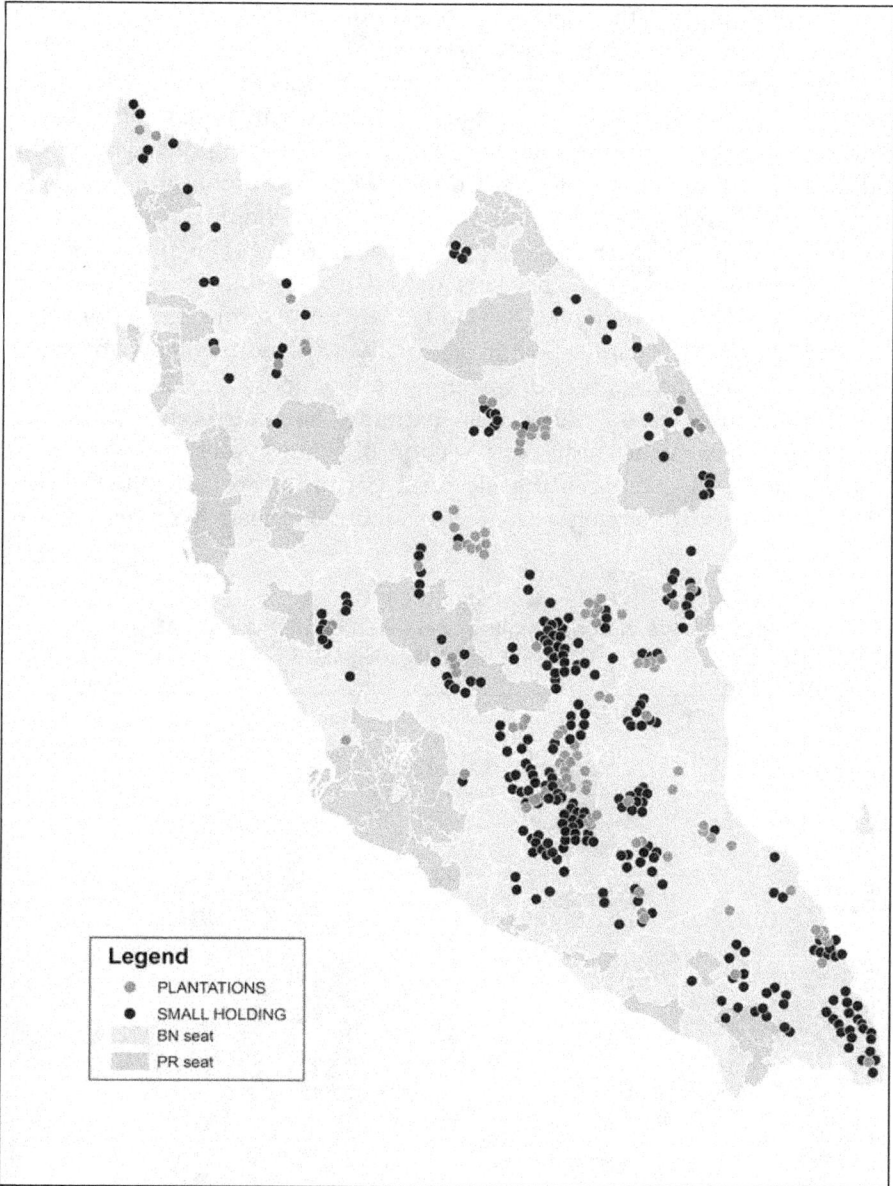

Legend

- ⬤ PLANTATIONS
- ● SMALL HOLDING
-   BN seat
-   PR seat

The Malay Vote and Islam

This section discusses the Islamic factor in securing the Malay vote. How important is this set against the competition between UMNO and PAS, the two leading Malay-Muslim parties on the Peninsula? UMNO and PAS are the two biggest Malay-Muslim parties who have used Malay and Islamic credentials as their identity, with PAS often proclaiming that it prioritizes religious over ethnic rights. Along with that, PAS has been persistent since the 1990s in promoting *hudud,* that is, Islamic criminal law, as noted in a previous chapter. Paradoxically, UMNO, through Mahathir, actually declared Malaysia to be an "Islamic state" in 2001. This sort of one-upmanship over Islam has been a consistent theme of UMNO–PAS politics, but it is doubtful whether extreme Islamic postures actually win more Malay votes for either party. I have argued throughout the book that it is actually centripetal, moderate, rather than extreme, and narrowly communal policies that win the large cross-section of ethnic votes.

Figure 11.8 compares the electoral performances of UMNO with PAS in terms of percentage of parliamentary seats won in twelve

Figure 11.8
Percentage of Parliamentary Seats Won by UMNO and PAS in General Elections, 1959–2013

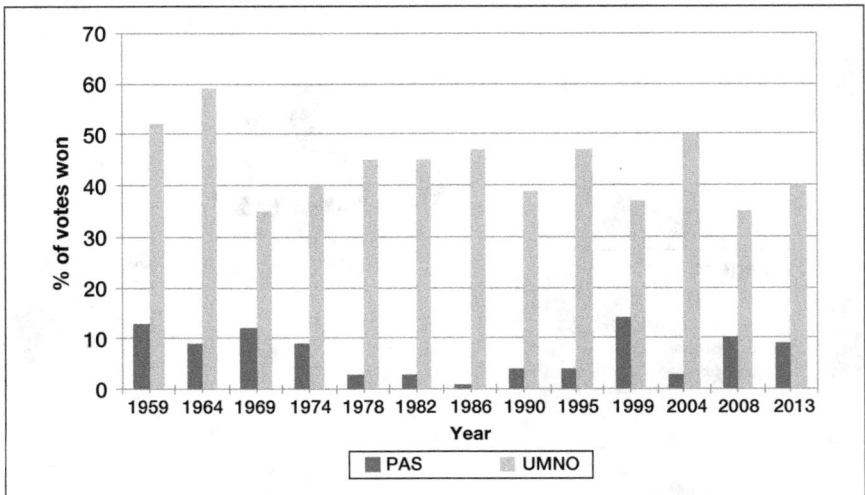

Figure 11.9
Percentage of Parliamentary Seats Won by PAS, 1959–2013

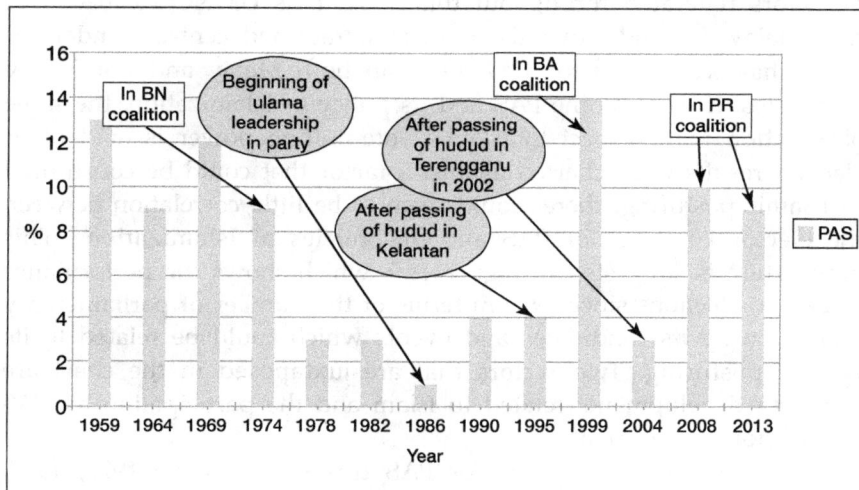

national elections. There is a wide gap between UMNO and PAS, as can be seen, with UMNO winning up to 64 per cent of all parliamentary seats in 1964 and PAS only managing 14 per cent in 1999, its best year. UMNO's worst electoral performances took place in 1969 and 2008, when it won only 35 per cent of all parliamentary seats.

Nevertheless, UMNO has always taken the electoral presence of PAS seriously, to the extent that it was driven to embark on an extensive Islamization programme since the Mahathir years in order to undercut the Islamic agenda of PAS.[6] In 1985, just a few years after PAS was taken over by its hardline ulama faction, UMNO began its shariah expansion project. In the mid-1990s extensive shariah reforms took place in terms of the promulgation of Islamic law and the expansion of the Islamic bureaucracy, but there is no evidence that this was critical to UMNO's electoral victories. The call for a greater emphasis on Islam (by the grass roots or the electorate) and the implementation of shariah law were hardly reflected in the electoral gains or losses of these two Malay-Muslim parties, as suggested by the electoral charts. I would argue that UMNO has so far succeeded in becoming the ruling party due less to its Islamic credentials than to factors reiterated throughout this book. It is UMNO's capacity to spin Malay demands towards more moderate and centrist tendencies which has won votes for UMNO, from both Malay and non-Malay electorates. If we examine PAS and its policy of Islamization, the same observation with respect to Islam's vote-pulling power is evident. If election results were charted against a factor that could be constituted as Islamic posturing, there would seem to be little correlation between the electoral success of PAS and its policies of Islamization.[7] This observation is suggested in Figure 11.9, which shows the performance of PAS in elections since 1959 in terms of the number of parliamentary seats won by its candidates and events which could be related to its Islamic posturing. Two factors that are juxtaposed in the chart are pertinent developments related to Islam and the participation by PAS in coalition governments.

The worst election years for PAS turned out to be 1978, 1982, 1986 and 2004. In 1978 PAS had left the BN coalition and contested on its own, after having gone through a crisis within the party and in the state of Kelantan where it held sway under the BN banner (see Chapter 5). In 1982 there were major changes within the party, which saw the exit of Asri Muda and the rise of the ulama faction. PAS was in a transition during the mid-1980s, switching from an "ethno-nationalist" orientation to one with a radical pan-Islamic tone. The Malay-nationalist faction under Asri Muda was forced to leave the party in 1982 and Yusuf Rawa, an ulama, was elected as its new leader in 1983 (Farish Noor 2004, pp. 326–28). When this new leadership was in power in 1986, PAS suffered its worst defeat ever. Islamic posturing appeared to be of no aid to check its slide in a period of economic recession. PAS also performed poorly in the election of 1995. The *hudud* legislation had just been passed in Kelantan in 1992. Its Islamic legislation was no match for the BN's economic achievements. Although it cannot be ascertained whether the poor showing of PAS was really due to this policy, what is clear is that showcasing Islamization does not actually deliver electoral dividends. PAS also trailed behind in 2004, winning only 3 per cent of parliamentary seats. Before this, in 2002, *hudud* legislation had been passed in Terengganu after the party had won the state government in 1999. Again, this policy of Islamization did not benefit the party when it came to the next general election.

The years 1959, 1969, 1974, 1999 and 2008 were the best election years for the party, when it won more than 10 per cent of the total parliamentary seats contested. The 1959 and 1969 elections saw PAS being led by more moderate Islamic nationalist leaders such as Burhanuddin Al-Helmy and Asri Muda, respectively, and in 1974 PAS was in the BN coalition. In 1969 it won 12 per cent of all parliamentary seats, its highest ever, thus excising a crucial proportion of Malay votes from UMNO and contributing to the latter's crisis. In 1999 and 2008, the two years when UMNO won the least percentage of parliamentary seats (about 35 per cent), these were also the years that PAS was in a partnership with the DAP and PKR in Barisan Alternatif and Pakatan Rakyat, respectively. We can thus surmise from these facts that the image of PAS during these good election years was moderated either by a softening of its Islamization agenda or by its power-sharing stance with its non-religious coalition partners.

Going by these trends it would be a mistake to assume that the Islamic posturing of PAS and its extolling of Islamic values were significant factors in capturing votes, even from Muslims. In fact it was precisely during the periods when it was aggressive in its Islamization programmes (such as the passing of the *hudud* laws) that saw it performing badly in national elections. On the other hand, the softening of its Islamization agenda clearly contributed to its electoral performance. Whenever PAS has entered into a partnership with other non-religious political parties, it has been successful in winning more parliamentary seats than when it has been on its own. The best ever election year for PAS was in 1999, when it won 14 per cent of all parliamentary seats in a partnership with multiracial parties, the PKR and the DAP.

Conversely, in the years UMNO performed poorly — 1969, 1990, 1999 and 2008 — as has been explained in previous chapters, this has had little to do with Islamic posturing. That is, Islam was hardly a variable in the electoral gains or losses of UMNO in those years. Considered to be the more moderate of the two parties on the question of Islam, there have no doubt been times when UMNO has tried to enhance its Islamic image. However, by and large UMNO used its resources to Islamize the government sector, thus wining much civil service support. But it also periodically controlled Islamic factions within the party and religious bureaucrats outside of it from veering towards extreme tendencies. Moreover, UMNO went out of its way to proscribe so-called "deviant" movements, like the Al-Arqam. In so doing UMNO would remain distinct from PAS, espousing the "moderate Islam" (such as *Islam Hadhari*) in fashioning its self-image. This essentially centripetal stratagem to move towards the middle ground was consistently executed by Mahathir, by Abdullah Badawi, and also Najib Razak. Najib has advanced his own preferred concept of *Wasatiyyah* (moderation) since taking the helm.[8] The aggressive posturing of Islamization on the part of PAS through the passage of *hudud* in Kelantan and Terengganu seems to have cost it votes in the face of UMNO's more moderate policies. The more radical religiosity of PAS does not seem to be endorsed by a large cross-section of Muslim voters at the ballot box. On the other hand, UMNO's strategy of Islamizing the state is calibrated to win enough Malay votes, while at the same time not driving too many non-Muslim voters away from the BN. The issue of *hudud* again took centre stage since 2014. This surfaced after PAS indicated its intention in April 2014 to implement *hudud* in Kelantan. PAS had planned to introduce enabling legislation for *hudud* through Parliament, angling for support from UMNO members. However, the Islamic party retracted its move after the Najib government apparently approved the setting up a national-level technical committee, with the participation of PAS, to study the long-term feasibility of *hudud*.[9] The attempt to introduce the bill was successful in June 2016 after it failed to see passage during the March–April 2015 sitting of Parliament.

I argue that tangible Malay rights are actually more important as an agenda for PAS than its ceaseless pursuit of *hudud*. In one of the earliest studies on the politicization of Islam in Malaysia, Judith Nagata (1980) was prescient in observing the inseparable link between religion and ethnicity: "In political rhetoric, the PAS plea for an Islamic state has long been interpreted as a demand for more Malay rights, an appealing concept to a community seeking truly national status. Where discussion of royalty is now prohibited, the Islamic state provides an alternative rallying slogan and symbol of ethnic identity" (Nagata 1980, p. 435). Likewise, for UMNO it would be the same: "Whatever the language used by UMNO, it is still the Malay community which is being mobilised and powerfully reinforced with the moral overtones of religion" (ibid., p. 436).

FINAL WORD

This book suggests that Malaysian politics have historically been premised on a hybrid model of "communalism" and "consociationalism". Most importantly, success in elections required a strategy of mediating communalism, centring policies towards a moderate middle ground. The ruling coalition, first the Alliance and then the BN, has been successful in orchestrating this model of politics since the 1950s, although there were times when its model was failing due to the weaknesses of coalition partners. By the end of the 1990s the engagement of *new politics* in power sharing among ethnically bounded opposition political parties became a new modality of electoral success. Since 2008 the emergence of a coherent new coalition of political forces deploying a stratagem of mediated communalism anchored to *new politics* has gained much electoral ground and become a real threat to the BN's grip on federal and state power. The threat will remain as long as the BN Leviathan is institutionally weak and the opposition coalition develops its institutional strength, remains coherent under an effective leadership and does not veer towards extremist communal policies. Ultimately, either coalition vying for power has to be cognizant of the necessary and sufficient conditions, both general and specific, for electoral success analysed throughout this book.

This book has tried to also put across three main arguments for electoral success. First, is the imperative of power sharing. A communally charged and regionally diverse political entity like Malaysia requires consociational power sharing arrangements within the rubric of grand coalitions of ethnic and regional forces. Second, policies which are spun to a moderate centre ensure the largest cross-section of votes and tend to produce winning electoral margins. Finally, path-dependent electoral success is achieved not just by a communal-centric approach, but also depends on structural elements, including the character of the electoral system, economic booms and downturns and global political contingencies, which are sometimes outside the control of political parties and governments.

Notes

1. Both academics are also likely to be considered to be part of the genre of work known as "historical institutionalism", to which I have alluded in the introduction.
2. Earlier work on authoritarianism invoked the similar notion of the "Bureaucratic-Authoritarian (BA)" state, a concept developed by the Argentine political scientist Guillermo O'Donnell. See Saravanamuttu (1987).
3. For a detailed history of FELDA, see Lee and Shamsul Bahrin (2006).
4. See the studies of FELDA seats in the 2013 general election by Khor (2015) and Maznah Mohamad (2015).
5. The FELDA map was supplied by Merdeka Centre. It indicated the location of schemes and thus allowed for the identification of the names of the fifty-four FELDA seats by Maznah Mohamad (2013).
6. For studies on this, see Nagata (1980), Liow (2009) and Maznah Mohamad (2010).
7. Political observers have suggested that under President Hadi Awang, the ulama faction of PAS has been on the ascendancy over the "Erdoganists" or moderates. This PAS split was detrimental to centripetal policies of moderation and, as shown in the previous chapter, led to the breakup of the party with the formation of the breakaway Parti Amanah Negara by PAS moderates. PAS politics took a turn towards greater Islamization, ironically, after the death of Tok Guru Nik Aziz, its former spiritual leader, who had always demurred association with UMNO and was steadfast about collaboration with PR parties.
8. Under Najib's tenure an International Institute of Wasatiyyah was formed at the Islamic University of Malaysia. See <http://www.iium.edu.my/wasatiyyah> (accessed 23 May 2015).
9. News reports have alluded to the setting up of this technical committee, comprising shariah experts, announced by deputy premier Muhyiddin Yassin. PAS decided not to introduce its private members bill in Parliament in 2014 after being invited to participate in this committee. See <http://www.nst.com.my/latest/umno-proposes-national-level-hudud-technical-committee-1.580535> (accessed 23 May 2014).

BIBLIOGRAPHY

Abdillah Noh. "Malaysia and the Consociational Option: Is There a Path Dependent Logic?" Working Paper No 2013/1. Tun Abdul Razak School of Government, Universiti Tun Abdul Razak, 2013.

Abdul Rashid Moten and Tunku Mohar Mokhtar. "The 1995 Parliamentary Election in Malaysia". *Intellectual Discourse* 3, no. 1 (1995): 77–93.

————. "The 2004 General Elections in Malaysia: A Mandate to Rule". *Asian Survey* 46, no. 2 (2006): 319–40.

Abdullah Ahmad Badawi. *Islam Hadhari: A Model Approach for Development and Progress*. Kuala Lumpur: MPH, 2006.

Abdullah Ahmad. *Tengku Abdul Rahman and Malaysia's Foreign Policy*. Kuala Lumpur: Berita, 1985.

Abdullah, Firdaus. "PAS and the 1978 Election". In *Malaysian Politics and the 1978 Election*, edited by Harold Crouch, Lee Kam Hing and Michael Ong. Kuala Lumpur: Oxford University Press, 1980.

Ahmad Fauzi Abdul Hamid and Muhamad Takiyuddin Ismail, eds. "Malaysia's 13th General Election: Reform, Change and Conservatism". *Kajian Malaysia* 32, supp. 2 (2014; special issue).

Amsden, Alice H. *Asia's Next Giant: South Korea and Late Industrialization*. New York: Oxford University Press, 1989.

Bailey, F.G. *Stratagems and Spoils: A Social Anthropology of Politics*. Oxford: Blackwell, 1969.

Balasubramaniam, Vejai. "Vote for Unity: Malaysia's Ninth General Elections". *Economic and Political Weekly* 30, no. 23 (10 June 1995): 1362–63

————. "The Politics of Locality and Temporality in the 2004 Malaysian Parliamentary Elections". *Contemporary Southeast Asia* 27, no. 1 (2005): 44–63.

Barraclough, Simon. "Communalism and Confusion: Towards a Clarification of Terms in the Study of Malaysian Politics". *Ethnic & Racial Studies* 7, no. 3 (1984): 413–21.

Brown, Graham. "Playing the (non)Ethnic card: The Electoral system and Ethnic Voting Patterns in Malaysia". CRISE Working Paper No. 21. Centre for Research on Inequality, Human Security and Ethnicity, Queen Elizabeth House, University of Oxford, 2005.

Campbell, David F.J. *The Basic Concept for the Democracy Ranking of the Quality of Democracy*. Vienna: Democracy Ranking, 2008.

Campbell, James K. and Yen Siew Hwa. "Trust in Mono-Ethnic and Mixed-Ethnic Associations in Penang". *Kajian Malaysia* 25, no. 1 (2007): 71–95.

Case, William. *Elites and Regimes in Malaysia: Revisiting a Consociational Democracy*. Melbourne: Monash Asia Institute, 1996.

———. "The 1996 UMNO Party Election: 'Two for the Show'". *Pacific Affairs* 70, no. 3 (1997): 393–411.

———. "Post-GE13: Any Closer to Ethnic Harmony and Democratic Change?" *The Round Table: The Commonwealth Journal of International Affairs* 102, no. 6 (2013): 511–19.

Cheah Boon Kheng. *Malaysia: The Making of a Nation*. Singapore: Institute of Southeast Asian Studies, 2002.

Chin, James. "The 1995 Malaysian General Election: Mahathir's Last Triumph?" *Asian Survey* 36, no. 4 (1996): 393–409

———. "The Maelanau-Malay Schism Erupts Again: Sarawak at the Polls". In *New Politics in Malaysia*, edited by Francis Loh Kok Wah and Johan Saravanamuttu. Singapore: Institute of Southeast Asian Studies, 2003.

———. "Chinese Tsunami or Urban Revolt? It is Both Actually". *The Round Table: The Commonwealth Journal of International Affairs* 102, no. 6 (2013): 499–501.

———, ed. *The Malaysian 13th General Elections. The Round Table: The Commonwealth Journal of International Affairs* 102, no. 6 (2013).

Chin, James and Wong Chin Huat. "Malaysia's Electoral Upheaval". *Journal of Democracy* 20, no. 3 (2009): 70–85.

Collier, Ruth Berins and David Collier. *Shaping the Political Arena: Critical Junctures, the Labour Movement, and Regime Dynamics in Latin America*. Notre Dame: University of Notre Dame Press, 2002.

Crouch, Harold. *Malaysia's 1982 General Election*. Singapore: Institute of Southeast Asian Studies, 1982.

———. *Government and Society in Malaysia*. Ithaca, NY: Cornell University Press, 1996.

Crouch, Harold, Lee Kam Hing and Michael Ong, eds. *Malaysian Politics and the 1978 Election*. Kuala Lumpur: Oxford University Press, 1980.

Dahl Robert A. *Polyarchy: Participation and Opposition*. New Haven, CT: Yale University Press, 1971.

De Mesquita, Bruce Bueno and George W. Downs. "Development and Democracy". *Foreign Affairs* (September/October 2005): 1–8.

Department of Statistics Malaysia. *Population and Housing Census of Malaysia 2010*. Malaysia: Department of Statistics Malaysia, 2010.

Diamond, Larry. *Developing Democracy: Toward Consolidation*. Baltimore, MD: Johns Hopkins University Press, 1999.

Faaland, Just, Jack R. Parkinson and Rais B. Saniman. *Growth and Ethnic Inequality: Malaysia's New Economic Policy*, 2nd ed. Kuala Lumpur: Utusan, 2003.

Faizal Hasiz. *Domination and Contestation: Muslim Bumiputera Politics in Sarawak*. Singapore: Institute of Southeast Asian Studies, 2011.

Farish Noor. 2004. *Islam Embedded: The Historical Development of the Pan-Malaysian Islamic Party PAS, 1951–2003*, vols. 1–2. Kuala Lumpur: Malaysian Sociological Research Institute, 2004.

Fields, Karl J. "KMT, Inc. Party Capitalism in a Developmental State". Japan Policy Research Institute (JPRI) Working Paper No 47. June 1998.

———. "KMT, Inc.: Liberalization, Democratization, and the Future of Politics in Business". In *Political Business in East Asia*, edited by Edmund Terence Gomez. London: Routledge, 2002.

Funston, John. "Malaysia's Election: Malay Winds of Change?" In *Trends in Malaysia: Election Assessment*, by Zakaria Haji Ahmad, Khoo Kay Kim, K.S. Nathan, Hari Singh, Meredith Weiss and John Funston. Singapore: Institute of Southeast Asian Studies, 2000.

———. "Malaysia's Tenth Elections: Status Quo, 'Reformasi' or Islamization?" *Contemporary Southeast Asia* 22, no. 1 (2000): 23–59.

Furnivall, J.S. *Colonial Policy and Practice: A Comparative Study of Burma and Netherlands India*. Cambridge: Cambridge University Press, 1948.

Gagliano, Felix V. *Communal Violence in Malaysia 1969: The Political Aftermath*. Ohio University Center for International Studies, 1970.

Gale, Bruce K. *Politics and Public Enterprise in Malaysia*. Singapore: Eastern Universities Press, 1981.

———. *Politics and Business: A Study of Multi-Purpose Holdings Berhad*. Singapore: Eastern Universities Press, 1985.

Geertz, Clifford. "The Integrative Revolution: Primordial Sentiments and Politics in the New States". In *Old Societies and New States: The Quest for Modernity in Asia and Africa*, edited by Clifford Geertz. New York: Free Press of Glencoe, 1963.

Goh Ban Lee. "The Demise of Local Government Elections and Urban Politics". In *Elections and Democracy in Malaysia*, edited by Mavis

Puthucheary and Noraini Othman. Bangi: Penerbit Universiti Kebangsaan Malaysia, 2005, pp. 49–70.

Gomez, Edmund Terence. *Politics in Business: UMNO's Corporate Investments.* Kuala Lumpur: Forum, 1990.

————. *Money Politics in the Barisan Nasional.* Kuala Lumpur: Forum, 1991.

————. *Political Business: Corporate Involvement of Malaysian Political Parties.* Townsville: Centre for South-East Asian Studies, James Cook University of North Queensland, 1994.

————. *The 1995 Malaysian General Elections: A Report and Commentary.* Singapore: Institute of Southeast Asian Studies, 1996.

————. *Chinese Business in Malaysia: Accumulation, Ascendance, Accommodation.* Honolulu: University of Hawai'i Press, 1999.

————. "Political Business Alliances: The Role of the State and Foreign and Domestic Capital in Economic Development". In *The State of Malaysia: Ethnicity, Equity, and Reform,* edited by Edmund Terence Gomez. London: Routledge, 2002.

Gomez, Edmund Terence and Johan Saravanamuttu, eds. *The New Economic Policy in Malaysia: Affirmative Action, Ethnic Inequalities and Social Justice.* Singapore: NUS Press, 2012.

Gomez, Edmund Terence and K.S. Jomo. *Malaysia's Political Economy: Politics, Patronage and Profits,* rev. ed. Cambridge: Cambridge University Press, 1999.

Grace, Jeremy. "SPR Delimitation: Malaysia: Malapportioned Districts and Over-Representation of Rural Communities". 2008 <http://www.tindakmalaysia.com/showthread.php/6896–SPR-Delimitation-Malaysia-Malapportioned-Districts-and-Over-Representation-of-Rural-Communities> (accessed 31 May 2015).

Hari Singh. "Political Change in Malaysia: The Role of Semangat 46". *Asian Survey* 31, no. 8 (1991): 712–28 .

————. "UMNO Leaders and Malay Rulers: The Erosion of a Special Relationship". *Pacific Affairs* 68, no. 2 (1995): 187–205.

————. "Tradition, UMNO and Political Succession in Malaysia". *Third World Quarterly* 19, no. 2 (1998): 241–54.

————. "Opposition Politics and the 1999 Malaysian Elections". In *Trends in Malaysia: Election Assessment,* by Zakaria Haji Ahmad, Khoo Kay Kim, K.S. Nathan, Hari Singh, Meredith Weiss and John Funston. Singapore: Institute of Southeast Asian Studies, 2000.

Hari Singh and Suresh Narayanan. "Changing Dimensions in Malaysian Politics: The Johore Baru by-Election". *Asian Survey* 29, no. 5 (1989): 514–29.

Hawkins, A.S.M. *Report on the Introduction of Elections in the Municipality of George Town, Penang, 1951.* Kuala Lumpur: Government Press, 1951.

Hawkins, David and Stuart Drummond. "The Malaysian Elections of 1969: Crisis for the Alliance". *The World Today* 25, no. 9 (1969): 394–403

Hilly, John. *Malaysia: Mahathirism, Hegemony and the New Opposition*. London: Zed Books, 2001.

Horowitz, Donald L. "Political and First-Past-The-Post". In *Elections and Democracy in Malaysia*, edited by Mavis Puthucheary and Noraini Othman. Bangi: Penerbit Universiti Kebangsaan Malaysia, 2005, pp. 385–401.

Huntington, Samuel P. *Political Order in Changing Societies*. New Haven, CT: Yale University Press, 1968.

———. *The Third Wave: Democratization in the Late Twentieth Century*. York: Simon & Schuster, 1991.

Hwang, In-Won. *Personalized Politics: The Malaysian State under Mahathir*. Singapore: Institute of Southeast Asian Studies, 2003.

Johnson, Chalmers. *MITI and the Japanese Miracle: The Growth of Industrial Policy, 1925–1975*. Stanford: Stanford University Press, 1982.

Jomo Kwame Sundaram, ed. *Mahathir's Economic Policies*, 2nd ed. Kuala Lumpur: Insan, 1989.

———, ed. *Tigers in Trouble: Financial Governance, Liberalization and Crisis in East Asia*. Hong Kong: Hong Kong University Press, 1998.

———, ed. *After the Storm: Crisis Recovery and Sustaining Development in Four Southeast Economies*. Singapore: Singapore University Press, 2004.

———. "Malaysia Incorporated: Corporatism a la Mahathir". *Institutions and Economies* 6, no. 1 (2014): 73–94

Jomo Kwame Sundaram and Ahmad Shabery Cheek. "Malaysia's Islamic Movements". In *Fragmented Vision: Culture and Politics in Contemporary Malaysia*, edited by Joel S. Kahn and Francis Loh Kok Wah. Sydney: Allen and Unwin, 1992.

Kahn, Joel S. "Growth, Economic Transformation, Culture and the Middle Class". In *The New Rich in Asia: Mobile Phones, McDonald's and Middle-Class Revolution*, edited by Richard Robison and David S.G. Goodman. London: Routledge, 1996.

Kahn, S. Joel and Francis Loh Kok Wah. *Fragmented Vision: Culture and Politics in Contemporary Malaysia*. Honolulu: University of Hawai'i Press, 1992.

Kessler, Clive S. "A Proposal for a Preferential Voting System". In *Elections and Democracy in Malaysia*, edited by Mavis Puthucheary and Noraini Othman. Bangi: Penerbit Universiti Kebangsaan Malaysia, 2005.

Khadijah Md Khalid. "Voting for Change: Islam and Personalised Politics in the 2004 General Elections". In *Politics in Malaysia: The Malay Dimension*, edited by Terence E. Gomez. Milton Park: Routledge, 2007.

Khong Kim Hoong. *Malaysia's General Election 1990: Continuity, Change, and Ethnic Politics*. Singapore: Institute of Southeast Asia Studies, 1991.

Khoo Boo Teik. *Paradoxes of Mahathirism: An Intellectual Biography of Mahathir Mohamad*. Kuala Lumpur: Oxford University Press, 1995.

————. "Unfinished Crises: Malaysian Politics in 1999". *Southeast Asian Affairs 2000*, edited by Daljit Singh. Singapore: Institute of Southeast Asian Studes, 2000, pp. 165–83.

————. "Limits to Democracy: Political Economy, Ideology and Ruling Coalition". In *Elections and Democracy in Malaysia*, edited by Mavis Puthucheary and Noraini Othman. Bangi: Penerbit Universiti Kebangsaan Malaysia, 2005.

———— "The Monkeys Strike Back: The 12th General Election and After". *Aliran Monthly* 28, no. 2 (2008).

Khoo Kay Kim. "Malaysian Elections 1990–1999: A Historical Perspective". In *Trends in Malaysia: Election Assessment*, by Zakaria Haji Ahmad, Khoo Kay Kim, K.S. Nathan, Hari Singh, Meredith Weiss and John Funston. Singapore: Institute of Southeast Asian Studies, 2000.

Khoo Khay Jin. "The Grand Vision: Mahathir and Modernisation". In *Fragmented Vision: Culture and Politics in Contemporary Malaysia*, edited by Joel S. Kahn and Loh Kok Wah. Sydney: Allen & Unwin and Asian Studies Assn. of Australia, 1992.

Khoo, Philip. "A New Dawn?" *Aliran Monthly* 28, no 4 (2008).

Khor Yu Leng. "The Political Tussle over Felda Land Schemes – UMNO Strengthens its Malay Rural Fortress in 13th General Election". *Kajian Malaysia* 32, supp. 2 (2014; Special Issue on "Malaysia's 13th General Election: Reform, Change and Conservatism", edited by Ahmad Fauzi Abdul Hamid and Muhamad Takiyuddin Ismail).

————. "The Political Economy of FELDA Seats: UMNO's Malay Rural Fortress in GE13". In *Coalitions in Collision: Malaysia's 13th General Elections*, edited by Johan Saravanamuttu, Lee Hock Guan and Mohamed Nawab Osman. Petaling Jaya and Singapore: Strategic Information and Research Development Center (SIRD) and Institute of Southeast Asian Studies, 2015.

Kua Kia Soong. *May 13: Declassified Documents on the Malaysian Riots of 1969*. Kuala Lumpur: Suaram Komunikasi, 2007.

Langdon, Frank. *Politics in Japan*, Boston: Little Brown, 1967.

Lau, Albert. *A Moment of Anguish: Singapore in Malaysia and the Politics of Disengagement*. Singapore: Times Academic Press, 1998.

Lee Hock Guan. "Mal-apportionment and the Electoral Authoritarian Regime in Malaysia". In *Coalitions in Collision: Malaysia's 13th General Elections*, edited by Johan Saravanamuttu, Lee Hock Guan and Mohamed Nawab Osman. Petaling Jaya and Singapore: SIRD and Institute of Southeast Asian Studies, 2015.

Lee Kuan Yew. *The Battle for Merger*. Singapore: Government Printing Office, 1961.

————. *The Singapore Story: Memoirs of Lee Kuan Yew*. Singapore: Times Editions, 1998.

————. *From First World to Third: The Singapore Story, 1965–2000: Memoirs of Lee Kuan Yew*. Singapore: Times Editions, 2000.

————. "Steadily Amplified Rural Votes Decide Malaysian Elections". *ISEAS Perspective*, no. 34, 6 June 2013.

Lee, Boon Thong and Shamsul Bahrin. *Felda's Fifty Years: Land Pioneers to Investors*. Kuala Lumpur: FELDA, 2006.

Levitsky, Steven and Lucan A. Way. *Competitive Authoritarianism: Hybrid Regimes after the Cold War*. New York: Cambridge University Press, 2010.

Liew Chin Tong. *Speaking for the Reformasi Generation: A Collection of Articles and Essays, 2003–2009*. Kuala Lumpur: REFSA, 2009.

————. "The Dominoes in Johor". *Malaysian Insider*, 13 January 2013 <http://www.themalaysianinsider.com/sideviews/article/the-dominos-in-johor-liew-chin-tong> (accessed 14 January 2015).

Lijphart, Arend. *Democracy in Plural Societies: A Comparative Exploration*. New Haven: Yale University Press, 1977.

————. *Electoral Systems and Party Systems: A Study of Twenty-seven Democracies, 1945–1990*. New York: Oxford University Press, 1994.

————. *Government Forms and Performance in Thirty-Six Countries*. New Haven: Yale University Press, 1999.

Lim Hong Hai. "Electoral Politics in Malaysia: 'Managing' Elections in a Plural Society". In *Electoral Politics in Southeast and East Asia*, edited by Aurel Croissant. Singapore: Friedrich Ebert Stiftung, 2002, pp. 101–48.

————. "The Delineation of Peninsular Electoral Constituencies: Amplifying Malay and UMNO Power". In *New Politics in Malaysia*, edited by Francis Loh Kok Wah and Johan Saravanamuttu. Singapore: Institute of Southeast Asian Studies, 2003, pp. 25–52.

————. "Making Elections Work: The Election Commission". In *Elections and Democracy in Malaysia*, edited by Mavis Puthucheary and Noraini Othman. Bangi: Penerbit Universiti Kebangsaan Malaysia, 2005, pp. 249–91.

Linz, Juan J. and Alfred Stepan. "Toward Consolidated Democracies". *Journal of Democracy* 7, no. 2 (1996): 14–33.

Liow, Joseph Chinyong. *Piety and Politics: Islamism in Contemporary Malaysia*. Oxford: Oxford University Press, 2009.

Loh Kok Wah, Francis, ed. *Sabah and Sarawak: The Politics of Development and Federalism. Kajian Malaysia* 15, nos. 1 & 3 (1997).

————. "Developmentalism versus Reformism: The Contest for Bukit Bendera, 1999". In *New Politics in Malaysia*, edited by Francis Loh Kok Wah and

Johan Saravanamuttu. Singapore: Institute of Southeast Asian Studies, 2003.

———. "Strongmen in Federal Politics in Sabah". In *Elections and Democracy in Malaysia*, edited by Mavis Puthucheary and Noraini Othman. Bangi: Penerbit Universiti Kebangsaan Malaysia, 2005, pp. 70–117.

———. *Old vs New Politics in Malaysia: State and Society in Transition*. Petaling Jaya: SIRD and Aliran, 2009.

Loh Kok Wah, Francis and Johan Saravanamuttu, eds. *New Politics in Malaysia*. Singapore: Institute of Southeast Asian Studies, 2003.

Loh Kok Wah, Francis and Khoo Boo Teik, eds. *Democracy in Malaysia: Discourses and Practices*. Richmond: Curzon, 2002.

Maarof bin Hj Salleh and Noorashikin Abdul Rahman. *Malaysia's 2004 General Elections: An Assessment*. Singapore: Institute of Southeast Asian Studies, 2004.

Mahathir Mohamad. *The Malay Dilemma*. Singapore: Donald Moore for Asia Pacific Press, 1970.

———. *The Challenge*. Petaling Jaya: Pelanduk, 1986.

———. "New Government Policies". In *Mahathir's Economic Policies*, 2nd ed., edited by K.S. Jomo. Kuala Lumpur: Insan, 1989.

———. *Malaysia: The Way Forward*. Centre for Economic Research and Services, Malaysian Business Council, 1991.

———. *A Doctor in the House: The Memoirs of Tun Dr Mahathir Mohamad*. Petaling Jaya: MPH, 2011.

Mahoney, James. "Path Dependence in Historical Sociology". *Theory and Society* 29 (200): 507–48.

Malaysian Insider. "Pakatan Trumps BN in Registering New Voters". 2010 <http://www.themalaysianinsider.com/malaysia/article/pakatan-trumps-bn-in-registering-new-voters/> (accessed 1 November 2010).

Marican, Pawancheek. *Anwar on Trail: In the Face of Injustice*. Petaling Jaya: Gerakbudaya, 2009.

Martinez, Patricia. "The Islamic State of the State of Islam in Malaysia". *Contemporary Southeast Asia* 23, no. 3 (2001): 474–503

Mauzy, Diane K. *Barisan Nasional: Coalition Government in Malaysia*. Kuala Lumpur and Singapore: Marican, 1983.

Maznah Mohamad. "The Unravelling of a 'Malay Consensus'". In *Southeast Asian Affairs 2001*, edited by Daljit Singh and Anthony Smith. Singapore: Institute of Southeast Asian Studies, 2001.

———. "Malaysia in 2002: Bracing for a Post-Mahathir Future". In *Southeast Asian Affairs 2003*, edited by Daljit Singh and Chin Kin Wah. Singapore: Institute of Southeast Asian Studies, 2003a.

————. "The Contest for Malay Votes in 1999: UMNO's Most Historic Challenge". In *New Politics in Malaysia*, edited by Francis Loh Kok Wah and Johan Saravanamuttu. Singapore: Institute of Southeast Asian Studies, 2003*b*.

————. "Malaysia – Democracy and the End of Ethnic Politics?" *Australian Journal of International Affairs* 62, no. 4 (2008).

————. "Fragmented but Captured: Malay Voters and the FELDA Factor in GE13". In *Coalitions in Collision: Malaysia's 13th General Elections*, edited by Johan Saravanamuttu, Lee Hock Guan and Mohamed Nawab Osman. Petaling Jaya and Singapore: SIRD and Institute of Southeast Asian Studies, 2015.

Maznah Mohamad and Wong Soak Koon, eds. *Risking Malaysia: Culture, Politics and Identity*. Bangi: Penerbit Universiti Kebangsaan Malaysia, 2001.

Means, Gordon. *Malaysian Politics*, 2nd ed. London: Hodder and Stoughton, 1976.

————. *Malaysian Politics: The Second Generation*. Singapore: Oxford University Press, 1991.

Merthyr, T.D. *Report of the Constituency Delineation Commission*. Kuala Lumpur: Government Printer, 1954.

Milne, R.S. *Government and Politics in Malaysia*. Boston: Houghton Mifflin, 1967.

Milne, R.S and Diane K. Mauzy. *Politics and Government in Malaysia*, 2nd ed. Singapore: Times Books International, 1980.

————. *Malaysian Politics under Mahathir*. London: Routledge, 1999.

Mohd Azizuddin Mohd Sani. "The Emergence of New Politics in Malaysia: From Consociational to Deliberative Democracy". *Taiwan Journal of Democracy* 2, no. 2 (2009): 97–125.

Nagata, Judith. "Religious Ideology and Social Change: The Islamic Revival in Malaysia". *Pacific Affairs* 53, no. 3 (1980): 405–39.

————. *The Reflowering of Malaysian Islam: Modern Religious Radicals and Their Roots*. Vancouver: University of British Columbia Press, 1984.

Nahappan, Athi. *Report of the Royal Commission of Enquiry to Investigate into the Workings of Local Authorities in West Malaysia*. Kuala Lumpur: Government Printer, 1968.

Nair, Devan C.V. *Socialism that Works – The Singapore Way*. Singapore: Federal Publications, 1976.

Nathan, K.S. "Outcome for the Barisan Nasional Coalition". In *Trends in Malaysia: Election Assessment*. Singapore: Institute of Southeast Asian Studies, 2000.

National Operations Council. *The May 13 Tragedy: A Report*. Kuala Lumpur: National Operations Council, Malaysia, 1969.

Netto, Anil. "Abdullah Badawi: Malaysia's Tinker Man". *Asian Times* (online version), 25 November 2003.

Ng Boey Kui. "Vulnerability and Party Capitalism: Malaysia's Encounter with the 1997 Financial Crisis". In *Mahathir's Administration: Performance and Crisis in Governance*, edited by Ho Khai Leong and James Chin. Singapore: Times Books International, 2001.

Ng Tien Eng. "The Contest for Chinese Votes: Politics of Negotiation or Politics of Reform?" In *New Politics in Malaysia*, edited by Francis Loh Kok Wah and Johan Saravanamuttu. Singapore: Institute of Southeast Asian Studies, 2003.

Nik Nazmi Nik Ahmad. *Coming of Age: A Decade of Essays 2001–2011*. London: Marshall Cavendish, 2011.

Nohlen, Dieter. *Elections and Electoral Systems*, 2nd ed. Delhi: Macmillan India, 1996.

Nohlen, Dieter, Florian Grozt and Christof Hartmann. *Elections in Asia and the Pacific: A Data Handbook Volume II: South East Asia, East Asia, and the South Pacific*. Oxford: Oxford University Press, 2001.

Noraini Othman. "An Agenda for Reform: The Electoral System and Prospects for Democratisation". In *Elections and Democracy in Malaysia*, edited by Mavis Puthucheary and Noraini Othman. Bangi: Penerbit Universiti Kebangsaan Malaysia, 2005.

Norris, Pippa, Richard W. Frank and Ferran Martínez i Coma, eds. *Contentious Elections: From Ballots to Barricades*. New York: Routledge, 2015.

O' Shannassy, Michael. "Beyond the Barisan Nasional? A Gramscian Perspective of the 2008 Malaysian General Election". *Contemporary Southeast Asia* 31, no. 1 (2009): 88–109.

Ong Kian Ming. "Examining the Electoral Roll". In *Elections and Democracy in Malaysia*, edited by Mavis Puthucheary and Noraini Othman. Bangi: Penerbit Universiti Kebangsaan Malaysia, 2005, pp. 292–315.

———. "Making Sense of the Political Tsunami". *Malaysiakini*, 11 March 2008.

Ong Kian Ming and Bridget Welsh. "Electoral Delimitation: A Case Study of Kedah". In *Elections and Democracy in Malaysia*, edited by Mavis Puthucheary and Noraini Othman. Bangi: Penerbit Universiti Kebangsaan Malaysia, 2005, pp. 316–45.

Ooi Kee Beng. *The Reluctant Politician: Tun Dr. Ismail and His Time*. Singapore: Institute of Southeast Asian Studies, 2006.

———. *Lost in Transition: Malaysia under Abdullah*. Petaling Jaya and Singapore: SIRD and Institute of Southeast Asian Studies, 2008.

Ooi Kee Beng, Johan Saravanamuttu and Lee Hock Guan. *March 8: Eclipsing May 13*. Singapore: Institute of Southeast Asian Studies, 2008.

Oon Yeoh. *Clean Sweep: The Global Triumph of Berish 3.0*. Petaling Jaya: SIRD, 2012.

Ostwald, Kai. "How to Win a Lost Election: Malapportionment and Malaysia's 2013 General Election". *The Round Table: The Commonwealth Journal of International Affairs* 102, no. 6 (2013): 521–32.

Pennock, J. Roland. "Political Development, Political Systems, and Political Goods". *World Politics* 18, no. 3 (1966): 415–34.

Pepinsky, Thomas B. *Economic Crisis and the Breakdown of Authoritarian Regimes: Indonesia and Malaysia in Perspective.* New York: Cambridge University Press, 2009.

———. "The 2008 Malaysian Elections: An End to Ethnic Politics". *Journal of East Asian Studies* 9, no .1 (2009): 87–120.

Pierson, Paul. "Increasing Returns, Path Dependence, and the Study of Politics". *American Political Science Review* 94, no. 2 (2000): 251–67.

———. *Politics in Time: History, Institutions, and Social Analysis.* Princeton, NJ: Princeton University Press, 2004.

Pillay, Chandrasekaran. *The 1974 General Elections in Malaysia: A Post-mortem.* Singapore: Institute of Southeast Asian Studies, 1974.

Poh Soo Kai, Tan Kok Fang and Hong Lysa, eds. *The 1963 Operation Coldstore: Commemorating 50 years.* Petaling Jaya: SIRD, 2013.

Puthucheary, Mavis and Noraini Othman, eds. *Elections and Democracy in Malaysia.* Bangi: Penerbit Universiti Kebangsaan Malaysia, 2005.

Putnam Robert D. *Bowling Alone: The Collapse and Revival of American Community.* New York: Simon & Schuster, 2008.

Putnam, Robert D., with R. Leonardi and R.Y. Nannetti. *Making Democracy Work: Civic Traditions in Modern Italy.* Princeton, NJ: Princeton University Press, 1993.

Quay, Audrey, ed. *Perak: A State of Crisis.* Petaling Jaya: SIRD, 2010.

Rachagan, Sothi S. "The Development of the Electoral System". In *Malaysian Politics and the 1978 Election,* edited by Harold Crouch, Lee Kam Hing and Michael Ong. Kuala Lumpur: Oxford University Press, 1980, pp. 255–92.

———. "Ethnic Representation and the Electoral System". In *Ethnicity, Class and Development: Malaysia,* edited by S. Husin Ali. Kuala Lumpur: PSSM, 1984, pp. 124–38.

———. *Law and the Electoral Process in Malaysia.* Kuala Lumpur: University of Malaya Press, 1993.

Rae, Douglas W. *The Political Consequences of Electoral Laws.* New Haven, CT: Yale University Press, 1967.

Ramakrishnan, P. "Maika: Bleeding Again". *Aliran Monthly* 23, no. 11 (2010) <http://aliran.com/aliran-monthly/2010/2010–5/maika-bleeding-again/> (accessed 31 May 2015).

Ratnam, K.J. *Communalism and the Political Process in Malaya.* Kuala Lumpur: Oxford University Press, 1965.

Ratnam, K.J. and R.S. Milne. *The Malayan Parliamentary Election of 1964.* Singapore: University of Malaya Press, 1967.

———. "The 1969 Parliamentary Election in West Malaysia". *Pacific Affairs* 43, no. 2 (1970): 203–26.

Reece, Bob. "Malaysia: Requiem for Democracy". *Far Eastern Economic Review (FEER)*, 18/24 May 1969.

———. "Some Teaparty". *FEER*, 8/14 June 1969.

———. "The Parting of the Ways?" *FEER*, 15/21 June 1969.

Reid, William. *Report of the Federation of Malaya Constitutional Commission.* London: Her Majesty's Stationery Office, 1957.

Reilley, Benjamin. *Democracy in Divided Societies: Electoral Engineering for Conflict Management.* Oxford: Oxford University Press, 2006.

Riker, William H. *The Theory of Political Coalitions.* Yale: Yale University Press, 1962.

Rose, Richard and Doh Chull Shin. "Democratization Backwards: The Problem of Third-Wave Democracies". *British Journal of Political Science* 31 (2001): 331–54.

Rudner Martin. "The Malaysian General Election of 1969: A Political Analysis". *Modern Asian Studies* 4, no. 1 (1970): 1–21.

Sabri Zain. *Face Off: A Malaysian Reformasi Diary (1998–99).* Singapore: BigO Books, 2000.

Sadiq, Kamal. "When State Prefer Non-Citizens over Citizens: Conflict over Illegal Immigration into Malaysia". *International Studies Quarterly* 49 (2005): pp. 101–22.

———. *Paper Citizens: How Illegal Immigrants Acquire Citizenship in Developing Countries.* Oxford: Oxford University Press, 2008.

Salazar, Lorraine Carlos. "Privatisation, Patronage and Enterprise Development: Liberalising Telecommunications in Malaysia". In *The State of Malaysia: Ethnicity, Equity, and Reform*, edited by Edmund Terence Gomez. London: Routledge, 2004.

Saravanamuttu, Johan. *The Dilemma of Independence: Two Decades of Malaysia's Foreign Policy, 1957–1977.* Penang: Universiti Sains Malaysia, 1983.

———. "The State, Authoritarianism and Industrialisation: Reflections on the Malaysian Case". *Kajian Malaysia* 2, no. 2 (1987): 43–75.

———. 'The State, Ethnicity and the Middle Class Factor". In *Internal Conflict and Governance*, edited by K. Rupesinghe. New York: St Martin's Press, 1992, pp. 44–64.

———. "Act of Betrayal: The Snuffing Out of Local Democracy in Malaysia". *Aliran Monthly* 20, no. 4 (2000).

———. "Is there a Politics of the Malaysian Middle Class?" In *Southeast Asian Middle Classes: Prospects for Change and Democratisation*, edited by Abdul

Rahman Embong. Bangi: Penerbit Universiti Kebangsaan Malaysia, 2001, pp. 103–18.

———. "Democracy and Modernity – When the Twain Shall Meet? Reflections on the Asian Conundrum". *Japanese Journal of Political Science* 7, no. 1 (2006): 41–58.

———. "The 12th General Election in Malaysia". *Opinion Asia*, 15 February 2008.

———. *Party Capitalism in Southeast Asia: Democracy's Bane?* Ishak Shari Memorial Lecture 2007 (Asia in the Twenty First Century). Bangi: IKMAS, Universiti Kebangsaan Malaysia, 2009*a*.

———. "Malaysia: Political Transformation and Intrigue in an Election Year". In *Southeast Asian Affairs 2009*, edited by Daljit Singh. Singapore: Institute of Southeast Asian Studies, 2009*b*, pp. 173–92.

———. "The Spoiler in Malaysia's Two-Party Politics". *Opinion Asia*, 30 August 2009*c*.

———. "More of a Double Blow than Status Quo". *Straits Times*, 15 April 2009*d*.

———. *Malaysia's Foreign Policy, The First Fifty Years: Alignment, Neutralism, Islamism*. Singapore: Institute of Southeast Asian Studies, 2010*a*.

———. "Encounters of Muslim Politics in Malaysia". In *Islam and Politics in Southeast Asia*, edited by Johan Saravanamuttu. London: Routledge, 2010*b*.

———. "The NEP, New Malay Middle Class and the Politics of Reform". In Edmund Terence Gomez and Johan Saravanamuttu, eds. *The New Economic Policy in Malaysia: Affirmative Action, Ethnic Inequalities and Social Justice*. Singapore: NUS Press, 2012*a*.

———. "Twin Coalition Politics in Malaysia since 2008: A Path Dependent Framing and Analysis". *Contemporary Southeast Asia* 34, no. 1 (2012*b*): 101–27.

———. "The March 2008 General Election in Malaysia as a Historical Conjuncture". In N. Ganesan, ed. *Conjunctures and Continuities in Southeast Asian Politics*. Institute of Southeast Asian Studies, 2013*a*.

———. "A People's Victory". *Aliran Monthly* 33, no. 3 (2013*b*).

Saravanamuttu, Johan and Rusaslina Idrus. "The Sarawak Polls of 2011: Implications for Coalition Politics in Malaysia". ISEAS Viewpoints, 4 May 2011.

Saravanamuttu, Johan, Lee Hock Guan and Mohamed Nawab Osman, eds. *Coalitions in Collision: Malaysia's 13th General Elections*. Petaling Jaya and Singapore: SIRD and Institute of Southeast Asian Studies, 2015.

Shamsul, A.B. "The Battle Royal: The UMNO Elections of 1987". In *Southeast Asian Affairs 1988*, edited by M. Ayoob and Ng Chee Yuen. Singapore: Institute of Southeast Asian Affairs, 1988.

Slater, Dan. "The Architecture of Authoritarianism: Southeast Asia and the Regeneration of Democratization Theory". *Taiwan Journal of Democracy* 2, no. 2 (2006): 1–22.

————. *Ordering Power: Contentious Politics and Authoritarian Leviathans in Southeast Asia*. New York: Cambridge University Press, 2010.

Slimming, John. *Death of a Democracy*. London: John Murray, 1969.

Smith, M.G. *The Plural Society in the British West Indies*. Berkeley: University of California Press, 1965.

Smith, T.E. *Report on the First Election of Members to the Legislative Council of the Federation of Malaya*. Kuala Lumpur: Government Printer, 1955.

Sothi Rachagan. *Law and the Electoral Process in Malaysia*. Kuala Lumpur: University of Malaya Press, 1993.

Starne, F.L. "The Singapore Elections of 1963". In *The Malayan Parliamentary Election of 1964*, edited by K.J. Ratnam, and R.S. Milne. Singapore: University of Malaya Press, 1967.

Tan Tai Yong. *Creating "Greater Malaysia": Decolonization and the Politics of Merger*. Singapore: Institute of Southeast Asian Studies, 2008.

Tan, Kevin Y.L. "Malaysia". In *Elections in Asia and the Pacific: A Data Handbook, Volume II: South East Asia, East Asia, and the South Pacific*, edited by Dieter Nohlen, Florian Grozt and Christof Hartmann. Oxford: Oxford University Press, 2001.

Tennant, Paul. "The Decline of Elective Local Government in Malaysia". *Asian Survey* 13, no. 4 (1973): 351–62.

Tunku Abdul Rahman. *Political Awakening*. Subang Jaya: Pelanduk, 1986.

————. *May 13: Before and After*. Kuala Lumpur: Utusan Melayu Press, 1969.

Vasil, R.K. *The Malaysian General Election of 1969*. Kuala Lumpur: Oxford University Press, 1972.

Verma, Vidhu. *Malaysia: State and Civil Society in Transition*, 2nd ed. Petaling Jaya: SIRD and Lynn Rienner, 2004.

Vogel, Ezra. *Japan as Number One: Lessons for America*. New York: Harper and Row, 1979.

Von Vorys, Karl. *Democracy without Consensus: Communalism and Political Stability in Malaysia*. Princeton, NJ: Princeton University Press, 1976.

Wain, Barry. *Malaysian Maverick: Mahathir Mohamad in Turbulent Times*. Houndmills, Basingstoke: Palgrave Macmillan, 2009.

Weiss, Meredith L. "Issues and Strategies of the Barisan Alternatif". In *Trends in Malaysia: Election Assessment*. Singapore: Institute of Southeast Asian Studies, 2000.

————. "The 1999 Malaysian General Elections: Issues, Insults, and Irregularities". *Asian Survey* 40, no. 3 (2000): 413–435

————. *Protest and Possibilities: Civil Society and Coalitions for Political Change in Malaysia*. Stanford: Stanford University Press, 2006.

————. *Electoral Dynamics in Malaysia: Findings from the Grassroots*. Petaling Jaya and Singapore: SIRD and Institute of Southeast Asian Studies, 2013.

————. "Malaysia's 13th General Elections: Same Result, Different Outcome". *Asian Survey* 53, no. 6 (2013): 1135–58.

Welsh, Bridget. *New Identities, New Politics: Malaysia's Muslim Professionals, NBR Analysis*. Washington, DC: National Bureau of Asian Research, 2008.

————. "Tears and Fears: Tun Mahathir's Last Hurrah". In *Southeast Asian Affairs 2004*, edited by Chin Kin Wah and Daljit Singh. Singapore: Institute of Southeast Asian Studies, 2004, pp. 139–55.

Wong Chin Huat and Soon Li Tsin. *Democracy at Stake? Examining 16 By-elections in Malaysia, 2008–2011*. Petaling Jaya: SIRD, 2012.

Zakaria Haji Ahmad. "The 1999 General Elections: A Preliminary Overview". In *Trends in Malaysia: Election Assessment*, by Zakaria Haji Ahmad, Khoo Kay Kim, K.S. Nathan, Hari Singh, Meredith Weiss and John Funston. Singapore: Institute of Southeast Asian Studies, 2000.

————, ed. *Government and Politics of Malaysia*. Singapore: Oxford University Press, 1987.

INDEX

About the Author

JOHAN SARAVANAMUTTU was formerly professor of political science at Universiti Sains Malaysia (Penang) and Visiting Senior Research Fellow at the ISEAS – Yusof Ishak Institute (Singapore). He is the author of *Malaysia's Foreign Policy, the First 50 Years: Alignment, Neutralism, Islamism* (2010). Other co-authored and co-edited publications include: *Coalitions in Collision: Malaysia's 13th General Election* (2015); *The New Economic Policy in Malaysia: Affirmative Action, Ethnic Inequalities and Social Justice* (2014); *March 8: Eclipsing May 13* (2008); and *New Politics in Malaysia* (2003).

Anwar Ibrahim at PR Ceramah in Seberang Prai (Penang) during 2008 election campaign

PAS poster for 2008 poll in Seberang Prai, Penang

Gerakan leader Koh Tzu Koon, candidate for Batu Kawan, in 2008 Penang poll

BN poster in Kota Bharu, Kelantan for 2013 general election

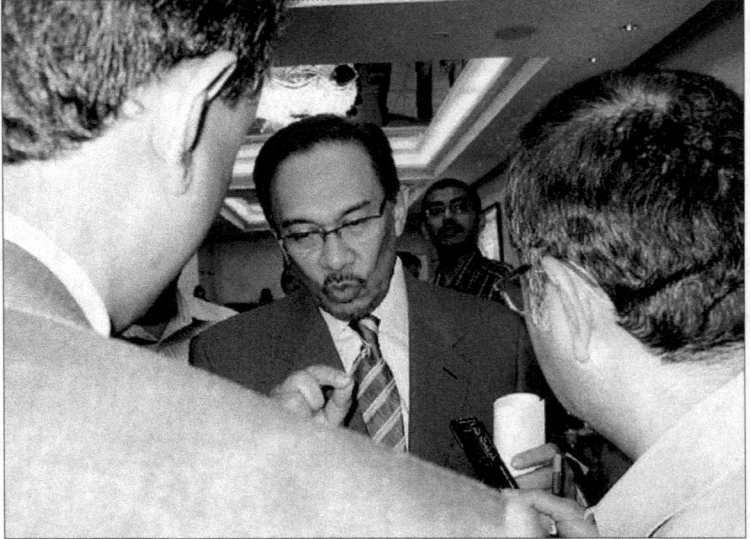

Anwar Ibrahim at Foreign Correspondents Association Press Conference
in St Regis Hotel, Singapore, 5 March 2008

PAS announcement for prayer gathering
starting at 3:50 a.m. at a field in Kota Baru,
Kelantan during 2008 election campaign

Anwar Ibrahim speaking at Foreign
Correspondents Association Press Conference
in St Regis Hotel, Singapore, 5 March 2008

BN poster highlighting
multiculturalism used for
Bukit Selambau by-election
of 7 April 2009

BN poster in Tamil script used
for Bukit Selambau by-election
of 7 April 2009

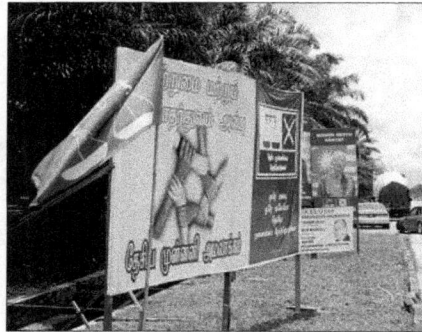

Bukit Gantang 7 April 2009
by-election posters

Anti-corruption poster used at Bukit Gantang 2009 by-election campaign

Bukit Gantang by-election PAS candidate Nizar Jamaluddin, 2009

Car poster of PAS for Bukit Gantang 7 April 2009 by-election

BN posters in Bagan Pinang
by-election, 11 October 2009

PR poster used in
Bagan Pinang
by-election 2009

UMNO poster with candidate
Mohd Isa Abd. Samad for
Bagan Pinang by-election 2009

BN poster for Hulu Selangor 25 April 2010 by-election
with picture of MIC candidate P. Kamalanathan

Hulu Selangor PR supporters at Hulu Selangor rally for by-election of 25 April 2010

PR supporters at Hulu Selangor rally for by-election of 25 April 2010

Poster of MB Ibrahim Khalid of the PKR put up for Hulu Selangor by-election of 23 April 2010

PAS candidate for Tenang by-election Normala Sudirman

PR poster for Tenang by-election 2011

BN event announcement during 2011 Tenang by-election at FELDA scheme

Protesting against inflation, rise in cost of petrol and sugar at Tenang by-election 2011

SUPP team led by George Chan in Miri, Sarawak 2011 poll.
The poster translates as "growing, living, servicing".

Kuching rally in Sarawak 2011 poll

PKR candidate Michael Teo for 2011 Sarawak poll

BN candidate Abang Johari for 2011 Sarawak poll

SUPP candidate for Sarawak poll on 16 April 2011

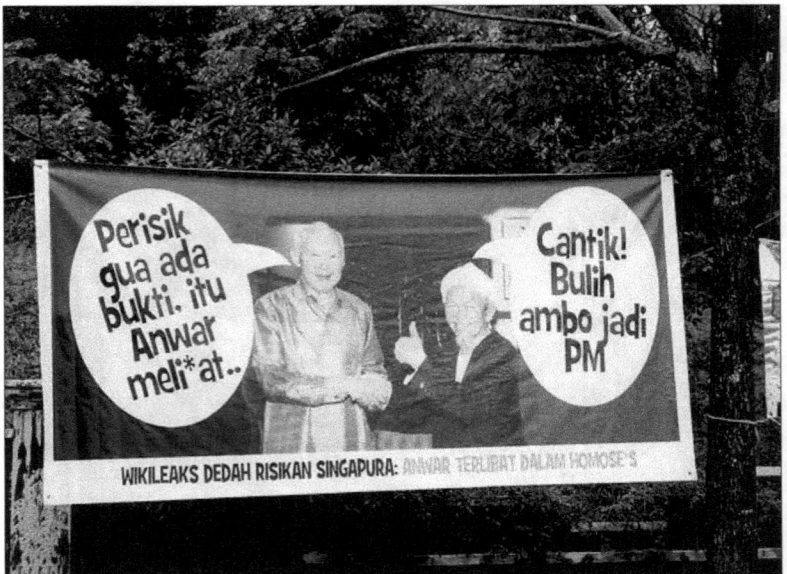

BN poster used in 2011 Sarawak poll with innuendo about Anwar Ibrahim

PKR Press conference Kuching after 2011 Sarawak poll

UMNO 2012 party convention

UMNO party convention exhibition on 30 November 2012

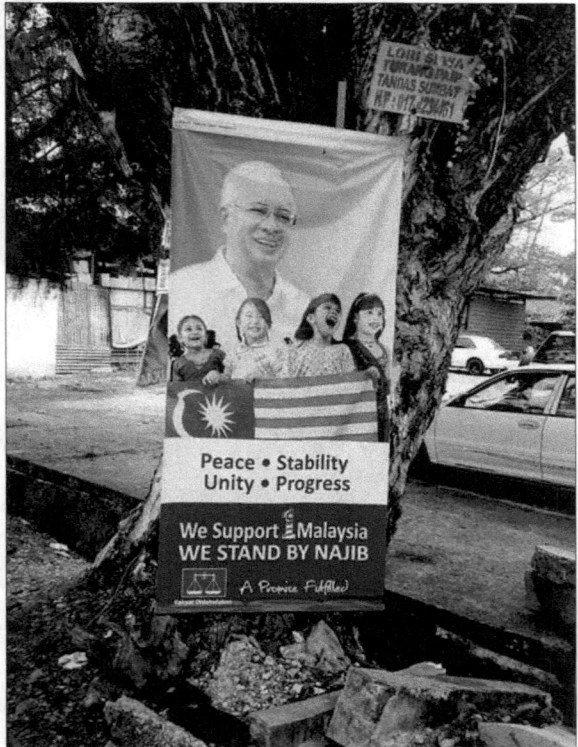

BN pre-election poster in Kedah, 2013

Arriving for the PSY event in Penang as part of the BN's 2013 campaign

Waiting for Korean sensation PSY in Penang on 11 February 2013

Ceramah of PAS and DAP candidates near Kluang during campaign of 2013

Charles Santiago, DAP candidate for Klang, on Nomination Day, 20 April 2013

DAP candidates Liew and Tan
for 2013 general election

DAP candidate Yap Soo Huey
for Pulau Tikus 2013 poll

DAP Penang candidates
for 2013 general election

PAS ceramah at Gombak, Selangor on 23 March 2013

PKR candidate for Wangsa Maju Tan Kee Kwong in 2013 poll

Poster for 2013 general election which translates as "Who is the most suitable candidate for PM?"

PR ceramah in Kuala Lumpur, 2013

PKR supporters in early celebration at Seberang Prai, Penang on night of 5 May 2013

PKR supporters in early celebration at Seberang Prai, Penang on night of polling, 5 May 2013

Voters cashing vouchers issued at BN dinner campaigns at Sungai Dua, Penang after the 2013 general election

Felda home in Johor

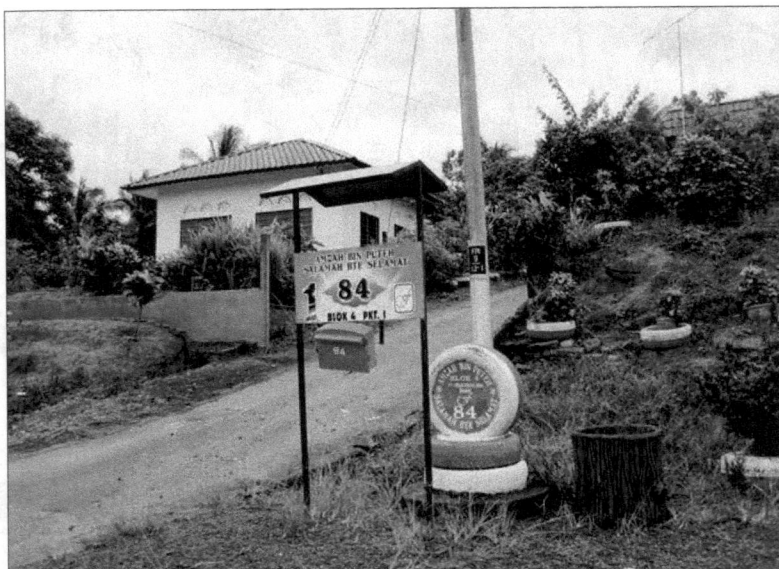

Felda home in Tenang, Johor

Felda home in Johor

PR poster for Kajang by-election, 23 March 2014

BERSIH 4.0 rally on the night of 30 August 2015 in Kuala Lumpur